Date Due

The international wine trade

La dignité du travail [The dignity of labour]

Detail of a mural painted by Jean Denis in 1931, representing Christ amongst winegrowers. The work spans the main staircase of the headquarters of the World Trade Organisation in Geneva. (Courtesy of WTO. Photograph by Laurence Bonvin.)

The international wine trade

PIERRE SPAHNI

Foreword by Hugh Johnson

WOODHEAD PUBLISHING LIMITED

Cambridge England

Published by Woodhead Publishing Ltd,
Abington Hall, Abington,
Cambridge CB1 6AH, England

First published 1995

British Library Cataloguing in Publication Data
A catalogue record for this book is available from the British Library

ISBN 1 85573 106 1

Designed by Andrew Jones (text) and The Colour Studio (jacket).
Typeset by BookEns Ltd, Baldock, Herts.
Printed by St Edmundsbury Press, Suffolk, England.

Contents

Foreword by Hugh Johnson . . . . *vii*

Preface . . . . *ix*

Introduction *1*

1 Production. 15
Viticulture 15 Winemaking 20 The environment 33
Finance 34 Innovation 38

2 Consumption. 44
Main features and trends 45 Traditional markets: the case
of France 50 New markets: the British and US models 55

3 Financial and administrative aspects of international
trade 87
Introduction 87 Prices; exchange rates 88 Transport
and insurance costs 91 Tariffs; excise duties and sales taxes 93
Technical specifications; labelling requirements; certificates
of origin and other documents 98 Export credit and
promotion 100 Distribution 102

4 The major import markets 104
North East Asia 105 North America 120 Western
Europe 143 Middle East and Africa 223 Latin America 226
Oceania 229

CONTENTS

5 Exporter profiles 232
The New World 232 The Old Continent 248

6 Formerly planned economies 272
Major importers 274 Leading exporters 281 Trade
between the EU and former COMECON members 286

7 After Marrakesh 292
Technical standards, sanitary and phytosanitary
measures 292 Geographical indications and appellations
of origin 293 Market access 294 Export subsidies 304
Domestic support 305

References *312*

Index *319*

Foreword

by Hugh Johnson

C an there be a more complex trade than commerce in wine? What other commodity is offered in such infinite variety, at prices from inconsiderable to fabulous, while changing constantly in quality and value according to its age, the weather conditions when it was made, even the precise patch where the vines grow?

Its markets are almost as various as itself, ranging from regions where it is as everyday as bread to milieus where it is elevated (if that is the word) to a fashion item. Governments vary so widely in their attitudes to it that in one country it is covered in health warnings, in another used as a tax cow, while in another the only official injunction is not to throw the empty bottle into the nearest ditch.

Precious and perishable as wine is, its trade is subject to all the pressures that affect any internationally-traded commodity, with the added complication that in most cases, and in all cases where its value is high, the trade flows both ways. With the exception of the former communist countries, where trade was grossly distorted by 'planning', the wine-exporting countries also indulge their taste by importing from their customers.

Thus a web of inextricable complexity is built up – inextricable, that is, until set out in remarkably lucid terms by Pierre Spahni. He is a geographer/historian (is there truly a difference?) with a statistician's rigour but a pilot's vision. Moreover it is clear from the outset that he loves 'this godly drink', as he calls it, and is fascinated by the intricacies that nature, tradition, geography, culture and taste have all contributed to its rich and wonderful weave. A compendium of dry facts would be useful; a wine-lover's analysis of the comings and goings of a myriad wines across the globe is truly absorbing.

Wine-professionals who look for a deeper understanding of their trade will be engrossed by this book. And so will wine-amateurs who have read the romance, studied the maps, but are still drawn in deeper to the marvellous amalgam of man and nature which is wine and its worldwide culture.

Preface

International wine trade is driven by the enjoyment of millions of consumers revealing quite different preferences, by their sheer curiosity and desire to deepen their knowledge of how wine is produced and how it can be best appreciated. Like this godly drink, people travel extensively nowadays. Many customers have thereby acquired a taste for wines of novel origins and styles. Telecommunications also introduced the 'global village', with its due share of fashions and fads. Each year brings scores of new offerings suiting just about every occasion and each consumer's wallet, for wines of similar quality come with noticeable differences in character, style and price, depending on where and how it was produced. Suppliers have reduced costs by streamlining winegrowing, winemaking and packaging operations. The markets they serve are also larger and often made of national and international segments pulled together to reach a certain critical mass. This re-engineering process was usually accompanied by a drastic improvement in the quality of the wines produced, better logistics and far more sophisticated marketing stressing the particularity of wines produced in the temperate zones girdling the earth. Better information is also beginning to filter from this traditionally secretive industry because firms increasingly need to attract outside capital. Wine has become a differentiated agricultural export item with a high value added to it and for which positioning in the countries' various segments is paramount. International trade is clearly not just moved by cost advantages (nineteenth century British economist David Ricardo used the famous example of exchanging 'wine for cloth' to illustrate the notion of comparative advantage between nations opening up to trade and the relative benefits derived from it – the 1709 Methuen Treaty between England and Portugal had wiped out Portuguese textile manufacture and marked the birth of its flourishing port industry). Trade is also driven by differences in production as well as in consumer preferences. The wine sector is forced to operate more efficiently and consumers can choose from an ever greater variety of wines: they are the sure winners of the 'trade game'.

International wine trade is thus a collection of potentially bi-directional flows between countries dotting the earth's surface. It is best represented by an asymmetrical matrix of flows of differing products shipped between markets organised in different ways and experiencing various stages of growth – from emergence in the case of the Asian Pacific Rim to some degree of maturity in Britain and straight decline in the USA, hopefully followed by some form of rejuvenation later. The ability of many importing countries to react by developing a credible domestic wine industry over the long term, and even to export afterwards, is a source of permanent change to this matrix. Price transmissions between markets is still relatively poor on the whole and one could hardly expect to be able to reason in terms of world prices and net trade volumes amidst such diversity of products, in stark contrast to most other agricultural commodities. Domestic taxation and social acceptance of alcoholic drinks also differs widely from one country to the next. An individual analysis of the major national markets is thus clearly required. Yet wine is considered a commodity for most agricultural policy decisions, particularly in Western Europe, where many governments have attempted to bolster the price of ordinary wines with taxpayers' money in exchange for rural votes. Denying foreign wines a fair access to their domestic market was usually their first but only successful step. Most other measures backfired because they pushed up the production of wines of the lowest quality and accelerated the decline of consumption in the traditional markets of Argentina, France, Italy and Spain – the four largest outlets for wine in the West during the 1970s. Ever greater reliance of their producers on foreign markets as their policies went bankrupt made them increasingly aware of the tangible benefits of freer trade and more willing to open up their own market in exchange for easier access to those holding the key to immediate and future growth.

The real value of trade (expressed in constant US$) soared during the 1970s but the rate of growth slowed down tremendously in the

1980s. Trade has even regressed in terms of volumes since the mid-1980s, chiefly as the result of tumbling French imports of cheap bulk for blending, contracting US imports and the economic collapse of the former Soviet bloc. Italy, the largest provider of cheap wines and rising star of the 1970s, was the main loser. The share of bottled shipments rose steadily over the past two decades and now appears to make up the majority of the volumes traded internationally. This is due mainly to direct sourcing by food supermarkets which have revolutionised the retailing of wines to consumers. This gradual modification of the composition of trade is reflected in the change in nature of the largest trade flow (in terms of value): French imports of Algerian bulk for blending topped the chart in the early 1970s, the US had that honour in the early 1980s with their orders of Italian Lambrusco and Veronese wines, whilst French shipments of essentially bottled wines to Britain became the largest single international flow of wine in the early 1990s. Germany provided the backbone to the growth in imports throughout that time, and French exporters managed to get the better of their Italian rivals who had concentrated too heavily on the cheap end of the US and German markets. France truly excelled in projecting an image of the highest quality and leapt forward in the UK, Germany and Japan. The technological revolution engineered by New World producers poses France and other traditional exporters with a serious challenge however. Also, the shift of the trade epicentre from the Mediterranean basin to the North Atlantic route and its subsequent re-centring in Western Europe, where most markets are either declining or approaching maturity, begs the question of whether it is realistic to expect further growth in the face of the relentless contraction of world consumption.

The short answer is 'yes' as nations have now committed themselves to facilitating access to foreign suppliers for a period of six years beginning in 1995 and, chauvinism aside, rising consumer interest in wine should necessarily call for more trade. Tumbling demand in the largest producing countries has freed up substantial production capacities in Europe. Some of them are being redesigned to produce wines intended to be marketed abroad. Growing pressures to export, easier access to markets, a general upgrading of consumer preferences plus the fact that the world still trades less than a sixth of its production: all these factors point to a continued increase in the real value of trade. Volumes could stabilise or even resume growth if the consumer base increased rapidly in the emerging markets of Latin America and Asia, though this is clearly not a critical issue. It is far more imperative that the spirit of freeing up trade be kept alive beyond the year 2001.

This book looks for simple clues to the patterns of international wine trade since 1970. Its purpose is to strip the subject to the bare economic factors underpinning international trade and thereby to complement – certainly not compete with – an outstanding body of wine literature devoted to technical, cultural, geographical and historical issues. Readers accustomed to a bucolic style may find this one 'a bit dry', but such is economic reality. A unique insight is given into the individual trade flows of twelve major importing countries. The level of competitiveness offered by the twelve markets is gauged and the positioning of the main strategic groups of exporters is also examined. Strategic groups are broadly identified as firms of identical nationality: these enjoy the same image for the quality of their wines and share a common level of assistance by their own government. Former communist countries are treated separately from market economies. Their statistics are of notoriously poor quality, for they were chiefly reported for the purpose of implementing an economic plan and not with the 'Western' view of providing market information. These economies are in full transition and the geopolitical map of some of the countries involved is still undergoing radical changes. The trade data featured herein are those communicated by the countries themselves to the United Nations. Emphasis is laid on the real value of the main trade flows; 1990 is taken as the reference year.

The discussion is arranged as follows: the first chapter examines technical factors giving rise to differences in pricing and in other characteristics of the wines which help position the final products. Chapter 2 deals with the forces at work behind the opposite trends in consumption revealed by traditional and Anglo-Saxon markets. An overview of the issues affecting international wine trade, particularly trade barriers, is offered in the third chapter. Chapter 4 is by far the most substantial and pragmatic one. The individual profiles of twelve major importing countries are drawn, covering more than 85% of world trade. Trends in the consumption of alcoholic drinks, wine market and import patterns, configuration of import and distribution channels, plus the country's trade policy: all these areas are scanned using the same procedure, so as to facilitate comparisons between markets. Medium term perspectives for wine imports are offered in most cases. Overall trends are reported for the remaining market economies and less developed regions of the world. Chapter 5 looks at trade from a different angle and takes the exporters' view. There, the analysis focuses on the challenge posed by New World producers to those based in Western Europe. The investigation progresses eastward in Chapter 6, to the previously planned economies of the former Soviet bloc. Major importers and exporters are dealt with separately here as well. The chapter ends with the planned integration of Eastern and Western European economies. Chapter 7 looks at the likely issues and developments awaiting us down the road from Marrakesh.

The Australian Wine Export Council (AWEC), the Centre Français du Commerce Extérieur (CFCE), the Institut National de Recherches Agronomiques (INRA) of Montpellier, the Instituto de Studios Economicos sobre la Realidad Argentina y Latinoamericana (IRREAL) of Mendoza, the Wine Institute of California and the Winemakers' Federation of Australia provided me with truly invaluable material. Many people in the industry also gave me generous help and advice. May they all find here the expression of my deepest gratitude and forgive me for not flaunting a list of their names and firms. I am much indebted to Chris Carson, Michael Finger, Dominique Foulon, Jon Fredrikson, Norberto Frigerio, Ronald Jansen, Jean-Pierre Laporte, Kirby Moulton, Bryce Rankine, Brenton Roneberg, Frédéric Rothen, Wade Stevenson and Koki Yokosuka, for giving me a good deal of their time and energy. Edwin Farver, Kathleen Heitz Myers and Noboru Ueno opened their fine bottles and hearts during my journey. I wish to extend my warmest thanks to them, also to Martin Woodhead and his winning team (Amanda, Neil and Simon) for making writing a delightful and exciting task. My love to my family and to Isabelle; this book is dedicated to her.

Introduction

W ine is an alcoholic beverage wholly produced from grapes, an agricultural crop. The need to survive in a difficult market – that of strongly differentiated and branded alcoholic drinks – has forced the wine industry to adopt an ever more competitive and international approach to marketing. The major handicap of the wine industry is that it is often caught in antagonism between long-established, stifling agricultural polices on the one hand (which breed many inefficiencies) and the need to respond quickly to rapidly changing and internationalising consumer preferences on the other. To a large extent, the juxtaposition of the obsolete and the state-of-the-art, of the arcane and the scientific bears witness to this, as does the persistence of production surpluses in many markets.

Wine is simple to produce: the transformation of grape juice into wine occurs naturally, as does its eventual evolution into vinegar. Good wines are typically elaborate products, however. Wine is also drunk in many contrasting ways and circumstances. Some people view it as energising and healthy, others as prone to abuse. Artists and priests have long blessed it. Worldly and mystical; jewel and commodity; wine has been traded actively down the ages.

A multidimensional product

Wine markets are notoriously heterogeneous. When a customer buys a particular wine, he (or she) is merely reacting positively to a collection of attributes – or characteristics – which are communicated to him (or her) through the product's mix. Some of the characteristics can be read directly from the label: dominant grape variety/ies in the blend, colour and origin of the wine, age, alcoholic strength and container size. Other, compound attributes like wine style and quality are more intuitive and difficult to assess. It is important to stress that customers are not so much interested in the individual characteristics of the wine they purchase than in the benefit they will derive from it. What counts is what the product will eventually do for them:[1] entertain, impress, accompany a meal, become a party's drink, a sauce, etc. Wine is even sold as a hobby kit providing all the necessary ingredients for turning enthusiasts into Sunday winemakers.

Customers' reactions differ because their individual preferences and tastes differ.[2] (Some marketing people would say that consumers' *wants* differ because their needs are shaped differently by their culture and/or by their individual personality).[3] Major differences in customers' preferences (wants) are likely to remain with us for some time, and these are the primary reason for market segments to exist.[4] Segmentation is carried further by those (clever) firms who have managed to convey an air of uniqueness to their wines, for this grants them a canny degree of monopoly power, limited only by the close – or distant – presence of substitutes. Marked product differentiation, particularly with respect to the country of origin of the wine, and ensuing market segmentation is a sufficiently strong base for generating 'two way' trade. The reason lays solely in the existence of widespread differences in customers' tastes and preferences within countries. The inclination to trade is reinforced considerably if there are likely economies of scale to be achieved by joining national

1 Hooley & Saunders, 1993, p 17.

2 Differences in individual reactions to the same good are an expression of differences in consumers' preferences and not a reflection of different perceptions as to the properties of the good (Lancaster 1979, p 17, in Kierzkowski, 1985, p 17).

3 Kotler & Armstrong, 1991, p 6.

4 Hooley & Saunders, 1993, pp 18, 137ff. They consider segmentation to be 'a logical extension of the marketing concept' and 'benefit segmentation' to be 'one of the most useful ways of segmenting markets for the simple reason that it relates segmentation back to the real reasons for the existence of segments in the first place – different benefit requirements'.

segments together: a firm's market increases.[5] Take the French for instance, who import cheap bulk wine from Italy (for the manufacture of aperitifs and the production of table wine) and export generally expensive bottled wines back across the Alps. The US is another prominent case of a major importer who turned into a main exporter. Germany, Australia, Hungary and Romania all have this ability to generate bidirectional trade flows. This increases consumer welfare, for the number of goods produced domestically is reduced to the more cost-effective products while the spectrum of consumers' choice is augmented by the number of imported goods.[6]

Prices usually reflect quality and customers are often left with them as the only gauge for it.[7] But in a differentiated market, competition is not just fought in terms of prices. Firms respond to differing consumer requirements by varying their product mix, of which price is an important but only one component; product, package and distribution are its remaining elements. Firms can go to great lengths to achieve segmentation. This results in highly differentiated offerings, based on the characteristics of the wines. Competitive positioning is tantamount to selecting and acting upon those attributes which can be accessed through the mix. Whether talking mix or preferences, it is useful to think of individual wines being positioned (close to others or alone in a niche) in a multidimensional space, with each dimension representing a single attribute of the wines: its price, origin, colour, alcoholic strength, character and style, and finally the container in which it is offered.

Origin is an important dimension, not just because the marketing of some wine is critically dependent on it (as in the case of most appellation wines), but also because it is subject to trade policies. Wine lends itself to discrimination by nations, either on an individual or on a collective basis (customs unions). Other macro issues shaping international wine trade flows, like countries' balances of payments and exchange rates, are also directly connected with the origin of the wines produced.

---

5 Kierzkowski, 1985, p 17.

6 Krugman & Obstfeld, 1991, p 140.

7 A recent study conducted in Western Europe by the Henley Centre found that wine and spirits, along with furniture, were amongst the few areas where consumers still considered highest price to be synonymous with highest quality, even at times of economic recession (*The Financial Times*, September 9 1993).

A multi-regulated industry

Wine legislation abounds. Starting with a first attempt at a legal definition at the end of the nineteenth century, production and marketing have become increasingly regulated activities. The core of the legislation was issued in the 1930s, with income and trade protection clearly in mind. The primary objective was to safeguard the health of the consumers *and* the economic interests of honest producers, both of which had to suffer from a systematic emergence of artificial wines at times of severe crisis. Such products had been manufactured and sold as wine with a view to reaping quick profits when supply was extremely scarce (as was the case in the 1870s and 1880s when European vineyards were literally devastated by phylloxera). They surfaced again in the 1900s, this time as a means of cutting costs when prices were diving in a Europe awash with wine. The deeds of a few unethical producers or merchants can have disastrous consequences on the image of the wines of a given origin. Recently, the Italian methanol and German and Austrian diethylene-glycol affairs have prompted many exporting nations to enforce or tighten up export quality controls.

Legislation on grape and wine production also seeks to warrant the generally positive impact which viticulture and winemaking have on rural employment and income, as well as on the environment. In most countries, areas, methods and levels of production are regulated by a swelling flow of agricultural legislation dealing with the delimitation of growing regions, the agreed types of vines, maximum levels of production, the use of techniques for transforming grape juice into wine (winemaking) and often the practice of blending wines as well. Distribution, advertising and labelling of the wines is usually regulated within the framework of food marketing laws. These stipulate that licences must be granted for importing and distributing wines and, sometimes, restrict them to state-run companies (mono-polies). An international standard code dealing with packaging, labelling and other technical issues may still sound like a distant reality, but there are a few mutual agreements recognising each party's winemaking (oenological) and marketing practices. The Australia–EU[8] agreement negotiated in 1992 is the first of the genre (the US–EU agreement is still waiting to be finalised). Finally, like any other alcoholic drink, wine must usually overcome the additional imposition

---

8 For the sake of simplicity, the term EU is used throughout this book when referring to the European Union and what was formerly known as the European Community and the European Economic Community.

of 'sin taxes', in the form of separate excise duties or higher consumer tax (higher than that which is normally applied to food products). The reason is that wine contains a fair amount (usually around 12%) of alcohol – a psychoactive drug which is now traded legally in most countries.[9]

Demand and trade are largely determined by culture and wealth (discretionary spending). Wine is deeply rooted in the Judeo-Christian world which has embraced its rites wholeheartedly, but it is also rapidly gaining ground in mainly Buddhist Asia. Only with Islamic countries does wine entertain an uneasy relationship. (The Koran bans consumption in this world but promises an after life adorned by it, prompting many enlightened governments in the Muslim world to cast a blind eye on the deeds of the individuals who have opted for the pleasures available in this world – rather than those on offer in the next.) Wine has thus been hard on the heels of the most advanced, tolerant societies from its Caucasian origins around 3000 BC through to present times. First sought as a rarity for the rich, it then spread gradually to the rest of the population, often as the result of its local production (vines adapt easily to a wide variety of climatic conditions but are mostly grown in temperate zones). The first accounts of wine exports are those from ancient Armenia to Babylon, down the river Euphrates. It was traded later from Canaan to Egypt, at the height of the Pharaohs' glory, who subsequently developed their own viticulture in the upper Nile valley. Then later from Asia Minor to Crete, on to Greece, to Rome and to Gaul...[10]

A ring of multinationals

If differing conditions of production, related to climates, soils and techniques in use, make it a differentiated product from the start, distinctions are often overdone for marketing purposes or sheer snobbery. (Coffee, for instance, reveals striking differences in quality and taste – owing much to the same factors imparting character to the wines – yet it is only marketed under a handful of varieties and a few powerful brand names.) Wine consumption is closely related to food, so that consumer preferences are even more likely to differ across national boundaries than they do within. Production and marketing

9 Recall US prohibition lasting from 1919–30.

10 Johnson, 1989.

technologies are quickly converging the world over however, so that tastes are rapidly internationalising (people travel extensively these days) and consumers cross varietal and geographical dividing lines with far greater ease than do professionals of the wine trade. They rely on a few producers' or retailers' brand names they consider 'safe', in order to choose from dozens of offerings. Brand image warrants quality and reliable brands have loyal customers. It is far more difficult for appellations to generate consumer franchise because of the sheer number of producers involved. Appellations have the undeniable advantage of allowing pooled advertising and promotion, and work as a good support for brands; the decision on whether to put the accent on the appellation or the brand is ultimately left with the individual producer or marketer. Many producers and wholesalers have their hands tied by legislation, however: appellations put considerable restrictions on planting and blending; Kendall-Jackson for instance prefers to use 'California' as an indication of origin for his thriving line of premium varietals (rather than Napa, Sonoma or any other viticultural area of the 'Golden State') because regional appellations are, in his view, excessively restrictive in terms of choosing the best grapes for the blend he wants to market. The ban imposed by French appellation authorities on the use of grape varieties on AOC labels is another example of constraining legislation;[11] innovation is much impaired as a result. But in a differentiated market – where each product aims to project its own air of uniqueness – creativity is vital.

Wine has to fight hard for shelf-space in supermarkets, specialist shops, restaurants and bars. It does so against cost-effective, standardised and heavily branded beverages: water, soft drinks, beer and spirits. Drinks multinationals have a proven ability to launch brand names successfully and they now need to continue to expand in a declining alcohol market. Vested interests make it difficult for firms to divest in any contracting markets. Competitive pressures are bound to increase in the alcohol drinks sector. Food retailers are also keen on building their own product lines (or brands) and are now operating well beyond their original, national boundaries. They tend to purchase at source and, in Western Europe, some of them have pooled their strengths in single international buying centres. They have usually stopped short of controlling suppliers because of the importance of consumers' fads and of the heavy investments required in production.[12] And why should they as long as wine production policies keep

---

11 *The Financial Times* 12 June 1993; with the exception of Alsatian wines.

12 Albert Heijn, the caring Dutch food retailer who has participation in a Spanish sherry producer, is one of the rare exceptions.

turning the international wine market into a buyer's market? Finally, shrinking home wine markets have forced many traditional producers to turn to foreign outlets to keep up sales.

Except in the bulk market, which is largely driven by price and currency fluctuations, the exporter-importer partnership is more of a long term bond, which is crucial to both firms' success.[13] Building up a name is an unremitting effort which requires a major input from the importer. There are savings to be made from interdependencies between marketing (and sometimes production) operations occurring in different, often adjoining countries: in logistics, in co-ordinating pricing and choosing distributors, in advertising as well as in the promotion of brands, e.g. ownership of a Hungarian wine producer may help a British spirits manufacturer increase its exports in Eastern Europe. Those who believe in brand control at all stages in order to preserve their margins are not shy of vertical integration, though this is usually confined to the hotel-restaurants-cafés (Horeca) and specialist shop sectors. The deregulation of the financial markets has made it much easier for firms to cross national borders and set up beachheads in the form of joint ventures, participations or mergers with local firms –or even their take-over (many are forced to tap the capital market in order to finance their own expansion anyway). So far, spirits multinationals have considered wine to be less profitable, more risky and more difficult to market than their core products, and their interest has been fairly limited. These are cash-rich giants who have set up a worldwide distribution network in most cases and whose original business is now on the decline. Many wine businesses are either too small to be concerned with the strategies of global players or simply fail to subscribe to the idea of globalisation of their own industry. They ignore international competition at their peril.[14]

Multilateral trade

If it is true that export activities have usually stemmed from chronic surpluses developing in specific wine-growing regions, it is equally true that trade has resulted in systematic, often successful attempts to

---

13 Sichel, 1989.

14 Hooley & Saunders, 1993, p 14 and 238. For them, an increase in competition is likely, chiefly for two factors: increased international trade and slower economic growth.

produce locally, where climate permits. The cost of sending wines round the world is substantial. Costs do not just involve the carrier's bill, but all sorts of additional expenses ranging from brokerage to breakage: an exporter has to insure itself against possible insolvency of the buyer; insurers, bankers, shippers and other intermediaries like to charge a fee for their participation in a deal, and marauding by rulers is still commonplace – today's potentates find it difficult to break with the medieval custom of levying a hefty duty on wine entering their fief.[15] Wines produced in Edinburgh may not have outlived the clarets shipped from Bordeaux to Leith, the local port, but neither did Paris wine growers manage to withstand the premiums set on their land by urban sprawl. Even so, vineyards which have sprouted (at different stages of history) in the immediate vicinity of the major ports of Venice, Bordeaux and San Francisco – now all deemed 'traditional' wine producing regions – have their roots deep in the wine trade.

Man-made barriers to trade are proving far more difficult to master than mere technical hurdles, for example shipping through the equator for Southern hemisphere exporters. Many of the quantitative restrictions prevailing today were introduced by producing countries in the 1930s with a view to shielding their domestic grape and wine growing sectors against foreign competition. Comprehensive legislation on appellations, which further restrict trade by seriously reducing opportunities for blending local with 'foreign' wines (and effectively set up cartels) were also initiated in the 1930s. Consuming countries levy usual tariffs on wine but then often raise hefty (sometimes discriminatory) internal duties, which they legitimise on the basis of its social cost. Raising prices has always been thought of as an effective way of keeping individual alcohol consumption and national finances in check. Yet a closer look at the domestic drinks market often reveals that wine happens to compete head-on with local production and/or other vested interests.

The formation of trade blocs through preferential trade agreements (of which customs unions are a special, free trade case) has brought about some levelling of trade barriers but not necessarily a reduction in them. Trade barriers (tariff and non-tariff measures) may fall substantially or even disappear amongst the bloc's trading members but tariffs are often getting attuned to a higher common external level *vis-à-vis* the rest of the world – the EU's Common Customs Tariff is a good example of this. In addition to any

---

15 It was customary for noblemen to charge a toll for wines passing through their land, usually in the form of wine. See Unwin, 1991, for more details.

convergence of protective measures taken at national borders, internal taxation regimes are also subject to some degree of harmonisation; the only real issue remaining for contention is heavier penalties levied on spirits than on beer or wine (when the rate of tax is expressed in terms of unit of alcohol present in the drinks). Finally, a better co-ordination of individual macroeconomic policies within trade blocs has also contributed to greater stability in wine trade flows.

Internal discriminatory taxation, prohibitive tariffs and other restrictive (non-tariff) measures still clutter the international wine market. The matter is further complicated by systematic granting of production and export subsidies of various ingenious forms by most of the governments involved. Some of the major importers are also producers and exporters, e.g. Germany, France and the USA. Fear of retaliation has thus prompted many players to refrain somewhat from dispensing with export subsidies – the prevailing code of conduct calls for producing nations not to grant such aid on wines shipped to another wine producing country. But is the cash dispensed by the US administration to foreign wine importers, for marketing expenses, any different from conspicuous export subsidies? And have domestic production subsidies not allowed EU wine producers to regain competitiveness in the international market-place and snap export contracts from honest rivals? A confusing subsidy battle is currently raging around the world. So, should Americans rejoice at the idea that they are sipping European wines on the back of EU taxpayers or should they join the vocal chorus of lobbyists claiming that US wines should be given fair access to European markets?

The issue of export subsidies is exacerbated by the fact that wine consumption in the older, traditional markets is falling fast and fails to be compensated for by the rise in demand on the new markets. The structural imbalance lies at the core of the EU surplus and some of the results of the EU's wine policy have been particularly messy. The EU has been pouring some of its surpluses into Brazilian motors for instance, and managed to jam not just Rio's streets (cars eventually became stranded when imports were abruptly suspended on the grounds of toxicity) but the unregulated market for ethyl alcohol as well, where the imbalance roughly matches the amounts of ethyl alcohol generated by the EU's wine intervention schemes (distillation of surpluses into ethyl alcohol).[16] The sums of taxpayers' money involved are simply ludicrous and further strengthen the call for liberalising international trade in an orderly fashion – in the

---

16 Swinbank & Ritson, 1992.

framework of GATT's successor, the World Trade Organisation (WTO). The WTO could also provide effective international arbitration in litigation regarding the use of geographical names (so-called 'semi-generic' wines).[17] Finally, it would help reduce the constant bickering about the presence or absence of traces of chemical substances and acidity levels for wine, as well as other sanitary and phytosanitary measures and technical standards. These are all too often used as a non-tariff barrier or as a means of pressure in today's brinkmanship negotiations (e.g. the proposed attempt, by the US administration in 1992, to penalise imports of French wines with a view to bringing the French government back to its senses on the oil-seeds issue). The recent Australia–EU agreement could provide a blueprint for international goodwill and gentlemanliness in many respects, as does the earlier agreement, by the Japanese, not to use misleading geographical names.

Supporting producers' prices on nearly equal terms with other agricultural crops, whilst steering consumers towards moderation, inevitably breeds distortions and inconsistencies. Man's ambivalence towards wine production and consumption has resulted in conflict between the policies generated at both ends of the market and a resounding waste of financial, human and natural resources in the case of the EU. The international wine trade has to wade through those policies in its quest for renewed growth. The CIF value of world trade fetched 8.8 billion US$ in 1990 and tends to stagnate.[18] That level had already been reached a decade earlier in real terms, but the 1980s were spent on a roller-coaster ride: trade lost nearly a third of its value in the first half of the 1980s and climbed back up again in the second (see Fig. A[19]). Volumes peaked half-way through, in 1985, at 5.4 billion litres. They have regressed slowly ever since and stood at 4.4 billion litres in the early 1990s.

Momentum for growth was often gathered in the 1960s, as in the case of Germany. In a contrasting move, France was reducing its massive 'imports' of Algerian bulk for blending at that time. Up until 1962, the year of independence of this French colony, shipments

17 Strictly speaking, though people often talk about 'generic wines' and 'generic advertising', see Chapter 1 on production.

18 Cost, insurance and freight – this is the value of the wines before payment of tariffs, duties and taxes in the importing country. This roughly corresponds to the FOB value (free on board) in the exporting country plus transport and insurance costs.

19 Movements in the CIF price and value of world trade are likely to be accentuated by the varying strength of the US$, in which they are expressed (this depends on how accurately differences in inflation have been transmitted to exchange rates).

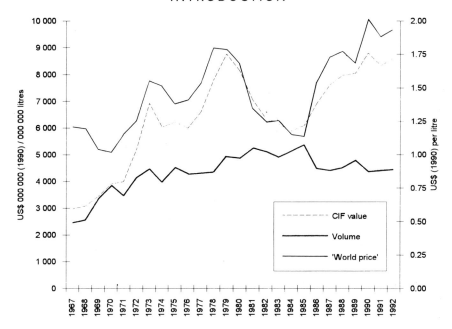

[A] World wine imports (source: United Nations).

between the two actually superseded the volume of wine traded in the rest of the world. French orders from Algiers fluctuated in a 1.5 to 2 billion litres band since the mid-1950s. Agreements on running them down, to about 700 million litres a year by 1970, were signed in Evian in 1964. 1970 was the deadline laid down by the Treaty of Rome[20] for setting up a common organisation for the EU's (or EEC's as it was then) agricultural markets.

The 1970s delivered dazzling rates of growth: 7.8% per annum in terms of real value and 3.5% a year on average for volumes. The trend was so strong that, discarding French imports for a moment, world trade increased nearly tenfold in volume between 1950 and 1979. The wine trade also weathered the shock caused by the 1973 oil price rise with little damage except for those who had ridden the 1972 and 1973 speculative wave too fast – prices had rocketed in Italy and France as the result of poor harvests and many traders had banked on further price increases. In Bordeaux for instance, many négociants found themselves caught with exclusive buying arrangements for wines they could not sell at a profit in the recessionary mid-1970s;

20 Setting up the European Economic Community in 1957.

11

they fell into the hands of their creditors, or insurance groups and global drinks marketers.

1980 was a turning point in many respects: the second 'oil shock' triggered recessions in the early 1980s in most industrial countries and world demand for wine embarked on a steady decline after increasing unabated for decades; world production followed suit, yet not sufficiently to keep the world market in balance. The lacklustre 1980s brought about a stagnation of trade in terms of volume in the first half of the decade as Germany started to cut down orders, and their contraction in the next; they declined at a yearly rate of 1% over that period. The collapse of French and Italian prices during the winter of 1979 sparked off a genuine 'wine war' between the two players and the introduction of two key price support arrangements by the EU a couple of years later – a minimum price for wine and the compulsory distillation of surpluses; some measures were also enacted with the aim of curbing output, gently paving the way for a gradual enforcement of national production quotas.

The value of world trade and its average price tumbled between 1980 and 1985, mostly under the pressure of soaring EU production surpluses – over 2.5 billion litres were removed each year from the French and Italian markets via distillation measures at that time. Value and price climbed back to 1980 levels as EU price support arrangements began to take effect, yet mostly as the result of the powerful shift from bulk to bottled trade that was spurred by food retailers. Not much ground was gained in the end: the value of world trade in the 1980s increased at a rate of only 0.5% a year. The levelling off of values and prices in the early 1990s, whilst volumes continue their gentle decline, prompts the critical question on whether international wine trade can resume growth this century, in value and volume, and where those 'green shoots' are likely to be found?

Western Europe and North America provided the engine for growth in the 1970s (see Fig. B). The contraction of the US market since 1986 – hitherto keeping abreast with the UK in the fight for fourth place in the world importers' league – was only partially offset by further increases in the American continent. The Soviet bloc has faced mounting economic difficulties ever since 1980 and its members cut their orders accordingly. COMECON's disintegration a decade later left its traditional wine suppliers looking desperately for substitute export markets. The world wine trade was thus left with only Western Europe (a sprawling EU who likes to further imports from Club members exclusively) and the Pacific Rim (Japan essentially) to fuel new growth. But is this trend sustainable in the face of a worldwide consumption declining at a rate of 1.7% per

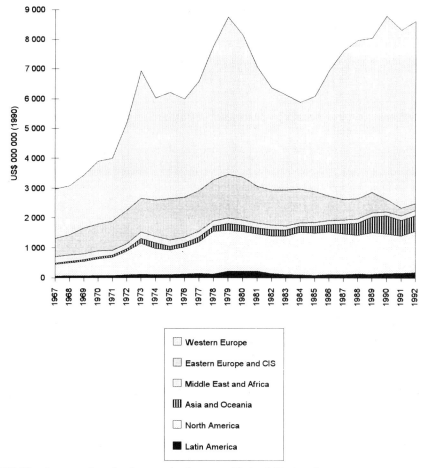

[B] The international wine trade (source: United Nations).

annum,[21] now that the British and other Northern European markets have reached a certain degree of maturity, that Germans have absorbed most of the impact of reunification and that the Japanese miracle has ground to a halt?

International trade in wine, as in other commodities, remains heavily concentrated in the hands of a dozen rich nations – the 'G7' plus a handful of Western European countries which are profiled later in this book. Many of the largest importers happen to be significant wine producers, and some are keen exporters as well, engaging in 'two way' trade. Large producers are most exposed to declining wine sales. Table A lists the major producing countries of the world.

21 From 28.2 in 1980 to 22.9 billion litres in 1992.

World wine production (million litres)

	1971–75	1976–80	1981–85	1086–90	%	1991	1992
Europe	24 881	25 845	26 195	22 756	78	20 014	23 857
America	4 496	5 088	5 235	4 552	16	3 935	4 064
Oceania	270	402	453	493	2	444	500
Asia	211	225	400	465	2	446	483
Africa	1 454	1 044	1 075	1 013	3	1 110	1 148
World	31 312	32 604	33 357	29 278	100	25 950	30 052

	1971–75	1976–80	1981–85	1986–91	%	1991	1992
France	6 874	6 726	6 746	6 534	22.3	4 269	6 540
Italy	6 956	7 462	7 215	6 023	20.6	5 979	6 869
Spain	3 219	3 383	3 396	3 366	11.5	3 139	3 704
Argentina	2 278	2 460	2 046	1 884	6.4	1 450	1 435
Former USSR	2 813	3 060	3 444	1 814	6.2	1 800	1 800
USA	1 322	1 654	1 771	1 712	5.8	1 514	1 562
Former FRG	809	783	980	1 092	3.7	1 017	1 340
South Africa	535	630	865	857	2.9	970	1 000
Portugal	1 033	948	908	846	2.9	983	756
Romania	791	802	870	750	2.6	481	750
Top 10	26 629	27 906	28 241	24 877	85.0	21 601	25 755
Former Yugoslavia	614	669	613	589	2.0	538	456
Australia	250	366	403	446	1.5	394	459
Greece	522	541	500	434	1.5	402	405
Chile	505	566	660	410	1.4	290	317
Hungary	509	525	499	406	1.4	461	388
Bulgaria	288	374	436	326	1.1	255	197
Brazil	211	270	401	292	1.0	306	358
Austria	224	294	287	285	1.0	309	259
China			150	273	0.9	300	310
Switzerland	95	104	131	128	0.4	125	124
Top 20	29 847	31 616	32 319	28 467	97.2	24 980	29 026
Former Czechoslovakia	109	142	130	120	0.4	155	134
Mexico			223	118	0.4	242	242
Uruguay	92	60	71	80	0.3	80	95
Algeria	697	230	101	69	0.2	46	50
Cyprus	104	100	93	67	0.2		
Japan	17	24	78	54	0.2	57	58
New Zealand	20	36	50	46	0.2	50	42
Morocco	106	88	39	43	0.1	39	44
Canada	62	48	47	39	0.1	37	38
Tunisia						41	41
Top 30	31 055	32 345	33 152	29 102	99.4	25 727	29 769

Source: OIV   *author's estimates in italics*

1

Production

Viticulture

Few people excel in viticulture nowadays. These rare cases should be noted however, not least because they reveal the vineyards' latent profitability – the aspect which people consider most.

(Pliny the Elder, *Natural History*, Book XIV, Paragraph 47, AD 77)[1]

Wine production is a sequence of tasks revolving around the transformation of grapes into a stable alcoholic drink, an operation which may take anything from 2 to 18 months. It ranges from crushing harvested grapes to dispatching bottled wines. The principal tasks are reproduced in Fig. 1.1. Winemaking cannot be dissociated from grape production (viticulture) for the quality of wine is largely determined in the vineyard.

However brilliant, a winemaker will not manage to make a great wine out of poor grapes. Viticulture is a science in its own right, as is oenology; grape growing and winemaking are becoming increasingly (if not wholly) a job for talented professionals. The required scientific technical knowledge, skills and financial stakes are too high to be left to the amateur or weekend farmer.

Vitis vinifera stems from Europe and Central Asia. The species is responsible for virtually all of the world's wine production. Its

---

1 'In nostra aetate pauca exampla consummatae huius artis fuere, uerum eo minus omittenda, ut noscatur etiam praemia, quae in omni re maxime spectantur', Gaius Plinius Secundus.

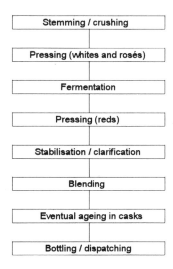

| Stemming / crushing |
| Pressing (whites and rosés) |
| Fermentation |
| Pressing (reds) |
| Stabilisation / clarification |
| Blending |
| Eventual ageing in casks |
| Bottling / dispatching |

1.1 Winemaking.

outstanding genetic capacity to adapt to its environment has resulted in a large number of vine varieties disseminating around the globe over the centuries, and in a wide spectrum of wines being made available throughout the world today. Man is also intervening directly in the selection process, first through vegetative (clonal) selection and, now, genetic engineering.

Clonal selection is operated in nurseries by cross-breeding new varieties from selected plants (*vitis vinifera* vines are hermaphrodites and prone to bud mutation). Thousands of clones are now available: they are much more resistant to viruses and bring much higher yields than in the past – and some would claim better quality. Even though there is considerable research undertaken at the moment, genetic engineering remains in its infancy. Progress with vines is slower than with other, simpler fruits such as cucumbers or tomatoes. Even the dwarfing of vines which are usually grown in pergola style is possible, which broadens the scope for mechanisation.

Most of the work is carried out by national research centres, with a consensus emerging rapidly amongst professionals, as to which varieties are best suited to wine production in any particular region, given the nature of its climate and its soil (deep, poor soils remain best suited for the production of wines). Much of the selection process has been done in isolation however, so less than a dozen vine varieties are truly ubiquitous: Cabernet Sauvignon, Chardonnay, Chenin Blanc,

Merlot, Pinot Noir, Riesling, Sauvignon Blanc, Semillon and Syrah.[2] These are deemed 'classic' varieties. They stand at the root of the export success of French and German wines and have been taken up by Australians, North and South Americans (USA and Chile), Eastern Europeans (notably Bulgaria, Romania and the former Yugoslavia who often achieve notoriety for their 'cheap versions' of the best varietal wines). Few other varieties have managed to cross national borders and many countries have continued to rely on their indigenous varieties, either because of lack of proven better varieties or for lack of trying. Italy, Spain, Portugal, Austria, Hungary, Argentina (with Criolla) are good examples of such particularism. Of the thousand or so significant varieties being used in the production of wine today, only three dozen have achieved international renown.[3]

This proliferation of names and places meets many a dedicated drinker's or collector's need for diversity but is hardly considered a sales pitch by the majority of consumers, who like to reduce risk by concentrating on classic varieties or on established appellations – regions with specific planting and production requirements such as the Chianti (which uses a great proportion of Sangiovese grapes in the elaboration of its wines), the Rioja (Tempranillo and Garnacha) or the Tokay (Furmint), to name a few.

Research and development conducted at public and private levels will continue to look for and come up with better and more economical vine varieties. As long as legislation on appellations evolves, this should add to the diversity of grapes rather than dent it. And similarly for the ensuing wines, which are often crafted from blending several varieties together.

Today's vintages are much more stable than in the past, both in volume and in quality. In addition to progress achieved in vine selection, the use of more resistant rootstocks (the understock upon which a fruiting vine variety is grafted) and the application of more effective chemicals have contributed to reducing the impact of natural hazards on production, particularly phylloxera, other soil pests and diseases. Hail and frost remain potentially damaging, though some preventive action can be taken against them, and these hazards can be insured against in most countries. All these factors have helped to

---

2 Robinson, 1986. Trade in cuttings is widespread but heavily regulated.

3 The 'major varieties' considered by Jancis Robinson, 1986, are: Barbera, Cabernet Franc, Carigan, Cinsaut, Gamay, Garnacha (Grenache), Nebbiolo, Sangiovese, Tempranillo, and Zinfandel for reds; Aleatico, Aligoté, Gewürztraminer, Malvasia, Melon de Bourgogne (Muscadet), Müller-Thurgau, various other Muscats, Paomino, Pinot Gris, Pinot Blanc, Silvaner, Trebbiano (Ugni Blanc), Viognier and Welschriesling for whites.

reduce risk and to stabilise income to growers who are increasingly faced with fixed costs.

Phylloxera is of North American origin. There, the indigenous vine family *vitis rupestis* has long been immune to the pest and is now almost exclusively used as a rootstock upon which any of the *vitis vinifera* varieties may be grafted. The recent resurgence of phylloxera in California's north coast region (the Napa and Sonoma valleys) is due to the growers' choice of the (now infamous) AR1 rootstock. The AR1 is a crossbreeding of *rupestis* and *vinifera* varieties. Its exposure to phylloxera was a risk which growers took willingly: it was thought to be minimal at the time and certainly no match to the fact that the AR1 was a bearer of high yields. At least 10 000 hectares (and perhaps as much as 16 times that figure) will need to be pulled up and replaced before the end of this decade, at an estimated cost of $30–60 000 per hectare.[4]

Planting a new vineyard or replanting an old one with a profitable grape variety is an investment which requires up to 10 years' payback (amortisation) period in free markets; grapes are a perennial plant – they last for several decades – and produce a yearly crop. Newly planted vines take 4–6 years to become fully productive. Switching from one variety to another by grafting a new variety on to an old vine (rather than digging it up) results in the loss of only one or two crops however. Yields usually start to fall after 10 years but quality continues to improve. Vines have an average economic life of about 30 years. Thereafter they are pulled up progressively and replaced with new plants.

Striking a balance between quality and yields is a difficult decision which growers must make not just at the onset of the investment programme (choice of land, grape variety, spacing between the vines and type of vine training) but throughout the growing season. Pruning, irrigating and, when necessary, thinning (removing excessive grape bunches during the growth process) seek to bring crop load and leaf surface into careful balance in order to ensure adequate ripening of the grapes (too many bunches per vine would prevent maturity from being reached, as would too few: the growth process would then be diverted into leaf production).

Berry development occurs in three phases. During the first, green stage flowering, berries experience rapid growth; they accumulate acids but little sugar. Growth then decelerates markedly. Two months after flowering, berries start to ripen. Ripening is the crucial stage

4 *Vinum*, 1993 (1), pp 42–5.

where grapes begin to accumulate sugars (glucose and fructose) and to lose acidity (tartaric and malic), whilst aromas start to build up.[5]

Grapes produce essentially two kinds of sugar, glucose and fructose. Fructose is much sweeter than glucose and is found in greater proportion in very ripe grapes as well as in varieties like Chardonnay. Zinfandel is an example of a high glucose variety.[6] Grapes also produce two main acids – tartaric and malic – which together are responsible for 90% of the total acidity of the wines.[7] Stems and seeds are not really essential, but skins are, especially for the production of red wines, for they contain pigments and tannins which impart colour and structure (ageing capability). Varietal flavour (aromatic) components are also present in the skins; they are deemed to travel from there to the flesh of the berries only at the end of the ripening process, close to maturity. New techniques have been developed for extracting these aromatic components whilst making white wines.

Maturity dictates the time for harvest and depends on the balance the winemaker wants to achieve between colour, flavours (aromas[8]), sugar and acidity content – more on this shortly. Some varieties ripen earlier than others and there are considerable differences in climate in both hemispheres, meaning the grape harvests take place virtually all year round, with heavy concentrations around September (Northern hemisphere) and March (Southern hemisphere). Adequate labour or machinery usually being in short supply, clever planning by some grape growers can thus significantly reduce costs (cost advantage).

Skilled labour remains the most expensive input and it is now increasingly being replaced with machines, even where it is in ample supply: sprayers, pruners and harvesters are common features in modern vineyards. Vineyards' declivity or poor access, and the search for the highest quality, e.g. harvesting in several batches to ensure optimal maturity of the grapes, severely constrain mechanisation, though small multifunctional caterpillars can now be used in terraced vineyards for instance. Mechanical harvesters allow for quick, nightly

---

5 Rankine, 1989, p 26; Foulonneau, 1991, p 29.

6 Rankine, ibid.

7 Ibid, pp 26–7.

8 Harvest time is important in this respect since it is dictated by the winemaker's choice between the production of wines having an immediate but short-lived (6–8 months) aromatic character (exploiting the free aromatic components) and that of wines acquiring a different, long-lived aromatic character by opting for a progressive transformation of the hidden aromatic components (*précurseurs aromatiques*). Foulonneau, 1991, p 31.

harvesting – which is a critical factor in hot climates. The most mechanised vineyards are those of the US (well over 85%), France, Germany and Australia (all in excess of 50%).[9] Quality producers are slowly coming to terms with the idea that manual pickers, however skilled, may eventually become prohibitively expensive and replaced with mechanical harvesters. Whether consumers are prepared to pay the necessary premium for picking grapes by hand depends ultimately on the perceived difference in the quality of the wines produced.

The basis of a thriving wine industry rests on skilful quality-minded and cost-conscious wine growers working in tight collaboration with the winemakers. Winegrowers must provide the desired grape constituents for the production of those wines that are in demand. Winemakers, for their part, must come up with quality products that are seen as unique whilst retaining recognisable features from one year to the next.[10] To this comes an additional, important constraint: winegrowers and winemakers must now show increasing respect for their natural environment, by making parsimonious recourse to chemical agents in the production of what is considered a natural drink.

Winemaking

Traditional winemaking in a sense of following what father and grandfather used to do is rapidly disappearing. We are in the age of innovation and experimentation with, in some cases, way-out ideas.

(Bryce Rankine, *Making Good Wine*, p 19)

The winemakers' original task of correcting possible deficiencies in a wine's appearance or taste has been gradually replaced over the past 20-30 years with a more creative function – that of crafting a wine's individuality from the grape's constituents. These owe their distinctiveness not just to the characteristics of the vine variety/ies the wines are made from, but also from the type of climate, soil, and vineyard management. The art of making good wine – and selling it – then consists in positioning it skilfully in the attributes' space. Price and

9 *Viti*, March 1987, pp 31–3.

10 Ough, 1992, p 2.

origin aside, this amounts to imparting the following dimensions to each wine:

1 its *colour*
2 its alcoholic *strength*;
3 its varietal *character* and winemaking *style*: fizziness, balance of odours and flavours;
4 a suitable *container* size, shape, colour and material.

Quality control has to occur right through the production process if a flawless wine is to be put to market (see Table 1.1).

It is the overall balance between colour, strength, style, character and container which ultimately positions a wine along the quality axis (which can be thought of as a higher dimension, regrouping the above four variables). Similarly, 'style and character' may be subdivided in the following lower dimensions: dryness/sweetness, fizziness, varietal character and age (their technical equivalents being respectively: acidity/residual sugar levels, CO_2, tannins and other phenolic components). The difficulty, when talking about quality, is that it is a highly subjective notion. Whilst producers and merchants are aware of the intrinsic quality of a particular shipment, consumers are much more receptive to the other elements of the marketing mix, especially package and price, which they often take as a guide.

Adopting a simple, multidimensional ordering of the wines, in accordance with their attributes, bears the advantage of flexibility over commonly accepted nomenclatures. Multidimensionality is a natural environment for economists and marketing people alike, and a powerful tool as well, that allows them to wade their way through the sheer number of identifiable elements present in each wine. Some elements come in fixed proportions: fixed acids, sugars, salts and phenolic substances all have their own taste and can be identified on an individual basis. Volatile substances (those which separate

Table 1.1 Characteristics of a wine

---

1 Price
2 Origin
3 Colour
4 Alcoholic strength
5 Varietal character and winemaking style:
   fizziness
   balance of odours
   balance of flavours
6 Container's size

---

themselves from wine by evaporation in the glass or in the mouth) are much more elusive, yet just as critical in influencing the overall taste of a particular wine; the most important ones are alcohols, volatile acids and hydrocarbons.[11] Hundreds of elements have been identified to date, some of which come in infinitesimal concentrations and are hard to track down analytically (they come in an infinite number of combinations and can easily mask each other).[12] However essential analytical checks may be, sensory evaluation remains the ultimate test.

Fermentation is central to the production of wines as well as beer or whisky. It is the transformation of the berry's sugars into alcohol (ethanol), carbon dioxide (CO_2) and heat (plus a few other elements) and is activated by the action of yeasts. These are present on the berries' skins, meaning that fermentation is a natural process (berries only need to break up for the fermentation to start) but nowadays winemakers prefer to deal with selected yeasts, allowing better control over the fermentation process.

Control over temperature during fermentation has significantly improved the capability of elaborating high quality white wines in countries enjoying a hot climate like Australia, California, Italy or Spain. Australia's near-obsession with the use of cooling systems at all stages of the winemaking operations (in order to develop and keep a maximum of aroma/flavour) and with the prevention of oxidation (this calls for carrying out all operations under inert gas, at low temperature) has certainly paid off and given producers a clear, if only temporary, technological edge. Control over temperature during the fermentation of reds has also improved the process by ruling out accidental stoppage of fermentation, which then needs to be reactivated – a sometimes difficult task. Once fermentation is over, red wines are also kept in anaerobic conditions by topping up the tanks or by using inert gas, in order to further the development of the bacteria responsible for the malolactic process – the transformation of malic acid into lactic acid (which is half as strong). Malolactic transformation or 'secondary fermentation' is always sought in red wines but usually not in whites.

Other new techniques have emerged for the vinification of white wines, notably the maceration of whole grapes (rare) or just of the skins (Dubourdieu's method) under CO_2 or inert gas before pressing. Their aim is to extract additional aromatic components present in the

11 Peynaud, 1987, p 147.

12 There are over 650 constituents according to Rankine (1989, p 293), and their number increases in line with improvement of analytical procedures, making wine 'a very complex beverage'.

skins. Maceration of red wines aims at extracting pigments, tannins and other elements bringing colour, structure and aroma, during a period of 1–4 weeks. The choice of technique depends on the variety of grapes used, on their degree of maturity and, most important of all, on the intended style of wine.[13] Burgundy's Pinot Noir, for instance, produces the best wines in the traditional manner but much less attractive wines under carbonic maceration (an intracellular fermentation producing very fruity wines, as in the case of Beaujolais' Gamay grapes which yield excellent *primeur* wines, e.g. Beaujolais Nouveau).[14]

Colour

Harvested grapes are first stemmed and crushed into must, in most cases, then transformed into wine through fermentation. Juices intended for the production of *white* wines are generally not destemmed and immediately pressed in order to avoid prolonged contact with skins and pips, then optionally cooled (in hot climates), treated and clarified before their transfer into fermentation tanks (fermentation of whites usually involves clarified musts).

Musts intended for the production of *red* wines are left to ferment with their skins for about a week, to allow the juice to extract pigments and tannins which give wines their colour and structure; thereafter they are drained and pressed. Note that a black grape does not necessarily yield a red wine; a well known example is the use of Pinot Noir in the production of champagnes. Rosés and their lighter counterparts, the so-called 'blush wines', only experience a brief contact with the skins.

Strength

Fermentation can be stopped before transformation of all sugars into alcohol, either through filtration and stabilisation of the wines (as in the production of sweet wines) or through the addition of alcohol (fortified wines). Finally, fermentation can be stopped and triggered

---

13 Not by mere economic considerations on availability/price of tanks, energy and labour cost.

14 *primeur* = made to be drunk young; Foulonneau, 1991, pp 113–33.

again later for sparkling wines, either in pressure tanks (*méthode Charmat*)[15] or in the bottles themselves (*méthode champenoise*).

Fortified wines (called dessert wines in the US) have alcohol added. Their production is widespread in warmer regions such as the Mediterranean basin, California and Australia, initially because adding alcohol was the only way to preserve sweetness.[16] Grape variety is not as important as for regular wines so high yielding clones are often used. Californian and Australian production of fortified wines has been falling ever since 1950. It remains the hallmark of the Spanish Jerez and Portuguese Oporto regions – producing sherries and ports respectively. Spain's sherry production requires extensive maturing and constant blending; this ensures consistency in quality is maintained over the years. The adjectives *fino, amontillado* or *oloroso* indicate increasing levels of sweetness.[17] Ports are made from very sweet grapes in a similar fashion; tawny ports are inter-year blends whilst vintage ports are not. Sherries and ports have an alcoholic content of about 18%. Madeiras and Hungarian Tokays are similar types of fortified wines.

Low alcohol wines apply the reverse principle: wines are made first, then part of the alcohol is removed. It is difficult to retain the flavour whilst dealcoholising the wines, and they are prone to subsequent microbiological spoilage, given the near absence of alcohol. Three techniques are commonly used: vacuum distillation (distillation occurs in vacuum at 30–50% of the temperature it would need otherwise; recovered aroma volatiles are concentrated and returned to the reduced wine), ultrafiltration and reverse osmosis.[18]

Sweet white wines have gained in appeal, particularly to women, thanks to improvements in winemaking and especially in filtration.[19] Where the addition of cane/beet sugar is not allowed, sweet white wines can be produced by postponing the date for picking the grapes

---

15 This process was introduced by Eugène Charmat in 1910; it is much less costly than the *méthode champenoise*, which requires disgorging the bottles in order to free yeast deposits. Much of the bottled fermented wines in the New World are disgorged into tanks (and sweetened to produce the desired style, e.g. brut, sec, demi-sec and doux, as in the *méthode champenoise* case), then rebottled; the only drawback is that the transfer equipment is very specific and expensive. Rankine, 1989, pp 62–73, Foulonneau, 1991, pp 168–72.

16 Rankine, 1989, p 73.

17 Ibid, p 75.

18 Ibid, pp 82–4.

19 Ibid, pp 51–3.

as long as possible in order to concentrate the sugar content, e.g. German *Spätlese Auslese* wines. This can also be achieved by freezing the grapes before pressing. Sometimes a special type of mould (*botrytis cinerea*) increases the grapes' sugar content and brings about other desired flavours as well. Alternatively, grape juice may be added to a stabilised wine after normal fermentation has occurred; the risk of the resulting wine restarting fermentation (because of the presence of grape juice) is then removed by sterilisation and filtration.

Where climate is unsuitable – cold temperatures considerably inhibit the formation of sugars in the berries – legislation allows for the addition of cane/beet sugar to the musts before their fermentation.[20] This practice is called sugaring or chaptalisation (from Jean-Antoine Chaptal, a nineteenth century specialist in the extraction of beet sugar and author of the well-known *Traité de la Vigne*). Chaptalisation is permitted in Austria, Switzerland and New Zealand. It is also common practice in the northern half of the EU, comprising the best appellation regions of Bordeaux and Beaujolais. The Commission has been attempting to limit this *modus operandi* for nearly a decade though, in an attempt to limit production surpluses – enriching wines increases output. It spent over 100 million ECUs a year subsidising the production of concentrated musts which can be used in place of sugar, but the measure soon became a standing joke as producers quickly found out that it could be used to evade newly imposed penalties on high yields.[21] This left the Commission considering outlawing chaptalisation altogether. An EU ban on sugaring would be hard to bring about since the idea keeps running into outright rejection by German and French AOC wine producers.[22] It would be difficult or costly to enforce and would only bring about marginal savings to the EU wine budget.[23] As for the estimated 200 000 tons of sugar used for chaptalisation each year, these would simply come to top EU production surpluses in that sector and call for an estimated 50–100 million ECUs in additional export subsidies for their disposal on the world market.[24]

---

20 Ough, 1992, pp 83–4.

21 According to an unpublished report by the Commission of the European Community in 1991.

22 Ibid.

23 39 million ECUs if aid for concentrated musts was maintained (according to estimates in the report above); this would be less than 5% of what was spent by FEOGA's Guarantee Section in the 1980s.

24 Ibid.

Character and style

Fizziness – the presence of carbon dioxide – is a natural outcome of the process of fermentation and is present in infinitesimal proportion in every wine. This attribute is easily controllable, and is also important in that it affects the diffusion of flavours, odours and alcohol in the human body (CO_2 activates its spreading through the blood system). Carbonated wines owe their bubbles to the addition of CO_2 from a source other than their own fermentation; they are considerably cheaper to produce and marketed as sparkling wines (or *Sekt*, or *spumante*) but cannot bear the mention *mousseux* in France.[25] Carbonated wines are often of much lower quality – and considerably cheaper – for the process is less costly, i.e. less labour intensive, and the base wine used for their production is usually of lesser quality (Germany imports a great deal of base wine from France, Italy and Spain). The remaining characteristics of the wines can be summed up in two principal categories.

1 A successful search for a *balance of odours* gives aroma to young wines and bouquet to aged ones. A certain opposition exists between fruit aroma, tannic constitution (tannin masks the fruit) and other flavours (such as vanilla) imparted by oak casks during maturation.[26]

2 A *balance of flavours* is achieved in a different way for white wines than for red wines. With white wines being largely exempt from tannic elements, the balance has to be found between acidity and sweetness (*moelleux*).[27] For red wines an equilibrium must be reached between acidity, tannin and sweetness.

Crafting a delicate balance of flavours, odours and fizziness for when the wines are expected to be drunk is the art of winemaking. Huge leaps forward have been taken recently in the chemical analysis of the wines, but sensory evaluation remains the winemaker's ultimate (some would say 'only') tool in assessing success in imparting character and style to the wines produced, and is a prerequisite for wine purchasers and importers.

The crucial operation of blending wines of the same origin is called *assemblage*; that of blending wines of different origins or vintages is known as *coupage*. *Assemblage* is not subject to major restrictions, except when different grape varieties are involved,

25 So-called *pétillants*.

26 Peynaud, 1987, pp 147–60.

27 Léglise, 1976, pp 101–3: 'The sweetness tones down the acidity and turns it into freshness, whilst the light tingle of acidity corrects the thick, heavy impressions of sweetness'.

whereas *coupage* is usually severely regulated. Blending is essential[28] (though many winemakers still fail to acknowledge the practice); this permits winemakers to accentuate or to attenuate the characteristics of the wines involved and, above all, to achieve consistency from one shipment to the next. *Coupage* is vital for the marketing of champagnes and sherries, for instance. Sherries' combined method of ageing and blending (known as the *solera* system) provides a good – if extreme – example of progressive blending of older wines with younger ones. Similarly for non-vintaged wines, the fact that they do not make reference to any particular year allows for a significant smoothing of variations in quality from one year to the next.

The ageing of the best red wines and that of whites of exceptional quality usually occurs in small oak barrels (of about 220 litres) and can last for a couple of years. Fresh, fruity white wines are ready to drink as soon as they have been clarified and stabilised and rarely benefit from ageing: their appeal depends on the aroma of the esters (combinations of acids and alcohols occurring during fermentation)[29], but ester retention is difficult (they disappear with time, at a rate which increases with temperature). These wines must be drunk whilst they are young, i.e. within two years.[30]

More complex white wines benefit from ageing in barrels (these are usually renewed every 2–3 years). Rosé wines are basically treated in the same fashion as white wines. Red wines are aged for much longer periods, because of the presence of tannins and other phenols, which continue to evolve favourably for some time.

The ageing period for reds is dictated by the style of the wines made: Gamay and Zinfandel are notoriously little aged because their appeal rests in their fruity character, the fact that they can be marketed just a few months after harvest has considerable appeal for the wine producer, e.g. Beaujolais Nouveau, Italian *novello* and California's 'white zins'). By contrast, Bordeaux reds are traditionally aged for two years in barrels.

Ageing in bottles is costly and rare (only top quality wines benefit from this; table wines would only lose in freshness and fruitiness), but some producers have opted for ageing part of their yearly production

28 E.g. Jess Jackson (of Kendall-Jackson, the current rising star of California): '... we have openly advocated the California appellation, which gives us the opportunity to blend the best fruit that's available, no matter where it comes from [within the state]', in *Wines and Vines*, March 1994, p 21).

29 Rankine, 1989, p 296.

30 Ough, 1992, p 216.

in that way, which they put to market later, at a significantly higher price. Excessive heat or cold has to be avoided during storage. Serious problems may arise in this respect when wines are shipped round the world; carelessness or industrial disputes can result in whole shipping containers (1000 cases or 9000 litres for bottled shipments, and twice that amount in the case of bulk) lying on a pier for several days and in a sharp deterioration of the quality of the wines concerned.

Container's size

Stability must be achieved and all proper analytical checks carried out before bottling occurs. One of the main functions of the container is to prevent any contact with air (resulting in oxidation of the wine). The most sophisticated bottling/filling devices use pre-evacuation of the bottle and pressuring with CO_2 or with N_2 before filling.[31]

Once corked, the bottles are decorated with a capsule either of plastic or metal; the more expensive lead capsules remained the hallmark of every leading wine for many years but have now become the subject of controversy and are on the wane). Caps lined with cork, metal or plastic are more economical than the cork and capsule couple, and are perhaps even superior to it for whites and wines which are meant to be consumed rapidly, but run into a significant degree of consumer resistance (the same thing happened when fruit juice cartons were first launched). They have already made serious inroads in the lower price range of wines and in the smaller container segments worldwide.

Regarding bottles, the choice of glass is important, yet still less critical than for beer which is much more liable to photochemical deterioration due to its lower alcohol content. The choice of glass for wine bottles is often more dictated by presentation on the super-markets' shelves and is now usually green or white.[32] Bag-in-boxes have only been widely accepted in Argentina and in Australia; cartons are used sparingly in Europe. Both kinds of cardboard containers have experienced problems with oxidation and have a serious drawback – that of conveying a cheap image to the wines; this can be easily worked around in the case of bag-in-boxes however, since their higher content (2–3 litres instead of the usual 0.75 litre) is associated with

---

31 Ough, 1992, p 232; Rankine, 1989, p 225.

32 Rankine, 1989, pp 234–5; also Ribereau-Gayon, 1991. There are problems in recycling green glass in the US, cf *Marché International des Vins et Spiriteux*, June 1993, p 16.

discount prices (as are wine jugs in the US). Moreover, they are especially suited for outdoor family gatherings and for serving wine by the glass in restaurants and bars, plus there are no glass bottles to dispose of.

At the other end of the spectrum, the now fastest growing segment in the US is that of 28.7 centilitre bottles, in six-packs, on the beer model. The continuing trend towards smaller packages is – as usual – exacerbated in the US, where it was nearly impossible to buy a glass of wine in a restaurant 20 years ago. Some are now going as far as serving a 'sip' to customers eager to try out various wines or unwilling to drink more than that for their lunch. The analogy between six-packs of cans/small plastic bottles versus a large plastic bottle for soft drinks, and six-packs of 27.8 cl bottles versus bag-in-boxes for wine is striking. Size of container and design of labels are increasingly dictated by distributors who are best placed to gauge consumer response; they can now do so within three weeks in Britain.

Additives and contaminants

One can add natural (non-synthesised) flavours, such as marsala and suze, to vermouths, and other fruit juice and natural flavours in the case of coolers and what North Americans call 'special natural wines' ('wine-based products' in the EU). SO_2 has proved an irreplaceable preservative so far. The list of other permitted additives depends on the legislation of the country concerned.

Contaminants include pesticide and fungicide traces in wines (for which maximum levels are stipulated in each producing country) as well as solvents and other materials which may come from carelessly prepared tanks, pipes and pumps. Any evidence of toxic levels in a wine results in its ban, e.g. primaricin or lead, yet usually with the result of serious trade frictions. Mutual recognition of oenological practices is a way of easing such tensions. Trade bickering aside, there are basically two universally recognised illegal compounds: diethylene glycol and methanol. Diethylene glycol is a toxic substance, which enhances sweetness and flavour (it is close to but should not be confused with ethylene glycol, an antifreeze substance); diethylene glycol was found in 1985 in a variety of German and Austrian wines and caused a considerable – if short-lived – blow to both wine industries, but not much else. Methanol, by contrast, is lethal (it can be distilled from wood[33] and is much cheaper to produce than ethyl

33 Methanol is therefore present in minute levels in spirits produced from wood, such as grape *marc.*

alcohol). Some Piemont winemakers used it to compensate for the deficiency of ethyl alcohol in 1986 – a direct consequence of barring the practice of sugaring. This resulted in the death of at least twenty Italians and in the blinding of many others and precipitated the decline of their exports to the US. Vile practices of this kind have inflicted considerable and, to some extent, irreparable damage to the world wine industry. A drastic improvement in export controls resulted from these two scandals around the globe.

Quality control

Quality control is performed through regular tastings and analytical checks. Tastings are meant to check that no undesirable substances appear or develop in the wines and to probe the presence of desired organoleptic features as well as their overall balance. Analytical checks are designed to follow the evolution of fermentation and maturation and enable winemakers to seek minimal presence of legal additives and to secure absence of flaws, such as lack of purity or funny tastes. Herewith wine producers are in a position to come up with exactly what customers expect from a natural drink. The quality of the container (material, size, shape, closure and labels) should mirror the intrinsic quality of the wines.

The laboratory is not just part of the modern winery's quality control programme, but also an instrument for winemakers' creativity. Ensuring greater consistency of the wines over the years whilst managing to give them a very personal, distinguishable touch has become less of a quandary. Experimentation and innovation are the hallmarks of the best producers. Only the largest wineries can commit substantial financial resources to R&D on a regular basis. This clearly gives them an edge over the average-size producer. National research institutes still carry out most of the research however, and results are then passed on to the many smaller producers. Their duties also include the continuing education and training of the next generation of grapegrowers and winemakers – a critical asset in international competition. Controlling the quality of the wines which are about to be exported is also vital if trade disruptions and tedious litigations are to be avoided.

The accreditation of a distinctive quality label is a marketing device which has its origins in the 1930s French system of geographical appellations – itself largely inspired from the geographical delimitation of the Douro's viticultural areas in the middle of the eighteenth century. This was intended as a purely defensive move originally, on the part of the traditional producers, against the emergence of mass viticulture and wine production in the French Midi. The idea was that producers who would subject themselves to stricter production requirements (lower yields per hectare and often organoleptic or analytical tests) would then be accredited a geographically-based quality label by a national authority – the INAO in France's case.[34] The French system was extended to the other five members of the EU (EC) in 1970, when a common organisation of their wine markets was finally set up (as in other agricultural products); it drew a sharp distinction between 'quality wines produced in specified regions' (appellation wines or higher quality wines hereafter)[35] and the rest, which were labelled 'table wines' (ordinary wines hereafter).

Ordinary wines can be subjected to specific national rules, e.g. French conditions for the production of *vins de pays*, but common (EU) production and marketing rules largely prevail in this sector. EU ordinary wines must be produced from agreed vines planted on EU soil (the import of wine grapes is strictly forbidden). They cannot be blended with imported wine unless they are meant for export. Ordinary wines must reveal an alcoholic strength of between 8.5 and 15% volume.

In the EU, appellation wines must be subject to stricter national provisions and have, so far, not been subjected to market intervention (price support) measures. For example, the French subdivide appellation wines into at least two further categories: VDQS (*vins délimités de qualité supérieure*) and the better AOC (vins à appellation d'origine contrôlée). Germans and Italians have done the same since 1970, the year of the EU's common legislation on wine coming into force: *Qualitätsweine mit Prädikat* (QmP) are of better quality than are mere *Qualitätsweine bestimmter Anbaugebiete* (QbA). Similarly, wines bearing the inscription *denominazione di origine controllata e garantita* (DOCG) prevail over *denominazione di origine controllata* (DOC) wines. Greece, Portugal and Spain had to adjust to the EU nomenclature upon joining the Community. Spain had started to put its system of geographical appellations in place as early as 1970.

The nomenclature adopted beyond Europe, in Australia, North and South America and South Africa is much simpler, yet not

---

34 Institut National des Appellations d'Origine.

35 Neither classification is wholly satisfactory and using simply 'quality wines' seems to contradict the fact that there are good quality table wines produced in the EU.

fundamentally different from that used in the EU. In the US, for instance, wines revealing an alcoholic strength of 15–24% are classed 'dessert' wines; Britons would refer to them as 'fortified' wines. Those with 7 to 15% alcohol fall in a broad category confusingly called 'table wines'; it is further (but informally) divided into 'premium' and 'non-premium' or 'jug' wines,[36] roughly matching the distinction between 'quality' and 'table' wines prevailing in the EU. Up until 1955, there was no official distinction between ordinary and higher quality wines.[37] The expression 'ordinary wine' is substituted for 'table wine' when dealing with the EU, to avoid confusing US readers.

The New World differs from old Europe in its controversial use of 'semi-generic' names such as Claret, Chablis, Burgundy, Lambrusco or Moselle. These names were implanted by European colonists and commonly used to depict varying wine styles. Their use is confined to North America and Australia, where they are permitted *if* they are accompanied by a geographic name referring to the region of production (e.g Californian Chablis). Semi-generics are positioned at the lower end of the quality scale, just above the mere 'generic' wines (whites, reds and rosés); they are virtually unused in international trade and rising consumer demands are clearly putting them on the wane at home. Semi-generics are gently upgraded into superior varietal wines, such as Chardonnays, Semillons, Cabernets and Zinfandels to name a few. Designations of geographical origin have found their way on the wine labels here as well. These are managed either by national or by more restrictive state regulations.

Where such legislation does not apply, producers' organisations have often taken the lead, by granting wines of superior quality a particular distinction involving regular checks of one form or another, e.g. Australia's Hunter Valley quality label accreditation programme. Many countries are reluctant to enact a proper legislation on appellations, for fear of acting precipitously and seeing it backfire in subsequent years – as was the case with Italy's Chianti region;[38] they prefer to concentrate on simple combinations of geographical, varietal and brand names.

---

36 These terms are not legally defined.

37 Stuller and Martin, 1989, p 69.

38 A new legislation is now planned, over 20 years after the Antinori winery started a popular rebellion against the stiff and largely unjustified requirements that wines entail a high proportion of Trebbiano and other minor grape varieties whilst Cabernets and Merlots were denied any part in the blend. Antinori thus started to market a top quality wine as *vino da tavola*.

The marketing of some of the finest Chiantis as *vino da tavola* (ordinary wine) for over two decades was an intentional joke aimed at a restricted audience. It epitomises the fact that legislation on appellations can work in an excessively restrictive manner and inhibit creativity which is so vital to the industry. Likewise, there seems to be little commercial justification for the ban issued by INAO on the use of varietal names in the case of French *appellations contrôlées* (except for Alsatian wines) or for the interdiction, by the EU, that reference be made to more than two varieties present in the blend.

The environment

The many treatments to which vineyards are subject in the wine-growers' fight against various pests and fungal diseases,[39] as well as the regular use of fertilisers and herbicides, can result in excessive diffusion, in the soil, of synthetic chemical agents. These can be transmitted to grapes through a vine's roots or eventually contaminate the groundwater system. Likewise, the spraying of vines too close to harvest time may result in toxic substances finding their way into the wine if no quality control is carried out. Growing public awareness of environmental issues and the failure of direct price support policies have recently prompted many governments to subsidise growers making limited use of chemicals and other toxic substances in managing their vineyards. These factors have contributed to the gradual emergency of a low-input (sustainable) viticulture.

There is a similar tendency to reduce the use of synthetic chemicals during the winemaking process. It is part of a wider trend in agriculture (and in cosmetics),[40] which is entertained mainly by retailers who have spotted a promising segment for truly 'natural' products. The launching of organic wines is a direct consequence of shifting consumer preferences. The issue is much easier to deal with in viticulture than in winemaking however, where organic wines are still noted for their faults in taste and appearance. Minimal recourse to synthetic chemicals, such as SO_2, has always been a major force in viticulture and in oenology. Genetics may soon come up with satisfactory solutions in this field.

---

39 Especially mildew and botrytis (mould/rot).

40 E.g. the Body Shop; also the positioning of many products on a 'health platform'.

Like any other activity, winemaking produces its own residuals. Solid waste consists of stems and peps, called *marc*. Liquid waste comes in the form of used water contaminated with detergents and sanitisers and/or waters revealing a high pH, their treatment may pose some problems: pH needs to be neutralised and the waters must be adequately evaporated. *Marc* can be easily recycled, either as a fertiliser in the vineyards or as an input for the manufacture of animal feed (as is draff – the by-product of whisky production); it can even be distilled into spirits. Oil has even been extracted from peps on a commercial basis in the US. No one should be lured into believing that treating waste is free: in the mid-1970s, expenses for waste treatment were put at an estimated 2–3% of the total cost of setting up a new winery in California.[41] There, permission to build a winery is granted upon submission of a satisfactory 'environmental impact report' that meets various requirements ranging from specific hydrological factors, e.g. soil and groundwater pollution to socio-economic and aesthetic considerations (the winery's design must blend in with the surroundings).

More importantly, however, the wine industry makes heavy use of corks, the best quality of which is becoming increasingly rare. Portugal's cork industry is the uncontested leader in this area. Corks are produced from the skin of a particular oak tree, which is capable of regenerating itself within 10 years, but the proportion of waste is high (more than two-thirds).[42] Widespread use of other bottle capping devices is still hampered by the entrenched views of consumers. Finally, recycling confronts manufacturers with a new challenge, and they are least interested in collecting, sorting, checking and sterilising used bottles because of the sheer costs this would involve. There are clear hints however that they may soon be forced to do so – as witnessed by Germany's 'green dot' indicating on packaging that the product's manufacturer has committed itself to doing precisely that.

Finance

Viticulture has moved away fully from the early days of mixed farming – vines were grown originally amongst trees and other crops.

---

41 Cooke et al, 1977, p 2.

42 Ribéreau-Gayon, 1991, pp 107–8.

Specialisation requires appropriate terrain (poor, deep soils which drain well, have adequate irrigation and plenty of sunshine are best suited for growing grapes) and if one ever notices anything growing between rows of vines, this is only an intended part of soil management and weed control. Wine producers' requisites for grape varieties and qualities are growing more specific each day. This has significantly eroded the value of multiple purpose grapes such as the Thompson Seedless, especially in California, where it is used both for wine and raisin production. Where such markets exist, the additional flexibility provided by the ability to allocate grape production to the table grape, raisin or wine market is rapidly losing its appeal. Poor results obtained in elaborating wine from such grapes have reduced their demand and lowered their price in the wine-grape segment. Careful consideration of which market to aim for needs to be given at the outset of any investment plan. Vineyards can always be converted by grafting another variety later on, but this involves considerable expense.

The progressive mechanisation of many routine tasks performed in the vineyards is not just calling for greater specialisation of equipment and higher capital investment, but also for a more professional labour force – most winegrowers now receive a higher-level education and training in viticulture and are being taught the basics of winemaking. Weekend grapegrowers (those who simply inherited their vineyards) often lack such skills and find themselves increasingly marginalised. A similar wind of change has swept through winemaking; those producers who are either unwilling or unable to keep in touch with the latest technology now end up in the backseat – invariably.

The production of grapes and that of wine are increasingly managed separately and in business-like fashion. Had they the means to do it, few wineries would actually be interested in owning all the vineyards required for producing the grapes they need. Possessing *part* of the vineyard can be a useful hedge against possible steep increases in the price of grapes though. The passing of short and long term contracts between grapegrowers and wineries bridges the two stages of the production process. Meanwhile, agricultural policies are being gradually phased out or redesigned in order to meet consumer demands more adequately. Adjusting production to demand remains difficult because of the high proportion of fixed costs and the concurrent elongation of the payback period for vineyards, to almost 10 years.

Fixed costs

Investing in a new vineyard begins with purchasing land, preparing the soil surface (and altering its chemical composition if necessary), fitting an irrigation system if required, and erecting supporting walls in the case of steep, terraced vineyards. Only then are vines planted and trellises erected. Machinery, such as tractors, spraying units, pruners and harvesters, does not necessarily need to be purchased, for it can in most countries be leased or contracted. In Australia, the break-even period is estimated to be 7–10 years.[43]

For a winery, the main part of the investment goes on purchasing land, buildings and cooperage – large multi-purpose stainless steel tanks with temperature and/or pressure control plus, eventually, an array of small wooden casks for ageing. The rest of the winemaking equipment (destemmer/crusher, fermenting/draining tanks, presses, centrifuges/filters, refrigeration units, a bottling line and, finally, all the necessary pumps and pipe work) is not cheap, but some operations, for instance crushing and bottling, may be contracted out at first and others, like pressing and bottling, can be cleverly scheduled to reduce capital investment.[44] A modular conception of the winery also allows for experimentation and gradual replacement of equipment over the years. Whenever required, tanks used for making red wines can also be used for rosés and whites, but not vice versa since the elaboration of reds requires evacuation of the skins.

The styles of wines one intends to produce (especially whether they are expected to be aged in wood) and the type of distribution channel one intends to serve together with the quality of that service (whether this involves doorstep delivery, whether retail sales are to take place on the winery's own premises and so on) have a major impact on the cost of setting up a winery.

Considerable economies of scale can be achieved in wine production: late 1970s estimates of the unit cost of setting up a winery in the northern coastal districts of California (where appellation wines are produced) put the unit cost of building up a winery with a yearly output of 10 000 cases at $24 per case, the unit price dropped to $6 for a total output of 175 000 cases, to $2 for 1.25 million cases and $1 for 5 million cases. Less than half that amount was

---

43 Davidson, 1992, p 107.

44 This is where bottlenecks usually occur; the current trend is to work with two shifts (Rankine, 1989, pp 38–40).

required for putting up a 3 million case winery in the central valley, which produces ordinary wine.[45]

Operating costs

Operating charges are fairly constant in vineyard management. They include fertilisers, pesticides and herbicides. The major costs are caused by labour, an area still prone to further savings. Full mechanisation reduces pruning costs by nearly half and slashes those for picking by two-thirds.[46] Returns to wine growers thus fluctuate with the size of harvest, in a proportion which depends on the degree of elasticity of demand. Most wineries are faced with an input constraint as they are either compelled contractually to take up all harvested wine grapes in the region, or feel obliged to do so owing to social pressures, or local customs. This means that in addition to bearing the brunt of the marketing effort wineries must also bear the risks (and rewards) associated with stocking all the wines produced – and harvests can experience marked fluctuations in quality and size from one year to the next.

The interaction between grape growers and wine makers depends much on the nature of the contracts passed between the two parties. Collective price bargaining takes place at around harvest time in most markets. Indicative prices are agreed upon for the various grape varieties, together with quality payment scales, usually, but not always, in line with sugar content. Payment is often made in various instalments throughout the marketing year, in order to smooth out cash outflow by the wineries. Governments may offer relief to the wineries in the form of preferential credit rates and/or a direct financial contribution for holding stocks at times of surplus production.

Financing

The sheer size of the initial investment (length of payback period) and the considerable expenses involved in R&D seem to point naturally towards increased concentration. This problem is neither new nor particular to the wine industry; atomistic structures have been perpetuated artificially in Western European agriculture, partly

---

45 Cooke et al, 1977.

46 Davidson, 1992, p 116.

intentionally and partly as the result of the nature of inheritance laws. The French and Italian governments, for instance, have long perceived a need to slow down rural exodus since the 1950s and helped wine growers pull their resources together in co-operative wineries, whilst national institutes carried out R&D for them. One of the major problems with such schemes is that, so far, only few co-operatives have displayed great management and marketing skills. At the wine production level, the rate of concentration is much higher in the ordinary wine segment, where economies of scale can be achieved and a critical mass must be attained to hold valuable brands, than in the sector of appellation wines.

Finally, the difficulty in getting fresh money for investments should be stressed, in an industry where many rich enthusiasts are prepared to run deficits for prolonged periods of time. This puts downward pressures on an already depressed average rate of return on investments in many countries. One way out of the high interest rates trap is for some wineries to 'go public' and raise fresh capital through the emission of new, public shares. Some have performed this task rather successfully, combining restructuring and recapitalisation, e.g. Hardy BR in Adelaide.

Innovation

The Western European wine industry is noted for its poor record in bringing new products to the market. There are two main reasons for this. The first is the constraints imposed upon industry structure by grape-related and wine-related legislation: the production side remains excessively fragmented and cosseted, so few are those European wine producers capable of investing large sums in the specific technologies required for producing and marketing novel wine-based drinks. The winemaking process has remained primarily in the hands of wineries run on a co-operative basis by grape growers; these were either unable to come up with the necessary cash or just unwilling to become mere purveyors of a primary commodity to other drinks manufacturers, for fear of losing their market to foreign wineries or to substitute products.[47]

The second reason for the lack of development of wine-based

---

47 E.g. concentrated musts, which are actively traded worldwide and much more cheaply produced by Eastern European and South American countries; Boulet et al, 1980, p vi.

drinks is that innovation was simply running *against* the mainstream of R&D carried out in the traditional field of winemaking. Raising the minimal natural alcoholic strength of the wines, i.e. the sugar content of the grapes, was an obsessive aim for (historically French-influenced) EU policy makers until recently; the fact that table wines are paid in line with their alcoholic content (the infamous 'degree per hectolitre' payment scheme) bears witness to this. However, grapes turn out to be excessively rich in sugar when considered from the opposite perspective of developing low alcohol low calorie drinks.[48] Reducing the sugar/alcoholic levels of the grape musts/wines is thus central to the manufacture of wine-based drinks. This can be achieved with the help of several techniques, e.g. filtering, condensation or ion exchange,[49] leading to either partial removal of the sugars in the musts or partial or total removal of the alcohol in the wines. The technologies required are not all new nor unfamiliar to those developed in traditional winemaking: low alcohol wines were first produced by German winemakers at the turn of the century, but have not really encountered worldwide enthusiasm; techniques that were recently developed for extracting a maximum of aromatic components from the musts are also widely used e.g. carbonic maceration. Yet even though there are undeniably some interactions between winemaking and the production of wine-based drinks, especially at the level of fundamental research, some of the technologies are highly specific and terribly expensive, i.e. out of reach of the typical winery.

The historical fight against low strength 'wines' helps to explain why the EU wine industry has been operating within such a narrow definition of the word 'wine', its alcoholic dimension being limited to values ranging from 8.5–15%, (the band sometimes being widened to 7–22% in order to include French *pétillants* and liqueur wines at the lower and upper ends respectively). This tight constraint was enforced for market organisational purposes, the aim being essentially to fight off wines with an insufficient sugar-alcohol content.[50] Wines must belong to this narrow 'strength band' or they fail to qualify for the various aids and tax incentives provided by the EU wine production regime. Anything above is considered as spirit and taxed accordingly. Far more important is the exclusion of the 'wines' falling into the lower band (under 8.5%) since consumers' preferences are generally shifting in that direction. These products, termed 'wine-

---

48 Escudier, 1993.

49 The use of ion exchanges is prohibited in the EU.

50 Boulet et al, 1980, p 77.

based' drinks are regarded as diluted alcoholic drinks, with some flavoured solution; the 'flavoured wines' category is expected to be enlarged to include them as well; preferential domestic tax (internal excise duty) treatment awarded to wine has already been extended to them in the EU Council's fiscal package adopted in October 1992.[51]

This legal straightjacket has made it quite uncomfortable (or less comfortable) for most EU wine producers or merchants to operate outside the prescribed band, on territories which they felt were already dominated by much larger spirits companies (above 22%) and soft drinks manufacturers (below 7%). The alternative solution – that of purveying these industries with the necessary raw material (concentrated grape juice or base wine) – was understandably of little appeal to cosseted EU wine producers, who feared they could be 'ransomed' by international drinks companies operating at either end of the spectrum.

The situation is far less static in the New World, and in particular in the US, where a few large wine producers have long invested in wine-related technologies: Gallo and Seagram operate all along the alcoholic dimension, from fortified wines to coolers (Gallo had pioneered this trend in the 1960s and 1970s already, with its 'pop wines',[52] which they had launched to make wine more popular, especially amongst the young). Even though the US legislation is not as dirigist as that of the EU, North Americans have also been faced with the problem of relaxing the minimal alcoholic content of the wines which was set to the international standard of 7%. In South America, Argentinians have done quite well with their development of low alcohol (5–7%) sangrias in the 1980s (the traditional, Spanish product usually reveals 7–14% and is also selling well).[53]

Wine-based products are thought to have an uncertain future because of the presence of close substitutes (wine coolers seem to be losing ground to beer and spirit coolers), even though they had the merit of espousing shifting consumer preferences rather closely, from strong alcoholic to much lighter, fruitier, refreshing drinks.[54]

Western European wine producers have also had cold feet in the area of packaging: here again they let their New World cousins

---

51 EU Council Directives 92/83–4/EEC, *Official Journal*, no 316.

52 These were not manufactured from grapes but from apple and other fruits; the word 'wine' was deliberately stretched in the industry's long term effort to bring existing consumers of alcoholic drinks over to wine.

53 E.g. Julian Chivite.

54 See Boulet et al, 1980 for more details.

introduce bag-in-boxes, cans (especially suited for coolers) and small bottles arranged in six-packs. Greater concentration and quasi-non-interference by the state have turned New World producers into keen marketers, for their choice is to either meet customers' ever changing preferences and purchasing habits or drop out of the competitive race.

To recap briefly, sparkling wines aside (these include carbonated wines), most wines fall into the category of still wines. Adding alcohol to wines turns them into fortified, i.e. dessert or liqueur wines like sherries, madeiras and ports. Vermouths are made from white base wine, flavoured with aromatic extracts (herbs) and added alcohol; wine coolers, low-alcohol wines and other wine-based drinks containing aromatic extracts (such as sangria) are increasingly attached to this category. It is worth stressing the basic distinction which is drawn between low alcohol (de-alcoholised) wines on the one hand and wine coolers on the other. Coolers are made by diluting wines of usual strength (10–12%) with carbonated water and fruit juice in a 1:2 proportion; this brings their alcoholic strength below 4–5%. Low alcohol wines have their alcohol content partly or fully removed but are not diluted with any other liquid. Strength below 5% can only be attained by selecting first-rate grape musts or wines (the varietal character becomes essential), dipping below 2% is usually only achieved by resorting to dilution with another solution, as with wine coolers, as de-alcoholisation below 2% runs the risk of seriously damaging the wine's organoleptic balance.[55]

Wines can also be distilled into brandies, e.g. Cognac, Aguardente and Ouzo, or into ethyl alcohol, for which there are hardly any viable commercial outlets at present (detergents, fuels) due to their costs. Some wines find other industrial uses, particularly vinegar. Figure 1.2 shows a breakdown of the principal grape products.

Musts for which fermentation has been prevented altogether are treated as mere grape juice. Should spirits be added to it (as with the Spanish *Mistelles* and French *Pineau de Charentes*, raising their strength to 17–20%, outside the scope of the EU's narrow definition of wine), they would be considered either as fortified wines or as spirits, depending on the nature of the legislation concerned. They are treated as wine for taxation and trade purposes anyway, as are wine coolers and low alcohol wines, both of which fall in the 'wine' category set up by the UN's standard international trade classification (SITC) and GATT's Harmonised System (HS) codes. Note that musts in

---

55 Escudier, 1993, p 406.

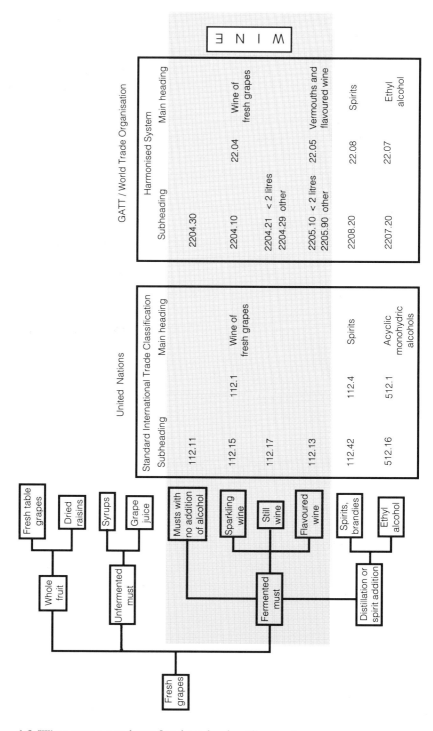

1.2 Wine grape products [and trade classification].

fermentation or with fermentation temporarily arrested by other means than the addition of alcohol – usually through impregnation with SO_2 or refrigeration – are treated separately by the SITC and HS codes, as number 112.11 and 2204.30 respectively. Both types of musts are generally intended to see their fermentation restarted in the recipient country, such as Japan and some parts of Eastern Europe and Russia). Unlike musts, wine coolers are little traded internationally; only the base wines are shipped through borders, they are mixed later with another solution by local drink manufacturers. Tables and figures bearing the title 'all wine' in the remainder of this book refer to SITC and HS codes 112.1 and 22.04 respectively; in other words, they include grape musts. Separate data on imports and exports of sparkling wine (SITC 112.15; HS 2204.10) and still wine (SITC 112.17; HS 2204.21 + 2204.29) as well as figures on trade in sparkling and still wines combined (SITC 112.12) are provided in Chapters 4 and 5. The HS code goes further than the SITC and offers a breakdown between shipments occurring in bottles (containers of less than 2 litres) and bulk. Many countries have adopted the HS nomenclature for wine trade but detailed series are not readily available on a systematic basis.

2

Consumption

Wine is a mature product. National markets are becoming increasingly segmented and aggregate world demand has been contracting since the early 1980s. Although new wine styles and novel wine-based drinks have generated comparatively poor sales to date, developing new products is still vital to the wine industry, since this helps renew and, in some cases, enlarge the existing consumer base by attracting new and primarily young customers from other corners of the drinks market. The launch of low strength wines and wine-based drinks is also intended to stem the haemorrhage of existing wine drinkers determined to lower their alcohol intake. The reduction in alcohol consumption is a general trend in most major market economies since 1980, e.g. demand in all G7 member countries is contracting except in the UK and, until recently, Japan. The shrinking environment in which manufacturers of alcoholic drinks are compelled to operate brings them to concentrate their efforts on capturing market share from one another.

'Moderate drinking' has had a reductive effect on the strength dimension of wine across all markets, old and new. Regarding wine's other characteristics, there is a divergence of trends between the traditional market on the one hand (where consumption is receding fast in purely quantitative terms) and new or emerging markets on the other, where wine is approached as a novel drink and where demand per capita is usually expanding quickly. The most successful wine marketers propose a mix which meets the changing preferences and budget constraints of their customers. Of all its characteristics, none seems more prone to fashion and fads than the place of origin of a wine.

Main features and trends

Country of origin

All too often wine producing nations prove impermeable to imported wines. Chauvinism is a major factor, reduced consumer choice as the result of trade restrictions is another. A country's exports can be easily discriminated against in the recipient country and used as a means of pressurising the other party into making concessions of a commercial or a strategic nature. *Realpolitik* aside, the normal commercial practice is that of granting mutual preferential treatment, on a bilateral as well as on a multinational basis, now usually in the form of tariff quotas. Consumers are leaning towards exotic products conveying an evasion from daily routine everywhere (the notion is central to all alcoholic drinks). A wine is thus often chosen on the grounds that it is reminiscent of distant places which a customer may have visited in the past: Napa Valley (San Francisco), Tuscany's Chianti (Florence), Yamanashi (Mount Fuji) to name but a few well-attended tourist regions that have succeeded in blending tasting with sightseeing and winery door sales. Another important factor related to the origin of the wines is customers' awareness of the political situation in a given exporting country. This parameter works mostly in negative terms (e.g. Yugoslavia). The surge in demand for South American and South African wines for instance, coincides with a return to democratic rule.

Colour

In the traditional markets, wine is a meal accompaniment and red meat the basic food.[1] Those countries are major consumers of red wines. Strong red ordinary wines are rapidly falling out of grace as their energising effect is now largely unwanted. Aside from their ability to enhance fish and other white meat dishes, white wines are drunk mainly on their own, and they are the major force behind the expansion of virtually every new market. Rosés have done well almost everywhere too. Their lighter coloration misleads people into believing they are lighter than reds in terms of calories and strength; they often constitute a white drinker's transition to the reds.

---

1 Wine has a nutritive function.

Style

The fundamental difference between traditional and new markets is that wines are considered a classical drink in the former and are mostly consumed for fun in the latter. Fizzy drinks are particularly suited to festive occasions and are a top seller in wine bars, together with sweet white wines – a favourite among women and a traditional entry point – the 'initiation wine' *par excellence*. Varietal character has gained in importance in both types of markets. The trend is also pointing towards drinking younger, fruitier wines such as Beaujolais Nouveau and white Zinfandels.

Packaging

New markets are much more receptive to innovations in terms of packaging – especially small containers arranged in multi-packs. Consumer resistance is greater in traditional markets, where people cannot seem to depart from the 'cork and glass bottle' model. This dimension is ultimately a function of lifestyles and these tend to be much more progressive, and certainly less inhibited, in the new markets. Distributors, such as supermarkets, work as a relay between the wine trade and consumers; they now largely dictate the terms as far as packaging is concerned. The same is true for price.

Price

Wine consumption is reputedly price inelastic in traditional markets and price elastic in the new ones, but this evolves in line with the gradual recognition of wine as a nutrient, i.e. meal accompaniment. Much the same can also be said for the elasticity of consumption with respect to income, which also varies markedly from country to country. The higher the degree of protection enforced at a country's borders, the higher the price of the wines and, usually, the larger the elasticities (wine becomes a non-essential item). The higher the price, the greater the potential for enlarging the existing consumer base too, as long as economic wealth and religious preferences permit. This point is well illustrated in the markets emerging along Asia's Pacific Rim, where wine is considered a luxury good and taxed accordingly. Tapping this enormous consumer reservoir is bound to be difficult and lengthy (though potentially extremely rewarding) as this involves switching from a narrow élite to a much broader consumer base.

Exchange rates, like tariffs, are part of the final price tag strung around wine bottles' necks. Tariffs and their equivalents are determined by the importing country. Barring a few significant 'two way' traders based in the EU, such as Germany and France, import prices have remained largely dictated by domestic market conditions prevailing in the country of export as well as by exchange rates which are basically a function of the economic strength of the two countries involved.

Traditional markets reveal some bipolarisation in terms of prices: cut-throat competition often prevails in the ordinary wine segment (in bulk trade on the international scene). The commodity end of the wine market is thus a classic stronghold for protectionist views and producing nations are usually well protected against foreign competition fought on price alone. In the higher quality segments, price is not the sole criterion as other attributes – particularly the image of the exporting country – are used to differentiate imported wines from each other as well as from domestic products. But 'value for money' invariably takes hold when recession or the taxman erode consumers' disposable incomes.

Three basic models

An increased role for international trade emerges from the drop in wine consumption witnessed in traditional, producing countries and the rise in demand characterising new, importing markets. The opposite trends in terms of consumption per capita are reproduced in Fig. 2.1 for a selection of countries. Another useful tool for analysis is the triangular Convergent Mix of Alcoholic Beverages model. It records consumption trends for wine, beer and spirits in most developed nations and argues for a convergence to a 40% share of total alcohol intake for wine, 40% for beer and 20% for spirits in developed market economies.[2] Table 2.1 offers a breakdown of the world's main consuming nations.

To gain a better insight in the evolution of demand in the new, importing markets as well as in the old, exporting countries, this chapter analyses the trends in alcohol consumption, wine demand and consumers' attitudes, including their purchasing behaviour. The French market helps illustrate the mechanisms at work in most traditional markets; these have been in a declining phase for at least 20 years and under strong pressure to sell outside their national borders

2 Developed by the Canadian Brewer's Association.

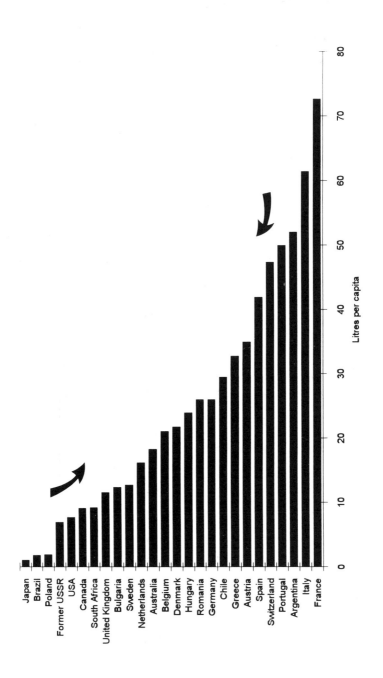

2.1 Wine consumption per capita in selected countries, 1990 (source: OIV).

Table 2.1 World wine consumption (million litres)

	1971–75	1976–80	1981–85	1986–90	%	1991	1992
Europe	22 936	22 605	21 693	17 585	74	17 337	17 169
America	4 297	4 955	5 275	4 907	21	4 522	4 459
Oceania	157	247	338	375	2	347	368
Asia	110	89	147	210	1	279	276
Africa	537	539	595	625	3	651	647
World	28 036	28 435	28 048	23 702	100	23 136	22 918

	1971–75	1976–80	1981–85	1986–90	%	1991	1992
France	5 489	5 157	4 616	4 172	17.6	3 802	3 690
Italy	6 052	5 133	4 630	3 738	15.8	3 490	3 527
USA	1 326	1 614	2 031	2 082	8.8	1 767	1 795
Argentina	1 947	2 171	2 019	1 780	7.5	1 781	1 678
Spain	2 589	2 332	1 968	1 728	7.3	1 681	1 550
Former USSR	3 050	3 603	3 603	1 673	7.1	1 900	1 885
Former FRG	1 255	1 491	1 590	1 564	6.6	2 078	2 078
Romania	618	683	683	660	2.8	449	460
United Kingdom	258	364	582	611	2.6	590	713
Portugal	750	769	795	584	2.5	620	554
Top 10	23 332	23 317	22 518	18 591	78.4	18 158	17 931
Former Yugoslavia	583	600	605	515	2.2	400	400
Chile	414	528	514	346	1.5	246	237
South Africa	261	249	308	332	1.4	367	352
Australia	131	207	301	330	1.4	305	324
Switzerland	275	285	308	314	1.3	305	304
Greece	332	378	380	307	1.3	324	315
Austria	283	269	266	262	1.1	261	260
Brazil	195	294	282	260	1.1	303	308
Canada	307	166	235	243	1.0	234	234
Hungary	348	370	312	236	1.0	310	310
Top 20	26 460	26 662	26 028	21 736	91.7	21 213	20 974
Netherlands	106	159	198	227	1.0	220	238
Belgium-Luxembourg	159	149	217	226	1.0	232	232
Poland	215	317	317	184	0.8	39	30
Former Czechoslovakia	157	180	207	182	0.8	172	139
Former GDR	100	140	140	*170*	0.7		
Bulgaria	173	183	183	130	0.5	99	99
Japan	36	41	57	112	0.5	127	121
Denmark	45	63	90	105	0.4	121	132
Sweden	61	77	86	105	0.4	101	104
China						96	96
Top 30	27 511	27 969	27 523	23 178	97.8	22 420	22 164

Source: OIV   *author's estimates in italics*

49

ever since. The haemorrhage is so serious that most have had to resort to cutting output. The new markets are explained with the help of two models – the UK for the 'importer only' case and the US for that of the 'importer-producer'. The British market is becoming increasingly flooded with competitive offerings from around the world, and is approaching maturity. The US swung into a phase of decline after nearly two decades of strong growth in the mid-1980s. Domestic producers not only managed to fend off foreign exporters; they also took the offensive and started to export their wines – with increasing success. Emerging consumer markets in South America and Asia might first appear marginal, but they are growing fast and may well hold the key for sustained long term growth in international wine trade. Their clientele belongs to a wealthy, trendy fringe of the population. This third model of wine consumption will be dealt with later, in Chapter Four, which will pursue the topic on the Asian shores of the Pacific.

Traditional markets: the case of France

Individual demand for alcohol in France – the world's highest in 1990 with just over 12 lpa – has been falling since its peak in the late 1950s.[3] Spirits consumption declined in the 1950s but has grown gently since then. Beer continued to gain in popularity until the mid-1970s and fell back thereafter. Wine remains the primary alcoholic drink in France in spite of its steady and rapid decline in volume: individual consumption nearly halved between 1960 and 1990, from 120 litres to 70 litres per head. Unlike beer or spirits, wine is almost exclusively drunk during meals.[4] Wine consumption is recentring around those occasional meals with guests. Reds are losing ground but continue to predominate over whites and rosés at a rate of 3:2.[5] Changes in lifestyle are chiefly responsible for the drastic cut in alcohol and wine demand by the French who increasingly tend to subscribe to the view that 'alcohol kills or makes you fat'.[6] The move was epitomised by the surprising adoption by parliament, in January

---

3 Litres of pure alcohol (lpa). Source: *World Drink Trends.*

4 Only 12.2% of still wines were consumed outside meals in 1990 (71.5% in the case of sparkling wines). Source: INRA-ONIVINS, 1991, vol 1, pp 27, 226.

5 75% red, 13% white and 12% rosé for super- and hypermarket sales in 1993. Source: Panel Secodip-Intercor.

6 INRA-ONIVINS, 1991, vol 1, p 226.

1991, of a law severely curbing advertising for alcoholic drinks, including wine, which came into force in 1993 (Loi Evin).[7]

The French wine market is subjected to basically two major trends: a transfer of demand to higher quality wines – drinking less but better – and a rapidly shrinking consumer base (see Fig. 2.2). The number of non-consumers soared from 24% to 38% of the population aged over 14 in just ten years (1980–90), and as much as half of the young adults admitted recently that they drunk none at all.[8] The 1980s have also witnessed a sharp reduction in the number of daily consumers (drinking 250 litres per year on average) and a rise in occasional consumers (who drink 34 l on average). By 1990, a narrow

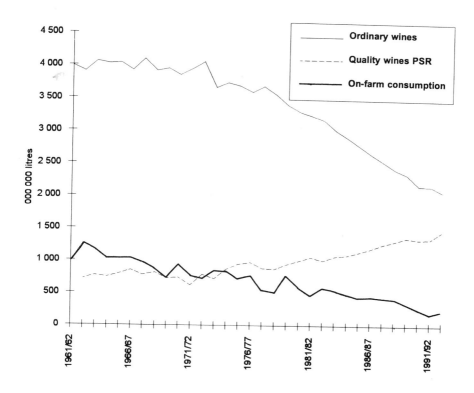

2.2 French wine consumption [including sparkling] (1961–1992) (source: Direction Générale des Impôts, Direction Générale des Douanes et des Droits Indirects).

7 Jena Laurent Maillard, 'La loi Evin', *Revue des Oenologues*, November 1991, no 61, pp 21–4.

8 Aged 18–30. Source: Sofrès-Europinion, in *Revue des Oenonologues*, November 1991, no 61, p 70.

majority (55%) of wine drinkers were occasional consumers.[9] This is new to France and nothing hints at a buck in trend.

Trends are subject to strong regional differences: it is the producing south which is most affected by the fall in demand. The largely non-producing north, where consumption is essentially occasional, continues to increase its share of the market as a result. Age, sex and income are other critical factors of differentiation. The average wine consumer is also getting older, presumably as the result of a conflict of generations. Those aged 15–35 account for proportionately less (22%) of wine consumption but, happily, the rate of contraction of demand is apparently slowing down. Also, in sharp contrast to the situation prevailing in the new wine markets, where women were largely responsible for the rise in demand, French women boast the highest rate of defection as well as the largest proportion of abstainers. Abstinence or very occasional demand are the hallmarks of the wealthier and of the more innovative segments of French society, e.g. yuppies and career women.[10] Regular wine consumers are recruited within the lower income brackets in most cases: the elderly and the retired, blue collar and agricultural workers.[11] Daily and other regular consumers purchase ordinary wines in the main.

Occasional consumers favour quality wines produced in specific regions (VQPRD in French). The high defection rate amongst daily drinkers and the general upgrading of customers' preferences means that increasing quantities of higher quality wines are being asked for by consumers and put to market by French producers: new appellations are created each year with the kind permission of the national watchdog, the *Institut National des Appellations d'Origine*. The consumption of VQPRD wines is expected to rise by 15–43% between 1990 and 2000.[12] Considering that domestic wine sales are expected to decrease by a further 14% to 48% between 1990 and the year 2000, VPQRD wines should represent 51–67% of French wine consumption by then (it now stands at 31%).[13] Wine demand could also become predominantly occasional by the turn of the century,

9 Daniel Boulet 'La transformation des comportements de consommation du vin en France', in *Revue des Oenologues*, November 1991, no 61, pp 17–20. NB: regular/habitual consumptions/daily as opposed to exceptional consumption/occasional.

10 INRA-ONIVINS, 1991, vol 1, pp 216, 225.

11 Ibid, pp 215, 224.

12 Ibid, p 219.

13 Ibid, pp 124–5.

both in terms of value and volume, as is the case in the non-producing markets.

Ordinary wines would also seem to suffer from a severe 'design' problem: over a third of the consumers actually diluted them with water in 1980. The proportion of 'diluters' sank to a fourth in 1990, and daily consumers were mostly responsible for this practice.[14] The vast majority of those who have renounced drinking wine have simply replaced it with water – usually from the tap.

In the rapidly ageing and shrinking ordinary wine segment, competition is fierce and mainly fought on price (even though this part of the market has been reputedly price inelastic on the whole); excellent logistics are essential for referencing in supermarkets which are their main outlet. The rising bargaining power of food retailer chains called for some restructuring on the production side. In the mid-1980s, there were four major firms operating on the ordinary wine segment: Castel, Société des Vins de France, Nicolas and Chantovent. Castel then engaged in a spate of large acquisitions, gobbling up Nicolas in 1988 and taking up all the ordinary wine operations of SVF in 1992 (among other firms), earning an estimated 20% share of the ordinary wine market. In addition to this, a collection of wine estates around Bordeaux, where Castel started as négociant, endow him with a combined 12–14% stake in French production.[15] Castels' turnover in wine – 450 million litres for 4.6 billion FFr (about 800 million US$) – puts it second worldwide, just behind Gallo who produces roughly 500 million litres a year.[16] The giant co-operative wineries UCCOAR and Val d'Orbieu were involved in similar restructuring deals recently (see Chapter 5). The effort that has gone into rejuvenation of the declining ordinary wine segment has led to a much more innovative stance in terms of container as well as greater reliance on brands in order to achieve differentiation. Most of the recent ventures and acquisitions evolved around brands, as it is often considered cheaper to acquire an existing one than to build up a new one. French analysts reckon that there is still no cause for concern that either a particular brand, or firm, should come to dominate the French ordinary wine market in the immediate future.

The higher quality wine segment is much more atomistic and traditional but not immune to competitive pressures either. It is considerably less branded and varietals still play a minor role – the

14 Ibid, pp 28, 227.

15 *Le Figaro*, February 8 1993.

16 *Impact*, January 1 1994. Estimates range between 480 and 540 million litres for Gallo.

accent is put on appellations (which, in France, bar the use of varietal names on the front label in most cases). The separation between the two sectors is becoming increasingly blurred as many firms have tended to diversify across segments. And VQPRD wines are not free of production surpluses either: market intervention is being seriously considered at EU level, and a 16% reduction in the vineyard area bearing a right to an *appellation controlée* (AOC) is deemed necessary to balance the market; Bordeaux was not spared.[17] Most adepts of higher quality wines are white collar workers and drinking wine is becoming more and more occasional. Work demands and rising concern for health and appearance have led them to reduce their level of wine consumption, particularly at lunchtime, and even to opt for abstinence altogether. Festive meals, with guests, are on the verge of becoming the only truly stable occasion for drinking wine.[18]

Meals with guests account for an enormous proportion of 75 cl bottles – 87%. This remains the most traditional container for wines, three-quarters of which are marketed in glass bottles (one third in litre containers and two-thirds in 0.75 l bottles). The remaining wines are shipped in 1 litre 'tetrapak' cartons, plastic bottles – mainly for bottom range wines – and small containers.[19] Cartons are essentially bought by men, for ordinary meals.[20]

Analyses of purchases by French households (outside Horeca) reveal that specialist shops (the biggest by far is Nicolas) attract a healthy 10% of French wine buyers, whilst over 20% of households buy directly from the wineries.[21] The traditional outlet, the *épicerie de quartier*, is constrained by space and is losing customers to supermarkets, from which the French are increasingly buying their wines: 45–48% did so in 1990, depending on whether one bought for an ordinary meal or for a meal with guests. An estimated 1.5 billion litres of still wines reached French customers via supermarkets' shelves in that year, representing 42% of total national sales (*consummation taxée*). Concentration is not as strong as one might anticipate however – the first ten supermarkets have a combined market share of 33% and the first five 22–25%, depending on the source of estimates. Many of the major wine retailers, e.g. Promodes,

---

17 Commission of the EU, 1993, and Berman, 1993.

18 INRA-ONIVINS, 1991, vol 1, p 225.

19 Gille, 1992, p 78.

20 INRA-ONIVINS, 1991, vol 1, p 179.

21 Ibid, p 135.

Intermarché and Casino, operate their own bottling plants. Super-markets have all developed their own brands or, failing to do so, insist on selling certain wines under exclusive labels. The market – and especially the ordinary wine segment – has become a mixture of producers' and retailers' brands, for supermarkets offer their own wines as well as producers' brands. Large producers who have established brand names, such as Castel, SVF, UCCOAR and Val d'Orbieu, are also providing supermarkets with vast quantities of wine in bulk, that are ready for bottling and selling under each retailer's own brand the following day. Supermarkets' best performers are mid-range wines: these are typically priced 7–24 FFr and now represent an estimated 60% of the turnover they realise on wine.[22] Finally, note that about 30% of the wines sold in France reach consumers through Horeca, a prime outlet for higher quality wines (half of national VQPRD sales occurred through this particular channel).

Adding up the opposite trends of France's two main segments, ordinary and quality wines, still shows declining overall volumes. Demand has become increasingly occasional and wines are losing in strength. Preferences are shifting from reds to whites and rosés, while French consumers remain largely uninterested in foreign bottled wines. Imported quality wines, for instance, account for about 6% of demand in that segment. France remains a significant buyer of bulk for blending though, representing a fifth of domestic sales of ordinary wine (more on this in Chapter Four). However dramatic these changes are to French observers, there is still a long way to go before approaching the Anglo-Saxon model sketched below with the help of the British and US markets.

New markets: the British and US models

The United Kingdom does have some 500 ha of vineyards scattered in the South of England, mainly in Essex, East Sussex, Hampshire, Kent and on the Isle of Wight. They produced 1.4 million litres of wine in 1990, enough to cover 0.2% of consumers' needs that year (660 million litres). Malta produces twice that amount and Switzerland 100 times as much as the UK, so Britain can be safely talked about as a traditional

---

22 Gille, 1993, p 80.

beer and spirits producer and as a wine importer.[23] Wine trade has a long history in Britain, but wine is still largely perceived as a novel alcoholic drink: a gentle, civilised beverage for the middle-aged and middle class; particularly appealing to women; suitable for going out and for parties, as well as for cooking, eating and relaxing at home. Wines must be mostly fruity and fun; they must also represent value for money, but need not necessarily be cheap, if they want to achieve listings in pubs and shops. There is little health concern amongst British wine drinkers (unlike in the US); this basically reflects the policy of the government, which has been at pains, for well over a century, to stress the benefits of wine consumption, especially when compared to that of spirits. The bias of the UK health policy towards wine and beer as opposed to spirits is reflected in its fiscal regime. The rate of taxation of alcoholic drinks is high, yet still in line with most other northern European countries, and wine demand is quite sensitive to price changes. This still gives much leeway for the government to alter the terms of competition between alcoholic drinks, from one year to the next, through the Treasury's budget.

Great Britain is one of the great sober nations of Western Europe; it ranked a poor 21st worldwide in 1990, revealing a consumption per capita of 7.6 litres of pure alcohol. Only Ireland (25th with 7.2 lpa) and the strongly regulated Sweden (32nd with 5.5) and Norway (34th with 4.1) managed to show lower figures.[24]

The levels of individual consumption of beer and spirits tumbled between 1875 – their all-time peak – and their low in the 1930s. This was a direct consequence of the temperance movement initiated during the Victorian era (1837–1901). Cobden's 1860 Commercial Treaty with France slashed duties on wine; this gesture was not just prompted by trade libertarians (free trade was in vogue), but also a deliberate attempt to persuade Britons to switch from spirits to wine.[25] Opposition to spirits and beer intensified during the last quarter of the nineteenth century and the decline in alcohol consumption perpetuated itself in the twentieth century, especially during the 1920s, as the result of higher taxes, stricter licensing laws

---

23 Another issue is 'British wine' (also called 'Made wine') which is not made exclusively of fresh grapes but represents 10% of what UK statistics refer to as 'wine consumption'. 'Made wine' is thus included in this particular section on UK 'wine' consumption, which draws on domestic statistics and surveys. See Chapter 3 for more details.

24 Source of data: *World Drink Trends*. Many would argue that Swedes and Norwegians drink nearly twice the published amount, bringing it to comparable levels to those revealed by the Danes and Dutch respectively (*The Economist*, 21 August 1993).

25 Crooks, 1989, p 14.

and the loss of the most valuable part of the consumer base during the First World War.[26]

UK alcohol consumption thus roughly followed a U-shaped curve this century, with two low points in the early 1930s and late 1950s respectively and a mini-revival in between; demand per capita has now basically returned to its early 1900s level. The evolution of the demand for alcohol closely reflects that for beer, of which Britain remains a major drinker. Wine has now almost rejoined spirits in terms of pure alcohol equivalents, but beer still outstrips them both, at a rate of more than 2:1.[27]

Whilst all alcoholic drinks experienced a decline during the first three decades of the twentieth century, wine managed to reverse its falling trend in the mid-1910s, until Nazi Germany cut off its supply in the late 1930s. The consumption of spirits perpetuated wine's decline well into the 1940s. Beer sales rose again significantly during the 1930s, until the end of the war, but then started to lose ground again, chiefly to wine, in the late 1940s. Wine shipments soared upon resumption of peace and trade with the Continent. Spirits soared again in the 1950s.

1960 marked the beginning of a period of sustained growth in alcohol consumption, and the rise in demand was particularly strong in the 1970s. Sales peaked shortly before 1980 however: the economic recession made average Britons cut down on consumption of beer and spirits. Wine weathered the crisis once more; but it is showing some signs of fatigue now that per capita consumption has crossed the 10 litres mark,[28] yet still after an outstanding 300% increase in consumption over 1970. Spirit sales grew fast in the 1970s but then started to recede gently during the following decade. Beer figures have remained almost stagnant over the past 20 years. The demand for beer, spirits and wine seems to have settled – if only momentarily – at around 6300, 240 and 730 million litres respectively (see Fig. 2.3).[29]

Consumer expenditure on alcohol – and beer – grew in line with that on food between 1975 and 1990. Spending on spirits grew considerably slower while wine outpaced them all (the rate of growth for wine was roughly equal to that of total consumer expenditure). In 1990, spirits, beer and wine accounted for 12%, 28% and 10% of

---

26 Young men, who are the heaviest drinkers. Crooks, 1989, pp 14–5.

27 Harding, 1991.

28 Nearly 16 litres per head if one discounts people aged under 15; C&E OPCS as in NTC.

29 In 1990 (C&E as in NTC): 63.1 million hectolitres for beer, 2.44 (27.21 million cases) for spirits, 7.34 for wine, including 0.7 'made wine'.

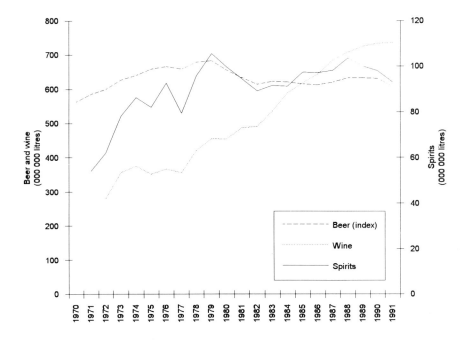

2.3 UK consumption of alcoholic drinks (1970–91) (source: HM Customs & Excise).

Britons' food budgets respectively. Food took up roughly an eighth of their total spending that year.[30]

The fall in the real price for wines and spirits helped them take market share away from beer, whose prices have risen gently over the past two decades (see Fig. 2.4). The demand for wine is particularly elastic with respect to income (2.6), ahead of spirits (2.1) and beer (0.9).[31] Richer consumers devote a higher share of their budget to wine as well. This is due partly to the fact that wine drinkers are usually recruited amongst the better educated, and partly to the ability of the more expensive wines to galvanize spending by the more affluent members of British society. Typically perhaps, the top tenth of households are reckoned to account for over a third of all spending on wine.[32] One should stress that this segment, like art, is a limited market and most vulnerable to recession. This is in sharp contrast to

30 Source: CSO (as in NTC).

31 Crooks, 1989, p 61.

32 The concentration of heavy alcohol drinkers is also an issue which is often forgotten: e.g. in Scotland 3% of the drinking population is thought to account for 30% of consumption; a similar situation prevails in the USA. Crooks, 1989, p 43.

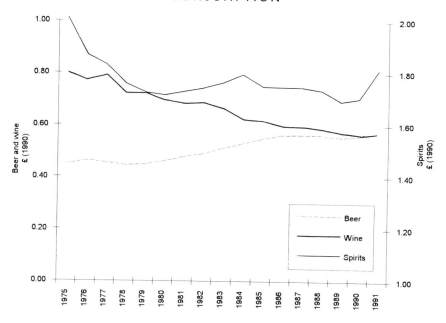

2.4 UK retail price of alcoholic drinks (litre of wine equivalent) (source: Business Statistical Office and Central Statistical Office).

beer which remains the poor man's drink; it behaves like an inferior good in the highest income brackets,[33] though many Britons are beginning to enjoy speciality beers and are starting to build up an appreciative and stable market, as with fine wines.[34] In addition to this, spirits and wine turn out to be more sensitive to price than beer (their own-price elasticity is estimated at −1.6, −1.3 and −0.8 respectively).[35] Spirits and wine tend to complement each other rather than work as substitutes.

33 Ibid, p 47.

34 '... after the blandness of much lager', *The Financial Times*, 19 January 1993. However unusually open to foreign beer products, the market share of pan-European brands is much smaller than for soft drinks; Dutch Heineken and Danish Carlsberg have market shares of 3.4% and 2% respectively.

35 As estimated over the years 1970–84, on the basis of Family Expenditure Survey data and corrected for under-reporting (using not FES budget shares but those from the National Accounts, which are more accurate); price elasticities are higher than those of the UK Treasury (−1.4 for beer; −0.4 for wine and −2.4 for spirits). See Crooks, 1989, pp 61, 76, an outstanding work for more details. Atkinson et al, 1990, have come up with roughly similar estimates concentrating around −1.1 for price and ranging between 1 and 1.5 for income.

The main impulse for the relative fall in wine and spirits prices, with respect to beer, did not come from the market however. It was given by the UK Treasury who lowered the rate of taxation on spirits and wine but increased that on beer. Taken together, the rate of duty (domestic duties are imposed on all alcoholic drinks consumed in the UK, whether imported or produced in Britain) and the consumer tax (VAT) make up more than 50% of the retail price of wine. The high incidence of taxation on the prices of alcoholic drinks means that the fiscal policy of the government dictates the terms of competition between them, by and large.

The UK Treasury vindicates its taxation policy on alcohol consumption on the grounds of its social cost, expressed in terms of additional health care expenses caused by addiction, i.e. alcoholism, and other external effects resulting from alcohol abuse, e.g. injuries caused by drunken-driving. Ever since the eighteenth century London 'gin epidemic', Britain has applied a differentiated tax or duty rates structure which clearly discriminates against spirits. The fiscal policy of the UK Treasury has also penalised wine until recently.

However sluggish, EU tax harmonisation has already stripped the Treasury of some of its powers in matters of alcohol taxation and brought about an equalisation of the beer and wine rates. This was no easy task. The EU Commission had to resort to dragging recalcitrant British, Irish and Danish governments before the European Court of Justice. Its 1983 ruling fell in the Commission's favour and resulted, the following year, in a slight increase in the UK duty on beer while the rate applicable to still wines was abated by 20% the following year (see Fig. 2.5).[36] Four years later, the duty rates were reduced for low strength beverages: low alcohol beer and wines as well as mixed drinks, including wine coolers. Duties on beer and wine are now similar but there remains a substantial tax bias against spirits.[37]

The reluctance of Northern European governments to give away powers in matters of alcohol taxation is quite understandable. Wine alone generated over £2 billion cash for the British Treasury in the 1990/91 fiscal year.[38] A common regime for duty and VAT was

36 The excise duty for wine with alcoholic content below 15% wine fell from £113 to 90.5 per hl: NTC, p 164.

37 If one subscribes to the sensible view that social cost is proportional to the strength of the drink; see Baker & McKay, 1990, p 6–7 for more details.

38 £855.342 million in duty and (an estimated) £1289 million in VAT receipts.

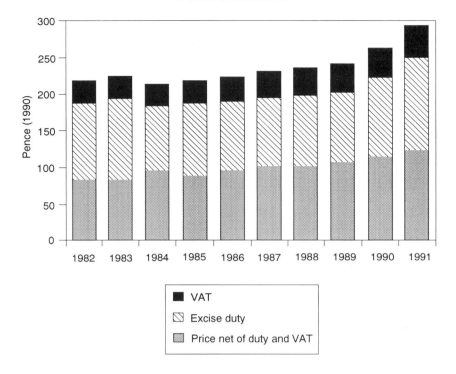

2.5 Wine and 'made wine'; level of duty and tax per litre (source: HM Customs & Excise).

enforced in January 1993.[39] The initial proposals of the Commission[40] represented a significant reduction in all UK duty rates (and Treasury revenue), yet an especially strong bias in favour of wine.[41] The stark opposition of some of the governments led to a status quo by and large: rates applied by individual member states may still vary significantly within a prescribed band which is expected to narrow down in the future, just like that of the European Exchange Rates Mechanism. This basic confrontation of vested interests (mainly between the various alcohol industries) takes place in each country; it is eventually arbitraged by the Treasury, which needs to maximise its revenue. Similar problems have developed in the USA.

Other important factors have contributed to the continuous rise in wine sales in the UK. The baby-boom years added many new customers to the wine consumer base. In the 1970s and 1980s,

39 Council Directives 92/83–84/EEC, 19 October 1992.

40 COM(87) 328, 1987, often referred to as the 'Cockfield proposals'.

41 See Baker & McKay, 1990, p 8–9, for more details.

drinking wine became fashionable and most of the growth came from the younger segment of the population, i.e. under 35[42] (the number of table wine drinkers jumped by 26%, from 25 million in 1982 to 31 million in 1992 while regular wine drinkers nearly doubled over the same period, from 3 to 6 m).[43] The sizeable increase in population which took place in the second half of the 1980s could have a similar effect in the early years of the next century.) In the late 1980s, the market was spurred by rising demand from existing consumers, aged between 25 and 50 who continue to provide the main drive to wine sales.[44]

The surge in wine sales was chiefly the result of changing customers' preferences and purchasing habits. A strong rise in home entertainment has made average Britons reduce visits to their local pub (unlike beer or spirits, wine is typically a couple's drink). French and Italian cuisines have also made considerable inroads in Britain in recent years (as in many other parts of the world) and wine drinking is closely associated with food. Foodhalls' wine departments have become a hallmark of the quality of the service offered to UK shoppers of late, while wines have continued to make advances on their own strength in local pubs, often via the ladies' lounge,[45] and in trendy wine bars, simply by becoming much more palatable and suitable to customers' needs. As in many other countries, image and fashion were all-important in the 1980s, and the 1990s are witnessing some return to older values.[46]

Vermouth and fortified wines' sales and share of the growing UK wine market have declined over the past decade (see Fig. 2.6). Sparkling wines have more than doubled their sales and their market share over the same period. The largest gainer in terms of sales volume

---

42 *Harpers Wine & Spirit Gazette*, 21 November 1980, reporting on EIU's Report no 87 on the wine industry.

43 Regular drinkers = so-called 'heavy users', defined as having drunk more than 3 bottles in a month (which is equivalent to more than half a glass a day); table wine includes appellation wine, e.g. sherry, port or vermouth drinkers). Source: NTC, 1993, p 106.

44 25–55 (NTC, p 106f) but really 25–49 in as far as 'penetration of weekly drinking' is concerned (NTC, p 104); below 40 according to FES survey, in Crooks, 1989, p 16; profile = 25–44 according to Euromonitor, as in MIVS, June 1990, pp 11–12.

45 It took a while for the wine glass to become socially acceptable in a male-dominated pub.

46 *The Drinks File*, 1993, no 2.

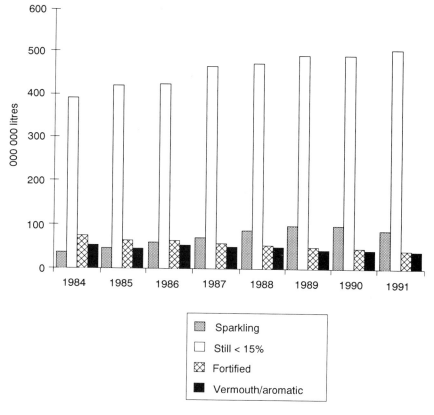

000 000 litres

Sparkling

Still < 15%

Fortified

Vermouth/aromatic

2.6 UK wine consumption [wines of fresh grapes] (source: HM Customs & Excise).

is still wine of less than 15% (sometimes, but confusingly termed 'light wine'[47] and referred to as 'still wine' henceforth).

Vermouths and fortified wines are more akin to spirits than to wine in the eyes of the consumers. Vermouth and sherry, both predominantly 'ladies' drinks' have actually seen their consumer base shrink over the past decade. Vermouths experienced soaring sales in the 1970s, and remained in fashion during the 1980s. They have now lost in appeal with young customers and have become regarded as an old ladies' drink. Sales have been falling in volume over the past decade and the total consumer base has shrunk by 37% to 9.5 million in 1992; and the core of regular users has diminished even more

47 'Light wines' really refer to wines of lower strength. It is preferable (and so much simpler) to talk of 'still wines' when dealing with wines of 10–15%. Those revealing a superior strength are already classified as 'fortified'. We shall refer to those revealing an alcoholic content of less than 10% as 'lighter' wines. Note: these are either partially fermented or partially de-alcoholised, depending on the method used.

rapidly, by 54%, to 0.6 million. Sherries have also lost in popularity, probably because of the confusion created by their seemingly directionless marketing;[48] their consumer base is typically older than that for table wine, concentrating as it does on the over 55s. Sherry sales have declined in volume over the 1980s as have all fortified wines except port, which has managed to keep its figures basically unchanged. The combined market share of vermouths and fortified wines had dwindled from 22% in 1984 to 12% in 1991.[49] Sparkling wines have been the fastest growing segment of the market over the past decade, thanks to soaring champagne sales and, recently, *cava* from Spain; sparkling and fortified wines have basically swapped market share in just seven years (between 1984 and 1991). Yet it is still wines which have gained most in terms of volume, by adding more than 100 million litres to their 400 million market since 1984.

These trends are further proof of the continuing drift away from high strength alcoholic drinks and wines towards beverages with reduced alcohol content. It is basically the combined result of the UK's fiscal policy and of greater concern with health issues on the part of consumers themselves, with perhaps a tinge of temperance (though still not comparable, yet, to the situation in the US).

Price

Regarding wine's other dimensions, price competition is fierce in the increasingly important 'off-licence' trade sector, i.e. specialist shops and supermarkets. In the early months of 1992, no less than 43% of the sales occurred in a 67p (US$1) range, between £2.33 and £3.00. Within that bracket, there was tight competition between German, French and, to a lesser extent, Italian wines. Some 40% of the offerings were positioned above that band and dominated by French products. Some 17% of sales were realised below the main price band. German, Italian and French firms fought each other in the £2.21–2.35 segment, whilst German and Spanish wines fought a fierce battle at the cheapest end.[50]

48 *The Drinks File*, 1993, no 2.

49 Market shares relate to wines made exclusively from fresh grapes (source: NTC).

50 Stats MR, as in NTC, p 92.

Origin

French, German and Italian wines monopolise three-quarters of the British market. The share of the original six members of the EU has been rising steadily since Britain joined the Community. Lately however, Britons have been turning increasingly towards New World wines, especially those from Australia, New Zealand and, recently, South Africa. Sales of Chilean wines have soared dramatically ever since the presidential palace returned to civilian hands. Although the biggest supplier by far, France lost market share to Germany, Spain, Portugal and to the New World producers in 1990 after major price increases. EU producers are also under pressure from the ever more aggressively priced East European wines.[51] Britain is a somewhat traditional outlet for these wines – Hungarian, Romanian and especially Yugoslavian wines have always been present – but competition has increased in the wake of the disintegration of the East European trading bloc COMECON, and particularly after the collapse of wine imports by the former USSR. Eastern European wines are now consistently achieving listings in the 'off trade' sector, though they are usually confined to the cheap end of the varietal segment. 'Value for money' is a key factor in Britain these days, but this should not be confused with buying the cheapest wines available however; New World wines were perceived as good value for money. Imports are dealt with in a more detailed fashion in the trade section.

Colour

Britain remains a white wine market in the main. The current market share held by whites is 60% but receding fast when compared to the 70% share they held in the mid-1980s.[52] Most white wines come from Germany and the discovery, in 1985, that some wine had been contaminated with diethylene glycol (so-called anti-freeze affair) may have been one of the major factors responsible for this dramatic development (white wines were still gaining market share until 1984). Another reason may lie in the increasing sophistication of British palates, now slowly moving towards red wines. Some of the fruitiest reds are produced in the New World and these seem to appeal more to the British consumer than do Bordeaux wines which virtually

---

51 *MIVS*, July 1991, p 5.

52 *The Drinks File* (for 1987–91). Wines from Spain for 1981–86.

dominate this corner of the market. Women seem to prefer the paler drinks – in 1991, 62% of the white wines and 67% of the rosés were drunk by women. The more colourful reds attract a narrow majority (56%) of men.[53] Women are more inclined to drink wine than men: they comprised nearly 60% of the wine drinking population in 1991.[54]

Character and style

Stars of the past decade were sparkling wines and fruity varietal wines. Whites, reds and rosés of less than 13% grew at a rate that was about twice that for the entire wine market. Note that the overall rate of growth has nearly halved in the 1980s (5.4% per annum) when compared to that of the 1970s (9.1% per annum).[55] Notwithstanding this, wine remains the most dynamic segment of the alcohol market. Other noteworthy features of the demand for wines in the UK include the seasonality of sales which peak at Christmas time, as do alcoholic drinks in general. Finally, off-trade sales have gathered pace over the years and continue to do so. This segment was valued at £4 billion in 1990 and roughly shared between supermarkets and specialist shops: their respective market shares were 53% and 47%.[56] Sainsbury, Tesco and Safeway all have exemplary wine departments and sell most of the wines under their own labels. The importing firms they control enable them to source the wines directly from the producers. Some supermarkets, e.g. Marks & Spencer go to great lengths in trying to educate their customers. A certain degree of confusion amongst customers has become noticeable of late though, together with a perceptible reluctance to try out new products. Their satisfaction with the current situation and loyalty to a few brands – including retailers' labels – may well be responsible for this. The risks which British customers seek to minimise most eagerly when they purchase a particular wine, are not just financial (e.g. opting for a bad price/ quality ratio) but also social (the chosen wine must not be judged unsatisfactory by family and guests) and functional (will the wine taste good and fit the dish?). Functional and social risks are perceived as being much more important than simply losing money, for they would seriously hurt buyers' self-esteem. To avoid this, customers are seeking

53 Source: PAS Drinks Market Survey, as in NTC, p 105.

54 Ibid.

55 Based on import statistics.

56 *MIVS*, February and June 1990, pp 16 and 11–12 respectively.

as much information as possible, much of which is readily provided on the bottle's label. They rely on the advice of friends, on the image of the store and on a limited range of 'safe' brands for the rest, which all act as a form of endorsement. Consumers' growing trust in super-market's own labels makes it difficult for producers' brands to hold up against them; these have seen their market share erode accordingly.[57]

The US is another recent market resting essentially on occasional drinkers of white wines. The level of individual consumption is lower than in the UK but overall demand is larger. It thus proved a true boon for West European exporters for 15 golden years – from the early 1970s until the mid-1980s when demand entered a contraction and maturation phase (health issues and brand names play a large role in shaping demand). Energetic reaction from domestic producers brought the Europeans to turn to the UK. Some US regions – particularly California – are endowed with climatic, natural and human resources which allowed a quick response to the soaring profits realised in the wine sector during the 1970s, and enabled them to compete effectively against wine importers when their survival was at stake. Spanish–Mexican missions are usually credited for starting viticulture in California in around 1770, but Californian wine production really began in earnest after it gained independence from the Spanish Crown in 1845, and particularly after the completion of the rail link between the two coasts in 1869, giving Californians access to the major urban centres of the US.[58] But those were rocky years: there were widespread fraudulent practices by east coast wine merchants, notably the mislabelling and marketing of Californian wines as European products, and the burst of the financial bubble of the 1870s brought along a string of financial disasters which spared only a third of California's 139 wineries; all others vanished. Wine trading ground to a halt in 1918, the year it was made illegal throughout the US (over a dozen states had already started to prohibit the sales of alcoholic drinks in the early 1850s). Prohibition merely shifted viticulture into peoples' backyards, so to speak, during the 1918–33 period (*more* wine was actually produced than ever before), but quality dropped immensely. A shattered industry was thus forced to operate a 'cold start' upon Repeal as most of the American vineyards were planted with inappropriate grapes, the winemaking profession was plagued with a crowd of amateurs and there were no legal distribution channels for alcoholic drinks in place. Nearly all the wines

---

57 This section is based on Mitchell and Greatorex, 1989 and Spawton, 1991.

58 This section draws on Singleton, 1992.

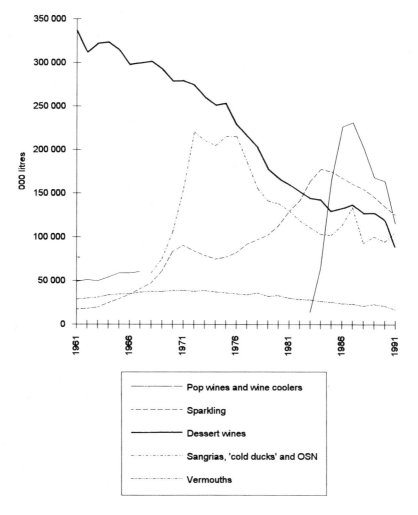

2.7 US consumption of selected wine products (wine coolers adjusted to reflect their wine content) (source: The Wine Institute of California).

put to market at the time were fortified wine (see Fig. 2.7); these made up the bulk of production until the late 1960s, when the entire market experienced a boom.

By 1990, the US were the world's fifth largest grape producer and California accounted for just over 90% of that. Viticulture is big business in the 'golden state': grapes only stand second to dairy produce with a production of about 5 million tons and a farm-gate value of over $1.5 billion at around 1990[59] and, for wineries alone,

59 1988–89 average; grapes tie second place with beef but have never been directly subsidised. See Singleton, 1992.

sales were estimated to reach $8 billion. California's grape production is split between dried raisin, wine[60] and table grapes at rates of 40-40-20%. These markets used to be largely intertwined but are now operating fairly independently (Thompson Seedless raisin grapes were long used for both raisin and wine production, but the wines elaborated from it were of poor quality); the shift to proper wine varieties only started in the 1970s but at 83% is now nearly complete.[61] The separation became particularly clear after the demise of ordinary 'jug' wines and wine coolers. The major wine varieties are Zinfandel and Cabernet Sauvignon for reds and French Colombard, Chenin Blanc and Chardonnay for whites. Cabernet Sauvignon, Chardonnay and Zinfandel saw the sharpest increase recently – between 20 and 40% in 1991 over 1990.[62] The state of New York is the second largest wine producer, with a share of 6%. South Carolina, Washington, Georgia, Oregon and Texas follow in that order and with market shares of less than 1%.[63] US wine production can thus be equated with Californian output to a large extent.

Today's US wine industry is the result of a powerful shift from fortified to generic or jug wine first, then further up the quality scale into varietals; a simultaneous shift occurred, from red and rosé to white and blush wines. Relentless research and experimenting in winegrowing and winemaking allowed for this increase in the quality of domestic wines, until they finally met US customers' need for a young, fruity and refreshing alcoholic drink. The consumer base widened steadily as a result, yet not sufficiently to turn wine into a 'national' drink. Demand soared between 1970 and 1987, its all-time peak (1984 if coolers' figures are either ignored or adjusted to reflect their wine content only);[64] consumption has been falling back almost as fast ever since then. This spelt a return to difficult times for US wineries faced with a relatively low level of profitability – the rate of

---

60 Including small amounts of grape juice/syrup production.

61 Singleton, 1992, Fig. 8.

62 Wine Institute.

63 Standard wine removed from fermenters; Wine Institute.

64 US demand for wine peaked in 1984 at 2.034 billion litres (cooler-adjusted figure) or in 1987 (2.119 billion litres) if coolers are included. Wine coolers soared from 1984 to 1987 and started to decline rapidly afterwards. The demand for wine used in the production of coolers represented 25% of California's wine production at its peak. Note that coolers' full sales figures (and not the estimated 'wine part' are used in US wine consumption official figures; the interested reader should divide them in half in order to extract the 'pure wine component' – such is the US rule of thumb (Wade Stevenson).

return on investments was deemed to be only about 7% at that time – and declining margins, as wine prices fell for most of the second part of the 1980s whilst grape prices increased.[65] Price wars raged in the ordinary jug segment and many foreign wines had to resort to abandoning the US market. All this took place in an atmosphere tainted by neo-prohibitionist tendencies and amidst one of the most unstable environments for corporate finance – that of the late 1980s and early 1990s.[66] The US wine industry is still left with the need to raise the awareness of wine amongst the US public by stressing all the benefits of moderate consumption whilst divorcing its image from that of 'hard liquors' (spirits) and also with the daunting task of lifting all inter-state trade barriers.

Individual US alcohol consumption, on the increase until 1981, has been declining ever since. First to fall were spirits, for which per capita consumption peaked in 1977–78. Beer consumption peaked in 1981 and wine followed suit a few years later. Average alcohol consumption per capita climbed higher in the US than it did in the UK, but has now fallen back to the British level. Although 65% of it is imbibed in the form of beer in both countries,[67] US spirits consumption remains notably higher than that in the UK and wine demand is much lower: it only stands at two-thirds of its UK level. In both countries wine outperformed beer and spirits in terms of growth: in the US, wine consumption per capita more than doubled over the last thirty years, from 3.6 litres per head in 1961 to 7.7 in 1990 (as a comparison, UK demand soared from 1.8 to 11.6 in that same time span). The sheer size of the US makes it a significantly larger market however; it is the fourth largest consumer worldwide, after France, Italy and the former Soviet Union.

Also, if wine consumption seems to have reached momentary stagnation in the UK, the (perhaps temporarily) mature American market has been declining for nearly a decade. Taxation is no minor factor: while the UK Treasury was favouring wine (to the detriment of beer), its US counterpart raised the federal excise tax sixfold in 1991. There is certainly no comparable bias towards wine on the part of the US regulatory authorities: the Bureau of Alcohol, Tobacco and Firearms (BATF) prevents wineries from making any link between

---

65 Kirby Moulton.

66 Leverage buy-outs, with the help of so-called 'junk' bonds.

67 UK consumption of beer is higher than that in the US, thus indicating that US beer is of higher strength than that sold in the UK.

moderate wine consumption and health in their promotional material, on the grounds that it breaches US law on alcoholic beverage advertisement.[68]

This prevents producers and marketers from positioning wine on a health platform in the media, and, in turn, might explain why so many Americans are still opposed to wine consumption on the grounds that it contains a psychoactive substance – alcohol. The National Institute of Alcohol Abuse and Alcoholism is a powerful institution around which most anti-alcohol groups like to rally; it keeps calling for increased taxation of alcoholic drinks in order to reduce abusive consumption and cover the 'social cost' of alcohol consumption. The two main indicators of alcohol abuse in the US – the level of cirrhosis deaths and casualties caused by drunken-driving – have been receding fast over the past twenty years. Also, there is no evidence that 'abusers' reduce their alcohol intake in the face of rising prices more than do moderate consumers; youths, for instance, would just appear to increase their consumption of marijuana.[69] But the federal, state and local governments do need some justification for raising 'sin' taxes. Those on alcoholic drinks were worth $17 billion in 1991 alone: 65% were the result of duties levied by federal and state governments, 25% came in the form of a sales tax imposed by state and local governments and the rest were the proceeds of licence fees, profits and a federal 'floor stock tax'. Tariffs amounted to 'only' $76 million, i.e. less than half a percent of total government revenue from alcohol revenue.[70]

Then again, America's values have often swung from one extreme to the other. What might have been excessive behaviour of the 1960s and 1970s gave way to a return to more conservative values in the 1980s and 1990s and attempts to restrict alcohol consumption by various pressure groups, like MADD (Mothers Against Drunk Driving). Attempts by embattled spirits producers to rally wine, beer and spirits under the same banner with the campaign 'an alcoholic drink is a drink is a drink' (spirits were first to suffer a reversal in trend) have badly hurt the wine industry. Neoprohibitionist attacks have been countered by the wine lobby, e.g. AWARE (the American Wine Alliance for Research and Education), amongst others, which attempts

---

68 The law prohibits any representation 'that the use of wine has curative or therapeutic effects if this representation tends to create a misleading impression' (Barrett, 1992).

69 Di Nardo and Lemieux, 1992, referred to in Heien, 1993. Dale Heien carries out an interesting review of literature in this area.

70 Source: Distilled Spirits Council of the US, November 1992, reproduced in Heien, 1993, p 5.

to give a more balanced view of wine's role in society. A reversal of the current negative trend is simply a matter of wine becoming fashionable again and of the product going into a new phase of its life-cycle eventually. US lifestyles have changed much over the past few decades and their ability to shape consumers' attitudes and preferences, and their behaviour, should not be underestimated.[71,72] US consumers' purchasing behaviour is quite impulsive (three hours before use on average), and nowhere in the world are brands so important and fads so full of consequences: pop wines in the 1960s, sangria and cold ducks[73] in the early 1970s, Italian Lambrusco in the late 1970s, other imported wine (as well as fashionable items like cars and clothes) in the early 1980s, followed by wine coolers and now white Zinfandel. All these fads appear to have brought the market up to its peak in the mid-1980s. Two resounding scandals – by Austro-German wineries in 1985 (diethylene glycol) and by Italians in 1986 (methanol) helped put demand on the decline in an ever more health conscious America. They certainly provided struggling Californians[74] with a golden opportunity to establish themselves firmly in the higher quality segment – virtually unprotected by the US trade regime. The US has been able to nearly treble the size of its domestic wine industry from 1960 to 1990.[75]

The near doubling of sales figures in 20 years, to 1.9 billion litres in 1990 was less the result of the cumulative effect of rising

---

71 Kotler, 1988.

72 A CBS *60 Minutes* TV broadcast in November 1991 devoted 12 minutes to a piece entitled 'The French Paradox' putting forward evidence of the much lower incidence of coronary heart disease amongst the French population in spite of their eating more dietary fat than regular Americans, then building the case that a moderate consumption of alcohol – of red wine in particular – may bring with it some health benefits. The broadcast was followed by extensive coverage of the issue by the printed press. The result was a momentous but radical buck in trend: supermarket scanning data showed an immediate increase of 45% on the previous year (mainly to the advantage of sweet reds). The programme was shown again in July 1992, with a similar effect on sales. The wine industry has been largely prevented from banking on the link between moderate wine consumption and good health by BATF, which did not hesitate to drag rebellious wine producers to court.

73 Cold ducks are red fruity wines produced by the champagne process.

74 California was faced with a serious production surplus in 1982 and some wineries went through an acute financial crisis in 1983 (Jarrique, 1987, pp 52–3).

75 From 557.6 in 1960 to 1697.3 million litres in 1990 (1529.1 if coolers are adjusted to their wine content – recall that their figure should be divided in half), according to the Wine Institute; this gives multipliers of 2.9 and 2.6 respectively.

population (+22%), and real income per capital (+30%) than that of a forceful shift of preferences towards lighter still wines, mainly whites. This was topped by two major bursts of activity in the market for wine-based products: cold ducks and sangrias were the fad of the 1970s and coolers that of the 1980s.

The impact of real disposable income of US consumers on wine demand is difficult to measure precisely, due to wide regional disparities, wide product ranges, changing preferences and, most critically, to the fact that the majority of wine drinkers still appear to be only occasional customers. There is a wide choice of income elasticity estimates to pick from, and although these vary considerably from study to study, they would tend to indicate that US demand for wine is, in general, rather *inelastic* with respect to variations in income over time.[76] The two recessions triggered by the oil crises of 1973 and 1979 did slow down the progression of the US demand for wine (see Fig. 2.8). The impact of receding incomes on (the generally more expensive) imported wines was tremendous, but they did little more than slow down the progression of domestic wines (see Fig. 2.9 and 2.10).

Wine is a positive function of individual wealth however, much more so than any other type of alcoholic drink. Here, as in the UK, beer appears to be the poor man's drink while wine enjoys an up-market image. The wine boom of the 1970s and early 1980s was definitely the work of 'yuppies'; at that time, demand concentrated around the younger (25–34) and wealthier Americans.[77] The wine consumer base may well have aged in the meantime (see below), but demand for wine remains tied to people's income status.[78]

In the US, still wines of less than 15% fall either in the 'jug' (ordinary) category or in that of 'premium' (higher quality) wines, which is split further into 'popular', 'super' and 'ultra' premium segments. These sub-categories are defined exclusively in terms of price points (see Table 2.2) and these vary over time. The vast majority of jug wines are generics, while most of the premiums are varietals. The fall in US wine consumption has been caused almost exclusively by the rapid loss of favour of 'jug generics', whilst 'premium varietals' are progressing steadily and rapidly. Price points are just as important in the US as in

---

76 See Pompelli, 1987, p 148 for a summary; Wohlgenant, 1985 also found demand (from 1963–82) to be both price and income inelastic.

77 *Impact* 1982, p 62, and Simmons Market Research in Pompelli, 1987, p 27.

78 National Family Opinion (NFO) Share of Intake Panel (SIP) survey, 1992 (in *MIVS*, November 1993).

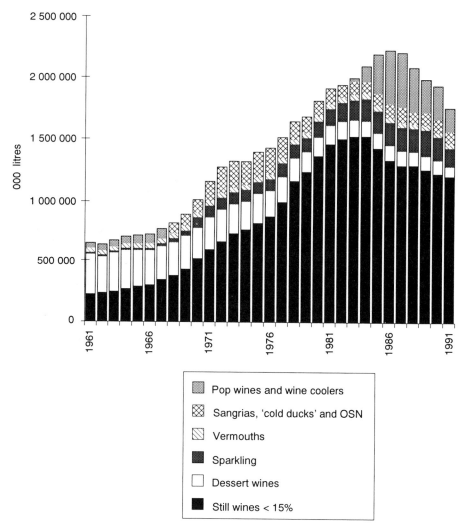

2.8 US wine consumption (domestic and imported) (source: The Wine Institute of California).

the UK; most of the sales still concentrate within a few price points at the lower end of the market. Gallo is the uncontested price leader in the jug segment; it also moved massively if belatedly into the low end of the varietal category – the so-called 'fighting varietals'.

US customers are, like their British counterparts, predominantly female; wine is the only alcoholic beverage for which sales depend on a majority of female consumers – 56% in 1992 (53% in 1981)[79] – even

79 SIP studies, 1992 and 1982 (in *MIVS*, November 1993 and *Impact*, 1982).

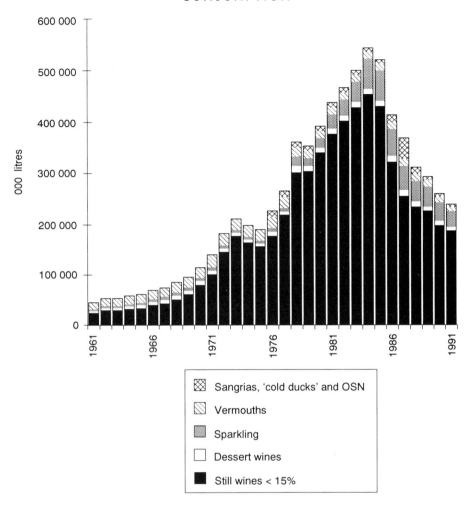

000 litres

Sangrias, 'cold ducks' and OSN
Vermouths
Sparkling
Dessert wines
Still wines < 15%

2.9 US wine consumption (imported) (source: The Wine Institute of California).

though alcoholic drinks tend to be a male's drink. Also, wine is increasingly drunk at one's home (77% in 1992 against 60% in 1981), particularly at dinner time (48% in 1992; 41% in 1981) or later in the evening (25% in 1992; 33% in 1981).[80]

People in their 30s dominate the market for alcoholic drinks in the 1990s but only account for 22% of wine consumption. Wine is just as eagerly drunk by those aged 40–49 (20%) and particularly by older people (aged over 60) who clearly leave malt-based drinks to concentrate on spirits and wine (28%). This is in sharp contrast to

80 Ibid; also in Pompelli, 1987, p 15.

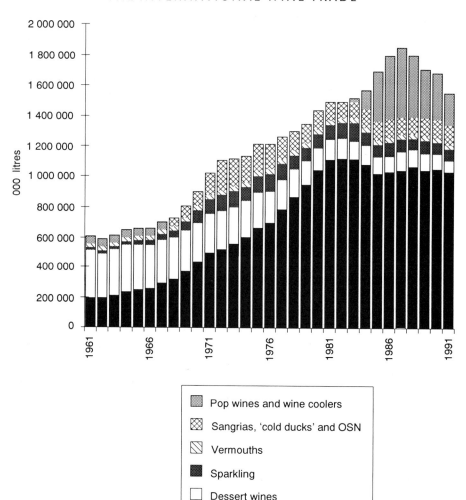

2.10 US wine consumption (domestic) (source: The Wine Institute of California).

coolers' sales, nearly half of which (43%) are realised by people in their 20s.[81]

Seasonality is an interesting aspect of wine in the US, the only beverage to suffer a significant set-back in sales during the summer, when it seems to give way to beer and soft drinks.[82] Americans are the world's heaviest major consumers of soft drinks. Looked at from that

81 SIP study, 1992.

82 See Pompelli, 1987 for more details, he estimated wine consumption on a seasonal basis.

Table 2.2 US wine categories and bestsellers in each

Popular premium ($3–7 per bottle at retail)		Super premium ($7–14)		Ultra premium (>$15)	
Gallo	19%	R. Mondavi	6%	Jordan	4%
Sutter Home	15%	Wine World	6%	Chalone	2%
Sebastiani	14%	Heublein	5%	R. Mondavi	2%
Top 3	48%	Top 3	17%	Top 3	8%

Source: Hambrecht & Quist (Fischer, in AIDV, 1992)

angle, their attraction to refreshing, low-strength wine coolers appears to be very natural.

The geographical distribution of sales reveals tremendous differences in wine consumption. The major consuming centres are the heavily populated west coast and the north-eastern part of the US, plus the states of Florida and Illinois. Over a quarter of the wine is drunk in the San Francisco, Los Angeles and New York areas.[83] The 13 litres per head consumed in 1990 by average Californians, for instance, puts them between New Zealanders and the Dutch, and well ahead of Britons; residents of Florida (9 litres per head) find themselves ranked in between Canadian and South African consumers. Utah, West Virginia, and Mississippi, who close the ranks, with levels ranging between two and three litres per capita, come just behind Tunisia.

Cultural differences help explain some of the variations in demand across states, but the principal reason lies in the fact that they have remained fairly independent in their taxing and controlling of the distribution channels for alcoholic drinks (they inherited the right to regulate the supply of alcoholic drinks upon Repeal in 1933). Most of the fifty states have opted for a mixture of local prohibition and private licensing, except Alabama, Delaware, Idaho, Maine, Mississippi, Montana, New Hampshire and Utah (who have either full or partial state monopolies) and Arizona, California, District of Columbia, Hawaii, Indiana, Nevada, North Dakota, Oklahoma and South Carolina, who have no local prohibition at all.[84] These trade restrictions are extremely costly to domestic and foreign wine suppliers, especially in terms of completing paperwork and keeping up with changes in states' legislations. There is a certain trend towards relaxation of state restrictions: half a dozen states have eased

83 Australian market study.

84 *Wines & Vines Buyer's Guide*, 1993, pp 346–58.

Table 2.3 US 'off' trade

	Supermarket chains	Warehouse clubs	Traditional wines and spirits shops
Domestic 'table' wines	49%	8%	26%
Imported 'table' wines	36%	3%	44%

Source: Nielsen Scan Track, March 1991, in Supermarket Business, March 1992, as in Fischer, 1992.

restrictions since the mid-1970s but New York and Pennsylvania still forbid the distribution of wine in supermarkets.[85] In the 'off' trade or outside 'Horeca', i.e. hotel-restaurant-cafés, including pubs and clubs, most of the wine is distributed through supermarkets (see Table 2.3). Some now claim that, legislation permitting, as much as 60–80% of wine sales may occur via supermarkets.[86] State taxation also varies widely from state to state: Oklahoma gives preferential treatment to local wines[87] and many consumers travel from neighbouring states to the less restricted District of Columbia and Nevada to buy their wines, thereby boosting their consumption to the highest levels in the US (19 and 16 litres per head respectively. Distribution problems related to the complexity of state laws remain a top issue in the US.[88]

Occasions

In the mid-1970s, between 50 and 60% of the purchases were for everyday use, 20–30% for special occasions, less than 10% for gifts and 10% for cooking.[89] The only serious exception is sparkling wines which are mainly drunk on special occasions. Sparkling wines are also the only wine type to be consumed predominantly away from home and, as such, have suffered greatly recently: their decline is mostly attributed to greater concern for drunken-driving. In 1992 (1981) 67% (59%) of the wines were consumed at home, 10% (20%) in other people's homes (parties) and a mere 15% (12%) in restaurants. The same study revealed that 73% (74%) of the wines were consumed at

85 Moulton & Zepponi, 1988; Stuller & Martin, 1989, p 63.

86 Michaud, 1991.

87 Stuller & Martin, 1989, p 62.

88 Ibid, p 227.

89 NPD survey, 1975, as in Folwell & Baritelle, 1978.

dinner – in increasing proportion – or later during the evening.[90] Also, as is the case in Britain, there is a tremendous concentration of consumption, with just over half of the wines sold to a mere tenth of the wine drinking population (over 80% of the wines to 30% of the wine drinking population).[91]

Communication

Regarding communication the opinions of just two critics wields incredible power over consumers' choices and, hence, on distributors. The first, and most influential, is a former lawyer's newsletter. *The Wine Advocate* uses an original 100-point scale, which its editor, Robert Parker, devised on the marking system used in secondary education.[92] The simplicity of the rating appeals to the ordinary consumer. New York retailers virtually carried Parker to sanctity, and he now wields the ability to turn a wine into a commercial success.[93] Marvin Shanken's biweekly *Wine Spectator* also uses a 100-point scale to review the wines. Evaluation is done by three editors, so its ratings are considered to be 'perhaps the most reliable in the nation'.[94] Other papers carry out wine reviews by wine columnists, such as the *New York Times* or *The Copley News Service* – to which no less than 200 local papers subscribe – but there seems to be no real match to Parker's *Newsletter* or Shanken's *Spectator*; some would go as far as saying that, barring a few big names and brands, one cannot get distributors to carry one's wine if it does not reach at least 70 points on either scale.[95] 'The fact that a highly regarded writer can sell wine is something with which the industry, however unhappily, must contend. Few other businesses support a coterie of journalists in such an intimate fashion'.[96]

90 47.9% (41.5%) at dinner and 25.4% (32.8%) in the evening. From SIP surveys, 1992 and 1981.

91 NPD survey, 1975, as in Folwell & Baritelle, 1978, p 35.

92 Stuller & Martin, 1989, p 314.

93 Stuller & Martin, 1989, p 314–6.

94 Ibid, pp 320–1; Marvin Shanken is "a tireless self-promoter who displays ready proclivity for flashy graphics and provocative headlines" and, to some, seems to relish in "exploiting troubles in the industry". He is also the publisher of *Impact* – a much quoted periodical dealing with the alcohol industry.

95 Jon Fredrikson.

96 Stuller & Martin, 1989, p 322.

Strength

US consumers have gradually moved away from the popular high strength wines of the 1960s to lower strength wines such as 'white zin' (around 10%) and coolers (4–5%).

Colour

The most surprising aspect regarding colour is that still red wine consumers are recruited amongst the younger part of the population (20–40) while still white wines are more of a mature man's drink (30–60). White wines provided the thrust for growth in the Californian wine industry, in spite of the prediction that educated consumers would soon turn to reds, simply because of the success of white and rosés in displacing spirits in the 'pre-dinner cocktails' segment.[97] A once red-dominated US wine market (47% market share in 1971; 28% for rosés and 25% for whites) had become the dominion of whites (57% in 1981, 25% for reds and 18% for rosés).[98] Rosés started to lose in importance in the early 1980s, but only to the benefit of blush wines (essentially white Zinfandel – see Fig. 2.11). The increase in US production was essentially in the white wine category. In 1990, Californian production of bottled wine was 16% red, 14% rosé, 53% white and 17% blush. The same year, imports of bottled wines were 37% red, 5% rosé and 57% white.[99] Although rosés and blush are made from red grapes, they are widely assimilated to white wines by consumers. The figure also reveals that canny Californians have actually managed to increase their sales since 1986, and not just by snapping market share away from Europeans in their declining domestic market, but by increasing their shipments to foreign markets.

Character and style

US consumer preferences lean towards fruity and rather pale varietal wines revealing a low alcoholic strength and much residual sugar. Sparkling wines have firmly established themselves after years of strong growth, whilst other wine-based fizzy drinks provided helpful

97 *Impact*, 1982, p 24.

98 Ibid, p 25.

99 Source: Wine Institute.

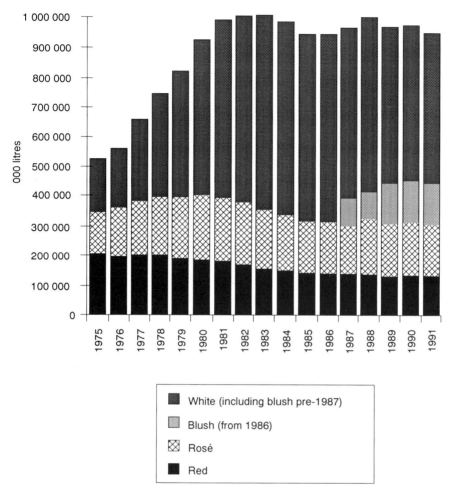

000 litres

White (including blush pre-1987)

Blush (from 1986)

Rosé

Red

2.11 Shipments by Californian wineries (by colour) (source: The Wine Institute of California).

but passing fads. Quality is rising continuously and varietals are soaring at the expense of generics.

Figure 2.8 shows the diminishing fortunes of dessert (fortified) wines. Sparkling wines enjoyed nearly continuous growth until the mid-1980s, but regressed later partly because of excessive pricing. Vermouths never really achieved much success. Wine-based drinks, which included pop wines,[100] sangria and cold ducks, went through a sales boom from 1970 to 1976 but faded out gradually afterwards;

100 Pop wines were immensely popular in the 1960s and in the early 1970s; they were made using nearly as much fruit concentrate (essentially pear) as grape juice; hence the 'wine' – and their progressive disappearance. Stuller & Martin, 1989, p 325).

coolers started in the early 1980s, peaked in 1987, and tumbled nearly as fast as they grew, with sales devastated by federal and state excise duty increases.[101] These carbonated drinks managed to tap the vast sales potential offered by sweet, bubbly, fruity drinks served with ice.[102] They were not targeted at wine drinkers but at beer and soft drinks consumers instead, in the hope that these would switch over to 'proper' wine later. That part of the scheme largely failed to materialise, for various reasons ranging from the absence of a sufficiently strong link between the two products to the fact that coolers proved the favourite illicit drink of teenagers. Their commercial success accelerated the wine boom in the early 1970s though and delayed the contraction of the market in the mid-1980s.

The real winners were still wines of less than 15% which enjoyed unremitting growth from the mid-1960s, when they overtook dessert wines, until their peak in 1984. Seagram's disposal of its ordinary wine business in the mid-1980s (the Paul Masson and Almaden brands in particular) was based on an early perception that the low-growth, low-margin 'jug generics' segment should be dropped. Gallo's belated move from generics to varietals could not pass unnoticed either, for it contributes to about a third of US production (the combined share of the Big Three – Gallo, IDV's Heublein which acquired the number 10 Glen Ellen in 1993, plus Canandaigua – is close to 60%).[103] Like Seagram, Heublein retreated in the premium segment by deciding to focus on its Beaulieu Vineyard, Blossom Hill and Glen Ellen brands and selling Inglenook and Almaden along with a few other wineries and a grape juice concentrate business to Canandaigua in the summer of 1994.[104] Generics are losing gradually in popularity, with consumers and marketers alike. Litigation with France, on the use of semi-generic names, played a role, but the overriding factor is consumers' perception of varietals as higher quality wines. Generics' share of Californian production of still wines just exceeded 80% in 1985; it has been falling steadily ever since. Varietals have been growing at 16% per annum and nearly closed on generics in 1992.[105]

---

101 Jon Fredrickson in *Wines & Vines*, April 1993, p 21.

102 Research Associates, in *Harpers* April 1980; Stuller & Martin, 1989, p 325.

103 *Drinks File*, October 15 1993.

104 This put the New York state based winery in second place, behind Gallo. Canandaigua is much more diversified than the Californian giant however; it is the fourth largest marketer of imported beers and the eight largest producer-marketer of spirits (*Wines & Vines*, August 1994).

105 Source: *Impact*.

The most fashionable product is white Zinfandel which made up as much as a third of Californian varietal production in 1990. Not exactly a new product (Robert Louis Stevenson was an early customer), it is one of the cheapest varietals to produce – like Beaujolais Nouveau it requires no ageing and is sold in a matter of months. Chardonnays have boomed recently and increased their share of Californian varietals to over a fifth, well ahead of Cabernet Sauvignons. The shift from generics to varietals was also felt in the sector of imported wines.

Origin

Figure 2.9 shows the fragility of imports, which had to weather one recession in the aftermath of the 1973 oil shock, then took off again, but did not survive the combination of a weakening US dollar and a succession of scandals in the mid-1980s. Imported sparkling wines did rather well, especially in the early 1980s, before being substituted in part by US coolers. The US offers a nice illustration of the substitution capabilities of domestic production to imports.

When sales were booming, US wines were confined to the lower quality segment (generic jug wines) and foreign ones were occupying the upper quality segment (premium generic wines). Even though domestic producers controlled more than three-quarters of the market in terms of volume in 1981, they only cashed two-thirds of the market valued then at just over $7 billion.[106]

Italian wines dominated imports during the boom years (1970s until the mid-1980s), but this was especially due to the Lambrusco phenomenon, a slightly carbonated wine which accounted for 64% of its exports to the US in 1980 (two-thirds sparkling red and one third white Lambrusco) and for a staggering 37% of all US wine imports.[107] The Lambrusco era is largely over, but Italian 'strongly-branded' wines have retained some of their appeal with US customers; German white wines happened to be in the right colour segment at the right time, unlike Spanish reds which were quite successful in the early 1970s but lost ground later (Portuguese rosés never quite made it either). The early 1980s proved quite successful for the French, who achieved a

---

106 Based on *Impact's* 1981 'consumer buying power survey' (*Impact*, 1982, p 11).

107 37.8 million US gallons vs 102.5. Source: *Impact* 1982, pp 28–9 (for Lambrusco), Wine Institute for total figures.

major turnaround with their appellations, in spite of recession and aided by the Italian scandal.[108]

Figure 2.10 highlights the relatively comfortable position of US producers who suffered a reduction of less than 10% between their peak in 1987 and 1990, while imports declined by more than half between their peak in 1984 and 1990, i.e. foreigners are back to where they stood in the mid-1970s. Basically, US producers moved into the higher quality segment through the breach opened by the various scandals. In doing so they have managed to shift most of the burden of receding consumption to the Europeans who now find their position also challenged by the New World wines, especially those from Chile. The move of the US producers was certainly aided by more protective legislation from Capitol Hill, but it was essentially the weakness of the US currency in the early 1980s that solved the issue for them. Also, US producers must be credited with a radical improvement in the quality of their wines and, most importantly, an effective monitoring of consumers' need for, essentially, 'a cold, light, refreshing beverage ... the hallmark of beverage marketing in the seventies'.[109]

Packaging

Containers have basically evolved from jugs to airline bottles, 187cl glass bottles arranged in handy six-packs. Bags-in-boxes were designed to overcome the problems of oxidation and recycling of glass jugs. They are widely used by restaurants and bars, but consumer acceptance has been lower than in Australia and apparently also in the UK.[110] As elsewhere in the world, cans have done poorly so far (except for coolers), plastic bottles are seen as inappropriate for good wine and tetrapak cartons are meeting just as much consumer resistance, thus leaving the wine industry to cling to traditional glass bottles. Lead capsules, which habitually adorned premium wines, have been gradually replaced with aluminium ones due to health concerns. Plastic capsules have been used for jug wines for some time, especially in the 1970s, when the price of plastic fell.[111]

---

108 *Impact,* 1982, pp 14–15, 22, 29.

109 Ibid, p 25.

110 Moulton & Zepponi, 1988, p 357.

111 Ibid, p 358.

Table 2.4 Top ten US imported table wine brands (thousands of 9 litre cases)

Rank	Brand/line	Country	Depletions 1980	1981	Estimated share of total imported table wine, % 1980	1981
1	Riunite	Italy	9 070	11 200	23.7	26.4
2	Cella	Italy	2 385	2 750	6.2	6.5
3	Bolla	Italy	1 540	1 590	4.0	3.8
4	Folonari	Italy	1 470	1 550	3.8	3.7
5	Zonin	Italy	1 200	1 500	3.1	3.5
	Top 5 combined		15 665	18 590	40.9	43.8
6	Giacobazzi	Italy	1 350	1 390	3.5	3.3
7	Blue Nun	Germany	1 260	1 300	3.3	3.1
7	Mateus	Portugal	1 240	1 300	3.2	3.1
9	Yago	Spain	1 060	1 100	2.8	2.6
10	Lancers	Portugal	900	905	2.4	2.1
	Top 10 combined		21 475	24 585	56.0	58.0
	Other brands		16 875	17 805	44.0	42.0
	Total imported table wines		38 350	42 390	100.0	100.0

Rank	Brand/line	Country	1991	1992	1991	1992
1	Riunite 'Classics'	Italy	2 050	2 030	10.3	9.2
2	Bolla	Italy	825	855	4.1	3.9
3	Folonari	Italy	745	750	3.7	3.4
4	Georges Duboeuf	France	550	715	2.8	3.2
5	Concha y Toro	Chile	435	655	2.2	3.0
	Top 5 combined		4 605	5 005	23.1	22.6
6	Cella	Italy	585	610	2.9	2.8
7	Mouton-Cadet	France	435	540	2.2	2.4
8	Marcus James	Brazil	385	520	1.9	2.4
9	Canei	Italy	505	500	2.5	2.3
10	Leonard Kreusch	Germany	430	440	2.2	2.0
	Top 10 combined		6 945	7 615	34.8	34.5
	Other brands		13 005	14 485	65.2	65.5
	Total imported table wines		19 950	22 100	100.0	100.0

Source: Impact

The Oxtoby-Smith study conducted in the mid-1980s on behalf of the California Commission, a volatile marketing order set up again in 1984, found amongst other things that most regular drinkers stuck with a few brands.[112]

The biggest US producers have retained their dominance of the market to a large extent and Gallo's position remains unchallenged. Similarly, the top five imported brands captured 41% of imports – themselves accounting for 21.3% of all wine sales in the US in 1980. Riunite enjoyed a 23.7% market share at that time (putting it in fifth position if it were included in the top US wineries chart), followed by Cella, Bolla and Folonari (see Table 2.4). Imports were brand-denominated and Italian wines suit the US recessionary economy particularly well with their low retail prices; Italian brands – mostly Lambruscos and Veronese wines – occupied the first six positions. Germany, Portugal and Spain were represented in the top ten but France's most sold brand (Seagram's Barton & Guestier) was only 11th; its second most sold brand was Baron Rothschild's Mouton Cadet (18th). The French had managed to place two brands within a less Italian-dominated Top Ten a decade later, however; meanwhile American consumers have dropped Portugal and Spain from their wine list and replaced them with hot Chileans and Brazilians.

112 Stuller & Martin, 1989, pp 70–1.

3

Financial and administrative aspects of international trade

Introduction

Thousands of offers are made every day on importers' faxes, describing wines on the basis of their origin, colour, strength, character and style. Technical information is produced on individual data sheets – certificates of chemical analysis – allowing for a quick profile to be drawn for each product. If a particular wine succeeds in catching the importer's interest and meets national standards regarding technical specifications, the exporter is asked to send samples for comparative tasting and for possible inspection of the shipment at delivery time, should the wines successfully pass the selection process. Picking a winner amongst the wines on offer is mainly a question of flawless appearance and taste – and price.

Participation in promotional efforts is also critical and must be set against the offer price: huge promotional discounts are proposed by some exporters to their business counterparts in strategic markets nowadays, which are partially refunded by governments. Incentives of this type have gradually come to replace all too conspicuous export subsidies.

The price likely to tip the balance in favour of any particular wine is not so much the contract price than its expected retail level – the result of the addition to the 'ex-winery' or free on board (FOB) price in which most contracts are stipulated, of transport costs, insurance premiums, likely intermediaries' fees, tariffs and domestic taxes. Ex-winery and FOB prices are usually expressed in the exporter's currency (cost, insurance, freight, or CIF contracts termed in the importer's money are much less popular), so exchange rates have to be fed into the equation too.

Prices, exchange rates and tariffs can reveal substantial differences depending on the exporting country; excise duties and sales taxes have been applied uniformly in all major markets ever since discrimination between domestic and foreign products has become unacceptable. Transport and insurance costs are basically a function of the mode of transport, the type of container and distance between the two sides of the deal. Agents' or brokers' fees are based on the nature of their service which can range from just lending one's signet for legal purposes, to providing full coverage of all the steps required for bringing the wine safely to the client's doorstep as well as fostering personal contacts on behalf of one party or the other, who may not have the means or the time to travel extensively.

Prices; exchange rates

Wine prices are usually negotiated 'ex-winery' or FOB[1] at the nearest commercial port when the wines are shipped or flown. The cargo becomes the importer's liability henceforth, who must arrange and pay for insurance and transport. FOB contracts are expressed in the exporter's currency, or in US dollars as is usually the case with inflation-prone South American states. Less common CIF arrangements are stipulated in the importer's currency; they also shift responsibility regarding transport and insurance into the exporter's camp. CIF prices are simply FOB prices augmented by transport and insurance costs.

Contract prices are thus essentially determined by domestic market conditions prevailing in the exporter's country and much less

---

1 Prices are occasionally quoted free alongside ship (FAS), the only difference being that the cargo is brought to the quayside but not actually loaded on to the ship. Many US data are expressed in FAS value; it is customary to treat them as FOB (the difference is minimal).

influenced by those at work in the import market. The main reason for the relative insulation of wine prices from 'international' market conditions rests with the fact that one trades in a highly differentiated good, particularly on the basis of its origin, i.e. its country or region of production. Also, wherever domestic production is a significant component of demand, it is often shielded against foreign competition.

Insufficient standardisation of the wines even at the renowned 'commodity end' of the market is the reason given for the absence of international wine exchanges, unlike for coffee or orange juice. Another may be the angst of producers, of the power wielded by arbitrageurs who buy cheap on one market and sell dear on the other until there are no more profits to be made. The major advantage with international commodity exchanges is that they offer head-on competition between all the major exporters and a unique source of readily available information on the prices of the goods traded there. The few centralised markets in which international wine sellers and bidders are free to compete from all corners of the world are auctions held by Sotheby's and Christie's in London, Geneva and New York, but these have as much impact on wine prices as markets in vintage cars have on pricing decisions taken in Nagoya or Detroit.

In the international wine market-place one is thus left to face different sets of prices in each country, denominated in local currency, and currencies have had markedly different fortunes over the years. The international wine trade is a web of import demand and export supplies. There is one set for each country as well as for each main category of wine. Arbitrageurs are a rare breed of well-informed, global operators who produce and market wines in several countries. Their situation provides them with good opportunities to take advantage of international price differentials by shifting goods from one market to the other. However impressive their balance sheets, their share of the wine trade is too small to endow them with any significant impact on international prices.

The absence of an international market-place and the maze of connections between the various national markets means that an adjustment taking place in any import market can only have a delayed and dampening effect on exporters' domestic prices. There are two good reasons for this. Firstly, any major changes in importers' domestic prices are only poorly transmitted back to exporters' domestic markets, that is after removal of the effect of excise duties, tariffs and exchange rates on prices. The second reason is the limited, albeit increasing, reliance on export markets revealed by wine producing countries: 15% of their output was exported during the 1980s and early 1990s on average, slightly more than the 13–14%

shipped overseas during the 1970s.[2] The maximum degree of overall exposure to foreign markets displayed by any single country in the second half of the 1980s was 25%, with the exception of Algeria, Bulgaria, Cyprus, Hungary and Tunisia. A similar situation prevailed in the early 1990s by and large, though Chile's degree of reliance on export markets is nearing that threshold, as had the former West Germany in the past.[3] Turbulences in even the largest importing market will thus not succeed in shaking any producer market; only firms who have excessively exposed themselves to an individual (or a set of closely related) market(s) may go down. Producers' markets are much more sensitive to changes in their own imports since their exposure is far greater on that flank. West Germany and Switzerland for instance imported 60% of their needs in 1986–90. The US and France reduced their exposure to imports to 15 and 11% respectively, down from the 19 and 15% they had revealed ten years earlier.[4] Prices are much more responsive to conditions prevailing on the international wine market in genuine 'two way' traders such as Germany or France. French and German prices would be affected by a major price rise in Italy or Spain for instance, though EU intervention or border protection would dampen the effect of a major shock occurring in a particular country. Prices certainly rose as the result of German unification which shifted the EU demand curve to the right.

Yet even if there were a clear transmission of prices back to their original markets, signals would still be lost in a sea of official interference. Wine prices are rigged in most producing countries. There is cartel-type collective price bargaining in virtually every producer market, usually involving grape growers' co-operatives and government intervention as a means of supporting producers' prices (and hopefully, their incomes at the same time). Grapes and wine *are* considered agricultural commodities at the producer's stage and policies designed for agriculture have usually been applied, with minor amendments, to the wine sector as well. Price support policies have largely failed to meet their objectives. Argentina and Chile have already freed their wine markets, and other countries are following suit.

Foreign retail prices are the result of the addition to CIF prices of economic rents resulting from quantitative restrictions, duties and other taxes plus the usual commercial margins taken by local distributors. Import (CIF) prices are themselves the exporters'

2 Based on OIV data.

3 Discounting the effect of the generally poor harvest in 1991; also based on OIV data.

4 Based on OIV data.

domestic prices expressed in the buyer's currency, augmented by shipping and insurance costs.

There is no 'world price' to speak of but a collection of CIF prices of various wine types of different origin competing against each other at the gates of a dozen critical markets, each market having its own tastes, requirements and currencies. The UK and US markets are a good proxy for international price levels. What these markets seem to indicate is that wine prices have tended to fall in real terms, since the mid-1970s, taking into account the rise in the quality of international shipments. This is only to be expected, for there is no reason why wine should have escaped the logic of ever-diminishing costs and prices, like any other manufactured product.[5] More importantly, the pressure of lingering structural surpluses has turned the international wine market into a buyers' market (chronic overproduction actually provides the initial impetus for developing aggressive export policies). Finally, many key import markets have healthy economies and strong currencies. Others can ill afford the luxury of imported wines; they are much better placed for exporting their own production, if they have any.

If variations in foreign retail prices have little consequence on exporters' domestic prices, this does not exempt individual wineries from having to react to price changes or exchange rate movements if they wish not to be priced out of a market and lose it for years. Variations in exchange rates can have devastating effects on a winery's fortunes. A change of strategy is necessary, calling for re-focusing on markets with stronger currencies or cutting prices drastically, as the Germans did in the mid-1980s (after the DM had risen against all major importers' currencies and on the heels of the diethylene glycol affair). Argentinian exporters, whose peso had been pegged on the US dollar recently, are experiencing a similar nightmare. Drastic changes in currencies (independent of conditions prevailing on wine markets on either side) can be offset with financial instruments for up to one year.

Transport and insurance costs

The traditional means of shipping wine in bulk was in barrels. They could be easily rolled on and off road and railway carriages as well as

---

5 See Henderson, 1984, pp 47ff.

ships until they reached their destination, usually a bottling plant situated in the vicinity of large consuming areas. The development of maritime routes and, later, that of railway and road networks meant a radical redesigning of trade patterns each time a new link was established between a wine growing region and a new large urban centre, or even between producing regions. Whether barges sent down the Euphrates, the Nile or the Rhine; Greek, Roman or Venetian ships cruising the Mediterranean sea, British vessels stopping in Bordeaux on their way to North Africa and America, French ships docking in Sète from Algeria and Sicily; trains linking the French Midi to Paris, California to New York, or Mendoza to Buenos Aires, every new link brought down transportation costs and, with it, access to hitherto unavailable markets, raising sales potential in untrodden places and competition in others. Barrels were replaced later with much larger tanks designed to hold any type of drinkable liquid and to roll on road, rail and sea – the wines could be pumped from one tank to the other if necessary. Meanwhile, sea shipping has been revolutionised by containerisation, so much of the wines sent in bulk from one continent to the other occurs in 20 000 litre containers which, like the old barrels, can be easily transferred from one means of transport to another, e.g. from lorry to ship and back to lorry again. Even Le Shuttle, which is expected to carry British customers to France has brought UK retailers to open branches on French soil, in order to take advantage of lower duty rates.

A chain of innovations on the drinks packaging side, such as cartons wrapped around twelve 75 cl bottles to make sturdy and shock-proof 9 l cases,[6] and their palletisation and containerisation (all using standard, interchangeable sizes) have considerably reduced the costs of shipping bottles directly from the wine growing regions to wholesalers' and retailers' depots. Dispatching full containers (of about 1000 cases) is the only economic way of exporting bottled wines. This halves the volume which can be shipped in bulk[7] but bears the additional advantage over bulk that small orders can be grouped to match smaller retailers' requirements: containers are broken down into pallets at the most efficient stage. Smaller exporters have also come to share sea containers and larger wineries have resorted to storing in duty-free depots situated close to their clientele,

6 Wrap-around cases eliminate partitions between glass bottles. The likelihood of impact and, hence, breakage is significantly reduced – the major cost associated with shipping wines in bottles rather than in bulk.

7 Containers usually hold 1000–1100 9-litre cases or, alternatively, 18–20 000 litres of bulk wine.

so as to be able to offer the shortest delivery time possible, e.g. in the UK for New World producers exporting to Europe. Southern hemisphere producers had to master the additional problem of sending wine across the equator, in very high temperatures. This was solved with the production of far more stable wines and by shipping them 'below deck', without having to resort to hiring expensive temperature-controlled containers used for the highest priced crus. In Western Europe, including the UK, virtually all trade takes place by road.

Transport and insurance costs depend on distance, but should not exceed 10% of the CIF price in any case. Freight, insurance and clearance charges (into bonded premises, duty not paid) currently amount to £3–4 and US$7 per case for Australian wine and even long journeys are deemed worthwhile, as the cost of shipping by sea is still minimal – it actually went down in the 1970s, as maritime shipping went through a deep crisis (carrying one ton of iron ore from Brazil to Western Europe cost nearly as much as a taxi fare between two Parisian train stations in the late 1980s; that of shipping Chilean wine by the container-load to Hong Kong now comes to less than US$0.5 per case.[8] It is not so much the cost of shipping the wines but that of travelling to visit the clientele at least once a year that prevents medium and small size wineries from selling abroad. Hence the continuing role for agents, brokers and other types of intermediaries who often act as representatives for several exporters. Their commission is usually well under 5% (sometimes as low as 2–3%) of the value of the wines passing through their hands,[9] unless they take an active participation in pushing the goods on to retailers' shelves as is often the case in the US, for imported and domestic wines alike. Figure 3.1 puts transportation and insurance costs into perspective, using the British market as an example.

Tariffs; excise duties and sales taxes

It is the overlaying of tariffs (raised on virtually all industrial goods), excise duties (raised on alcohol and tobacco) and finally sales taxes (VAT and the like, raised more or less uniformly across consumer goods) by

8 Private interviews; Vigarié, 1987; *The Financial Times*, 28 May 1994.

9 Usually after payment of tariffs.

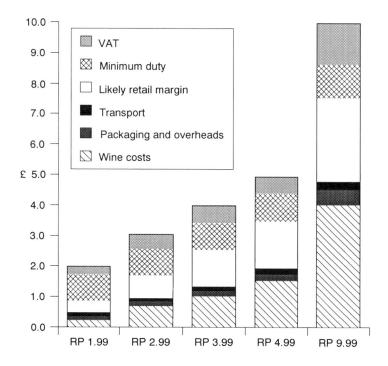

3.1 Breakdown of the retail price of wine in the UK (source: *The Financial Times*).

government treasuries which cause the greatest impediments and distortions to trade. Together they can cause a doubling or trebling of the CIF prices by the time the wines reach consumers, as they can vary enormously from one country to the next, even in the EU. Tariffs are also often used to discriminate against possible suppliers, on the basis of their nationality.

Harmonisation of excise duties and sales tax is an arduous task, particularly excise duties which bring so much easy cash to government treasuries. In the US, and even within the EU which had pledged to overhaul the system in the run up to the 1993 single market, convergence has not yet been attained (see Table 3.1). The time taken to remove other trade impediments at the commodity end of the market, meant that it took at least 12 years longer than expected to see free trade enforced; EU harmonisation is dealt with in greater detail later.

The reduction of tariffs and quantitative restrictions is taking place within the framework of bilateral and multilateral agreements: trading blocs attempt to free up trade within their borders whilst erecting a common fence against third parties and, sometimes, subsidising the dumping of surpluses on third markets. Just about every major wine importing nation imposed trade restrictions during the 1930s (including licensing restrictions); these were progressively lifted in the post-war period within the framework of bilateral agreements. The most significant multilateral concessions occurred within trading blocs, e.g. the EU, Mercosur and NAFTA. Wine was largely left out of successive GATT[10] rounds because it belonged to the sensitive agricultural sector. The Uruguay Round managed to include agriculture for the first time though; the signing of its Final Act in Marrakesh, in April 1994, gave new perspectives for growth in the international wine trade. GATT is the only institution spanning trading blocs, including the former socialist Eastern European economies now in transition to market economies. Its successor, the World Trade Organisation (WTO) is the most promising framework for reducing domestic and export subsidies (commonly used by the EU wherever it feels unexposed to retaliation), as well as for improving market access by converting all quantitative restrictions to wine trade into tariffs and reducing them in an orderly fashion later – after having ensured an initial minimal access at a near-zero tariff rate.[11] The issue on tariffication and tariff equivalents for wine is crucial to boosting trade.

GATT may not only prove the best framework for eliminating export subsidies and improving access to foreign markets, it also appears to be the most appropriate platform for accelerating patchy and agonising discussions aiming at smoothing out technical barriers to trade: (like the EU–US discussions that have been going on for a decade yet produced no tangible result so far). The ambitious GATT agreement seeks to lower technical barriers to trade by harmonising international standards. These are defined as the development, adoption and application of any standard, test method or certification system. The amended *Standards Code* of the final Act was made applicable to all WTO members – and not just to the Code's signatories as was previously the case. The Agreement also seeks to bring about a similar arrangement for sanitary and phytosanitary measures used specifically in agricultural trade, as well as to ensure better protection of trade-related intellectual property rights, including geographical designations (appellations) and trade marks.

---

10 General Agreement on Tariffs and Trade.

11 This is in order to prevent the most protectionistic countries from imposing excessively high tariffs.

Table 3.1 Excise duties and VAT rates within the EU

Products/taxes	Still wines		Sparkling wines		Spirits		Intermediary products	
Country	Excise	Value added tax	Excise	Value added tax	Excise	Value added tax	Excise	Value added tax
Belgium (in Belgian francs)	Special duty: 14.71 (per litre)	20.5%	0 Special duty: 51.49 (per litre)	20.5%	90 Special duty: 545 (per litre of pure alcohol)	20.5%	*Non-sparkling:* 19 (< 15% vol) or 27 (> 15% vol) (per litre) *Sparkling* As above Special duty for Belgium: 32.49 (< 15% vol) or 24.49 (> 15% vol) per litre	20.5%
Luxembourg (in Luxembourg francs)	0	12% (< 13% vol) or 15% (other)	0	15%	90 plus 320 spirits consumption tax	15%		15%
Spain (in pesetas)	0	15%	0	15%	847.41 (per litre of pure alcohol)	15%	69.34 (per litre)	15%
Greece (in drachma)	0	18%	0	18%	1 450.21 (per litre of pure alcohol)	18%	118.659 (per litre)	18%
Ireland (in Irish punt)	2.15 (per litre)	21%	4.30 (per litre)	21%	21.83 (per litre of pure alcohol)	21%	3.11 (per litre)	21%
Italy (in lira)	0	13%	0	19%	11.466 or 10.220 (per litre of pure alcohol)	19%	778.35 (per litre)	13%
Netherlands (in guilders)	Alcoholic content 8.5% up to 15% = 1.075 (per litre) > 15% up to 18% = 1.87 (per litre)	17.5%	> 8.5% up to 18% = 3.665 (per litre)	17.5%	31.78 per litre of pure alcohol subject to a minimum tax of 27.35	17.5%	*Non-sparkling* < 15% = 1.3275 > 15% = 1.87 (per litre) *Mousseux:* 3.665 (per litre)	17.5%

Portugal (in escudos)	0	5% (ordinary or common wines) 16% others	0	16%	1 348 (per litre of pure alcohol)	16%	80 (per litre)	16%
Germany (in Deutschmarks)	0	15%	2 per 75cl bottle	15%	25.50 (per litre of pure alcohol)	15%	*Non-sparkling:* 1 (per litre) *Sparkling* 2.66 (per litre)	15%
United Kingdom (in pounds sterling)	1.3477 (per litre)	17.5%	2.2255 (per litre)	17.5%	19.81 (per litre of pure alcohol)	17.5%	2.0733 per litre	17.5%
Denmark (in krone)	6.55 (per litre)	25% VAT plus variable tax on container	6.55 + 3.30 per litre	25% VAT plus variable tax on container	143 (per litre of pure alcohol) + 37.5% of the taxable value (excluding VAT)	25% VAT plus variable tax on container	9.85 per litre for wines with an alcoholic strength ranging between 15 and 22%	25% VAT plus variable tax on container

Source: CFCE

Technical specifications; labelling requirements; certificates of origin and other documents

Analytical, certification, sanitary, labelling and environmental requirements imposed by trading partners on each others' exports usually come out of genuine health and environmental concerns; they also aim at protecting the interests of honest local merchants by cracking down on fraud. No one disputes the right of nations to pursue such objectives honestly, i.e. if they can refrain from using such measures with a view to restricting trade.

Some work aiming at harmonising technical standards has been done in the framework of the annual gatherings of government officials hosted by the OIV, FAO's *Codex Alimentarius*, or of various bilateral agreements.

The most arduous side of the task is the harmonisation of long (and seemingly endless) lists of acceptable levels of potentially harmful substances present in wines. Many importing countries put constraints on the level of those two additives which are not naturally present in wine: SO_2 (sulphur dioxide) and sorbic acid (regarded as very safe).[12] Total (tartaric) and volatile (acetic) acidity levels are also usually kept under check. Other substances such as cadmium, lead, fluor and methanol can be subject to upper limits too, as are pesticides and fungicide residues, particularly procymidone and MITC. But requirements differ widely from country to country. The Canadian province of Ontario is probably the most restrictive of all, having established maximum levels for a dozen substances *and* 14 residues of pesticides and fungicides.[13] Several cases have cropped up which have severely disrupted trade flows mainly between the EU and the US. Being preventive whilst remaining pragmatic is the current objective of trade settlements; the US, for instance, established interim maximum levels for procymidone to ease the tension between the EU and the US.[14]

Making winemaking standards conform looks less daunting, as this can rest on the assumption that what is safe for an Australian or American to drink should prove just as safe on a French dinner table. There remain a few contentious issues though, such as the ban placed by the EU on imports of wine made using the ion exchange process, a technology used widely in food and beverage processing throughout

12 Ough, 1992, p 287.

13 INV, 1991.

14 Fitch, 1994.

the world but not permitted in winemaking in the EU.[15] The EU also refuses entry to low acid wines as well as those wines in which the initial acidity content has been raised by more than 4 g/litre, on the grounds that these oenological practices are not allowed within the EU. Bilateral agreements sometimes offer provisional derogations, but the best chance for oenological standards to get attuned on a long term basis rests with the ability to strike a worldwide, multilateral agreement.

Labelling requirements are another area of contention. Issues range from the peculiar interdiction, by the EU, that indication of more than two varieties be made for a multi-varietal blend to the insistence, by the US, that wine bottles carry one of the official health warning statements. But even the most awkward restrictions can only result in the printing of separate labels to be affixed on the bottles shipped to a particular destination. Misleading names and denominations are gradually being phased out through bilateral agreements. Of particular concern are semi-generic names – European traditional and geographical terms which have entered into generic use overseas, as a description of a particular wine style, e.g. burgundy and claret.[16]

Permitted container sizes seem to be just another obstacle to trade, whilst genuine environmental restrictions may result in some PVC bottles or other containers being banned, or in forcing distributors to collect and recycle or reuse wine bottles. Importers may also have additional requirements of their own, from container type and size to participation in the design of labels or even random inspections of wineries. These constraints can be turned around and used as an additional way of monitoring changes in consumers' preferences occurring in foreign markets.

Certification involves providing a clear identification and description of the wines, including the results of various types of analyses, e.g. alcoholic strength, acidity level and SO_2 content. It is general practice for bilateral agreements to opt for an accelerated procedure, whereby imported wines undergo only a few analyses and certification documents delivered by authorities of the exporting country are accepted at face value by the recipient country. Documents bearing all the necessary details about the origins of the wines are accompanied by a certificate of analysis or a declaration that the wines have been analysed and conform to the importer's

---

15 Seemingly, for reasons other than consumer health (Clawson, 1993).

16 It should be stressed that EU producers have also used names for wines produced in the Union, e.g. 'tokay'.

requirements. These, plus a copy of the invoice are then bundled together in one single 'accompanying document'.

The bill of lading is a transport document commonly used in international trade. The carrier issues two signed copies to the exporter upon receipt of the goods and one copy is mailed by the exporter directly to the importer (the other is kept safe). A bill of lading acts both as a receipt for the goods by the carrier to the exporter and as a title to the goods by the importer. Bills of lading are often used in documentary credit as a means of eliminating the risk of insolvency on the part of buyers in the case of CIF contracts, as their agreements to pay are replaced with bank guarantees of payment.[17]

WTO could speed up the whole process of mutual recognition of winemaking standards and practices as well as the reciprocal protection of geographical indications and traditional expressions by taking the EU–Australian agreement as a blueprint for a global, multilateral agreement.

Export credit and promotion

The degree of assistance provided by governments to exporters varies enormously in intensity and form. This depends much on an exporting nation's resources and may range from providing market information, export credit insurance and missions, to straight export subsidies. Exporting nations are understandably shy about the form and degree of assistance provided to wineries in order to help them gain access to foreign markets and hold it subsequently.

Market information and advisory services

Most wine exporting countries have an overseas trade department providing interested firms with advice and information on foreign markets, technical standards, major importers and distributors and on how best to approach them, and competition as well as trade statistics. These are usually drawn from trade representatives scattered around the world and who are often connected loosely with overseas embassies. Overseas trade missions are also often provided for,

---

17 See Watson, 1990, Chapters 8 and 14 for more details.

whereby a group of exporters is taken on an organised tour in order to meet potential buyers. Business can even be guaranteed to exporters in some cases, against payment of a fee or 'business insurance premium'. Inward trade missions do the opposite: they bring potential importers to visit the exporting country, and are critical for smaller wineries which do not have the means to visit and prospect many export markets.

Credit insurance

National export credit insurance schemes help exporters to cover risks inherent to the buyer and to the country of export – so-called buyer/credit risk and country risk. A comprehensive export guarantee policy would typically involve covering against importers' insolvency, their failure to honour their debt within a given period after payment is due, or simply refusing to accept the goods they ordered – all buyer's risk. Socio-economic events such as war or the imposition of exchange controls preventing honest importers from honouring their debts would also be catered for. Even exchange risks arising from any of the above can be covered to a limited extent.[18] Proper exchange rate risk has to be hedged against with the usual means put at one's disposal by financial markets, as mentioned earlier. The French state-funded Compagnie Française d'Assurance pour le Commerce Extér-ieur (COFACE) introduced a scheme designed for small firms with a yearly turnover of less than FFr 1.5 million (US$0.27 m); it can be subscribed to via France's ubiquitous Minitel system.[19] Export credit insurance should be wholly financed by premiums, but many national schemes run substantial deficits which are covered by governments.

Market information and (export) credit insurance help exporters lower their marketing costs, as do various other programmes, such as Australia's Export Management Grant which awards partial and degressive refunds on marketing expenses (such as air fares). And so do various forms of generic promotion, whether sponsored by a national exporter's body, such as the Australian Wine Export Council set up in 1991 with the clear task of devising, financing and

---

18 Watson, 1990, pp 43, 114–17. Export credit provided by OECD members (with the exception of Turkey) is the object of 1976 and 1978 agreements aiming at avoiding a damaging competition between members in this sector and is monitored accordingly (OECD, 1990).

19 *La Journée Vinicole*, 6 July 1993.

implementing a worldwide generic wine promotion programme for Australian wines, or a regional group of wine producers and shippers, such as the Conseil Interprofessionnel des Vins de Bordeaux or the California Wine Institute, both of which were amongst the largest spenders on generic advertising in the UK in 1991. Large surplus producing countries have sometimes helped exporters to lower their price altogether, by providing them with export subsidies and measures with similar effects. The EU is the largest provider of such help – usually amounting to the difference between the price prevailing within the EU and those on international markets[20] – yet admittedly not to places where it could face retaliation. Some 64.5 million ECUs a year were nevertheless spent to this end in 1986–88 on quantities representing nearly a third of the EU's exports; a further 45 million ECUs were granted to exporters in 1989 and some 60 million ECUs were budgeted for 1990 and 1991.[21] The issue of export refunds is linked with that of domestic production subsidies. There is now growing pressure to phase out and ban this type of aid, as well as any measures used by the trade to circumvent such interdiction.

Measures with similar effects have cropped up, particularly the US Market Promotion Progam (introduced by the 1990 Farm Bill and replacing the previous Targeted Export Assistance Program) granting US exporters a 25% refund and foreign importers an additional 25%. This type of aid was designed to help exporters finance part of their marketing expenses on foreign soil. The money (15 million 'promotional dollars' a year) was apparently used as a straight promotional discount (i.e. price reduction) in most cases, which would amount to subsidisation of US exports at a rate of 50%.

Distribution

Importers' requirements depend on their own technical and marketing abilities, the configuration of a country's import and distribution network, their position within that system, and their marketing muscle. Working with national operators may result in razor-thin

20 Basic Regulation 882/87, art 56. Export refunds are also available for grape musts and liqueur wines but not for quality wines (Swinbank and Ritson, 1992, p 28), for these are not subject to a direct price support policy (unlike table wines).

21 Official Journal of the EU, OJ L30 of 4/2/199, in Swinbank and Ritson, 1992, p. 19.

margins and perhaps even participation in promotional expenses; the competitive environment in which they operate is likely to make them import in bottles, or in bulk through a wholesale firm they own, using their well qualified wine department staff. Regional importers and distributors are more likely to be part of a longer, slower distribution channel as it may regroup orders for many different types and sizes of retailers.

There are three major types of retailing channels in each market: specialist shops, supermarkets and 'Horeca' (hotel-restaurants-cafés, and also pubs and clubs). The rise of supermarkets as a major force in retailing wines and the concentration occurring in the two other sectors is a major feature of the 1980s. Exporters have responded by setting up ventures on the importer's terrain, in order to reduce delivery time and keep control over their products and their margins. The ideal case for them is to 'export to themselves', as do most international marketers, some of which have even moved their export marketing departments to a foreign country. The configuration of the national distribution networks will continue to evolve with the needs of the consumers and the growing quest for freer trade. Import and distribution monopolies in several Scandinavian, Canadian and US states for instance, are under strong pressure to be dismantled. Those of the former Soviet bloc members have collapsed with the 1989 revolutions and Western-style import and distribution networks are gradually emerging in their place.

The next chapter bundles market trends, trade policy and import–distribution channels into 12 major individual profiles.

4

The major import markets

Wine imports are concentrated in the hands of a dozen privileged countries: the 'G7' nations – Canada, France, Germany, Italy, Japan, the UK and the US – plus a handful of Western European states: Belgium, Denmark, Holland, Sweden and Switzerland. In 1990, these twelve countries alone contributed to 70% of world GDP.[1] The same twelve nations imported 85% of the volume of wines shipped around the globe in the early 1990s and their orders totalled 88% of the value of international wine trade (see Table 4.1). The 'Big Three' in value – Germany, Britain and the US – are not the top three importers in volume terms. The US, who rank third with 12% of the value of world imports, have only a 4% share in volume, for these are almost exclusively bottled shipments of often higher quality wines. This is in sharp contrast to the situation in France which imports mostly cheap bulk for blending.

Growth in international wine trade has been sluggish in recent years; it was wholly based on German, British, Belgian, Dutch and Danish performance, who had to compensate for falling figures elsewhere in the early 1990s, particularly in the former Soviet bloc. The US, Canadian and Swiss markets are basically stable and hopes on soaring Japanese orders were dashed in the early 1990s when it had to come to grips with economic recession.

The first portrait in the gallery of wine importers' comes from

1 Source: World Bank.

Table 4.1 Main importers, US$ 000 (1990)

All wines*	1988	1989	1990	1991	1992	1993	Value share, % 1991–93	Volume share, % 1991–93
Germany**	1 266 262	1 178 895	1 501 102	1 613 780	1 606 873		19.0	25.2
UK	1 553 303	1 470 553	1 770 978	1 586 771	1 635 674	1 548 638	18.8	15.9
USA	1 052 223	1 085 270	1 011 564	964 494	1 101 604	990 409	12.0	4.1
Belgium-								
Luxembourg	512 366	482 260	607 122	594 201	661 954		7.4	5.5
Netherlands	441 735	414 067	477 103	485 088	525 391		6.0	5.5
Switzerland	471 897	469 798	537 757	474 233	432 391	391 520	5.1	3.9
France	382 107	373 141	400 965	409 705	423 492	354 950	4.7	13.4
Japan	255 969	343 984	423 522	335 138	319 194		3.9	1.7
Canada	237 984	302 163	305 682	279 330	282 975	273 921	3.3	3.3
Denmark	201 056	176 096	219 480	220 547	257 034		2.8	2.9
Italy	166 075	192 919	222 271	222 681	202 804		2.5	1.8
Sweden	145 739	151 128	161 231	147 038	163 225	183 105	1.9	2.4
Other	1 281 433	1 406 773	1 148 495	983 418	1 004 024		11.7	14.5
World	7 968 149	8 047 047	8 787 272	8 316 424	8 616 635		100.0	100.0

* Including musts and vermouths
**1988–1990: FRG only
Source: United Nations

North-East Asia. Japan represents a third type of wine consumer market behind the traditional and the new, Anglo-Saxon models sketched in Chapter 2. Japan is a typical emerging market as far as wine is concerned and the most developed in a region deemed to deliver most of the world's economic growth over the next few decades. It exemplifies a breakaway from traditional Asian lifestyle and gradual embracing of Western consumer culture, and foreshadows what might happen all along the Asian Pacific Rim. The review of the main importers then proceeds eastwards across the Northern Hemisphere, to Western Europe, before turning south through the Middle East and Africa, then heading west over South America and ending on the Australian continent.

North East Asia

Japan

The stunning rates of growth in the Japanese demand for foreign wines has aroused much interest amongst wine exporters. Imports grew from virtually nil in 1970 to nearly 100 million litres in 1990,

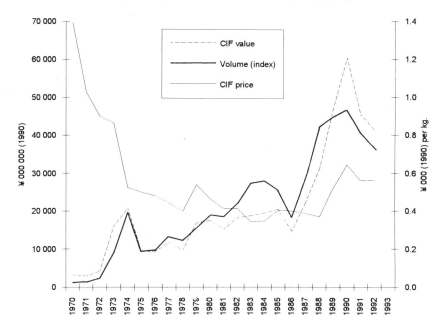

4.1 Japanese imports (112.1) (source: United Nations).

representing 60 billion yen CIF (US$414 000), see Fig. 4.1. The sheer enthusiasm of mainly traditional European wine exporters has dimmed recently: growth has momentarily disappeared and even given way to negative rates since the burst of the 'bubble economy', as wine imports are prone to be hard hit by any reduction in disposable income. But Japan has delivered strong recoveries in the past.

The main attraction of the Japanese market is its sheer potential for long term growth: per capita consumption is extremely low (1.1 litres)[2] and the total population base is huge; over 123.5 million people living in an area 25% bigger than Italy, and mainly in urban areas (77%). In 1990, the Japanese spent ¥6.6 trillion (US$45.6 billion) on alcoholic drinks. Just over half of this expenditure was on beer (54%), nearly a quarter on *sake* and *sochu*, 15% on whiskies and brandies, and only 3% on wine.[3] Total alcohol consumption per capita is still moderate by international standards – Japan ranks 26th with 6.5 lpa – but it is rising steadily, with a 40.6% increase over 1970. What is more, spirits consumption has been receding since the mid-1980s, leaving all the growth for beer (+85.9% over 1970) and wine (+240.6%). On this basis of 1990/1970, Japan ranks as the world's

2 Data refer to 1990 unless stated otherwise.

3 *Monthly Report on Liquor and Food Statistics.*

fourth fastest growing wine market, after the UK, the former East Germany and Denmark.[4]

The shift to beer is mainly from men and that to wine from women; the rise in wine consumption is tied to the westernisation of lifestyles and is most pronounced in the major conurbations: Tokyo/ Yokohama and Osaka. The Tokyo region accounted for more than 40% of Japan's expenditure on wine in 1990.[5] Marrying wine with Japanese food is still thought to be a major task – it competes essentially with the much cheaper and much more popular beer. Also, much of the success of wine is correlated with the successful inroads made by foreign restaurants in large cities – witness the mushrooming of French and Italian restaurants in Tokyo for instance, and the resulting explosion in French and Italian wine sales (the lack of success of Spanish wines seems to be attributable to the virtual absence of Spanish restaurants in the capital). Many firms thus feel that being firmly connected with the catering business provides the most solid base for growth, especially if one likes to operate at the higher end of the wine market. Dining out is still unusual in Japan and habits of this type are bound to change only slowly. Another critical factor in pushing up wine consumption in Japan, and especially that of imported bottled wines, is the explosion of overseas holidaymaking by the Japanese, especially the younger generation. They want to drink those wines back in Japan.

Japanese people have a wholly different perception of wine than have Westerners, e.g. the average wine drinker likes to sip only one glass per drinking occasion.[6] There is also a clear preference for sweet whites and rosés, which outsell reds by a ratio of 3:1.

Japan also foreshadows, to some extent, the future evolution of wine consumption and trade in the most active part of the globe – North East Asia. The most attractive market beside Japan and Hong Kong is Korea. The Chinese provinces of Guandong, Jiangsu and Shandong as well as the city states of Shanghai, Tianjin and Beijing could follow suit, though mainland China does have a winegrowing potential which should not be dismissed lightly: only 10% of China's grape production of 700–800 000 tonnes is thought to be crushed for wine production and the government is actively promoting the production of wine. The Xinjiang region is the major producer,

4 Source: *World Drink Trends.*

5 Tokyo has a per capita consumption which is about 3 times higher than the Japanese average. Source: *Monthly Report on Liquor and Food Statistics.*

6 Nippon Research Centre.

marketing essentially sweet wines.[7] For the time being however, perhaps the next ten years or so, growth seems likely to be limited to Japan and Korea. The much more tropical South East Asia (Singapore, Thailand, Malaysia and Indonesia) gives less scope for growth in wine trade. These markets have been dominated by European suppliers and the French and Germans in particular, but producers situated on the Pacific shores, e.g. California, Australia, Chile and Argentina via Chilean ports seem best placed for securing access to these lucrative markets over the longer term.

Market and import trends

Demand fell back seriously in the early 1900s; this was mainly due to the burst of the economic bubble. The most expensive wines, notably French products, have been hardest hit. This has happened on two occasions in the past, most markedly during the recession caused by the first oil crisis in 1974 and 1975, then also during the slowdown caused by the recession of 1980-81. The momentary setback of the mid-1980s was of an entirely different vein.

The 1985 fall in imports and the dramatic cutback in the following year, bringing volumes temporarily below the 40 million litres mark, was due to a serious fall in demand for German wines in the wake of the diethylene glycol affair as well as to a significant downturn in the demand for Spanish and Yugoslavian wines. The recovery of 1987-90 was due to the cumulative effect of the resumption of German imports and soaring demand for US wines, whilst wines from Australia, Argentina and, later, Italy started to break serious ground in Japanese territory, see Fig 4.2 and 4.3.

There was a strong speculative note underlying the steep rise in imports of 1990: many of the orders had been placed by trading firms wholly unacquainted with wine, and the Japanese market was simply unable to absorb all the foreign shipments. Bottled orders had to be cut back drastically the following year, by over 16% in volume, mostly to the dismay of French exporters. The pricking of Japan's 'bubble economy' in 1992 brought another cut in orders, this time more on the bulk side of the trade (−26%).[8]

---

7 *Revue de l'Académie Suisse du Vin*, June 1992, pp 73–4; and *La Vigne* (as reported in *Bulletin de l'OIV*, no 735–6, pp 442.

8 Source: Japan Tariff Association.

4.2 Japanese imports from main suppliers (CIF, 112.12) (source: United Nations).

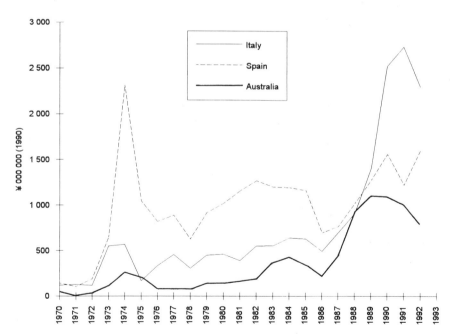

4.3 Japanese imports from selected suppliers and challengers (CIF, 112.12) (source: United Nations).

Trade policy

Internal taxation comprises a consumption tax (currently 3%, which affects all consumer goods) plus a liquor tax which Europeans would refer to as an excise duty. In 1987, a GATT panel ruled that Japan's liquor tax system, which favoured alcoholic drinks produced domestically – albeit using vast quantities of imported bulk – over bottled imports, was simply discriminatory. The indirect tax incentive to import bulk was particularly strong for whisky and wine. Sweeping changes were brought about to the Japanese liquor tax in the wake of the GATT ruling; they took effect in January 1989. A few squabbles remain about the exclusion hitherto of domestically produced *sochu* (a potato-based spirit) from the tax. More recently, falling sales of Japanese-made whisky and rising popularity, especially with the 20–40 age range, of low alcohol drinks in cans (which can be distributed by the ubiquitous street vending machines) has prompted the government to consider the introduction of a much reduced, special tax rate on drinks with an 8–12% alcohol content. This *mizuwari* (literally 'water diluted') drinks market is especially interesting for spirit-based coolers.[9] Still wines are subject to a tax of ¥46.3 per litre and fortified wines to a basic tax of ¥85 per litre, augmented by ¥7.1 per litre for each additional degree of alcohol in excess of 13%.[10]

Regarding border protection, Japan does not erect any type of technical, i.e. non-tariff, barriers. Wine is subject only to its domestic Food Sanitation Law; an invoice (in English), a certificate of origin and a certificate of analysis are the only documents required.[11] Import disruptions often take the form of voluntary self-restraint, following a ban on sales imposed for health reasons, as in the recent MITC case. Following the discovery by US authorities, in early 1992, of traces of methyl isiothiocyanate in Italian wines, most Japanese importers suspended their imports from Italy (the MITC insecticide is sometimes used to control fermentation but is banned from use in food in Japan, in the US and in Italy as well as in many other countries).[12]

Japan does not follow any particular tariff policy other than applying a differentiated system which offers preferential rates for musts and wine shipped in bulk from developing countries, e.g. Eastern Europe, North Africa and South America. The 1992 tariff

9 *Nihon Keizai Shimbun*, 15/3/93.

10 Such was the situation in July 1991.

11 CFCE (1992, Japan, p 40).

12 *The Financial Times*, 22 April 1992.

schedule, for instance, provided for a ¥24 rate for imports of wine in bulk and for a free rate for musts, against a statutory rate of ¥64 in both cases. Bottled imports are not subject to differentiated tariff treatment, but to a tariff of 21.3% of its CIF value within a min/max bracket of ¥93/156.8 per litre.[13] This system clearly favours cheap imports in bulk from developing countries, which are generally, if not wholly, used for blending with wines produced from domestic grapes. The resulting blend is marketed as 'Japanese wine', at the lower end of the price scale – below the ¥1200 mark. These are Japan's ordinary wines and the largest segment by far with an estimated 80% of all wine sales.[14]

The 'Japanese wine' segment is critical to the survival of domestic grape and wine production. Like the rest of agriculture, viticulture is faced with comparatively high production costs, mostly because Japan's hot and humid climate requires that grapes be grown in pergola style,[15] thus barring full mechanisation of pruning and harvesting. Japan does produce outstanding wines of its own. High production costs mean that they have to compete with some of the better wines from around the world (above the ¥25 000 mark),[16] notably French wines which are perceived as being the best available. The marketing of 100% Japanese wines is thus fairly limited and confined to a specialist connoisseur niche. The vast majority of the crush is blended with foreign wines imported in bulk or with wines produced from imported musts and grapes, and is then put to market as 'Japanese wine' (see Fig. 4.4). Japanese legislation requires a minimum of 5% of indigenous product to be present in the blend and bottling to take place within the country for the resulting product to be considered 'Japanese'. There is nothing outrageous in such practices, and certainly nothing wrong when considered from a Japanese perspective as this is quite consistent with 'mixing rules' applying to other agricultural sectors, e.g. the manufacturing of milk reconstituted from milk powder, fats and other constituents purchased in various parts of the world.

Japanese wine production is fairly concentrated: 1989–91 average estimates put Suntory's market share at 21%, Mercian (formerly

13 Japan Tariff Association, 1992.

14 CFCE (1992, Japan, p 64).

15 This is mainly due to the presence of fungus, but pergolas allow for a greater leaf surface; another problem is the occurrence of typhoons in September (harvest time), which can cause dilution.

16 They have come into competition with estate bottled Beaujolais, Sancerre, etc, but not wines near the very top end.

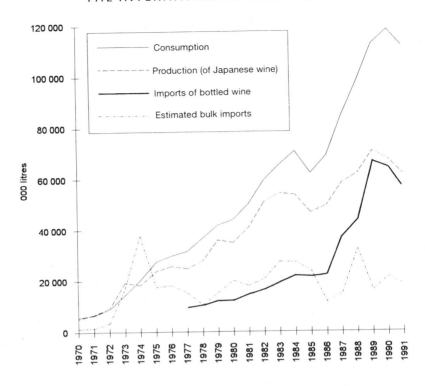

4.4 Japanese wine consumption, production and imports (source: National Tax Administration Agency).

Sanraku) at 20%, followed by Manzu (formerly Kikkoman) with 10% and Sapporo with 9%, leaving over a hundred other wineries to fight for the remaining 40% market share.[17] But the rate of concentration is smaller in wine than that prevailing in the domestic production of beer, controlled by Kirin (48%), Asahi (25%), Sapporo (19%) and Suntory (8%). Market dominance is greatest in the production of whisky: Suntory captures a 72% market share, followed by Nikka (18%), Kirin-Seagram (5.5%) and Mercian (2.3%).[18]

Wine production in Japan is relatively new, having started to develop during the Second World War, and demand only became significant in the 1970s. Japan is well aware of its limited possibilities for producing excellent wines: the northern island of Hokkaido offers micro-climates that are akin to the world's best winegrowing regions,

17 *Wands*, reported by CFCE (1992, Japan, p 45).

18 Source of market share data: *International Drinks Bulletin*, vol 5, no 19, November 1990.

but the majority of the wine is made in Yamanashi prefecture, south of Tokyo, which derives most of its income from fruit production and tourism. Riesling, Cabernet Sauvignon and Japan's best-known indigenous grape, the Koshu variety (which probably originates from Tadjikistan and came to Japan via China – unlike the other varieties which were imported from Europe only a century ago, in the Meiji period. Another limiting factor is the fact that grapes delivered for crush are commanding a much lower price than those marketed as table grapes. This may well change progressively as Japanese agriculture is liberalised, but for the moment, roughly a tenth of grape production is allocated to winemaking (with 85% marketed as table grapes and the rest being processed as canned fruit, grape juice and for other minor uses). Japan's total grape production peaked at 350 000 t in 1979 and has been declining ever since; it is now standing at around 270 000 t. A gently rising proportion of grapes has been diverted to winemaking since the 1979 peak, resulting in a doubling of quantities delivered for crush, from 15 000 tons (representing 4.2% of grape production) to just over 30 000 tons in 1990 (representing 11%).[19] A rough estimate would put the proportion of truly domestic wine at 37%[20] of the quantities which are currently classified as Japanese wine.[21] Japanese wines are about two-thirds white and one third rosés/reds.[22] This part of the market is bound to lose steadily in importance in the long term, as will Japanese reconstituted milk. 1992 has already shown a significant cutback on the days of bulk imports: more than a third down on their 1988 level – a local maximum, still below the 1983 and 1984 import levels – and more than a quarter down on their 1991 level. How fast the Japanese wine segment will decrease in the future depends on consumer awareness, which is notoriously low in Japan, for wine as for all other consumer goods.

The importance of brand names in Japan cannot be stressed enough. The most popular and most advertised brands are Suntory's Madonna, Mercian's Select and Kirin's Dance. Table 4.2 gives the most successful imported brands in 1992.

Regarding global brands, it is extremely costly to build up a name

19 Ministry of Agriculture, Fisheries and Food (MAFF).

20 1987–91 average (author's estimate, based on the assumption: litres of wine produced = wine crush tonnage times 0.8).

21 All bulk imports – whether blending with indigenous wine or not – fall in this category for statistical purposes since they must be bottled on mainland Japan. This does not preclude some importers/wineries from bottling/marketing them 'as is', i.e. without blending them.

22 Noboru Ueno.

Table 4.2 Most successful imported brands in Japan (1992)

Major imported brands	000 cases			Origin	Importer
	1990	1991	1992		
Valckenberg	420.0	400.0	420.0	Germany	Suntory
Calvet	470.0	370.0	330.0	France	Suntory
Piat d'Or	275.0	265.0	238.5	France	Nikka
Wine Club	122.0	181.5	220.8	USA	Kirin Beer
G.A. Schmittsches		80.0	110.0	Germany	Mercian
Fontanafredda	146.0	142.7	97.5	Italy	Montebussan
Mortier	110.0	100.0	95.0	France	Meijia
Cruse	90.0	110.0	90.0	France	Mercian
Bordeaux & Bourgogne		100.0	90.0	France	Suic
B&G	96.0	92.0	85.0	France	Kirin-Seagram
Drathen	120.0	90.0	85.0	Germany	Asahi Ber
Auge		48.0	72.0	France	Kikkoman
San Francisco		80.0	72.0	USA	Kirin-Seagram
Mateus	160.0	125.0	70.0	Portugal	Suntory
Delo		70.0	67.0	France	Nihon Shurui Hambai
Sichel		60.0	50.0	Germany	Jardine

Source: Japan Wines & Spirits Importers' Association

in Japan (because of the huge advertising expenses involved), yet Japanese consumers now seem to be just as reluctant to buy imported wines marketed under Japanese brand names, e.g. Suntory and Mercian have had to discontinue their efforts in that direction. National and regional distributors do participate in promotion efforts however and seem to be content with relatively small margins. Some foreign producers help promote their brands: the California Wine Institute for instance spent US$3 million in 1990 for that purpose.[23] Also, note that there is little central buying by the large national operators and no links between alcoholic drinks producers and retailers.

Import and distribution channels

The bulk side of the import market is concentrated in the hands of ten trading companies. Some of them, such as Mitsubishi and Sumitomo are large conglomerates with very limited interest in wine; they mostly act as brokers, pushing the samples and eventually the final products

---

23 Australian Wine and Brandy Corporation.

(whether wine or musts) to the doorsteps of the 'wine factories' which blend imported bulk with truly domestic wines. Wine factories are located in the vicinity of major ports, mostly in the Tokyo Bay, e.g. Kawasaki. Others, like Suntory and Mercian are responsible for blending and subsequent marketing of those wines; these two firms are major players in the upper quality segment as well since both import and market large quantities of imported bottled wine. Of the two, Suntory is the largest; it moved from spirits into wine (as did other liquor marketers faced with the maturity/decline of this market) and owns or controls a number of high quality wine producers abroad. Mercian is a diversified alcohol, chemical and foodstuff producer which generates more than three-quarters of its ¥84 billion turnover from producing and/or marketing indigenous and imported wines and spirits.[24] Amongst other things, it owns Château Reysson in France and Markham Vineyards in Australia and is producing 100% Japanese wines at its Katsunuma winery in the Yamanashi Prefecture.

Bulk imports of wine and musts usually take place in 20 000 litre containers and prices are negotiated ex-winery or FOB, in local currency or in US$ (importers are usually large enough to command significant discounts on shipping and insurance costs; they are also sophisticated enough to hedge against currency movements). Regarding musts, fermentation is usually prevented with the addition of SO_2 (rather than via the addition of alcohol, which commands higher tariff rates) and concentration occurs before shipping. In Japan, yeasts and water are added back to it and some SO_2 removed in order to trigger fermentation. Argentina, Spain, Eastern Europe and South Africa are all traditional suppliers of bulk or musts. Since the collapse of the Russian market however, Romanian and Bulgarian producers have reduced their bulk production in order to concentrate on the higher-valued bottled shipments. This has driven the price of bulk up and many Japanese importers away from their offerings. (For bulk as for bottle, Japanese wine marketers usually start with their domestic price points system and 'work back' the purchasing cost at which they would like to find wines offered; only then do they proceed to 'shop around' the world for the best quality available at that price.) For musts and bulk alike, tasting remains a necessity for assessing their quality. The next most important factor to a Japanese importer is the grape variety.

The import of bottled wines, unlike the bulk side, shows no sign

---

24 Figures for 1990 and 1991, then equivalent to US$670 million. Source: Mercian 1991 Annual Report.

of concentration. Some 100–200 firms are active there, though 60 firms or so are believed to handle three-quarters of the imports and less than a dozen of them have specialised in wine. Many firms engaged in this activity in the heyday of imports but lacked experience in dealing with wine. They were quick to opt out of the market as soon as competition grew fiercer. Barring a few cases however,[25] all best-selling imported brands are marketed by wine, beer or spirits producers, as shown in Table 4.2. Other importers are joint ventures, such as Kirin-Seagram, formed in 1973, which imported French *Barton & Guestier* (1985) and American *San Francisco* (1972). Jardine is one of the few wholly foreign ventures (between the Hong Kong based Jardine Wine and Spirits, Guinness's United Distillers and Moët-Hennessy); it imported German *Sichel* (1950) among other things. Jardine's strength lies in its firm ties with the on-premise sector (hotels, restaurants and bars) which it caters for with a selective portfolio of some 200 still and sparkling wines, along with brandies, Scotch whiskies and other spirits. A sizeable portion of Jardine's portfolio is at the high end, e.g. it includes Domaine Chandon's sparkling *Reserve* and Heitz' famous *Martha's Vineyard Cabernet* to name but a few of Napa Valley's crus). In 1992, some 40% of bottled imports were estimated to be in the ¥1000–1500 range and that this sector had remained largely unaffected by recession. Mostly hit was the upper end of the market, i.e. upwards of ¥10 000. As brand names are essential in Japan, exclusive contracts for bottled imports, running for several years, are not uncommon.

Be it in bulk or in bottle, the import of wines is firmly in Japanese hands. Importers are faced with particularly complex logistics. Japan's multi-layered distribution system comes from the need to offer consumers a broad palette of offerings in spite of an acute shortage of shelf and storage space as well as from the habit, for consumers, to buy one bottle at a time. Until recently, 80% of all retail sales were estimated to occur through heavily protected local specialist shops – the *sakayas*. Getting a retail licence for alcoholic drinks remains difficult in Japan. An increasing number of supermarkets[26] are being granted a liquor licence but the pace of reform is judged to be extremely slow, and not just by Western standards. The major fear is that many of these small shops are doomed to disappear. Some of them may turn into convenience stores, others into local discount

25 E.g. Tokyo area's powerful milk marketer Snow Brand.

26 Daiei is the largest supermarket chain, followed by Ito-yokado, which runs 7/11s and has large suburban outlets (*The Financial Times*, 15 June 1993).

liquor stores, such as Kawachiya,[27] as recession bites and Japanese consumers are increasingly turning away from prestige brands and looking for better value for money.[28] But these already face fierce competition from ever more popular discounters which are mushrooming on the fringe of all major cities and resort to parallel imports of well known brand names in clothing and fashion as well as drinks.

In 1991, just over half of total imports were sold through the on-premise market, which is dominated by French wines with 51% followed by Germany with 18%, USA 13% and Italy 11%.[29] The rest is split between the once all-important gift segment dominated by France with 60%, and followed by Germany with 24% market share, which is now in rapid recession, and home consumption, which is gaining in importance; French wines still figure prominently with 38% market share, but German wines are hard on their heels with 30%, followed by the USA with 15% and Italy with 6%. The origin of the wines is shifting considerably now that people are becoming more cost-conscious. Each country's image appears to be a key element in the success of its wines. Fluctuations in exchange rates is another important element.

In general, import of wine (as that of spirits, clothes and other fashion items) has been strongly aided by the rise of the yen against all other major currencies in the 1970s and 1980s (the Japanese currency had been significantly undervalued under the fixed exchange rate mechanism).[30] Table 4.3 gives a detailed evolution of imports from the major supplying countries.

Mostly hit have been top of the range French imports such as champagnes and AOCs, owing to improved awareness amongst Japanese wine consumers, who are becoming increasingly acquainted with US and Australian wines. French brands have all been badly hit by recession, while some German and US brands have even managed to increase their sales in such tough conditions. Yet French wines continue to enjoy the best image around; they are the strongest performers in the upmarket and on-premise segments, while German wines have also managed to keep a relatively high profile. German and US wines do best in the retail market; these are mainly white, cheaper wines and the influence of women is ever-growing as consumption

---

27 *The Financial Times,* 12 August 1993.

28 Supermarkets vie with both convenience stores and discounters (*The Financial Times,* 15 June 1993 and 12 August 1993).

29 Source: Wands, September 1992.

30 Krieger, 1993, p 486.

Table 4.3 Japanese imports, 000 yen (1990)

All wines*	1988	1989	1990	1991	1992	Value share, % 1991–92	Volume share, % 1991–92
France	16 024 898	28 638 758	39 950 720	27 717 728	24 902 669	60.6	31.2
Germany**	5 045 366	5 772 119	7 645 533	5 642 444	5 562 483	12.9	15.7
USA	3 184 655	3 910 935	3 372 478	2 649 650	2 489 220	5.9	10.3
Italy	1 044 479	1 580 456	2 747 839	2 954 827	2 486 453	6.3	5.9
Spain	1 427 595	1 488 296	1 745 101	1 341 656	1 703 879	3.5	5.1
Argentina	1 053 128	956 286	1 075 216	1 007 253	1 040 664	2.4	9.7
Australia	937 045	1 101 393	1 099 135	1 003 861	779 927	2.1	3.5
Portugal	510 415	785 273	879 683	941 234	628 923	1.8	1.8
Chile	362 439	351 511	472 911	444 914	325 230	0.9	3.9
Bulgaria	389 467	315 695	432 277	319 920	307 302	0.7	4.3
Other	1 328 809	1 302 135	1 605 331	1 561 634	1 014 915	3.0	8.6
World	31 308 295	46 202 857	61 026 225	45 585 121	41 241 665	100.0	100.0
Sparkling							
France	2 250 583	4 151 458	7 025 360	6 196 434	6 023 556	82.5	49.4
Spain	261 627	324 047	476 945	403 293	551 074	6.4	19.7
Italy	127 029	190 833	387 032	381 112	336 179	4.8	12.2
USA	60 812	95 275	149 280	202 494	149 560	2.4	6.4
Germany**	59 866	130 950	204 179	166 092	142 581	2.1	8.0
Australia	6 081	16 563	22 046	132 300	32 728	1.1	2.9
Portugal		11 325	13 545	8 872	5 775	0.1	0.3
Austria		4 389	13 545	30 661	5 054	0.2	0.5
Hungary	1 487	1 274	1 729	391	3 971	0.0	0.1
S Africa	4 595	5 096	7 061	913	2 286	0.0	0.1
Other	13 784	9 060	37 176	14 613	17 086	0.2	0.3
World	2 785 864	4 940 270	8 337 896	7 537 176	7 269 851	100.0	100.0
Still							
France	13 601 203	24 246 919	32 516 859	21 239 733	18 699 351	57.8	31.9
Germany**	4 980 905	5 630 976	7 427 954	5 475 569	5 418 698	15.8	17.5
USA	2 789 512	3 377 085	3 074 784	2 430 585	2 339 058	6.9	11.4
Italy	782 042	1 218 044	2 132 853	2 352 301	1 956 916	6.2	5.3
Spain	758 258	953 597	1 084 870	820 676	1 055 223	2.7	3.9
Australia	924 342	1 084 829	1 069 308	871 561	747 199	2.3	3.9
Portugal	510 415	773 948	865 562	932 362	623 147	2.3	2.1
Argentina	325 276	271 951	338 473	367 543	365 177	1.1	6.3
Chile	308 790	290 213	415 418	393 899	308 987	1.0	4.2
Bulgaria	387 305	313 996	432 277	319 920	307 302	0.9	4.9
Hungary	76 623	98 248	76 081	113 381	132 835	0.4	0.5
S Africa	59 731	33 268	42 075	40 838	108 771	0.2	0.7
New Zealand	133 516	89 754	120 461	156 437	101 431	0.4	1.0
Romania	125 678	183 754	122 478	182 010	99 747	0.4	1.9
Yugoslavia					91 806	0.1	0.6
Slovenia					53 664	0.1	0.3
Austria	37 839	52 380	98 415	187 881	51 016	0.3	0.3
Switzerland	18 514		40 058	27 791	44 519	0.1	0.0
China	92 704	36 100	41 210	43 187	35 014	0.1	0.3
Other	538 253	477 506	633 429	492 536	119 119	0.9	3.0
World	26 450 906	39 132 567	50 532 565	36 448 212	32 658 981	100.0	100.0

*Including musts and vermouths **1988–1990: FRG only Source: United Nations

slowly shifts from restaurants and bars into Japanese homes. Italian wines benefited most from the rising popularity of Italian fashion and restaurants, until 1992, when the MITC affair put them on hold. Portuguese wines consist mainly of one brand and have been falling sharply. Spain has been losing ground ever since 1984. One of the best performers of the late 1980s is Australia, which saw sharp increases until the recession hit Japan. Together with the US, it is one of the few suppliers experiencing an increase in export volumes in 1992 (see Table 4.3). Like the US, Australia was at first penalised by a fairly bad image. Both countries are relatively close, hence a common destination for Japanese holidaymakers, and the two countries are new wine producers, lacking the lustre of French wines. Exports of Californian jug wines projected a cheap image on all US wines. Australians were faced with the additional problem of confusion with Austria in the wake of the diethylene glycol affair – both names are spelt nearly identically in Japanese, but both seem to have benefited from recession thanks to their good quality/price ratios, better connections with supermarket chains (especially for US producers) and an apparent absence of commitment to traditional wine suppliers, i.e. 'the best deal around prevails'.

To recap briefly, the burst of the Japanese economic bubble resulted in a temporary squeeze in consumers' disposable income as well as in corporate budgets for entertaining expenses, causing a serious break in the exponential trend of wine imports. This also generated significant compositional changes in the nature of imports, shifting the balance towards the more efficient New World producers. Cheaper bulk imports, which are favoured by Japan's trade policy and reinforced by its commercial policy asking only for a fractional presence of truly domestic wine in order for the resulting blend to be marketed as 'Japanese wine', have also been kept alive (the decline of this segment has been delayed by recession).

Outlook

Asians have a radically different perception of wine. The rise in demand comes from the Westernisation of Japanese lifestyle, predominantly in the food, clothing and entertainment sectors. Bringing wine into the Japanese diet which is based heavily on rice will take a long time. Wine is best marketed in association with Western food and the sprouting of foreign restaurants and their continuing success will remain the privileged channel for bringing wine to the Japanese people. This is also true for the much less developed markets of the Pacific Rim. Prospects for long term development of wine consumption, and hence trade, are good, despite the momentary lull in imports caused by the Japanese recession.

The most interesting wine markets of the Pacific Rim after Japan are Hong Kong, where people drank 1.7 litres per head on average and imported some 4.6 million litres in 1992, mainly from France and from the US,[31] and South Korea which abolished all import quotas on wine and reduced duty rates recently – South Korea would appear to produce five-sixths of the estimated 6 million litres it consumes each year.[32] Taiwan's Tobacco and Wine Monopoly imported 1.7 million litres in 1990, half of which came from the US.[33] Singapore and Thailand's markets are growing, but sales remain largely confined to hotels. Like the other countries of South-East Asia, e.g. Malaysia and Indonesia, their climate is tropical and much less suited to wine consumption by the local population.

North America

Canada

The most distinctive feature of the Canadian wine market is that it does not form a single national entity but consists of ten autonomous monopolies. The Canadian constitution grants provincial governments extensive powers in matters such as commercial licences. Each of them has set up its own liquor control board which regulates the import and distribution of alcoholic drinks within their jurisdiction. Imports from other states (including those of wine produced in other Canadian provinces) are thus determined by the rules set up by these large monopsonies/monopolies. Some liquor boards provide a fairly competitive environment, as in the case of the *Société des Alcools du Quebec*. Others, such as the Liquor Control Board of Ontario, continue to apply discriminatory practices against out-of-state producers, in spite of the international obligations undertaken by the state of Canada, notably under GATT.

---

31 CFCE (1992, Hong Kong, p 74).

32 CFCE (1992, South Korea, p 34).

33 Hong Kong's 14 March 1993.

State monopolies aside (as many as 18 US states enjoy that privilege,[34] Canada also offers striking similarities with its powerful neighbour in terms of alcohol consumption. In 1990 for instance, Canadians and Americans ranked 23rd and 24th heaviest alcohol drinkers worldwide, with a per capita intake of around 7.5 lpa.[35] Both countries saw a sharp and steady decline of the demand for spirits over the 1980s, while beer consumption kept basically steady (declining marginally), leaving wine as the only alcoholic drink capable of generating growth in the 1980s. The growth in wine consumption was even more rapid in Canada than in the US, starting at a lower level in the early 1960s (2.2 litres in Canada against 3.5 in the US) and peaking at just over 10 litres in the years 1985–88, against a US peak of 9 litres in the years 1985–86; in this respect, Canadians are even more akin to the British who started with 1.8 litres and levelled off at 11.5 in 1989–90. The demand for wine in Canada has been receding ever since the mid-1980s however. In 1990, it fell back to where it stood a decade ago:[36] below the 9 litres mark. The rise of neo-prohibitionism in the US at that time must have played a major hand in curbing Canadian wine consumption.

Canada does have close cultural ties with the US. Some 90% of the gently rising population lies in a 200-mile band along the American border and more than 60% are concentrated in the two provinces of Ontario and Quebec.[37] These two provinces and those of British Columbia and Alberta together make up 90% of Canada's wine market.[38] Ontario alone accounts for half of Canada's wine consumption.[39] The French culture of the inhabitants of Quebec and Canada's historical ties with the French crown (Canada was explored and settled by French immigrants in the sixteenth century, then lost to the British in the mid-eighteenth) makes it a natural dominion for French wines. Yet the French, together with all their West European counterparts in Germany, Italy and Spain kept losing ground during the 1980s. The major beneficiaries were American, Australian and

---

34 According to J. Tremblay, PDG *Sociétéde Alcools du Québec* (Montpellier Conf. on intl. trade, Feb 1993).

35 Source: *World Drink Trends.*

36 Ibid, 1980.

37 Krieger, 1993.

38 CFCE (1992, Canada, p 62).

39 Ziraldo, 'United States-Canada Free Trade Agreement and North American Free Trade Agreement: Canadian Industry Perspective', in International Wine Law Association, 1992, p 115.

Chilean exporters who have succeeded in meeting the enthusiasm shown by many Canadians for white wines since the late 1970s (+150%). Hardest hit were domestic wine producers, mostly located in Ontario.[40] They used to enjoy an immense popularity in the late 1970s[41] but have seen their wines fall out of favour over the past twenty years. Canada's domestic wine production had to be cut back accordingly, from just over 47 million litres in the late 1970s and early 1980s to 38.6 in the second half of the 1980s.[42] Canadian wines have, so far, borne the main brunt of the recession whilst foreign wines have come out largely unhurt on the whole. Imported volumes have flared briefly at nearly 170 million litres in 1984 and then stabilised at around 140 million. 3% of imported volume consists of Italian and French vermouths,[43] while 97% are still and sparkling wines. The remainder of the analysis concentrates on them.

Market and import trends

Looking at the real value of imports shown in Fig. 4.5 sheds a different light on Canadian trade. Imports eased off after the first oil shock in 1974, and again in 1978. Their real value then fell until 1983 in spite of continuously rising volumes. The years 1974–1983 witnessed a formidable fall in the real value of the CIF price,[44] from C$ 3.4 to C$ 1.7. Such was the extent of the plunge in import prices that Canada managed to increase volumes even in the recessionary early 1980s. CIF prices started to pick up again in 1984 and reached C$ 2.4 in 1990 whilst volumes remained basically unchanged, for a total of C$ 345 million.

A closer look at individual trade flows reveals a recent shift away from German, Italian and especially Spanish wines to the better priced – but not necessarily lower quality – wines from Chile, Australia and the US (see Fig. 4.6 and 4.7 and Table 4.4). Regarding French wines, the current worldwide trend of 'drinking less but better' seems to

40 Ontario has a vineyard of around 11 000 ha in the Niagara Peninsula; British Columbia, the other Canadian producer, has about 1300 ha (CFCE, 1992, Canada, p 61). Quebec has a few wineries which assemble and bottle wine (some produce wine from imported grapes).

41 Particularly in Ontario (MacKinnon and Larue, 1990, p 2).

42 The average wine production of Canada was 47.6 million litres in 1976–80, 47 million in 1981–85 and 38.6 million in 1986–90 (OIV).

43 Two thirds and one third respectively; all data are 1989–91 averages, calculated from United Nations statistics.

44 Expressed in 1990 terms; recall that the CIF price is net of tariffs and taxes.

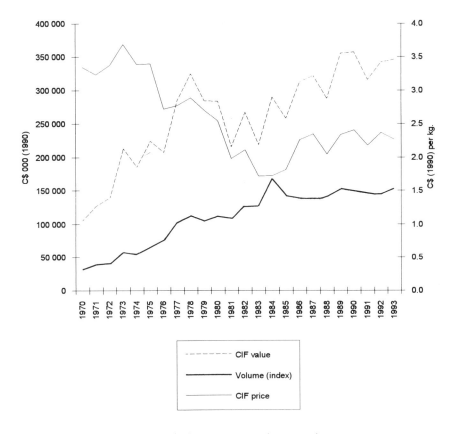

4.5 Canadian imports (112.1) (source: United Nations).

apply in Canada as well. The fall in the CIF prices, from the mid-1970s
to the mid-1980s was attributable in large part to the weakness of the
suppliers' currencies versus the Canadian dollar. The exceptions are
the US dollar which gained slightly throughout that period, as well as
the Deutschmark and the French franc which rose sharply in the
1970s. The general weakness of the Canadian dollar versus its trading
partners over the second half of the 1980s again brought about a rise
in CIF prices. US exports to Canada rose sharply in the early 1980s,
when Californian producers faced production surpluses for the first
time and prices fell as a result, making them more competitive than
any other supplier except Chile. The extremely low value of US wines
also reflects the increasing amounts of cheap bulk sent across the
border, and also the fact that the US enjoys preferential treatment
since the entry into force of the Canada-US Free Trade Agreement in
1989.

Table 4.4 Canadian imports, 000 c$ (1990)

All wines*	1988	1989	1990	1991	1992	1993	Value share, % 1991–93	Volume share, % 1992–93
France	154506	195514	192436	156479	156229	151002	46.2	36.5
USA	20783	30937	28807	35708	47041	52190	13.4	19.9
Italy	39403	47480	51456	46699	48221	51778	14.6	14.6
Chile	3291	5344	8681	12282	20709	23233	5.6	8.4
Germany**	28824	27648	26019	21946	19971	17583	5.9	5.0
Australia	7535	10513	14701	13086	15289	17181	4.5	4.0
Spain	17219	17757	15604	12115	14110	12523	3.9	4.8
Portugal	6800	7492	7842	7863	7381	7561	2.3	1.7
Hungary	2921	3376	2914	3162	3765	3600	1.0	1.5
Greece	2474	3015	2754	2500	2811	3412	0.9	1.2
Other	5559	6339	5545	4081	6598	6043	1.7	2.5
World	289317	355415	356759	315921	342125	346109	100.0	100.0

Sparkling

	1988	1989	1990	1991	1992	1993		
France	16278	24746	19737	14160	15352	13521	49.6	22.4
Spain	5770	7339	6039	4929	4533	3975	15.5	24.7
Germany**	5675	5947	4737	4882	3464	3898	14.1	21.3
USA	721	1413	1616	1944	2894	2926	8.9	14.0
Italy	2719	3794	3607	2602	2886	2472	9.2	12.3
Austria	27	176	88	65	106	218	0.4	0.5
Australia	83	56	97	91	149	203	0.5	0.9
Chile		5	99	36	208	181	0.5	1.2
Hungary	106	124	93	184	303	116	0.7	1.7
Greece					3	9	0.0	0.0
Other	17	29	56	208	220	28	0.5	1.0
World	31397	43628	36169	29101	30117	27548	100.0	100.0

Still

	1988	1989	1990	1991	1992	1993		
France	132862	164828	167920	137340	136493	132811	45.9	37.1
USA	20056	29523	27191	33764	44148	49261	14.4	20.6
Italy	30354	36599	40718	37869	39758	43367	13.7	13.3
Chile	3291	5340	8582	12246	20500	23052	6.3	8.9
Australia	7452	10457	14604	12995	15140	16978	5.1	4.2
Germany**	23150	21701	21282	17064	16507	13684	5.3	4.5
Spain	11442	10417	9565	7186	9577	8548	2.9	4.3
Portugal	6792	7487	7814	7670	7188	7554	2.5	1.7
Hungary	2815	3252	2821	2978	3462	3484	1.1	1.6
Greece	2474	3015	2754	2500	2808	3403	1.0	1.3
Bulgaria	1108	1281	672	542	1449	1527	0.4	0.6
New Zealand	255	570	355	391	977	1337	0.3	0.2
Argentina	825	726	1761	1071	1523	919	0.4	1.1
Israel	715	514	488	376	433	622	0.2	0.1
Yugoslavia					723	264	0.1	0.2
Romania	138	353	186	159	295	167	0.1	0.1
Switzerland	195	237	235	296	170	135	0.1	0.0
Tunisia	263	243				135	0.0	0.0
Denmark			105	178	149	134	0.1	0.0
Other	1964	2100	1590	916	680	491	0.2	0.2
World	246152	298644	308641	275541	301980	307873	100.0	100.0

* Including musts and vermouths   ** 1988–1990: FRG only   *Source: United Nations*

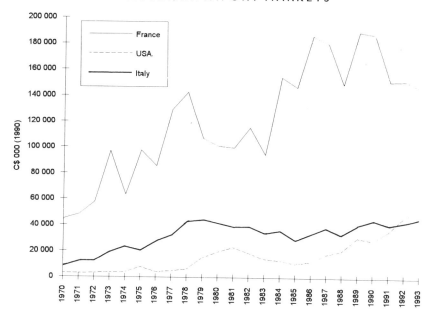

4.6 Canadian imports from main suppliers (CIF, 112.12) (source: United Nations).

Other factors have helped Canadians operate their shift away from traditional West European supply sources. If the French turned out to be the immediate beneficiaries of the European débâcle triggered by successive scandals involving adulterated German and Italian wines, recent changes in Canada's trade policy definitely favour US producers.

Trade policy and distribution channels

The policy of the powerful provincial liquor boards[45] which requires imported wines to go through a tedious and costly referencing procedure before being granted access (if any)[46] to the boards' own marketing channels (the sole legal commercial channels in Canada)[47] and then charges a hefty fee for just handling the wines, has been

---

45 Especially those of Ontario and Quebec; the remaining eight Liquor Boards are either fairly liberal or of marginal economic value to exporters.

46 The success rate of the applications is 2–3%.

47 Two exceptions exist: Ontario wine producers are allowed 'wineries' door sales' (amounting to an estimated 25% of their turnover) and Quebec's licensed *épiceries* can market wines bottled in Quebec.

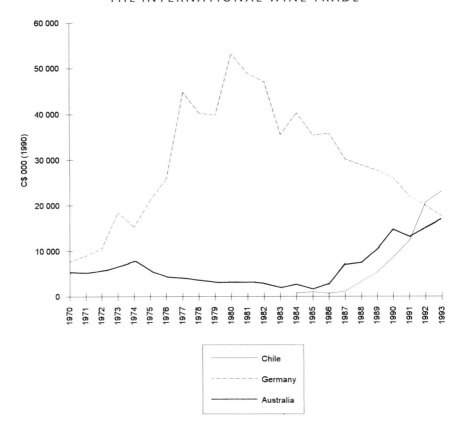

4.7 Canadian imports from selected suppliers and challengers (CIF, 112.12) (source: United Nations).

subject to intense scrutiny and international criticism. Producers must ensure their own promotion[48] and may face de-listing if they fail to meet minimum sales quotas; price is the critical factor in the boards' listing decisions and must be kept unchanged for at least a year; the producer may also be asked to bear transport and insurance costs to Canada.

Most of the recent changes in Canada's trade policy came on the heels of a 1987 GATT ruling which called for the removal of the liquor boards' most blatant discriminatory trade practices, particularly the application of differential mark ups. Ontario exemplified such discrimination until fairly recently, by applying a mark up of 66% on

---

48 Usually through an appointed local agent who takes a 10–15% commission on the FOB price. Their commission must be included in the CIF prices proposed to the Liquor Boards for referencing (CFCE, 1992, Canada, p 69).

foreign wines and 1% on local products, whether 100% domestic or blended. This mechanism managed to more than treble the price of a bottle from the docks to the shelves. Take a CIF price of C$ 1.68, for instance; after payment of C$ 5.37 in Federal Excise Tax, a Federal Sales Tax of 18% and a Provincial Sales Tax of 12% (all of which apply indiscriminately to domestic and foreign wines) and the applicable mark up, its retail price became C$ 6.65. The cellar door price of an Ontario wine of C$ 2.77 however merely translates into a retail price of C$ 6.25 after being subjected to the same array of taxes but only to a mere 1% markup.[49]

Canada and the US signed a free trade agreement which stipulated significant successive cuts in the provincial liquor boards' mark up differentials between US and domestically produced wines as soon as the treaty came into force, on 1 January 1989, leading to their being totally phased out in 1995. (These dispositions have since been taken up by the more comprehensive NAFTA agreement which became effective in 1994.) Similar provisions were stipulated by the EU-Canadian agreement which followed suit, though the speed of the reduction in the mark up affecting US wines is more rapid than that for EU wines (leading to a total phasing out by 1996).[50]

The issue of mark up is a thorny one, for empirical work supports the view that the Canadian demand for foreign wines is quite sensitive to price changes whilst that for domestic wines is quite inelastic.[51] For instance, rather than lower the mark up on foreign wines, the Province of Ontario opted for raising the mark up on provincial wines until differentials would disappear by the agreed deadline. Ontario and British Columbia have also introduced a new 16% service fee to replace revenue lost in reduced mark ups.[52]

Mark up differentials are due to be phased out more rapidly in the case of domestic wines blended with imported ones than for purely domestic wines.[53] As in Japan, some of the imports take place in bulk and are used either for bottling 'as is' or for blending with domestically produced wine. In the first case, the wines usually bear the

---

49 This example is extracted from MacKinnon and Larue, 1990, p 18; other similar examples are provided in CFCE (1992, Canada).

50 CFCE (1992, Canada, pp 80–1).

51 Own-price elasticity of −0.6 for Canadian wines, −1.32 for French, −1.46 for Italian and −1.0 for German wines; with corresponding income elasticity of 1.01, 1.06, 0.6 and 1.72 (MacKinnon and Larue, 1990, p 17).

52 Clawson, in International Wine Law Association, 1992, p 111.

53 CFCE (1992, Canada, p 77), Ziraldo, in International Wine Law Association, 1992, p 117.

Table 4.5 Canadian bulk imports

	1990		1991		Prices (C$/litre)	
	Volume (thousand litres)	**Value** (C$000)	**Volume**	**Value**	**1990**	**1991**
Whites <13.7%	31 257	21 639	32 749	21 533	0.69	0.66
France	9 516	11 314	11 691	10 271	1.19	0.88
US	10 912	4 480	11 932	5 176	0.41	0.43
Chile	3 910	1 556	3 268	1 789	0.40	0.55
Reds <13.7%	13 183	11 240	11 759	9 807	0.85	0.83
France	5 416	6 979	5 490	6 019	1.29	1.10
Italy	1 333	1 258	1 227	965	0.94	0.79
US	1 875	1 045	3 083	1 665	0.56	0.54
Argentina	2 319	676	712	309	0.29	0.43

Source: CFCE

appropriate indication of origin together with the name of the bottler, or are simply marketed under the liquor board's own label – as is often the case with the *Société des Alcools du Quebec*. In the second case, wines are simply put to market as 'Canadian wine'. Bulk imports still amount to a third of total trade in terms of volume but only represent a bare tenth of their total value. France and the US are Canada's major trade partners. Bulk is a tough market however (it is almost entirely driven by price) and they now have South American producers hard on their heels (see Table 4.5).

Outlook

The GATT agreement will lead to a reduction of tariffs and to an erosion of the preferential treatment awarded to US wines by NAFTA. International (mainly US) and perhaps internal pressures should continue to mount, for liberalising import and distribution channels by stripping the boards of their monopsonistic and monopolistic powers (hopefully not leading to the introduction of provincial excise duties). The sunny days of the boards seem to be numbered in any event. US state monopolies, which Canada charged with discriminatory practices against foreign beer and wine producers and exporters in a recent complaint lodged at GATT,[54] face a similar fate.

---

54 Canada lodged a complaint and GATT ruled in favour of the Canadians in 1992 (Ziraldo, in International Wine Law Association, 1992, p 117).

United States

Once the largest and most open market of all, the US became, in the second half of the 1970s, a new Eldorado for Western Europe which was increasingly awash with production surpluses. Americans were discovering wine, their taste for European lifestyles and fashion goods seemed insatiable and a rising currency made it all the more possible for over a dozen years after the demise of the gold standard. The mid-1980s brought about an abrupt end to the gold rush. A succession of scandals at the time when US consumers were experiencing a swing of mood about wine, signalled the beginning of the European retreat. A weakening dollar, lower domestic prices and a much improved quality of domestic wines also helped push them back to sea. Growing calls for protectionism by some US producers, financial instability and rising neo-prohibitionism helped turn this once invaluable and much sought after outlet into a much less accessible and far more risky market.

Market and import trends

There are no musts imports by the United States. Vermouths grew relatively strong in the early and late 1970s but never quite made it in the US: volumes went briefly through the 20 million litres mark but now stand at only half that level, representing in 1990 4% of the total imported volumes under the heading 'wine' and only a little more than 2% of their value. Here, as in Canada, most of the wine trade consists of still and sparkling wine (tariff position No 112.12). US imports are sensitive to changes in prices.[55] These are, in turn, heavily dependent on movements in exchange rates. The relative strength of the US currency against those of its major trading partners pushed the real price of imports down until 1984; imported volumes progressed almost steadily as a result. The subsequent weakening of the US dollar helped bring import prices up again; their 'recovery' was also due in part to a general shift to higher quality wines as importers of cheap generic wines were compelled to leave the saturated ordinary (jug) wine market in the hands of large Californian producers.

US demand for foreign wine is elastic with respect to both price and income. Estimates carried out during the boom years (1960–84) suggest a reduction in both types of elasticities as one approaches the all-time peak year of 1984. Elasticities also vary considerably

---

55 CIF prices: tariffs only amount to a small, non-discriminating barrier – except against cheap bulk.

depending on the origin and the quality of the wines concerned. Price and income elasticities of imported wines are deemed greater for imported than for domestic wines. Also, the higher the quality of the wines, the grater their exposure to changes in consumes' incomes but the smaller their sensitivity to variations in prices.[56] This corroborates the accepted view, amongst traders, that the lower end of the market is essentially driven by price considerations whereas wines situated at the high end of the spectrum tend to benefit from a strong image and consumer loyalty.

The real value of imports (expressed in 1990 US$) experienced significant swings in its fortunes, more than doubling between 1970 and 1978 but then keeping nearly steady at just over $1 billion for another 12 years. Only in 1991 did shipments slip back below the $1 billion US$ mark (see Fig. 4.8 and Table 4.6).

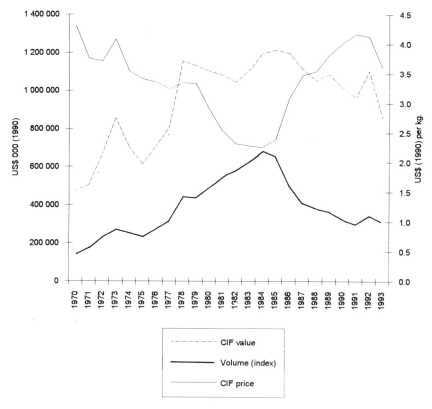

4.8 US imports (112.1) (source: United Nations).

56 Lindsey, 1987, pp 294, 297, 317, 328–9; White and Blandford, 1988, pp 37–40.

Table 4.6 USA imports, 000 US$ (1990)

All wines*	1989	1990	1991	1992	1993	Value share, % 1991–93	Volume share, % 1991–93
France	540 519	471 677	462 311	525 613	424 938	48.3	27.5
Italy	306 343	313 657	287 773	328 716	226 781	28.9	40.6
Spain	83 148	83 633	72 333	75 098	55 724	7.0	8.5
Australia	18 316	20 519	25 918	33 241	35 713	3.2	3.6
Chile	11 604	17 014	23 775	36 232	30 570	3.1	6.3
Germany**	56 224	50 465	40 133	40 835	28 066	3.7	4.5
Portugal	35 109	28 134	23 731	24 327	21 820	2.4	2.4
Brazil	3 737	2 902	3 544	5 856	6 681	0.6	1.8
Slovenia				2 105	3 344	0.2	0.8
Argentina	2 066	2 083	2 860	3 398	3 114	0.3	0.6
Other	28 188	21 480	22 122	26 218	19 765	2.3	3.3
World	1 085 253	1 011 564	964 500	1 101 638	856 517	100.0	100.0

Sparkling

Sparkling	1989	1990	1991	1992	1993	Value share, % 1991–93	Volume share, % 1991–93
France	208 755	186 576	170 944	159 437	155 102	63.4	29.7
Italy	72 767	67 693	60 277	56 081	45 330	21.1	39.0
Spain	45 761	45 562	41 999	35 973	29 298	14.0	28.9
Germany**	1 327	1 554	1 937	1 054	1 323	0.6	1.1
Belgium	521		377	371	790	0.2	0.1
UK	507	193	137	781	491	0.2	0.1
Australia	153	258	290	305	333	0.1	0.3
Chile	92	111	438	196	175	0.1	0.4
Portugal	378	216	57	124	164	0.0	0.1
Israel	93	48		43	54	0.0	0.0
Other	1 022	617	532	774	832	0.3	0.4
World	331 375	302 828	276 988	255 140	233 893	100.0	100.0

Still

Still	1989	1990	1991	1992	1993	Value share, % 1991–93	Volume share, % 1991–93
France	329 701	282 709	289 673	364 222	268 296	43.9	28.1
Italy	213 949	226 553	210 335	254 229	168 320	30.1	38.3
Australia	18 163	20 261	25 628	32 935	35 380	4.5	4.6
Chile	11 512	16 903	23 336	36 036	30 395	4.3	8.0
Germany**	54 877	48 856	38 182	39 724	26 724	5.0	5.5
Spain	36 367	37 027	29 568	38 670	26 170	4.5	4.1
Portugal	34 633	27 917	23 675	24 203	21 656	3.3	3.1
Brazil	3 737	2 902	3 544	5 856	6 681	0.8	2.4
Slovenia				2 105	3 344	0.3	1.1
Argentina	2 051	2 020	2 834	3 356	3 114	0.4	0.7
Hungary	2 859	3 169	3 286	3 576	2 400	0.4	0.9
Greece	2 925	2 566	3 360	4 715	2 296	0.5	0.8
UK	3 285	1 997	2 285	2 594	1 971	0.3	0.1
S Africa				1 847	1 917	0.2	0.2
Israel	2 221	1 339	1 250	1 888	1 532	0.2	0.3
Belgium				1 073	1 433	0.1	0.1
Switzerland	644	1 203	885	1 489	1 228	0.2	0.2
Romania	2 312	1 680	1 734	864	1 002	0.2	0.3
Bulgaria	2 468	1 816	1 621	1 037	881	0.2	0.3
Other	7 636	6 308	6 338	4 912	2 629	0.7	0.7
World	729 341	685 226	667 535	825 332	607 368	100.0	100.0

* Including musts and vermouths   ** 1988–1990: FRG only   *Source: United Nations*

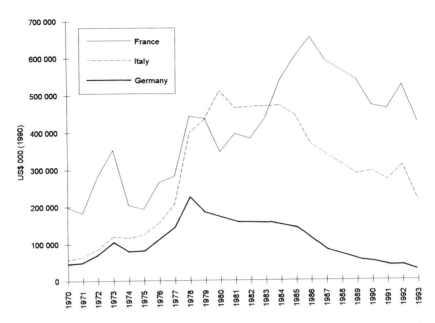

4.9 US imports from main suppliers (CIF, 112.12) (source: United Nations).

Looking closer at the evolution of the shipments from individual countries shows decidedly different fates. If the French enjoyed a relatively strong position right from the start, it is the Italians who were quickest to bank on US consumers' soaring enthusiasm for imported wines and other fashionable goods during the 1970s. Between 1975 and 1984, their shipments into the United States grew more than fourfold in terms of volume (the French 'only' tripled their sales volume to the US in the same time span). This was 'big time' for slightly carbonated red Lambruscos and white Veronese wines essentially; success gravitated around a handful of well-performing brands (see Table 2.3).

Only in 1980 did Italian shipments manage to surpass the French in terms of value however, so low was their average price, see Fig. 4.9. The downfall of cheap Italian wines was clearly precipitated by the methanol 'affair' which burst into the open in early 1986 in Italy.[57] The Italians were bound to lose ground in the embattled 'jug' segment anyway, but they now appear to be staging something of a comeback.

The principal beneficiaries of the Italian débâcle were the French. The main thrust for French success in the first half of the 1980s had come from the strength of the dollar against the French franc. French

57 See Hallgarten, 1986, pp 184–90 for details.

exporters had also managed a discrete progression with varietal wines and more strongly branded wines. However strong the quality image of French wines, exports were to prove just as vulnerable to the ailing dollar: prices soared and shipments fell drastically in the mid-1980s.

Noteworthy is the relatively high positioning of the French wines amongst those supplied by other nations. The explanation lies partly with the dearness of sparkling wines (especially champagne) which accounted for only 16% of the volumes shipped in 1990 but generated 40% of the revenue. The remaining wines were mostly higher quality still wines which were almost equally split between whites (53%) and reds (47%). There were some shipments of the cheaper varieties: *vins de table* (29%) and even fewer *vins de pays* (7%), but the great majority of the still wines (63%) were AOCs: not just reds from Bordeaux and Beaujolais, but also well performing and relatively expensive whites from Burgundy.[58]

The Germans, like the Italians, were caught in the jug segment and fought heavily on price. They managed to do so in spite of a relatively strong Deutschmark throughout the 1970s. Initial success aside – especially with their *Liebfraumilch* blends – German wines sales never seemed to gather as much momentum as did either the French or the Italians. Their efforts were severely hampered by the Austro-German diethylene glycol[59] affair which was unveiled in Austria in 1985, a full year before the Italian scandal. They never really recovered from this.

Spanish wines enjoyed a good deal of success in the 1960s with their sherries and in the early 1970s with sangrias, but then saw their fortunes decline steadily, essentially because their red wines were in the 'wrong' colour segment, see Fig 4.10. However, Spain managed to keep the value of its shipments unchanged amidst the general European débâcle in the late 1980s. This enabled it to surpass Germany, both in volume and value, to become the US's third largest supplier. Spanish wines seem now to be benefiting from a belated,

---

58 Source: French export data (CFCE).

59 Diethylene glycol (DG) was used in order to provide wines with more body and sweetness, and essentially more *moelleux*. The affair would have remained undetected for years, were it not for the 'sheer greed and stupidity' of one of the Austrian producers who insisted on reclaiming VAT on DG, thereby alerting the local tax inspector. Many of the wines involved were used for further blending by German producers and merchants. The Germans were heavily involved. DG was also found in 100% Italian wines (DG can improve the often harsh, tannic taste of poor red wines and 'also increases the level of dry extract in a wine that has been diluted with water'. See Hallgarten, 1986, pp 26–37 for more details.

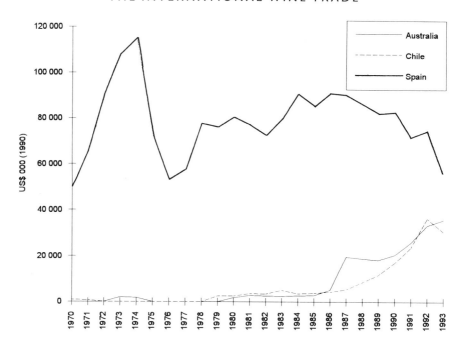

4.10 US imports from selected suppliers and challengers (CIF, 112.12) (source: United Nations).

slow shift of consumer preferences towards quality reds – a sign that the American market may be maturing after all.

Spanish exporters have performed well in the US sparkling market during the 1980s[60] and have continued to do so even in the context of a declining market, since 1984 (sparklers' sales fell by 3.7% in 1992, whereas still wines managed to redress, albeit momentarily). They derived half their revenue from that segment in 1992.[61] Spearheading their efforts for years were *cava* producers. Spanish sparkling wines sold at less than Italian *spumante* and at roughly a quarter of the price of their French *mousseux* recently.[62] *Cava* sales fell by a heavy 13% in 1992 however, whilst *spumante* and champagnes declined by only 1 and 2% respectively.[63]

The Spanish comeback in the still wine category appears to rest in

---

60 Spanish sparklers have been 'the star of the 80s', *Wines & Vines*, July 1989, p 22.

61 Source: Wine Institute; data reproduced in *Wines & Vines*, July 1993, p 24.

62 The average CIF price of sparkling wines originating from Spain was 3.7 against 4.4 for Italian sparklers and US$16.3 per litre for those of French origin, 1989–91 period. Source: United Nations.

63 Fredrikson, in *Wines & Vines*, April 1993, p 23.

good part on their good performance in the highly competitive 'fighting varietals' segment. All large domestic producers (especially Gallo and Heublein) were forced to move up from a saturated cheap generic jug wines market[64] to varietals and the challengers from the Southern hemisphere were quick to join the race (Chile with some excellent and cheap Cabernets, Merlots and Chardonnays; Australia with clearly outstanding wines and, lately, Brazil). Australia and Chile saw their export volumes roughly double between 1990 and 1992, allowing Chile to overtake Germany as the US fourth largest supplier (behind Italy, France and Spain) and Australia to swap sixth place with Portugal (now seventh). Portuguese wines have seen their fortunes decline throughout the 1980s; ports are less in favour with US consumers eager to reduce the strength of the wines they drink; even rosé sales have managed to decline threefold between 1987 and 1991. Portugal and Italy had one problem in common: sales had concentrated for too long on just a handful of successful brands. Finally, the year 1992 also witnessed the overtaking of Yugoslavia by Brazil, for eighth place. One additional reason for the US to favour imports from the Southern hemisphere economies is that they belong to their 'dollar zone'. Chilean exporters for instance, have long opted for pricing all their exports in US dollars.

In the US, large sales figures are almost invariably linked with strongly banded products which are distributed *and* promoted across the nation: in wine as in other areas of US business, the 80/20 rule largely applies, meaning that 80% of volume is channelled to consumers by 20% of the distributors, large distributors command large discounts however.[65] Well known imported brands have, thus far, been linked with the so-called 'national' importers.

Import and distribution channels

National importers have developed a truly nationwide distribution network which includes all the 18 monopolistic states. There are about thirty such importers,[66] mostly located in the New York region.

---

64 Around 1990, it was estimated that the jug segment would take up 72% of Californian production in volume but only bring in 42% of sales revenue (Frederikson, in *Wines & Vines*, June 1990, p 36.

65 In 1982 for instance, Gallo was offering its largest distributors discounts of 20% (*Wines & Vines*, August 1992, p 18). Also, according to *Impact*, the top 10 wine brands (the top 9 being American, with Riunite taking the last place) accounted for nearly 40% of sales in 1988.

66 There used to be twenty of them in the mid-1970s. CFCE, August 1976, pp 57–8.

They used to deal primarily with spirits and their yearly turnover is typically in excess of $100 million. Key to their strength is their direct involvement in the promotion of the wines they import – usually on a 50/50 basis with the exporter if they do not already own the brand under which the wines are marketed in the US. Import orders take place by the container load and containers are shipped directly from the exporter's winery to the importer's regional customers. Prices are usually FOB (shipping port) per case. Independent national importers are something of a rarity. Their initial activity was in the spirits trade and their allegiance to global distillers (especially the Canadian-based Seagram and Hiram-Walker) has remained unaltered in spite of their re-centering their activity on wine. Others have been taken over by large foreign (mainly) wine exporters, as was the case with Austin Nichols, bought by Pernod Ricard (who then owned Société des Vins de France, France's largest wine producer) and Schiefflin by Moët-Hennessy. Some national importers are simply the affiliates of large industrial/food conglomerates such as Beatrice Food or of the Tobacco giant RJ Reynolds.

The fact that wines would not be physically handled by national importers, the heavy concentration of wine consumption in large conurbations (recall that over a quarter of wine sales are concentrated in the New York, Los Angeles and San Francisco areas) and the desire, especially for retailers, to enjoy larger than razor-thin margins, have all contributed to resorting to regional importers who may not be able to handle the 'hottest' brands but are in a position to offer similar services to both exporters and retailers and, in addition usually ensure the physical distribution of the wines to the retailer's loading bay. Regional importers are characterised by a greater specialisation in wine than their national counterparts. Like national importers, they usually become exclusive agents for the wines they purchase and sell, if only on a regional scale.

There are also brokers/importers. As is usually the case with brokers, they do not buy and sell but only help supply meet demand (or vice versa) and usually deal with all the paperwork, often involving several US states. They often act on the demand of larger retailers who seek to purchase lesser known – and thus cheaper – wines of good quality, even just in order to make a temporary attractive deal or offer, in the most direct way, and thereby improve their margin. As with wine brokers in general, their main attraction is in the competitiveness of the deals they offer – they act as small exchanges. Retailers and wholesalers often resort to their services in order to 'fill in' their product lines. This pushes the problem of financial risk back into the hands of exporters (or their credit-insurance institutions), for many

US firms have acquired the unfortunate reputation of being bad debtors recently.

The classical three-tier distribution structure involves an importer, a wholesaler and a retailer. This system is the outcome of the legal peculiarities of American federal and state laws (recall that for alcoholic drinks, the retailing and, in some states, the wholesale distribution function must be divorced from either import or production) and the ensuing difficulty, for exporters, to deal with a truly single market. Deregulation in certain states, ever more competitive pressures and rising doubts about the efficiency of the old structure have led to a considerable shortening of distribution channels recently, though wine prices still face a multiplier of 3 or 4 between their export value and their tag price on supermarket and liquor stores in the US on average. Regional wholesalers, large liquor store chains, food retailers, and even hotel chains are now dealing directly with their foreign suppliers and only resort to importers in order to comply with legal requirements, i.e. they must use their import licence. An electronic service has enabled orders to be issued directly from the US to French subscribing firms for several years now.

The result of shortening of the import and distribution channels in the US is that demand is likely to become more fragmented as an increasing number of retailers will find it profitable to move away from mainstream national brands. The rapidly changing structure of the US wine market and in particular the increasing international presence of foreign wine producers in their own backyard (through acquisitions, mergers and other types of alliance taking place largely in California) have reinforced this trend. How far this has gone is ultimately a question for US consumers to answer, who like to purchase most of their wines in supermarkets (there is a higher proportion of purchases in liquor stores for imported than for domestic wines) and who pick them from the shops' shelves on a mainly spontaneous basis – 51% in 1986.[67]

A major factor in helping to reduce imports, mainly from the EU, was the rising competitiveness of domestic production, in both quality and price. The largely Californian domestic wine industry had been in a state of near-surplus since 1982: in 1983, Californian wineries refused to take up part of the grape harvest for the first time since repeal of prohibition. Domestic wine prices had been falling since 1978, in real terms, and grape growers' resentment was increasingly

67 1986 *Point of Purchase* Advertising Institute study, as reported in *MIVS*, November 1987, p 9.

turning against what they felt was unfair competition by EU producers who were seen as draining their subsidised wine lake into foreign markets, including the US. American wine producers had been hard on the heels of the most successful importers in terms of production technology. The raging internal price war which market leaders had waged against each other on the jug market in 1983 had left the production sector much leaner: there were many casualties in the shape of smaller wineries and Coca-Cola of Atlanta, who had entered the wine market with great pomp in 1973 but were leaving the battlefield just ten years later. Better quality and lower prices: the competitiveness of US wines was greatly improved and the US consumer market lay virtually on their doorstep. The much more protectionistic line adopted by Washington from the mid-1980s to date, who made it clear that similar access to the EU market was desired, has helped Californians vintners repel foreign wines.

Trade policy

US tariffs are specific and modest by international standards. They have been reduced considerably since the 1950s, mainly under GATT, from about 100% of the CIF value of the imported wines at the time (on an *ad valorem* basis) to a current 5%.[68] Still wines with a strength of less than 14% for instance, now face a tariff of 37.5 cents per US gallon (9.9 cents per litre) when packaged in containers of less than 4 litres. Tariffs usually increase with the strength of the wine and sparkling wines – which are considered as luxury goods in just about every country – get taxed much more heavily: 62.5 cents/gal (16.5 cents/litre). The system does discriminate against bulk imports however: still wine under 14% alcohol for instance gets charged a steep 1.17 $/gal (30.9 cents/litre). Similarly, vermouths face a 55% surcharge if they are imported in bulk.[69] Little wonder then that bulk represented only 1.1% of the shipments in the early 1990s.[70] A similar barrier used to exist for spirits but was removed at the 11th hour of the GATT's Tokyo round of negotiations – a US concession worth an estimated $30–40 million a year.[71]

68 Clawson, in OIV, 1993.

69 CFCE (1992, United States, pp 16–17); concerning the situation of January 1991.

70 1990–92 average; the calculation was carried out for still (<14%) wine only, for which data were readily available.

71 Ivie, International Wine Law Association.

A federal excise duty is applied to both foreign and domestic wines, which again increases with the strength of the drink; the economic 'rationale' of the federal government is similar to that of the UK Treasury. Much coverage has been given to the raising of the tax in January 1991, from 17 to 107 cents per gallon. The 1991 federal tax hike – which coincided with an increase in the California state tax – was held as chiefly responsible for the drop in US consumption that year.

The US provides assistance to its wine exporters in the form of a Market Promotion Program (MPP) which was anchored in the 1990 Farm Bill (the bill replaced the former Targeted Assistance Program with the MPP; aid is administered by the US Department of Agriculture). There is also export assistance financed by the Californian wine industry association, the Wine Institute of California, now to the tune of $17.1 million – more than four times the $4.1 million made available to them in 1986.[72] These programmes were designed mainly in response to the wine policy and attitude adopted by the EU.

The US government has considerably hardened its stance towards the EU. US grape and wine producers launched a two pronged attempt at stemming wine imports from Western Europe. The first was an attempt at exacting equal tariff treatment from the EU with respect to US wines. A diluted text was eventually adopted by Congress in 1984 after the American Soybean Association rallied the wine producers' camp[73] (it basically leaves the decision with the US President on how to retaliate in the event of persistent disagreement on the issue) and was included in the Omnibus Trade Bill enacted later that same year, which encompassed a much wider range of commodities.

The other major source of pressure for making entry more difficult for EU wines came from domestic grape growers who lodged two successive complaints against EU exporters at the US International Trade Commission (ITC), charging them with unfair competition and calling for compensation.[74] The first case alleged that Italy and France were using export subsidies and dumping practices in connection with their exports of ordinary wine to the US. These allegations were considered to be unfounded after careful examination of the charges, but the passing of the Wine Equity Act by Congress

---

72 *Wines & Vines*, December 1991, p 28.

73 It was initially opposed to it for fear of retaliation by the EU, a major market.

74 Californian growers enjoyed widespread support from the US Department of Agriculture.

the same year encouraged the growers to present a second case, this time against Italy, France and Germany. A similar verdict fell in October 1985, even though it was felt that the generous system of EU production subsidies provided some level of indirect help to EU exports. Interesting was the fact that, in the first ITC case, the court had to decide on whether to include or exclude Canadian-based Seagram from the proceedings because of its position as both a major producer and an importer. The uncollaborative attitude of two major US wine producers/marketers, who refused to communicate their price data to the investigators working on the second case, was quite revealing of the lack of cohesion within an industry which was becoming increasingly international.[75]

But the trade frictions between the US and the EU administrations were far from over. A new row erupted soon after, regarding the latest enlargement phase of the EU, to include Spain and Portugal. The application of the principle of Community preference, one of the tenets of the Treaty of Rome, was tantamount to a loss of the Spanish and Portuguese markets for US agricultural exporters (and GATT's Article XXIV-6 is explicit about requiring compensation in such cases). The stance adopted by the EU representatives led the US administration to make a 'hit-list' of retaliatory tariffs, on which white wines figured prominently. An agreement emerged in January 1987, which gave preferential access to US maize 'corn' for a period of 4 years but ignored pleas about access to Portugal's soya oil market; a pro forma, unbinding tariff quota was thus maintained by the US on goods selected for possible retaliation.[76]

Regarding the (hitherto unsolved) issue of mutual recognition of each other's oenological practices and use of semi-generic names, negotiations on so-called 'wine accords' have been dragging on for well over a decade. The use of semi-generic names is peculiar to the US, Canada and Australia. Semi-generic names are European geographical names[77] used to represent a certain type or style of wine, e.g. sherry, port and champagne. They were introduced by immigrant winemakers in order to relate their wines to what they used to do before they left Europe, and have become part of the American language. In the US, their use is only permitted if the region of production of the wines is stated alongside, e.g. Californian Chablis.

---

75 Gallo and Heublein refused to communicate their price data. See Jarrige, 1987, pp 52–70 for more details on these issues.

76 See Jarrige, 1987, for more details on these issues.

77 The word 'claret' is an exception.

The debate is largely fuelled by the French who did not oppose their use for decades, and yet have now suddenly come to view them as part of their intellectual property.

There are only a few oenological practices on which agreement has not yet been reached (the process of ion exchange, [78] permitted in the US, is probably the most important). Here again, much progress has been made but negotiations have stalled as the result of a hardening of attitudes on both sides of the Atlantic.

Norms relating to container size and labelling have been largely accepted by the wine trade. Noteworthy is the required presence of a 'warning label' on each bottle, against possible hazards related to wine consumption and the presence of sulphates in wine (SO_2). Wine labels must also offer information on the identity of the producer and of the importer, in addition to other items related to the country of production. A certificate of analysis and of origin of the wines shipped into the US is also a prerequisite. The US Food and Drug Administration periodically issues a list of permitted substances in wine and their level of tolerance. This, again, has proved a favourite point of friction between the EU and the US. In 1989, some French wines were denied access to the US market on the grounds that they contained unacceptable levels of procymidone (an easily identifiable chemical which is used heavily in champagne for instance, to combat mould).[79] Wine bottles with a lead closure became the next target in 1990 and 1991. Italian wines contaminated with MITC (methylisothyocyanate) were banned in the US in 1992, as in Japan.

The weakness of the US currency eased much of the tension by simply postponing the issue, but importers and exporters are visibly running out of patience with the technocrats; a code of normalisation of technical requirements has been in the works ever since the conclusion of the Tokyo round of negotiations at GATT. Traders feel that it would clearly be in the offing if there had been any political willingness to free up wine trade. Renewed trade disruption always

---

78 The ion exchange process was developed in Australia and has been in use since the mid-1950s. It can stabilise wines against potassium bitartrate crystallisation and also raise their acidity. At the core of the process lies the use of an ion-exchange resin – an insoluble gel capable of exchanging ions with the surrounding liquid. See Rankine (1989, pp 135–8 and 173–9) for more details. EU food and drink manufacturers are allowed to use the ion exchange process, but not winemakers, although there is no scientific evidence that consumers' health could be endangered in any way. Restrictions on the import of wines made in accordance with this process are thus regarded as an arbitrary standard or technical barrier (Clawson, 1993, p 3).

79 Foulon, 11 Feburary 1992, Montpellier conference on '*Le marché mondial du vin: entraves aux échanges commerciaux*'.

manages to cause uneasiness amongst traders and 1992 was no exception: imports rose partly as the result of inventory build-ups in anticipation of renewed trade frictions between the EU and the US.[80] Running out of stock is the last thing that successful retailers can afford and this is one of the reasons why they are increasingly turning to domestic producers. Federal and state governments' treasury officials are in no hurry to free up their markets either, because they would lose a valuable tax revenue cash-cow and much of their independence in the process. Finally, recall that the US is running a parallel debate on the advantages and disadvantages of sobering up. All these trends could point to a bleak future for foreign wine exporters to the US, had it not been for the determination of the US administration to push harder for easier access to other markets for its own wines.

Outlook

The US is still a market to reckon with. Medium term perspectives may not look too good for West European wine exporters except for those operating in the higher quality segment. Over the longer term however, the attractiveness of the American market to importers will depend critically on its producers' ability to get the average American consumer to adopt wine as a regular beverage when the opportunity rises; the pendulum is bound to move back into more libertarian territory at some time.

NAFTA will mean easier access to an enlarged market for US producers. Progress achieved in Canadian territory, their prime client and next-door neighbour, is likely to soothe concern over market access by Californian producers for a short while and thus divert attention from overseas markets. Mexican producers may find they have a long way to go before they can make significant advances in the US (Mexico is proving an increasingly valuable outlet for Californian wines). Meanwhile Chile (NAFTA's next applicant) appears to have conquered the palates and purses of many US consumers. Argentina may win their hearts and East Europeans are not far behind: Hungary has already applied, in 1991, for tariff exemption as an emerging nation.

GATT may prove the best forum for technocrats to solve their frictions, by ensuring a fair liberalisation of all markets. Meanwhile on the ground, Californian producers have been increasingly swallowed up by foreign corporations eager to participate in the domestic

80 Jon Frederikson in *Wines and Vines*, July 1993, p 20.

market. Some, like Nestlé with Beringer and Moët & Chandon with Domaine Chandon, entered the market in the early 1970s and left their mark, e.g. the sparkling segment was transformed by Chandon's arrival). Others came in much later, in the financial shake-up of the 1980s which literally shattered the industry; this is the case of the purchase of the Heublein wine holdings by Grand Metropolitan's IDV from an embattled J Reynolds conglomerate. In 1990, the top ten foreign investors in the California wine industry (Grand Met's IDV, Nestlé, LVMH, Seagram, Allied Lyons, Suntory, Adelaide Steamship, Eckes, Racke and Four Seas, in that order) controlled an estimated one third of US wine production and had a combined sales figure of about $675 million. A large foreign – mainly European – presence on the US production side would best warrant amicable relationships between the US and the EU administrations.

Western Europe

Japan and North America aside, all other major wine import markets are located in Western Europe. (The international wine trade was born on the eastern shores of the Mediterranean, so to speak, and later evolved around it.) A tentacular EU houses most of them, having become the dominant force in international wine trade because it regroups both the interests of the world's four largest exporters (58% of world production) *and* subjects all its club members to a single, 'incestuous' policy.[81]

A situation of free trade is still decades away, even within the highly protective perimeter around the EU. The reason lies in the ambivalent nature of wine: an agricultural commodity which rapidly becomes a differentiated and even high value-added good, depending on the amount of care, skill and marketing that is put in and round the bottle. As an imported alcoholic drink (that was originally meant for the wealthy), it shares with tobacco the distinctive privilege of steep taxes which can vary widely from one country to the next. And opinions could hardly diverge more than between retentive treasury representatives of an essentially beer-producing north and those of the south of the Union where nearly all winemakers are concentrated. France's allegiance falls clearly with the 'Club Med' in this respect.

---

81 The image is borrowed from Ian Wilson-Smith, in AIDV, 1992, p 17.

Germany has been a producer of both beer and wine for too long to join ranks with either clan: its realistic policies may offer once again the basis for compromise. Great skills may be required to achieve fiscal harmonisation within the EU. Even though the principle was agreed upon a long time ago and subsequently turned into law, with effect in January 1993, excise duty rates can fluctuate within a band that is large enough to accommodate previous rates. Wild differences in the levels of 'domestic' taxation are still hampering the development of wine trade however. Business sources and past experience would suggest the beginning of the next century as the most realistic date for the establishment of truly free trade in wine *within* the EU.[82]

The EU may stand level with the US and Canada on the taxation front. Regarding the distribution of alcoholic drinks however, the EU does not suffer any comparison with the impediments imposed by the US three-tier system. Channels have undergone a radical transformation in the run up to the single market: most supermarkets and specialist shop chains buy directly at source (often getting producers to bottle wines for their corporate brand label) and 'central', pan-European buying is increasingly popular, even involving non-EU countries. The forceful concentration and uniformisation of distribution outlets runs parallel to a convergence in lifstyles across Western Europe, in spite of the remaining strong regional particularism in tastes. A majority of European consumers prefer to purchase their wine from supermarkets.[83] The food and drink retailing sector is already highly concentrated in the North of Europe. Market leaders like Aldi are thus left with Mediterranean countries for pursuing their expansion.[84] Table 4.7 gives a synoptic view of the rates of concentration in the distribution of wines by food supermarkets in selected EU member states.

It is in relation with third countries that the EU is proving most discriminating, enforcing EU preference amongst Club members by imposing quasi-minimum import prices to non-members, and promoting exports via export subsidies on markets where it does not fear retaliation. The EU's Common Customs Tariff (CCT) applies to imports from non-ECU countries; it provides for import duties to be raised on all categories of wine entering the EU (these 'import duties' will be referred to as 'tariffs' in order to avoid confusion with the 'excise

---

82 Ibid, p 18; movement of wine in bulk between Italy and France was disrupted for more than 12 years *after* the establishment of a common market in wine, in 1970.

83 Source: Food Marketing Institute and Coca Cola, in *Drinks File*, May 14 1993.

84 Peron and Camous (1989).

Table 4.7 Wine distribution by food retailers: market shares of the top five chains

France	%	Germany	%	Belgium	%	UK	%	Netherlands	%	Spain	%
Leclerc	8	Aldi	15	Delhaize	16	Sainsbury	17	Albert Heijn	31	Pryca	6
Intermarché	8	Rewe Lb	7	G.B.	16	Tesco	14	Edah	7	Continente	4
Système U	3	Edeka	7	Aldi	15	Asda	7	Albrecht	9	Dia	4
Auchan	3	Tengelmann	4	Colruyt	11	Argyll	5	S. Unie/Ziko	8	Eroski	4
Carrefour	3	Coop Gp	3	Cora	5	Dee	4	TSN	5	Al campo	3
	25		36		63		47		60		21

Source: SECODIP

duties' applied individually by most member states within their jurisidiction). The CCT provides for tariff quotas (reduced tariff rates for specified quantities negotiated bilaterally) to most producers in the Mediterranean basin, e.g. Algeria, Tunisia and Cyprus.[85] These apply on top of any eventual 'countervailing charge' imposed on all shipments reaching EU borders below a specified minimum price, called the 'reference' price. Designed in theory to prevent third countries from dumping wines on the EU, while in practice shielding EU ordinary wines from competition, this system basically works like a minimum import price for this type of wine – the more expensive quality, and usually bottled, shipments go through virtually untouched. The recent GATT agreement led to a scrapping of countervailing charges by January 1995. Tariffs were raised accordingly (more on the Uruguay Round negotiations in Chapter 7).

In as much as the regime on 'domestic' taxation (what is 'domestic' in an economic and political union?) is likely to be challenged from within the EU, the liberalisation of the EU border regime is bound to collapse under outside pressures, like those of the US demanding equal access, yet preferably under the aegis of GATT's successor, the World Trade Organisation, which alone can ensure equity in the treatment of others. However long overdue, the enforcing of a common market in wine within the EU and the subsequent enlargement of the Club's members from the original six to the current twelve, definitely boosted international wine trade figures. The EU policy of continuing support to domestic producers, denying access to third country suppliers and aggressively promoting exports has been highly damaging to bulk trade worldwide, however, in the author's opinion. The effect has been less for bottled trade, which may have seen its success precipitated by the necessity for –

---

85 Another way to look at it is the application of full, reduced (within quota limits) and zero rates (to EU members).

and ingenuity in – getting round such restrictive policies (and those of the US), just like in the good old days when Belgian and Dutch traders had to circumvent the intricacies laid by French lords and developed a flourishing wine trade which they came to dominate in the sixteenth century. The inclination of the Belgians and Dutch towards free trade provided the impetus for their customs union, Benelux, in 1948 and, ten years later, for full economic union. And there were credible precedents: the Belgium-Luxembourg Economic Union (BLEU) set up in 1922 had already freed up the movement of goods between those two countries and set up a common customs tariff applied to imports from third countries. Belgium and Luxembourg lie at the very core of the European Economic Community established by the Treaty of Rome in 1957. The profile of the world's largest importers continues with them. The Netherlands are next, followed by the other three 'original' signatories of the Treaty of Rome: Germany, France and Italy who are also major world wine exporters. The first enlargement was northbound and produced a collection of wine importers of the purest vein, Denmark and the UK, and thus a string of hopes to solve the problem of chronic production surpluses by the EU.

Belgium–Luxembourg

The Belgium–Luxembourg Economic Union is a 240 million litre import market. A tenth is vermouth, the rest still and sparkling wine representing 217 million litres in 1990 and worth BFr 19.2 billion CIF (US$580 million), see Fig. 4.11. Volumes alone put the BLEU a mere 10% behind the US that year, but their value trailed significantly (by 42%) behind American levels. Lower transport and insurance costs do not wholly make up for the difference. The main reason for the much lower average CIF import prices lies in the persistence of bulk trade between Belgium and its traditional sources of supply in Europe: in the still[86] wine category, 41% of reds and rosés and 36% of the whites crossed the border in bulk shipments in 1990 and 1991; their price was only 40–42% that of the wines imported in bottles.[87]

Luxembourg has vineyards of 1000 ha producing some 15 million litres on average and representing only 6% of wine consumed by the 10 million residents of the BLEU.[88] Luxembourg's production and

---

86 Alcoholic content below 13%.

87 1990–91 averages. Source: BLEU Customs.

88 1986–90 averages (OIV data).

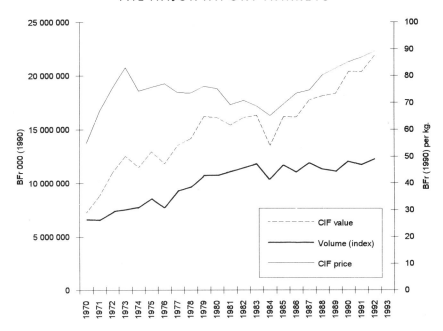

4.11 Belgium–Luxembourg imports (112.1) (source: United Nations).

consumption rose sharply, by about 50%, in the first half of the 1980s. Belgian per capita demand for wine increased steadily between 1960 and 1990, partly as the result of consumers shifting away from beer (a saturated market since the early 1970s) and spirits (sales have been dwindling since the late 1970s). Growth in wine demand slowed down considerably in the late 1980s and consumption per capita now appears to stand at around 24 litres. The import boom which started in the early 1960s and lasted for a solid twenty years (traded volumes rose fourfold) is thus largely over. But trade could gain momentum again if EU tax harmonisation were to reduce domestic excise duties and VAT rates down to levels prevailing in wine producing countries. Duties and VAT together amount to roughly a quarter of the retail price of ordinary wines marketed in Belgium at present.[89]

Wine consumption attitudes are split in accordance with Belgium's main linguistic division between French-speaking Walloons on the one hand, who make up 40% of the population but drink over 70% of the wine,[90] and the Dutch-speaking Flemish community on the other (Belgium separated from Holland in 1830). Flemish people tend to be much more occasional wine drinkers than are Walloons, and this

89 CFCE (1992, Belgium, p 18).

90 Ibid.

is reflected throughout the country as a whole: 53–54% drink occasionally, 30% are regular consumers and 16–17% are non-consumers.[91] Regular wine drinking occurs mainly at home and during meal times, much in accordance with the French 'model', but wine does enjoy a more prestigious status than do all other regular drinks. Belgium is still a predominantly red market (75%), but whites have been making headway since the mid-1980s.[92] Consumers' interests in rosés is among the highest in Europe.[93]

Over 60% of Belgian customers buy their wines off supermarket shelves; over a quarter do so at specialist shops and over 8% in the producing country itself, usually France.[94] Belgians are experienced wine purchasers and good bargain-hunters on the whole. The recession and the proximity of France have helped price become a decisive factor in choosing between wines. Economic slowdown did not spare Belgium during the oil crisis of the mid-1970s and then again in the early 1980s; recession seems to have lingered ever since then, and has affected wine trade significantly. Historical ties aside (Antwerp was the leading European wine distribution centre in Europe in the sixteenth century) the kinship of Walloons with the French across the border makes it easy for Belgian wine retailers to source themselves directly in France's producing regions and for French exporters to operate in Belgian territory.[95] Contracts are stipulated in French francs, ex-winery, in most case. Belgium has become a formidable market for French wines over the years (see Fig. 4.12).

Market and import trends

French wines fit Belgian cuisine quite well[96] and have enjoyed a market share of 60% and 74% in volume and value respectively over the years 1970–90, see Table 4.8. Their dominance was acquired in the early stages of the building up of a 'common market' in wine in 1970; it has not been put under serious threat by any other country since. French exports into Belgium have benefited from a steady depreciation

91 Ibid.

92 Increasing 60% between 1985 and 1989 (CFCE, 1992, Belgium, p 20).

93 Ibid, p 17.

94 Source: Suma Research, in CFCE (1992, Belgium,, p 20).

95 E.g. Schenck, a major wine importer.

96 CFCE (1992, Belgium, p 27).

4.12 BLEU imports from main supplier (CIF, 112.12) (source: United Nations).

of the French franc against the Belgian currency, which lost a third of its value between 1970 and 1990. French dominance is most conspicuous in the sparkling category (over 80% market share):[97] about half the volumes came from Champagne itself and generated nearly 80% of the revenues; their remaining sparkling wines came from other parts of France, from Germany (who came a distant second, with only a tenth of the market share in terms of volume) and from Spain who have been strengthening their position in recent years (see Fig. 4.13).

Yet French dominance is not just confined to the bubbly elements; it extends to still wines as well. In the early 1990s,[98] two-thirds of French exports to the BLEU consisted of appellation wines. Red and white Bordeaux had the lion's share (a hefty third) of the AOC market; their immense lead somewhat dwarfs the success of red Côtes du Rhône, red Beaujolais as well as red and white Burgundies. Some 40% of AOCs were imported in bulk and bottled in the BLEU. Trading in bulk remains particularly strong at the cheap end of Bordeaux and other skilfully advertised generics with a good image,

97 In 1990 and 1991 on average (CFCE data).

98 1990–91 average, based on French export data.

Table 4.8 Belgian imports, 000 BFr (1990)

All wines*	1988	1989	1990	1991	1992	Value share, % 1991–92	Volume share, % 1991–2
France	13 525 092	13 997 088	15 208 000	15 177 737	16 370 717	75.1	65.3
Portugal	1 849 966	1 629 586	1 745 833	1 807 267	1 795 583	8.6	6.9
Italy	1 049 388	1 106 041	1 177 567	1 133 993	1 059 755	5.2	10.9
Germany**	456 230	536 270	795 333	782 955	820 155	3.8	6.6
Spain	719 709	652 076	687 033	698 229	733 913	3.4	5.9
Netherlands	174 651	184 179	202 233	265 917	371 883	1.5	1.1
Greece	123 040	124 987	118 733	108 464	103 150	0.5	0.8
Bulgaria	78	21 905	80 100	136 312	86 486	0.5	0.9
Chile	13 654	9 261	20 167	43 859	66 324	0.3	0.5
USA	26 800	17 717	35 300	40 604	41 023	0.2	0.3
Other	152 259	145 282	167 100	171 163	167 224	0.8	0.9
World	18 090 867	18 424 393	20 237 400	20 366 499	21 616 214	100.0	100.0

Sparkling							
France	2 394 361	2 529 825	3 036 600	2 762 831	2 985 097	91.8	83.4
Netherlands	10 650	5 355	22 533	38 270	122 430	2.6	1.7
Germany**	54 966	47 837	58 000	66 118	55 772	1.9	7.8
Italy	35 149	29 072	41 467	36 330	36 370	1.2	2.8
Spain	34 095	35 837	44 300	47 048	20 223	1.1	2.2
Portugal	12 483	12 966	29 133	24 724	14 566	0.6	0.7
S Africa	3 121	1 893	4 467	3 748	6 082	0.2	0.4
UK	195	40	1 267	10 159	3 071	0.2	0.2
Austria	624	2 174	2 133	1 184	1 429	0.0	0.1
USA	39		1 433	329	1 064	0.0	0.1
Other	14 707	11 556	20 467	10 422	11 951	0.4	0.7
World	2 560 390	2 676 556	3 261 800	3 001 164	3 258 057	100.0	100.0

Still							
France	10 717 842	11 028 841	11 965 733	12 219 544	13 185 188	75.2	69.7
Portugal	1 837 171	1 614 929	1 714 267	1 782 510	1 781 017	10.5	7.9
Italy	738 824	787 654	822 800	836 513	768 702	4.8	9.3
Spain	605 017	589 542	625 233	617 744	691 187	3.9	6.2
Germany**	225 248	251 827	252 167	245 565	285 336	1.6	2.1
Netherlands	161 660	159 898	147 800	218 145	238 110	1.4	1.0
Greece	121 947	123 981	118 067	107 215	102 177	0.6	1.0
Bulgaria		21 865	79 967	136 312	86 486	0.7	1.0
Chile	13 654	9 221	20 167	43 826	66 324	0.3	0.6
USA	26 761	16 872	33 867	40 275	39 959	0.2	0.3
S Africa	17 477	13 409	18 567	20 877	31 322	0.2	0.2
Switzerland	13 342	13 892	14 967	19 102	20 162	0.1	0.1
UK	5 461	5 637	12 433	15 157	16 482	0.1	0.0
Hungary	3 901	9 785		11 573	15 813	0.1	0.1
Morocco	7 178	4 389	9 200	8 844	11 191	0.1	0.1
Argentina	15 136	20 496	20 167	6 608	7 055	0.0	0.1
China		5 235	6 233	6 247	5 656	0.0	0.0
Algeria	23 523	25 368	19 600	21 897	4 531	0.1	0.1
Yugoslavia					4 501	0.0	0.0
Other	41 390	27 985	33 833	34 785	24 480	0.2	0.2
World	14 575 534	14 730 825	15 915 067	16 392 741	17 385 679	100.0	100.0

* Including musts and vermouths ** 1988–1990: FRG only *Source: United Nations*

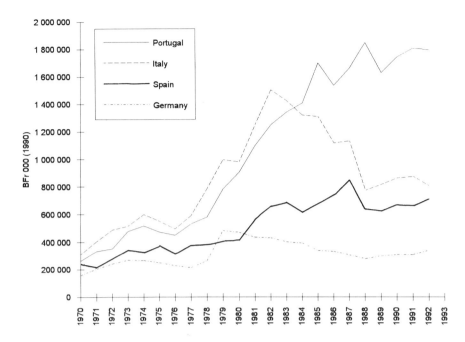

4.13 BLEU imports from selected suppliers and challengers (CIF, 112.12) (source: United Nations).

where this remains a very good source of profit to importers and distributors. The proportion of bulk shipments rises as one crosses over to ordinary wines: it is nearly 50% for the successful, higher quality *vins de pays* (reds in the main) and 60% for the *vins de table* which still make up the core of this category of wines but which are suffering from constant decline and steady displacement by *vins de pays*[99].

In 1970, Greek wines used to enjoy a similar market to that of the French in terms of volume, but were considerably cheaper. Greek shipments were replaced with ordinary wines produced in Italy within a dozen years of the scrapping of wine tariffs and quotas in the EU. Italian exports to the BLEU soared and peaked in the early 1980s, at 40 million litres; sales figures fell steadily thereafter and Italian decline was, here also, precipitated by methanol. German wines suffered much less from diethylene glycol: they sold at bargain prices for years but managed to stage a comeback in the late 1980s (German prices fell steadily, in spite of the firming up of the Deutschmark against the Belgian franc throughout the 1980s, ending up below Spanish levels and almost as cheap as Italian wines).

99 Ibid.

Portuguese and Spanish wines progressed well over the past 20 years in spite of being left on the EU's doorstep. They have benefited from EU membership – 'community preference' – since 1989, albeit with some temporary transitory restrictions in the case of Spain. Wines from the New World have not yet managed any significant move into the Belgian market: combined sales of North and South American still wines, plus those from Algeria – a former popular source for Belgians and French alike – only achieve a 0.6% market share in their category (see Table 4.7). Algeria is, like Greece, a major casualty of West European economic integration.

Import and distribution channels

Concentration and direct sourcing are the driving forces behind the changing configuration of wine import and distribution channels. 45% of the wine consumed in Belgium is drunk in public places, i.e. the Horeca sector. The rest is meant for home consumption and here, 80% of household wine and spirits purchases takes place in supermarkets. The wines marketed through the Horeca channel tend to be different from those displayed on retailers' shelves, for fear of damaging price comparisons (margins are substantially higher in the Horeca sector, ranging between 200 and 300% whilst a typical supermarket's mark up is 25%).[100]

Most of the supermarkets' wine sales are concentrated in a handful of firms: taken together, the first five channel 63% of the wines. Their service is regarded as quite good as most of the supermarket chains rival each other in their attempt to emulate the quality of service provided by specialist shops. Some go as far as offering advice in their wine section, e.g. Delhaize Le Lion.[101] Only half of the Belgian consumers would cross the road to pick a wine from a specialist (retail) shop when buying for a special occasion.[102] This unusually high degree of trust put by Belgian customers in their food retailers is rooted in the need for guidance in the maze of confusing French denominations. The success of supermarkets' own labels bears witness to this and, in turn, provides an explanation as to the persistence of bulk imports by some food retailers: Delhaize Le Lion, for instance, buys 80% of its wines in bulk and bottles them in Belgium.[103] Other supermarket chains select their wines and have

100 CFCE (1992, Belgium, p 35).

101 Ibid, p 34.

102 Ibid, p 27.

them bottled and labelled in the region of production.[104] Strong competition and minimal margins have persuaded all supermarket chains to adopt direct sourcing in the production regions, either by the producers themselves or through the services of local wine brokers, or *courtiers*. They would only resort to Belgian importers and brokers in order to complete their 'portfolio' of wines. Specialist shops and independent distributors are losing market share; they either tend to regroup their orders and use centralised purchasing to enhance their bargaining power, or simply go out of business. The size of the duty free market supplying the international workforce of the EU and NATO is hard to assess, yet would appear to be significant. This particular channel is even more important to the spirits industry, whose products face even higher excise duties.

The Horeca sector is far less concentrated and buys from various sources, though essentially from established fine wine importers/ wholesales and 'multiple-products' importers (dealing with a large spectrum of food products, including wine) who can offer them additional services, e.g. private labels. They also buy wine from wholesalers and occasionally from supermarkets, partly for tax reasons.

Belgium and Luxembourg have witnessed a considerable short-ening of the traditional importer-wholesaler-retailer channel over the years: in the late 1980s, 60% of imports of spirits and wines were realised by the largest eight firms active in this field.[105] Holland aside, nowhere is the grip of supermarkets on wine distribution and trade as forceful as in Belgium.[106]

Outlook

1992 figures would suggest that wine imports could rise further. A few factors could lead to a growing wine trade: a reduction in excise duties, a white wine boom amongst the Flemish segment of the population and a rise in the Belgians' disposable income. In spite of all its shortcomings EU monetary convergence implies that Belgian wine imports are likely to become much less influenced by movements in exchange rates between member states and more a function of exporters' purely domestic wine market conditions.

103 Ibid, pp 34, 36.

104 And also blended if necessary.

105 See table showing 1987 main wine and spirits importers, in CFCE (1992, Belgium, p 29).

Netherlands

Belgium's Flemish community and the Dutch have a common language and culture. No wonder, then, that Dutch and Belgian wine imports reveal a fairly similar pattern over the period 1970–90. Trade almost doubled in volume in that time span and roughly trebled in real value, see Fig. 4.14. Although generally stagnant since the mid-1980s in terms of volume, imports have continued to progress in real value in both countries. The 220 million litres of wine imported by the Netherlands in 1990 were worth Fl 870 million (US$ 480 million) at CIF level. Dutch trade figures were only 8% below those of Belgium in terms of volume, yet over 20% smaller in value. Dutch price-consciousness may come from the ingenuity and shrewdness of their ancestors – especially those traders based in Rotterdam, who used to dominate European wine trade in the seventeenth century.[107]

The Dutch had an earlier and milder recession than Belgians after the second oil crisis in 1980 and its impact on wine trade has been much less severe, for a good reason: whilst recession was biting

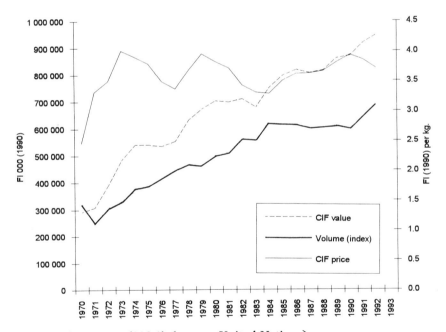

4.14 Dutch imports (112.1) (source: United Nations).

106 Ley, in *NEID Information*, June 1992.

107 Dutch shippers introduced the use of sulphur in order to keep the wine; *allumettes hollandaises* are still in use today.

hardest, Dutch customers were still able to benefit from falling CIF prices. Wine was not alone either, in suffering from contraction of sales over the past decade, whether caused by the crippling of disposable incomes or by anti-alcohol campaigns: beer figures have remained flat throughout the 1980s and individual demand for spirits – the Dutch favourite traditional drink – has declined steadily, prompting some consumers to switch over to wine. Wine was thus relatively late in 'running out of growth'; volumes only levelled off in the mid-1980s. They picked up again strongly in the early 1990s, prompted by price falls.

Holland has a very stable population of 15 million. It is not the wealthiest country in Western Europe, ranking a modest 16th worldwide in terms of GDP per capita in 1990,[108] behind all the countries analysed so far in this book except Belgium, but its traditionally open and tolerant society contributes much to enhancing the quality of life of its citizens. Many of its people like to rely on means other than alcohol for their relaxation. The Dutch drink less than the Belgians for instance, but more than the British, Americans and Japanese.

The Dutch wine consumer base is relatively large, around 60% of the adult population in 1990,[109] especially when one considers that wine consumption would only concern a small (albeit wealthy) fringe of the population before the Second World War. Drinking wine remains the hallmark of the better off today, to a large extent, and women make up the majority of wine drinkers. Wine is enjoyed outside meal times in most cases – only 26% seem to drink wine during meals[110] – and thus remains largely an occasional drink. Holland behaves much in accordance with the Anglo-Saxon model: white wines were most popular with women and provided the initial thrust; they continue to grow, but only slightly. Reds are now in favour and their market share is on the increase, currently at around 56%. The share of whites remains basically stable at 42% whilst rosés are retreating fast, from 4.5% in 1985 to 1.5% in 1992.[111]

Dutch wine customers are extremely sensitive about price. Brand names and region designations of origin play an important but secondary role in the selection of wines.[112]

---

108 *The Economist,* 1993.

109 CFCE (1992, Netherlands, p 16).

110 According to Burke interview, in CFCE (1992, Netherlands, p 44).

111 *Drinks File,* 16 April 1993.

112 CFCE (1992, Netherlands, p 44).

Market and import trends

French products enjoy a tremendous quality image, as in Belgium, as well as a reputation for high price. Red generics from Bordeaux have once more acquired the lion's share. Côtes du Rhône, Burgundies and Languedoc wines follow suit, but at a considerable distance. White wines from the Loire and Alsatian white varietals are also performing well.[113]

France's nearest rival was and remains Spain, see Fig. 4.15 and Table 4.9, whose sherries are particularly successful and capture a major share of the higher strength segment.[114] Spain's lighter wines have also made good progress recently. Spain actually sold more wines in the Netherlands than France in the early 1970s. Spanish prices soared briefly in the mid-1970s; shipments kept fairly steady to date, in volume, but declined in value as real prices kept falling for a decade, until the mid-1980s. Much of the fall in price was due to the prolonged weakness of the peseta.

Germans still hold about a third of white wine sales in Holland, see Fig. 4.16. The German wines' boom came to an abrupt halt in 1984 and sales dipped in 1985 as the result of the diethylene glycol affair.

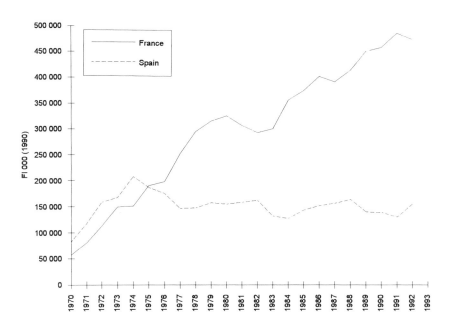

4.15 Dutch imports from main suppliers (CIF, 112.12) (source: United Nations).

113 CFCE (1992, Netherlands, p 53).

Table 4.9 Dutch imports, 000 Fl (1990)

All wines*	1988	1989	1990	1991	1992	Value share, % 1991–92	Volume share, % 1991–92
France	413 484	449 621	457 791	486 743	476 481	52.7	47.0
Spain	164 040	139 836	139 198	130 138	155 650	15.6	17.0
Germany**	68 807	77 082	69 773	71 554	74 761	8.0	10.7
Portugal	47 443	47 538	53 683	59 617	59 797	6.5	4.2
Italy	39 956	49 329	50 613	55 192	53 875	6.0	9.0
Belgium	48 664	56 176	55 802	53 042	50 382	5.7	4.8
Bulgaria	2 023	4 458	6 697	9 412	9 246	1.0	1.6
UK	17 942	16 371	15 609	15 651	8 725	1.3	1.9
S Africa	1 115	1 425	1 914	4 299	6 431	0.6	0.7
Chile	377	350	1 161	2 857	5 995	0.5	0.4
Other	10 772	10 938	14 322	18 440	18 785	2.0	2.7
World	814 623	853 125	866 562	906 945	920 128	100.0	100.0

Sparkling

	1988	1989	1990	1991	1992	Value share, % 1991–92	Volume share, % 1991–92
France	37 896	47 473	42 154	46 903	39 781	77.3	54.4
Spain	1 938	3 375	3 707	4 839	4 762	8.6	17.9
Belgium	2 441	2 313	2 003	2 430	3 642	5.4	6.9
Germany**	2 158	2 795	2 461	2 317	1 792	3.7	10.9
Italy	776	1 053	1 567	1 374	1 202	2.3	6.1
UK	31	41	24	47	223	0.2	0.1
S Africa	20	28	44	99	197	0.3	0.6
Australia	12	117	314	151	42	0.2	0.4
Greece	26	2	4	16	34	0.0	0.1
Portugal	12	15	9	13	18	0.0	0.1
Other	609	817	928	1 205	1 093	2.0	2.6
World	45 919	58 029	53 216	59 393	52 788	100.0	100.0

Still

	1988	1989	1990	1991	1992	Value share, % 1991–92	Volume share, % 1991–92
France	374 782	401 378	413 975	437 600	431 976	52.4	48.9
Spain	161 703	136 136	135 193	124 933	150 356	16.6	17.9
Germany**	65 335	71 497	65 172	67 176	66 499	8.1	10.6
Portugal	47 431	47 523	53 666	59 586	59 766	7.2	4.5
Belgium	42 934	50 168	50 613	48 442	45 416	5.7	4.8
Italy	34 269	41 900	44 347	47 230	45 267	5.6	7.4
Bulgaria	2 023	4 458	6 697	9 412	9 246	1.1	1.7
S Africa	1 094	1 396	1 871	4 200	6 233	0.6	0.7
Chile	371	332	1 128	2 826	5 985	0.5	0.5
Argentina	165	997	2 639	4 146	3 860	0.5	1.2
Australia	3 994	2 400	2 196	2 443	3 418	0.4	0.3
Greece	2 657	2 306	3 022	3 020	3 286	0.4	0.5
USA	738	1 336	1 809	2 046	2 331	0.3	0.2
UK	1 049	1 223	1 55	1 401	1 960	0.2	0.2
Romania	155	428	712	1 011	837	0.1	0.3
Hungary	189	428	707	850	740	0.1	0.1
Ireland					701	0.0	0.0
Yugoslavia					462	0.0	0.0
Israel	175	198	331	409	364	0.0	0.0
Other	1 989	1 896	1 638	3 149	1 619	0.3	0.2
World	741 053	765 997	787 270	819 882	840 324	100.0	100.0

* Including musts and vermouths   ** 1988–1990: FRG only   *Source: United Nations*

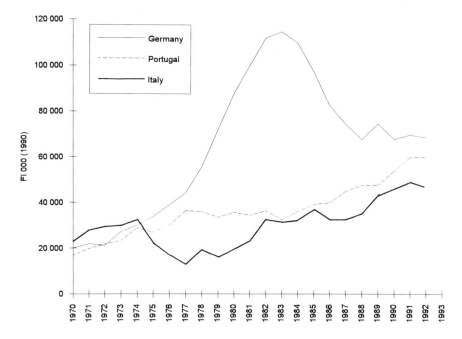

4.16 Dutch imports from selected suppliers and challengers (CIF, 112.12) (source: United Nations).

Liebfraumilch and other whites dropped out of fashion in spite of substantial price cuts. Some would argue that the policy of attempting to win back market share by cutting price actually helped their image deteriorate even further, as was undoubtedly the case in Britain. German whites are now positioned at the bottom of the price range.

Italian wines have never really caught the Dutch consumers' attention. Portuguese wines sustained progression in spite of being left out of the EU, through the success of vintaged ports; the relative dearness of aged wines allows them to pass with ease over the minimum import price hurdle set by the EU. Greece became an early casualty of the application of the principle of EU preference. Here, as elsewhere in the Union, cheap imports were swiftly replaced with shipments from Italy in the main.

There are no other significant challengers in terms of market share, even though Argentinian wines and Bulgarian varietals have made some progress lately, in the bottom and medium price ranges.[115]

114 Three-quarters of the liquor wines' segments (CFCE, 1992, Netherlands, p 17).

115 See CFCE (1992, Netherlands, p 43) for Bulgarian wines and CFCE (1992, Netherlands, p 17) for positioning.

Other New World wines are making headway, but their combined market share still lies well below 5%.

Import and distribution channels

The remaining 200–250 traditional wine importers still active in the Netherlands control an estimated 40% of the exchanges.[116] They are rapidly dwindling in number and in importance as concentration of the retail sector gathers pace. Specialist shops and food supermarkets – the two main channels for wine – either source themselves directly in the foreign producing regions or have developed their own import structure.[117] Others, who deal principally with spirits, have fallen prey to 'global' operators, e.g. Seagram, Pernod and Moët-Hennessy amongst others.[118]

In stark contrast to Belgium, the Dutch Horeca sector's estimated 10–12% market share[119] is still a relatively poor channel for marketing wines. A small but growing amount of wine is also sold to private customers by direct mail, an effective way of retailing relatively expensive wines to a wealthy but discerning clientele.

Specialist shops, known in Holland as *slijters* and *delicatessen*, have a legal monopoly for spirits and, to a large extent, for higher strength wines (above 15%) which supermarkets are barred from selling. Specialist shops realise most of their turnover on spirits and only a quarter on wine. They have increasing difficulties competing with supermarkets and are continually losing in market share, now running at about 17%, as well as in independence. Many shops have thus joined forces and regroup their orders, which they place either with established Dutch importers or directly with foreign producers. Others have fallen under the control of supermarkets. For this is where the real buying power rests in Holland these days: in the hands of pan-European food retailers who rely more and more on direct import *and* central buying for their wine selections.

About 70% of all wines consumed in the Netherlands are marketed via supermarket shelves. Of these, over 30% reach customers through one chain alone. There are two major features characterising leading retailer Albert Heijn. Firstly, it built its success

116 CFCE (1992, Netherlands, p 18).

117 E.g. Gall & Gall, CFCE (1992, Netherlands, p 18).

118 CFCE (1992, Netherlands, p 27).

119 CFCE (1992, Netherlands, pp 52–3).

on developing an extended product line, *Huswijn* (house wine) under its own label; these are good quality ordinary wines imported in bulk and bottled in Holland. Second, it took control of the major chain of specialist shops in 1988,[120] which accounts for 20% of the *slijters'* sales.

In the Netherlands, as in Belgium, the five largest supermarket chains control at least 60% of all wine sales. Economic integration is quite advanced amongst the northern four founding members of the EU, i.e. Belgium, Luxembourg, Netherlands and Germany, and particularly strong in the case of the distribution of food and beverages: one will note, for instance, that the third largest wine retailers in both Belgium and Holland are controlled by Germany's largest, Aldi.

Outlook

Prospects are similar to those for Belgium: the Netherlands remains an important market as demand looks set to grow further. The modification of excise duties introduced in January 1993 (as elsewhere in the EU) brought with it a 30% increase on still wines with a strength of less than 15%.[121] It halved the rate applicable to those containing less than 8.5% alcohol, in a move designed to curb alcohol consumption.

Germany

The Federal Republic of Germany (FRG) is the colossus of the international wine trade. It inherited this status in the late 1970s when overtaking France as the world's largest importer in volume and its position has remained unchallenged to date. Imported volumes went through a phase of sustained growth until 1981, then into a phase of decline until 1990, when reunification provided a strong boost. The US superseded Germany during the first half of the 1980s in terms of value, and the UK did the same between 1983 and 1990.

Reunification with the former German Democratic Republic (GDR) on 3 October 1990 raised it to even further prominence in Western and Central Europe; the GDR was dismantled into five *Länder* (Mecklenburg-Vorpommern, Brandenburg, Saxony-Anhalt, Saxony and Thuringia) who joined the FRG and its 16 million citizens were simply

---

120 Gall & Gall, CFCE (1989, Netherlands, p 27); (1992, p 21).

121 *MOCI, Moniteur du Commerce International,* 4 January 1993.

added to the 61 million Germans living west of the Oder-Neisse line.

This largely unforeseen expansion of the EU to the east brought with it a sudden swelling of the ranks of its wine consumers – much to the delight of EU surplus producers and particularly Spain – who could bank once more on 'Community preference' to boost their sales, though mainly achieved by diverting trade. The former GDR used to import an estimated 200 000 litres[122] before reunification and much of it came from Hungary and other Central European states, all members of the former Communist trading bloc COMECON.[123]

The former GDR market has not yet reached a level of sophistication comparable to that of the western *Länder*; nor is it as well documented. The profile thus focuses on the former West Germany for the period up until 1990.

German wine production consists mainly of white wines (over 80%) and has followed an upward trend ever since the end of the Second World War: average output in the 1980s was nearly three times that of the 1950s.[124] Domestic consumption and demand for exports have, together, grown even faster than has the indigenous production and the degree of 'self-sufficiency'[125] has dipped accordingly, from 70% in the 1960s to around 55% in the 1970s and 1980s.[126] The remaining 45% of wines are imported (see Fig. 4.17).

Most of this remarkable growth in West German imports occurred in the twenty years leading to the common organisation of the EU market in wine, and not after. Volumes soared from 103 million litres in 1951 to 621 million in 1970, and the 1 billion litres imported in 1990, for a CIF value of DM 2.4 billion (US$ 1.5 billion), only represented a further 50% increase on 1970 volumes. Imports receded in volume during most of the 1980s; growth resumed in the mid-1980s, but only in terms of real value (see Fig. 4.18).

German wine consumption rose from 12 litres per head in 1960 to 25 litres in 1980 and on to 26 litres in 1990, the world's 12th highest. Growth neared stagnation in the 1980s under the combined effect of recession and the diethylene glycol and methanol affairs. Yet this was no isolated trend: individual consumption of beer (the highest in the world at over 140 litres per head) has been subject to gentle decline ever since the mid-1970s and demand for spirits has

---

122 Source: OIV.

123 See *Das Weinjahr*, 1986, pp 209–10 for more details on Hungary.

124 1 billion litres for 1981–90, against 0.335 for 1951–60. Source: OIV.

125 The ratio of production to total demand, including demand for exports.

126 Source: OIV.

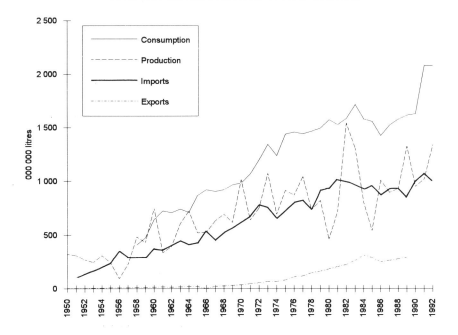

4.17 German wine consumption, production and imports (source: OIV).

fallen sharply throughout the 1980s, from over 3 to 2.2 lpa in 1990.[127]

Wine consumption remains occasional in the former West Germany – only a quarter of the population drink it at least once a week.[128] It concentrates on white wines, which enjoyed a 64% market share in 1990, against 9% for rosés and 27% for reds.[129] Also noteworthy is the comparatively large slice of the budget taken by sparkling wines and that consumers' preferences are slowly but steadily leaning to reds – a sign of the maturing of the German market.

Consumer panel studies show that rarely consuming households (with less than 5 litres) represent a tiny but stable proportion of German households (2%). The number of those considered 'regular drinkers' – with purchases in excess of 40 litres – rose from 14% in 1965 to 22% in 1985 and accounted for nearly 68% of all household expenditure on wine. Occasional consumers saw their number decrease from 58% to 51% and their wine expenditure share fall even more rapidly, from 47% in 1965 to 30% 20 years later. The rise in number and expenditure share of the regular drinkers has its origins

127 Source: *World Drink Trends.*

128 Source: CFCE.

129 Source: CFCE.

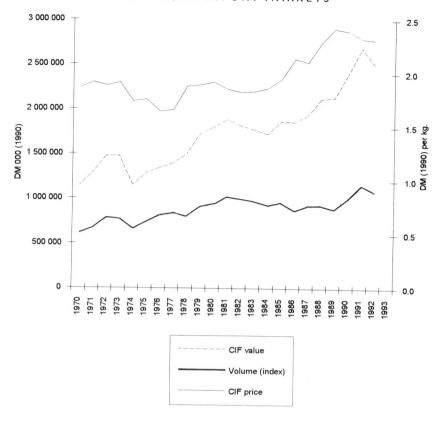

4.18 German imports (112.1) (source: United Nations).

in the 1970s; the phenomenon peaked in the early 1980s, as did wine imports in general.[130] Most striking is the proportion of single and two-person households, which make up nearly two-thirds of the wine consumer base.[131] The concentration of expenditure on a decreasing number of households is a trait of the evolution of the German wine market.[132]

Imports consist mainly of red wines; these had a 60% share in volume, against 30% for whites and 10% for rosés in 1985.[133] The most valuable part of German wine imports is destined to be marketed accordingly, whether bottled in the region of production or by

---

130 *Das Weinjahr*, 1986, p 45 and *Marketing Jahrbuch Wein*, 1991/2, p 90, based on household panel data.

131 CFCE (1992, Germany, p 67).

132 *Das Weinjahr*, 1986, p 57.

133 Ibid, p 60.

importers – still after additional sweetening in the case of some whites shipped from Tunisia and the former Yugoslavia.[134] German white wines reveal a high level of residual sugar, a salient feature which matches the predominantly festive character of wine consumption in Germany.

Other, vast quantities of wines are imported for further elaboration by German wineries. In 1985 for instance, 16% of imports were 'base wines' used in the production of sparkling *Sekt* and a further 1% – mainly reds – were imported for blending with domestic wines.[135] There were also large shipments of industrial wines used for the production of spirits and vinegar.

There is some degree of interdependency between import and production in Germany. Yearly fluctuations in production are amplified by the northern situation of German vineyards and cannot be compensated by variations in stocks alone. Neither is the market immune to shocks occurring on the demand side, at home and abroad.

The linkage between domestic and foreign market conditions is particularly well illustrated by the evolution of consumption, exports, production and imports in the 1980s. In 1981 and 1982 for instance, Germany made record purchases outside its borders, mainly from Italy, in an attempt to make up for the production deficit caused by a succession of unusually small harvests in 1980 and 1981. Supply conditions later swung from shortage to surplus in just two years: there were exceptionally large harvests in 1982 and 1983, domestic demand receded temporarily between 1984 and 1987 and export markets weakened as well in 1985–1986; the result was a curb in imports, by over 10%, between 1982 and 1989. Imports would only resume growth after reunification in October that year.

The simultaneous development of often common infrastructures for the production, import and distribution of wines – and their (less conspicuous) link with spirits – means that much of the shipments to Germany is done in bulk (60% in 1985).[136] Imports are largely in the hands of wine (and spirits) wholesalers and other wine middlemen, such as brokers' *Agenturen*; this sector remains relatively fragmented, in spite of the wave of concentration that swept across Northern Europe's food retail sector. (Wine scandals are not alien to this trend: retailers – especially food supermarkets – do not wish to take *any*

---

134 Though this segment appears to be contracting. CFCE (1992, Germany, p 84).

135 *Das Weinjahr*, 1986, pp 106–8, 165–6 and *Marketing Jahrbuch Wein*, 1991/2, p 66.

136 Calculation based on data from the Stat. Bundesamt, in *Das Weinjahr*, 1985, pp 166–75.

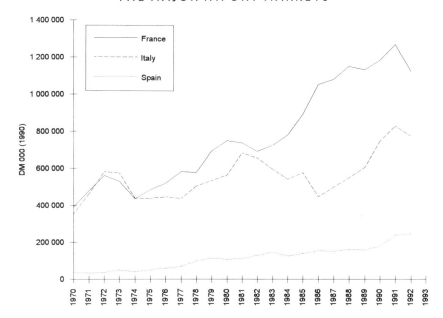

4.19 German imports from main suppliers (CIF, 112.12) (source: United Nations).

legal responsibility regarding the import of ever too often fraudulent wines.)

The battle for market share in all three categories of imports, whether bulk for further elaboration, bulk for bottling or mere bottled imports, has been led by French and Italian exporters in the main, see Fig. 4.19 and Table 4.10.

Market and import trends

Sparkling wines
Bubbly wines are big business in Germany: 350 million litres of sparkling wines were sold in 1990, representing about 20% of total wine consumption,[137] and 16 million litres were exported.[138] Only a fifth of the sparkling wines marketed in Germany had been imported as finished products and roughly a sixth of these was champagne.[139] The remaining 80% were German-made, vat-fermented *Sekt*, produced

---

137 Total consumption of 1630 million litres in 1985. Source: OIV.

138 Including some 440 000 litres sold duty free to NATO forces stationed in Germany.

139 *Das Weinjahr*, 1986, pp 214, 216; *Marketing Jahrbuch Wein*, 1991/2.

Table 4.10 German imports**, 000 DM (1990)

All wines*	1988	1989	1990	1991	1992	Value share, % 1991–92	Volume share, % 1991–92
France	1 149 864	1 130 890	1 183 400	1 269 447	1 123 179	46.1	25.5
Italy	574 388	628 923	771 678	860 871	800 417	32.0	41.2
Spain	171 677	165 926	191 478	260 008	274 460	10.3	16.4
Greece	39 353	42 516	51 443	58 792	52 145	2.1	2.4
Portugal	47 119	43 277	46 432	50 949	45 684	1.9	1.1
Yugoslavia					37 892	0.7	1.8
Austria	9 131	11 633	15 282	19 006	25 255	0.9	0.6
Hungary	17 683	14 856	12 947	16 797	23 208	0.8	1.5
Bulgaria	5 161	6 140	10 509	16 153	17 524	0.6	1.3
Romania	10 901	9 781	9 588	9 295	11 217	0.4	0.8
Other	97 973	92 113	119 660	128 449	93 244	4.3	7.2
World	2 123 251	2 146 055	2 412 416	2 689 767	2 504 225	100.0	100.0

Sparkling

	1988	1989	1990	1991	1992	Value share, % 1991–92	Volume share, % 1991–92
France	340 794	353 223	380 538	432 273	367 711	64.6	32.5
Italy	112 031	89 956	107 193	147 231	168 980	25.5	54.0
Spain	24 278	27 980	36 081	41 123	43 622	6.8	10.5
Austria	1 234	1 274	1 681	2 366	2 956	0.4	0.4
S Africa	180	217	284	373	567	0.1	0.1
Hungary	141	113	116	200	477	0.1	0.1
USA	46	98	93	251	360	0.0	0.0
Portugal	63	106	59	205	139	0.0	0.0
Bulgaria	224	217	201	104	89	0.0	0.0
Yugoslavia					23	0.0	0.0
Other	16 735	20 518	18 519	14 132	15 404	2.4	2.3
World	495 725	493 702	544 766	638 257	600 329	100.0	100.0

Still

	1988	1989	1990	1991	1992	Value share, % 1991–92	Volume share, % 1991–92
France	806 076	775 655	801 043	834 922	751 797	41.7	26.9
Italy	437 448	514 264	639 287	679 894	603 243	33.7	41.7
Spain	138 200	131 098	144 205	196 896	205 042	10.6	15.1
Greece	38 827	42 040	51 249	57 222	52 084	2.9	2.8
Portugal	47 056	43 147	46 373	50 744	45 511	2.5	1.3
Yugoslavia					37 869	1.0	2.1
Hungary	17 542	14 743	12 829	16 597	22 730	1.0	1.8
Austria	7 764	10 219	13 482	16 623	22 070	1.0	0.7
Bulgaria	4 937	5 923	10 308	16 028	17 388	0.9	1.5
Romania	10 901	9 781	9 569	9 295	11 217	0.5	1.0
USA	5 912	4 731	5 035	8 143	10 207	0.5	0.1
S Africa	3 246	4 983	4 501	5 924	7 939	0.4	0.2
Croatia					6 540	0.2	0.3
Tunisia	9 135	5 672	6 308	7 671	6 525	0.4	0.7
Slovenia					5 598	0.1	0.3
Switzerland	5 702	4 465	5 676	5 158	4 363	0.3	0.1
Chile		700		2 318	4 251	0.2	0.1
Turkey	2 399	2 452	3 037	3 282	3 945	0.2	0.1
Australia	778	1 088	1 583	1 361	2 011	0.1	0.0
Other	51 454	44 567	63 353	63 801	10 432	2.0	3.2
World	1 587 378	1 615 527	1 817 839	1 975 879	1 830 760	100.0	100.0

* Including musts and vermouths   ** 1988–1990: FRG only   *Source: United Nations*

in the greatest part (90%)[140] from the 200 million litres or so of base wine (*sektgrundwein*) imported on average over those years, mostly from Italy (79%) and France (18%).[141]

Business is heavily concentrated; the largest 14 producers and importers marketed 87% of the wines in the mid-1980s.[142] A handful of giant domestic producers tower over this sector – the three largest are Faber, Henkell and Söhnlein. Four major international spirits and vermouth producers/marketers also figure in the top 14: Cinzano, Seagram, Simex (from Crimea) and Chandon.[143] Concentration grew in the second half of the 1980s as the result of several acquisitions. At the end of the 1980s, the three major groups were:[144] Günther Reh (Faber, Schloss Böchingen and Wissemburg Kellereien, with a combined turnover of 105 million bottles/79 million litres), Oetker (combining Henkell and Söhnlein, with 85 million bottles/64 million litres), and Seagram-Deutschland with 20 million bottles/15 million litres. Together, the Big Three captured just over half of the German sparkling market in 1988, then worth about 304 million litres.[145]

Italian *spumante* – flavoured, muscat based, wine produced mainly in the Asti region and marketed by Cinzano – and other sparkling, or pearl wines, are selling at very low prices. Spanish *cava* is also successful but slightly more expensive; Codorniu and Freixenet basically constitute a duopoly in this area. A high strength sparkling wine imported from former Russia, *Krimsekt*, sold well despite its relatively high price. Champagnes are France's largest export category by volume; other, cheaper sparkling wines imported from France were struggling hard in a market dominated by domestic producers.[146]

Nevertheless, imports of sparkling wines grew over 12 times between the mid-1960s and the mid-1980s – 10 times in the first decade alone.[147] Demand is highly seasonal however: 40% of sales are realised in the last six weeks of the year and there is a second peak in the spring, around Easter. The upward trend in consumption does not

140 CFCE (1992, Germany, p 84).

141 *Das Weinjahr*, 1986, pp 174, 177.

142 Ibid, p 215.

143 Ibid, pp 217–18.

144 CFCE (1992, Germany, p 85).

145 405 million bottles (339 domestically produced − 12.5 to export markets +69 million imported bottles). CFCE (1992, Germany, p 85).

146 Ibid, p 86.

147 *Das Weinjahr*, 1986, p 216.

seem to have reached its ceiling yet, and certainly not in view of the success encountered by their cooler cousins, especially in the former GDR.

Coolers and cocktails, such as sangria, is a much younger market in Germany and, arguably, still in its embryonic phase. Sales are far less seasonal than that of *Sekt*. In 1991 and 1992, cooler sales amounted to an estimated 30 and 40 million bottles (22 and 30 million litres) respectively. Major producers of *Sekt*, spirits and wine as well as a major wine importer are all active in this growing market, and the new *Länder* are showing the greatest potential for further growth. Coolers and cocktails involve little imports except, perhaps, in the case of Spanish sangria. New producers of wine coolers have sprung up in the former East Germany as well.[148]

Still wines

Consumer preference remains strongly geared towards German white wines, as in the sparkling market, but the trends revealed by the German market during the 1980s would point to a certain degree of maturation: there has been a marked shift to rosés – especially in the non-producing north and in the younger segment of the wine-drinking population – and to reds as well.[149] Imported wines benefited from this trend. The ever-increasing share of wine expenditure by higher income households,[150] has played a role in furthering demand for appellation wines in Germany.

French and Italian wines have the highest penetration rate after German domestic wines but they now have Spain hard on their heels, in terms of volume at least (see Table 4.10). Competition is fiercest in the ordinary wine segment where differentiation is not so much based on regional denominations than on the nationality of the wines. This corner of the market is most sensitive to price and much is still imported in bulk and bottled by well-equipped German wineries.

The steady growth of French exports to Germany in value since the mid-1980s was due to the resounding success of France's higher quality wines especially AOCs. In 1987, Germany became France's first market for its AOCs, overtaking the UK.[151] The shift towards higher quality shipments by the French was dictated by their embattled position at the cheap end of the market. In 1985, as much as a third of

---

148 *MIVS*, January 1994, pp 5–6.

149 *Das Weinjahr*, (1986, p 57); CFCE (Germany, p 67).

150 CFCE (1992, Germany, p 67).

151 CFCE (1992, Germany, p 83).

French imports by volume were shipped as base wine for the manufacture of *Sekt* and as industrial wine for distillation; together they accounted for between a quarter and a fifth of the 300 million litres imported in the early 1990s. About as much wine (60–70 million litres) was quality red, virtually all of which was shipped in bottles. The vast majority of the 30+ million litres of quality whites were also bottled shipments. Imports of ordinary reds (70–80 million) and whites (30 million) occurred mostly in bulk. Germany is France's first market in value and second in volume; it is Italy's first market on both account.[152] Figure 4.19 shows the evolution of the shipments of both countries in terms of real value.

Italian exports to Germany surged as soon as a common organisation of the EU market in wine was set in place, in 1970. Italian shipments rose again in the mid-1970s and in the early 1980s, which were periods of pronounced weakness of wine prices throughout the EU. Italian prices for ordinary wines dipped far below French levels in 1980 and plunged to new depths in 1981, boosting Italian exports to Germany and then receding steadily in volume until they reached the 400 million litres level in 1985. The combination of the methanol affair with ill-timed distillation by the EU, which sent Italian prices way above French levels, pushed imported volumes below those from France who clearly benefited from the problems of the Italians in the ordinary wines sector.[153] Italians recaptured that sector, which they traditionally held, together with Italy's first rank in terms of volume in 1988. The 470 million litres imported from Italy in 1990 included some 160 million litres of base wine for *Sekt*, nearly 70 million litres of ordinary reds and 100 million of ordinary whites (mostly in bulk) as well as over 40 million litres of quality reds and some 30 million of quality whites (nearly all in bottles). Italy and France have both suffered from Spanish successes in the still wine segment in the early 1990s.

Half of Spain's 40 million litres exports to Germany were bottled sherries (in 1985). The rest were reds of less than 13% (two-thirds in bulk), aromatic wines (essentially sangria, again two-thirds in bulk) and some still whites of less than 13%. Spanish reds – most of which are of higher quality – were identified as the most serious threat to the French, though they clearly suffered, then, from a lack of consistency in their pricing policy (prices were far too dispersed and confusing to consumers, e.g. Rioja's would range from 4 to 26 DM, for an average

152 Caire (1989).

153 CFCE (1992, Germany, p 83).

price of 4.5.[154] Spanish shipments increased threefold between 1990 and 1991 but only increased by over a third in value. Most of the increase concerned quality whites in bulk, which jumped from 5 to over 80 million litres.[155]

As for the remaining suppliers, note that the 50 million litres of wines shipped by the former Yugoslavia were still reds in 90% of the cases and nearly all of it was imported in bulk. The 10 million litres of Hungarian imported by the FRG in 1990 were down to a third of the volume of trade between those two countries in 1981. Hungary used to rank fifth in the suppliers' league in terms of volume, behind the Big Three and Yugoslavia; it has since been overtaken by Bulgaria (12 million litres in 1990), Cyprus (27 million) and two EU states – Greece and Portugal with 29 and 11 million litres respectively,[156] (see Fig. 4.20). The diethylene glycol affair dealt a cruel blow to Austria's exports to Germany, which tumbled from 19 million litres in 1985 to 4 million litres in 1990. This put the country just behind Tunisia who

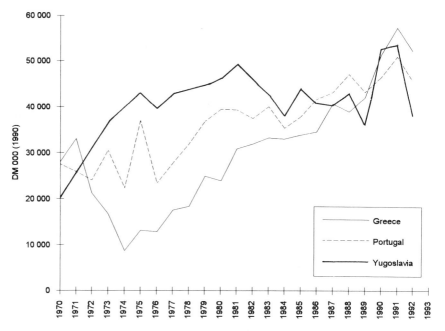

4.20 German imports from selected suppliers and challengers (CIF, 112.12) (source: United Nations).

154 Caire (1989).

155 *Marketing Jahrbuch Wein*, 1990/91 and 1991/92.

156 *Das Weinjahr*, 1986, p 210 and *Marketing Jahrbuch Wein*, 1990/91.

exported 57 million litres that year. Much of those imports is done in bulk and carried out by a small club of importers.[157]

Import and distribution channels

A look at the distribution sector for wine in Germany sheds light on the configuration of the import sector. In 1991, 2 billion litres of domestic and imported wines consumed reached German consumers through the following channels: the Horeca sector accounted for 30% of the sales in volume; direct sales to consumers accounted for 15%, and the remaining 55% of the wines reached customers via retailers, i.e. supermarkets and specialist shops.[158]

The proportion of the catering sector has remained virtually unchanged since the 1970s.[159] Direct sales are the principal outlet for domestic foreign wines (mailing is a popular marketing channel in Germany) but only a marginal way for distributing foreign wines to German customers. Specialist shops, e.g. Jacques Weindepot[160] is still a relatively little developed outlet for wine and spirits.[161] The vast majority of the foreign wines reach customers through the food retailing sector: general stores, e.g. Karstadt, Kaufhof; supermarkets, e.g. Tengelmann; discounters, e.g. Aldi and wholesalers, e.g. Metro.

A striking characteristic of the food retailing sector is that, despite its strength (it is gaining in market share each year), it is still reluctant to source itself directly in foreign wine producing regions and prefers to rely on importers' expertise, whether German wine wholesalers who import in bulk, bottle, label and deliver according to retailers' specifications, or wine agents who select the wines for their large customers and arrange for their import and most of the remaining logistics. The three main reasons for the relative absence of direct imports (when compared with Belgium or the Netherlands are (a) the regional character of the German food distribution system, (b) its reluctance to bear any liability arising from the sale or import of fraudulent wines and (c) the presence of a competent domestic wholesale sector for wines.

A dozen German importers could be considered as 'national' in

---

157 CFCE (1992, Germany, p 84).

158 According to the Geisenheimer Institut für Betriebswirtschaft, in *Drinks File*, 1992.

159 It was then put at 28–30% by the same Institute (Bock, 1977, p 17).

160 *Die Weinwirtschaft – Markt,* 5 March 1993, p 17 and 24–26 November 1993, p 21.

161 Unlike for the rest of the food sector. CFCE (1992, Germany, p 91).

view of their size, with turnover in excess of DM50 million in 1990: Reidermeister & Ulrichs, Langguth, Racke, Pieroth, Schenk, Egger & Franke, Buxtorf, Amman, Schlumberger, St Ursula-Binderer and JWD.[162] Not only are they able to supply customers through each of the major retailing channels, but also to provide the food retailing sector with most of the wines it needs. These are usually well equipped wineries which import large quantities in bulk and are fully capable of meeting supermarkets' requirements in terms of price, promotion (labelling, point of sale material, etc), wide selection of wines and logistics. Their ability to provide stable qualities is a key asset, as the food retailing sector is extremely keen to avoid fluctuations in this respect. These are fairly anonymous wines which are bought, imported and packaged by the German importers.

A few large foreign co-operative wineries have also established footholds in Germany recently (with the 'single market' very much in mind) in order to supply food retailers directly with their own wines. They must ship, import and deliver the bottles to the supermarkets' distribution centres by the truckload, which requires a certain production capacity. Although many a co-operative winery is known for 'bottling whatever is being produced' and for its disregard for marketing, there are notable exceptions. Many of them have opened offices in Germany: France's Union des Vignerons des Côtes du Rhône; which markets a quarter of Côtes du Rhône's Appellations Contrôlées under the *Cellier des Dauphins* brand; Val d'Orbieu who represent 17 co-operative wineries in the French south-west; the Alsace's Wolfberger who acquired Kiefer, a Saarland-based traditional wine importer; the Italian giants Gruppo Italiano Vini and Corovin; and the Austrian Winzer Krems.[163] Spanish co-operative wineries are nearly absent as much of the trade is done in bulk by large Valencian shippers – and by two large producers in the case of *cava* (their problem lies in their involvement with other agricultural crops and absence of specialisation in wine). The greatest chance for foreign co-operative wineries resides in the slowly rising importance of bottling in the region of production as a guarantee of integrity of the wines. This has already worked well for Austrian wines: Winzer Krems now claims control of two-thirds of Austrian exports to Germany.[164] More distant foreign exporters have considered sending bulk to Germany

162 Ibid.

163 5 March 1993, 16–24.

164 Ibid, p 22.

and using the sophisticated domestic wine industry for packaging and distribution to consumer markets in Western and Eastern Europe.

Hundreds of smaller German importers supply the German market with the remaining wines. Their market share may only amount to an estimated 30% – at least in the French case[165] – but they are highly specialised and work with much more comfortable margins than do the suppliers of the large food retailers. International marketers of branded spirits, sparkling and still wine, such as Seagram, should not be forgotten either, who could least afford to miss the unique opportunity offered by the crumbling of the wall in late 1989: access to a region with 16 million dwellers and an enormous growth potential as far as wine is concerned.

Outlook

Reunification has brought with it sweeping changes: whilst per capita demand for beer was essentially identical on both sides of the Oder-Neisse, that for spirits was significantly higher in the East (5.2 lpa, the highest in the world in 1990) than in the West (2.2 lpa, ranking 12th after the US and Canada). The opposite was true for wine: 20 litres for 18th ranking in the East; 26 for 12th in the West. Viewed from the angle of former West Germany, the transition to a bigger market has maintained the level of individual beer consumption by the German nation basically unchanged at 143 litres per capita in 1991; it has raised that for spirits dramatically (2.7 lpa) and lowered that for wine by 5% (25 litres per capita).[166]

The integration of the 5 new *Länder*[167] failed to translate into the instantaneous boom in wine sales which many had anticipated though. After several years, the West German wine industry had to realise that consumption patterns in the Eastern part of the country – where people drink roughly as much beer but comparatively more spirits and less wine[168] – could only come into line with those of their Western counterparts over the medium to long term (5–10 years), for at least two reasons. Firstly, it would take much longer than expected for incomes in the new *Länder* to become level with those in the former FRG. Secondly, former GDR citizens have acquired different

165 CFCE (1992, Germany, p 87).

166 Source: WDT.

167 See page 160.

168 Source: WDT.

tastes from those prevailing in the West during their 44 years of incorporation with the former Soviet bloc.

East German consumers have thus an even greater preference for sweet and sparkling white wines than have their fellow citizens in the West. The former GDR hardly produces any wine, so they are also less fussy about the origin of the wines they purchase, their choice being largely dictated by price considerations and only rarely by prestige (East Germans spend nearly 20% less on an average bottle of wine.[169] Convergence of tastes between the two should increase in line with the rapid expansion of Western German retailers to the East. These usually content themselves with pushing for existing product lines – albeit more of the cheaper sort – and most wines come from the EU (only rarely have Western-based retailers reacted by offering a radically different portfolio of wines to customers in the East). The odds are thus clearly in favour of West German and EU wines, particularly those situated in the middle and lower price ranges. For instance, recall that imports of Spanish wines soared in volume during the early 1990s but posted far more modest increases in terms of value. Shipments of lightly sparkling wines, table wines and vermouths from Italy as well as sangria and still white wines from Spain, have been met with increasing success in the Eastern part of the country. French wines other than ordinary wines and cheap generics from established wine growing regions are deemed too expensive at the moment.[170]

German reunification has already brought some life to flagging West German import figures. This was simply due to the fact that the New *Länder* were increasingly supplied by Western-based firms. Domestic grape production being more or less fixed (the EU Commission keeps pushing hard for the introduction of national production quotas), a rise in East German consumption to the basically stable levels prevailing in the Western part of the country[171] would mean that another 200 million litres may have to be sourced outside Germany by the turn of the century. EU producers are set to benefit mostly – if not wholly – from this new burst of activity unless Hungary, Bulgaria and Romania were offered to take part in a free trading area with the EU before then. Recent wine trade agreements between them and the EU grant them (and EU exporters)

---

169 Source: Nielsen (in *Die Weinwirtschaft – Markt,* 11, Juni 1993).

170 *Die Weinwirtschaft – Markt,* 11 Juni 1993.

171 21 litres per head in the years 1987–1990 according to the Ifo-Institut für Wirtschaftsforschung (in *Marketing Jahrbuch Wein* 1992/93, p 83).

preferential tariffs for limited volumes of export.[172] One should nevertheless consider the East German market – once a secure outlet for wine producers belonging to the Soviet bloc – as having been successfully transferred within the protective walls of the EU. A similar fate looms for Poland as well as for the Czech and Slovak Republics who have all applied for EU membership. Claiming back lost territory will be a formidable task for Eastern European wine exporters.

France

France remained the world's largest wine importer in terms of volume until the late 1970s, when West Germany took a definite lead. Trade was shaped by colonial preference before 1970 and by EU preference thereafter, yet ultimately sanctioned by the preferences of French consumers. Apart from its traditionally large imports of bulk for blending with its own, declining production of ordinary wines. France has shown comparatively little interest in buying foreign products so far. Imports have thus declined along with domestic consumption, since the 1960s, in volume and value (see Fig. 4.21).

The 1.5 billion litres imported each year on average in the course of the 1950s fell to 1 billion in the 1960s, 800 million in the 1970s and 600 million in the 1980s. Imports seem to have stabilised in the early 1990s, see Fig. 4.22; some 500 million litres were brought into France at that time, for a value of just over 2 billion French francs. These are mostly cheap bulk imports of still wines, an estimated 80% of which is intended to be blended with domestic produce and marketed as a Community blend or, more frequently, as French ordinary table wine.[173]

France used to 'import' nearly all its wines from Algeria, the North African colony, where many of its winegrowers had fled and established a new viticulture, with financial assistance from the French government, in the wake of the destruction of their vineyards by phylloxera in the 1870s and 1880s. Many of the destroyed vineyards were replanted later with hybrid vines, derived from crossbreedings between *vitis vinifera* and American varieties, which were resistant to phylloxera and mildew, but bore high yields and generally poor wines. These were then systematically blended with

172 So-called 'tariff quotas' – this issue is dealt with in greater detail in Chapter 6.

173 Gille, 1992, p 201–2.

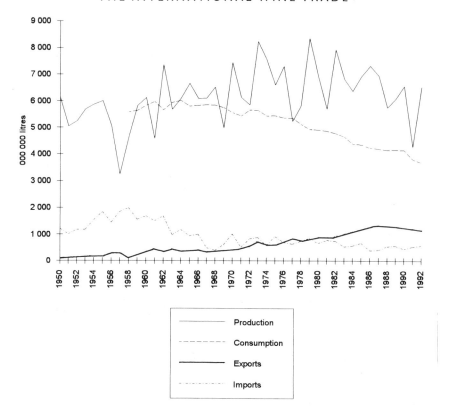

4.21 French wine consumption, production and imports (source: OIV).

better wines from Algeria, the so-called *vins médecins*. (French consumers demanded relatively high strength wines at that time.)

France has been overproducing wine since the rebuilding of its vineyards at the end of the nineteenth century. The chronic surplus was estimated at 700 million litres on the eve of Algerian independence in 1962, and shipments from the colony totalled 1400 million litres in those years on average. France's wine policy was completely interventionist in the early 1960s, so no one doubted that a swift solution would be brought to the surplus issue. Agreements were signed between France and Algeria in Evian in 1964, which provided for a smooth running down of Algerian shipments to about 700 million litres, corresponding to the size of the surplus, by 1970.

The first day of January 1970 was the agreed deadline for setting up all of the EU's common market organisations for agricultural commodities. Goods would be freely traded within the Union's external borders from then on, and wine would be no exception. However reluctantly, France had to deregulate its wine economy

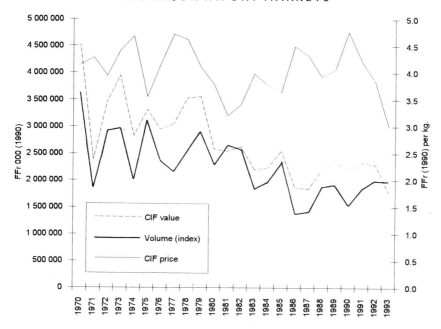

4.22 French imports (112.1) (source: United Nations).

substantially in order to integrate with the far more liberal German and Italian markets.[174] Wines from Italy were almost immediately substituted for imports of Algerian wines. (France resorted to importing large quantities of Algerian wine in 1973 only, in order to compensate for a succession of small harvests, in 1971 and 1972, in both French and Italian vineyards). Negative Monetary Compensatory Amounts (MCAs) were introduced between France and its five other EU partners after the devaluation of the French Franc in August 1969 as a temporary expedient for preserving fictitious common prices in the agricultural sector. They equalled the amount of the devaluation and worked as an import subsidy as well as a tax on exports. The aim was to avoid shocks caused by swings in exchange rates: food imports by France would have become instantaneously more expensive at a time of high inflation and agricultural exports to other member states suddenly more competitive when their production was already in surplus. MCAs were thus welcomed upon their introduction but sparked controversy later, mainly because of the distortions they

174 See Spahni, 1988, Chapter 3, for a comprehensive discussion of French and EU integration.

introduced in EU agriculture.[175] Germany devalued in October of that year and positive MCAs were applied there.

MCAs were first introduced for table wine in 1971, for Germany and the Benelux countries, and were made applicable to all EU Members in 1973. Following the introduction of contraction rules and that of a minimum price for wine in 1982, MCAs for wine were calculated on that basis and only applied if strictly necessary. In practice, this meant creating exclusively negative MCAs which applied only to producing countries with a weakening currency. MCAs disappeared almost completely (except for Greece) for some time but were re-introduced recently following turbulence on exchange markets. In January 1994, for instance, only negative MCAs applied to exporters such as Italy, Greece and Spain.

MCAs are accounted for by CIF prices, but only proportionately to the value share of ordinary wines in all wine exports. Variations in exchange rates are thus transmitted to CIF prices imperfectly, because MCAs partly offset such variations, for ordinary wine only and for falling exporter's currency.

In the case of French-Italian trade, however, the amount of the MCA, which penalised Italian 'exports' to France was also applied to French 'exporters' to Italy, this time as an equivalent subsidy.

The attractiveness of Italian wines was all too often exacerbated by the inherent weakness of the Italian currency. This led to violent social unrest in the French Midi and to illegal disruptions of Italian imports by France, in 1975 and 1981.[176] Each of the riots, dubbed 'wine wars', brought the EU to reinforce its price supporting arrangements for ordinary wine.[177] In short, MCAs were largely unable to offset fluctuations in currencies because of the absence of an effective minimum intervention price for wine[178] (unlike for most major commodities), and the issue was simply resolved by hiking

---

175 See Tarditi, 1978, and Ritson & Tangermann, 1979 for more details.

176 By imposing an import tax in 1975 (based on a lapsed provision; see Spahni, 1988, p 62 for details); by blocking Italian wine at the border in 1981. See Cour de Justice des Communautés Européennes, 22 March 1983.

177 *Garantie de Bonne Fin* and preventive distillation were introduced in a first review of the EU wine policy (EC Reg 1160/76); a minimum price for wine and support distillation were introduced in a second review, in 1982 (EC Reg 2144/82); lame structural measures were also enacted in 1980. See Spahni, 1988, Chapter 4, for more details.

178 See Tarrou, 1976, Bousigon, 1979, and INRA-ENSA-Montpellier, 1987, p 105, for more details.

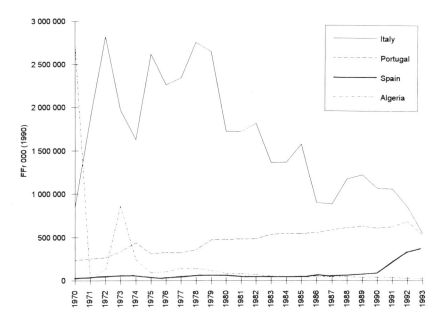

4.23 French imports from main suppliers (CIF, 112.12) (source: United Nations).

prices in both countries with distillation, i.e. EU taxpayers' money. Herewith, yielding to exaction, the EU embarked on the most wasteful support programme in wine history.

Greek wines also became attractive in the mid-1980s and Spain started to join the party in the early 1990s as transitory trade restrictions of wines were gradually lifted: Spanish shipments to France have been soaring in recent years (see Fig 4.23, 4.24 and Table 4.11). In 1991, at least 82.85% of imports from Spain were in bulk – mostly white wines with many appellations – and 93.3% of Italian exports to France were bulk wines also, mainly reds.[179] Only an estimated 20% of Italian imports are sold as such; the rest is used for blending.[180] Importing bulk for blending remains profitable to a large extent and shipments of this nature are now running to the tune of 4–500 million litres a year. The virtual collapse of French consumers' demand for ordinary wines – whether denominated as EU blends or in French disguise[181] – resulted in a steady reduction of this type of trade

179 Author's estimates.

180 Gille, 1993, pp 201–2.

181 The French like to talk of 'naturalisation' or *'francisation'* of imported wines (Gille, 1993, pp 210–12).

Table 4.11 French imports, 000 FFr (1990)

All wines*	1988	1989	1990	1991	1992	1993	Value share, % 1991–93	Volume share, % 1991–93
Italy	1 207 371	1 258 146	1 097 447	1 090 453	889 998	574 737	40.1	56.1
Portugal	613 726	630 095	607 686	624 039	682 643	524 728	28.7	9.3
Spain	66 748	76 858	98 539	241 359	356 753	421 178	16.0	27.5
Not specified	125 812	140 575	152 838	148 049	131 894	63 276	5.4	0.7
Germany**	13 892	15 725	17 636	29 093	18 726	28 866	1.2	0.8
Algeria	46 795	34 679	36 755	36 442	23 618	22 059	1.3	0.8
Morocco	20 615	20 213	21 379	27 138	22 627	19 214	1.1	0.8
Belgium	12 969	12 232	8 766	14 484	13 884	16 509	0.7	0.1
UK	4 064	4 053	4 112	3 312	4 461	12 856	0.3	0.0
USA	7 505	7 678	7 783	9 658	20 063	12 249	0.7	0.2
Other	80 270	132 976	124 914	102 570	112 312	75 179	4.6	3.6
World	2 199 768	2 333 229	2 177 856	2 326 597	2 276 980	1 770 851	100.0	100.0

Sparkling

	1988	1989	1990	1991	1992	1993	Value share, % 1991–93	Volume share, % 1991–93
Italy	14 229	12 337	13 764	25 455	20 814	21 807	33.6	54.1
Not specified	32 038	24 437	27 207	33 004	31 955	17 616	40.7	9.0
Germany**	3 861	3 638	2 569	17 703	4 046	9 142	15.2	30.5
Spain	4 968	5 978	9 190	6 700	2 744	3 747	6.5	4.8
Belgium	121	66	119	38	220	1 481	0.9	0.3
UK	2 099	66	60	278		897	0.6	0.3
USA	114	53	49	234	821	509	0.8	0.3
China						103	0.1	0.0
Austria	13	53	38	27	15	14	0.0	0.0
Australia		7			5	5	0.0	
Other	146	659	521	1 193	466	1 630	1.6	0.7
World	57 589	47 293	53 517	84 633	61 085	56 951	100.0	100.0

Still

	1988	1989	1990	1991	1992	1993	Value share, % 1991–93	Volume share, % 1991–93
Portugal	613 567	630 042	607 544	623 974	682 453	523 504	30.8	9.7
Italy	1 157 708	1 208 494	1 047 580	1 027 751	828 432	516 693	40.0	56.7
Spain	57 544	63 242	76 378	218 317	323 983	373 827	15.4	26.9
Not specified	93 570	115 847	124 790	114 805	99 148	43 917	4.3	0.6
Algeria	46 795	34 679	36 755	36 442	23 618	22 059	1.4	0.8
Morocco	20 462	20 213	21 379	25 787	22 627	19 214	1.1	0.8
Germany**	9 643	11 981	14 953	11 390	14 405	19 135	0.8	0.5
Bulgaria				4 832	15 081	11 805	0.5	0.5
USA	7 391	7 625	7 735	9 424	19 242	11 730	0.7	0.2
UK	1 965	3 757	4 052	2 849	4 461	11 431	0.3	0.0
Belgium	3 816	3 335	3 943	9 102	5 543	9 175	0.4	0.1
Greece	47 819	103 668	86 465	61 139	57 335	6 792	2.1	1.9
Macedonia						6 414	0.1	0.1
Australia		1 404	2 357	3 753	5 743	6 082	0.3	0.2
Argentina	967				2 759	4 466	0.1	0.1
Austria						3 560	0.1	0.1
Hungary	1 329	2 122	2 428			3 462	0.1	0.0
Lebanon	2 353	2 893	1 896	2 342	2 989	3 191	0.1	0.0
China					2 393	3 107	0.1	0.0
Other	21 289	20 595	26 593	26 081	25 130	21 312	1.2	0.7
World	2 086 219	2 229 897	2 064 847	2 177 987	2 135 343	1 620 876	100.0	100.0

* Including musts and vermouths   ** 1988–1990: FRG only   *Source: United Nations*

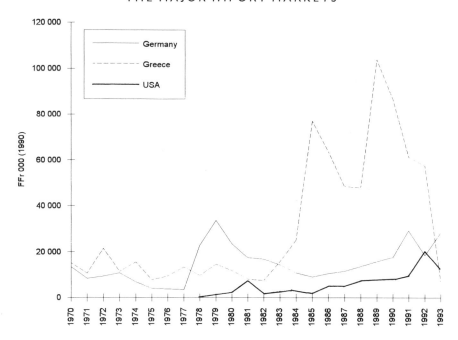

4.24 French imports from selected suppliers and challengers (CIF, 112.12) (source: United Nations)

in the 1970s and the 1980s. Overall trade fell just the same, given the scant attention paid by French consumers to foreign bottled wine.

Ports are but one outstanding exception. France is the world's largest foreign customer of genuine ports by far: in 1989, nearly 30 million litres were ordered, grabbing a 42.2% export market share that year.[182] Their losing favour towards the end of the 1980s was due to substantial price rises. The French have also expressed a marginal, but nevertheless growing interest in German and US still wines (see Table 4.11). The high price of most champagnes has brought many customers to pick an increasing number of Italian, German and Spanish sparkling wines off supermarket shelves, and Australian wines have made a shy debut lately, in the wake of the acquisition of Orlando by the French drinks giant Pernod-Ricard. Few supermarkets import directly however.[183] Casual observers walking through the aisles of an average Parisian food supermarket are struck by the truly bewildering choice of domestic wines – supermarkets have over a hundred

182 *Marketing Jahrbuch Wein*, 1991/92, p 168.

183 Gille, 1993, pp 201–2.

references on average[184] – whilst foreign offerings can only be noted for their virtual absence and poor display, usually placed on bottom shelves. This may have to do with France's insistence on showing a net trade surplus in wine which was achieved in terms of volume in the late 1970s.

The case of Italy supports the opposite view, namely that international wine trade is about dealing with a much differentiated product and the more open the markets, the greater the benefits to all parties involved. Italy is now importing nearly as much wine from France, in terms of value, as it is shipping there (US$180 million versus 200 million in 1990).

Italy

Individual demand for alcohol is comparatively low in Italy: the country ranked 14th worldwide in 1990 (37th for spirits and 39th for beer; it achieved 2nd place for wine, with 61.4 litres per head after France's 73.1 litres).[185] Alcohol consumption reached a plateau in the late 1960s and early 1970s. It began to contract afterwards and tumbled in the 1980s, both as a result of dwindling wine and spirits sales (even whisky, which kept scoring successes until recently, has seen import figures starting to dip since 1990). Only beer continues to increase, though there may be hints of saturation in this sector as well. Sales of low alcohol drinks and non-alcoholic beverages are experiencing a boom at present.

Per capita wine demand halved between 1970 and 1990, from 113.7 to 61.4 litres and fell further in 1991 to 56.8 litres (the rebounding of demand in 1982 can be largely ignored).[186] The downfall was worsened by the methanol affair in the mid-1980s and only little relief was brought by the moderate rate of growth in population, which increased by 7% between 1970 and 1990. The long term trend for domestic consumption keeps pointing down in the 1990s, albeit at a less dramatic rate (see Fig. 4.25).

184 In 1993, the average French supermarket had 119 wine references spread over 36 metres of shelves; 5% of them were foreign offerings (194 references over 94 metres and 6% foreign wines in hypermarkets). Neither data showed any particular trend over the past five years, except for the number of references per supermarket which increased by 6.5% on 1988. Source: Panel Secodip-consommation, in *Journée Vinicole*, 26–27 July 1994.

185 Source: *World Drink Trends*.

186 The alleged 24% increase should be considered as a break in the series, stemming from the sudden 'discovery', by Italian authorities, of huge, undeclared stocks.

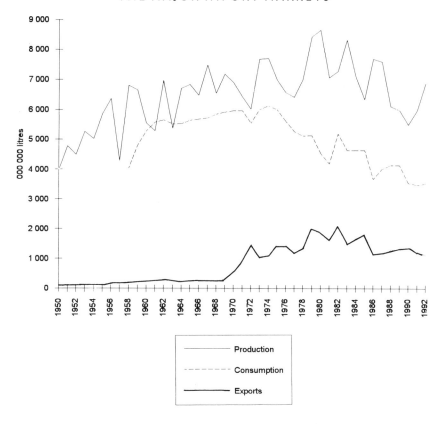

4.25 Italian wine consumption, production and imports (source: OIV).

Roughly 20% of Italians are either rare consumers of wine or abstainers; 16% like to drink it only occasionally whilst a majority of the population take it regularly, during meals. This largely explains the predominance of reds (62.1%) over whites (29.1%) and rosés (8.8%) within the still wine category. There are noticeable regional differences though, the most striking being that the centre of the country clearly favours white wines. Also, younger consumers have a clear bias for whites; older for reds.[187]

In Italy, as in France, it is the cheap end of the ordinary wines segment which has been most hit by the defection of consumers. These wines are typically sold in 1 litre bottles, or jugs (*fiasci*) of greater content. Considerable efforts have been deployed to rejuvenate this ailing segment of the market over the past decade: new brands, labels and containers have been designed in order to boost their lacking image. Italian legislature has been particularly unsuppor-

[187] CFCE (1992, Italy, p 23).

tive of their efforts: cans and other novel types of containers were only allowed in 1988. One litre cartons are doing well with inexpensive wine; they are cheaper and easier to handle than glass bottles, and are particularly suitable for palletisation weighing only a tenth of a typical glass bottle, thereby further reducing transportation costs.[188] Consumers can dispose of them effortlessly.

Appellation wines are increasingly in demand and also produced in greater number – DOC wines make up 10–12% of production (Venice, Tuscany and Piemonte are the major regions of production). These are white wines in the main and their demand is essentially occasional.[189]

Demand for sparkling wines has been burgeoning after the halving of the VAT rate in 1987, from 38% to 18% (yet still double that applicable to most still wines), and is now stagnating if not receding. Over 90% are domestic *spumante*, and a few come from Spain (*cava* essentially), but the vast majority of the shipments originate from France.[190] Champagne exports to Italy have been very successful until as recently as 1990; Italy was champagne's third or fourth largest outlet in the early 1980s, which then made up between a quarter and a third of all Italian imports by volume. Champagnes represented 9–10% of Italian imports by volume and over 70% by value in 1990 and 1991.[191]

The remainder of French exports to Italy are split almost equally, in terms of value, at both ends of the spectrum. Quality appellation wines usually come in bottles: red and white Bordeaux, white Burgundies and considerably cheaper AOCs are all popular, most successful by far are the Beaujolais Nouveau (the Italians were quick to emulate them by launching their own *novello* which at the time of writing has received a mixed reception). The great majority of the volumes are ordinary wines however, shipped in bulk and for a tenth of the price of AOCs on average.[192] These are mainly reds used for blending as well as the production of vinegar, plus white base wines used for the production of sparkling wines (as in Germany). Italy has also on occasion imported large quantities of ordinary bulk for blending with its own production, as in 1973, following two meagre harvests at home.

188 Ibid.

189 Ibid.

190 Ibid.

191 Author's estimates, based on CFCE data.

192 Calculations based on 1990 CFCE data.

Greece has provided Italy with large quantities of very cheap bulk since 1985, as well as musts. Portugal is shipping fairly regular quantities to Italy, which are almost equally split between ports and still wines, including reds for blending.[193] CIF prices of Greek and Portuguese wines have decreased steadily since the mid-1970s and this may be due in part to the weakness of the drachma and of the escudo versus the lira,[194] unlike France, whose currency has been appreciating against the lira for over twenty years. The evolution of the average CIF price for Italian imports (see Fig. 4.26) is reflecting changes occurring at both the cheap and top ends of the markets, as well as the particular evolution of prices of champagne. Orders of German and Spanish wines have picked up lately. Half the value of shipments from Spain are *cava*. Figures 4.27 and 4.28 show Italian imports from major suppliers.

Barring price sensitive demand for cheap bulk for blending or for further processing (which depends much on supply and demand conditions prevailing in the EU as a whole), the most worthwhile part

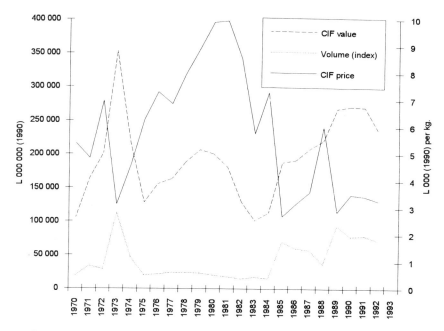

4.26 Italian imports (112.1) (source: United Nations).

193 *Marketing Jahrbuch Wein,* pp 168–70.

194 Such moves have not been fully compensated by MCAs, which were supposed to be phased out but were reintroduced between some of the trading partners (cf above).

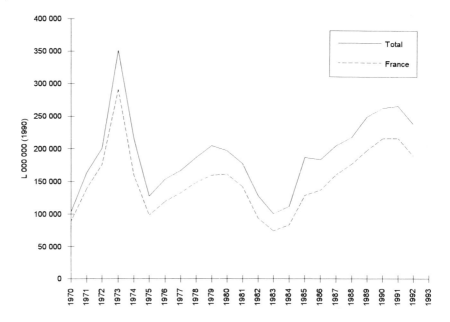

4.27 Italian imports from main supplier (CIF, 112.12) (source: United Nations).

of Italian imports is meant essentially for the urban élite of the North of the country, including Rome. This type of trade is clearly vulnerable to recession, and has risen sharply since the mid-1980s in line with economic recovery in Italy.

Foreign companies still have some way to go if they want to increase their rate of penetration of the Italian market, constrained as it is by the lagging development of the food retail sector – only an estimated 30% of all wines were retailed via supermarkets and wholesalers' in 1990. Many Italian households continue to rely on sales purchases directly from the wineries, who sell 50% of their wines in this way (bulk is often delivered to the customer in cask, who then bottles it himself).[195] The remaining 19% of the wines are sold through high-profile specialist shops known as *enoteca*. These, together with restaurants, remain the prime outlet for retailing foreign quality wines.[196]

Imports appear to be firmly in the hands of the wine and spirits trade based in the north, who are either producers or established importers of wines and spirits (and food) who then sell on to retailers.

195 Bottling equipment is commonly sold to particulars in Italy.

196 CFCE note, Milan, May 1992, based in part on *Il Corriere Vinicolo*, 2 March and 6 April 1992.

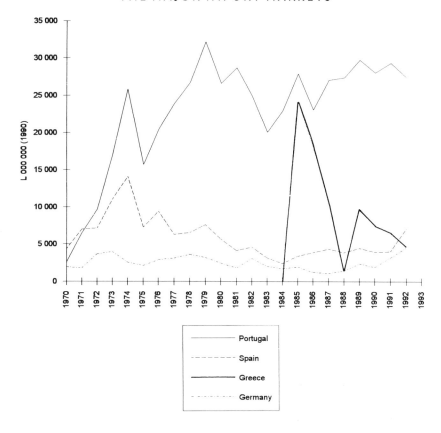

4.28 Italian imports from selected suppliers and challengers (CIF, 112.12) (source: United Nations).

Direct imports by supermarkets and specialist shops remain patchy and embryonic when compared with those that have emerged in the major Western European wine importing countries, with the exception perhaps of France. But so is the market, which many expected to remain impenetrable to foreign wines, simply in view of domestic surpluses, setbacks on export markets and rising competition. By joining the ranks of the major importers, Italy has demonstrated that it too is capable of generating 'two way' trade. Imports from France may still be hampered by unpleasant memories of violent disruptions of shipments the other way round (the 'wine wars'), but Italians are slowly opening to foreign wines and the country remains a potentially strong market: Italy's 57 million inhabitants made it the 16th largest country in the world in 1990, after the UK, and its GDP of just under US$1 trillion makes it the 6th biggest economy, slightly ahead of the UK.

Table 4.12 gives a detailed breakdown of Italian wine imports.

Table 4.12 Italian imports, 000 lira (1990)

All wines*	1988	1989	1990	1991	1992	Value share, % 1991–92	Volume share, % 1991–92
France	178 273 999	200 352 855	217 928 916	217 573 238	190 466 975	80.0	51.9
Portugal	27 381 124	29 756 428	28 015 663	29 345 454	27 353 298	11.1	14.5
Spain	4 517 988	5 228 663	4 642 169	5 035 335	7 622 906	2.5	7.3
Greece	1 380 660	24 425 700	9 566 265	7 596 621	4 715 744	2.4	17.3
Germany**	2 347 121	2 500 601	1 897 590	3 226 616	4 568 240	1.5	6.8
UK	492 044	1 322 476	1 397 590	2 642 708	668 174	0.6	0.3
USA	622 766	624 057	428 916	480 387	495 351	0.2	0.1
Belgium	262 913	539 488	380 723	383 844	445 816	0.2	0.1
Yugoslavia					431 506	0.1	0.2
Austria	157 160	208 505	344 578	195 411	391 878	0.1	0.2
Other	5 343 446	1 926 119	3 193 976	3 544 159	2 565 920	1.2	1.3
World	220 779 221	266 884 892	267 796 386	270 023 774	239 725 809	100.0	100.0

Sparkling

	1988	1989	1990	1991	1992	Value share, % 1991–92	Volume share, % 1991–92
France	158 966 797	173 320 113	186 249 398	186 130 600	167 394 613	95.7	89.1
Spain	2 360 340	2 924 902	2 846 988	3 027 715	3 209 876	1.7	7.4
Germany**	922 398	1 458 077	1 033 735	2 329 817	429 304	0.7	1.3
UK	7 344	223 086	549 398	2 347 264	372 064	0.7	0.8
Austria	32 313	29 162	22 892	30 242	90 264	0.0	0.1
Portugal	183 598	65 613	395 181	800 257	61 644	0.2	0.8
Yugoslavia					12 109	0.0	0.0
USA		1 458	91 566	4 653	4 403	0.0	0.0
Switzerland	1 469		24 096	6 979	2 202	0.0	
Greece							
Other	4 218 356	906 924	1 739 759	1 911 078	1 296 720	0.9	0.5
World	166 692 615	178 929 334	192 953 012	196 588 604	172 873 198	100.0	100.0

Still

	1988	1989	1990	1991	1992	Value share, % 1991–92	Volume share, % 1991–92
Portugal	27 197 525	29 690 815	27 620 482	28 545 198	27 291 655	42.2	17.5
France	17 737 070	24 384 874	29 174 699	29 314 049	21 264 881	38.2	47.6
Greece	1 380 660	9 783 694	7 454 217	6 497 432	4 715 744	8.5	19.0
Germany**	511 138	917 130	863 855	850 273	4 109 214	3.7	8.0
Spain	1 499 631	1 542 645	1 083 133	994 505	3 891 260	3.7	6.0
USA	622 766	622 599	337 349	475 734	490 948	0.7	0.1
Yugoslavia					324 730	0.2	0.3
UK	464 137	1 032 318	745 783	271 017	296 110	0.4	0.2
Croatia					280 699	0.2	0.3
Austria	123 378	167 679	321 687	148 885	211 350	0.3	0.1
Slovenia					133 194	0.1	0.1
Switzerland	177 723	134 143	112 048	60 485	125 489	0.1	0.1
Chile	49 939	17 497	37 349	30 242	123 287	0.1	0.0
Belgium	76 377	530 740	155 422	93 053	119 985	0.2	0.1
Lebanon				29 079	74 853	0.1	0.0
Not specified			30 120		52 837	0.0	0.0
Ireland					46 233	0.0	0.0
Hungary	7 344	55 407	77 108	24 426	44 031	0.1	0.0
Israel	23 501	16 039		27 916	37 427	0.0	0.0
Other	753 488	752 368	1 096 386	1 132 921	211 350	1.0	0.7
World	50 624 675	69 647 947	69 109 639	68 495 214	63 845 278	100.0	100.0

* Including musts and vermouths   ** 1988–1990: FRG only   *Source: United Nations*

United Kingdom

The UK was the world's largest importer in terms of value in 1990: its £993.3 million (US$ 1.77 billion) put it ahead of West Germany (US$ 1.5 billion) even though it trailed behind the Germans by some 25% in terms of volume. Of the 748 million litres Britain imported that year, some 6.6% were vermouths and a small but fast rising quantity of musts (0.4%). The remaining 93% were still and sparkling wines.

Musts are something of a novelty, rising from nearly scratch to 2, 3 and 6 million litres in 1989, 1990 and 1991 respectively; they come mainly from Italy and are primarily used for the production of 'British wines', i.e. home-made wines which are all too often confused with real 'English wines' produced from grapes grown in England and Wales. Vermouths were quite fashionable in the 1970s and imports peaked at 76.4 million litres in 1979, but then fell back to around 50 million litres, a level at which they stabilised during the 1980s, though shipments have declined slightly recently, standing at 45 million litres in 1991.[197]

Sparkling wines performed well, increasing by 275% in volume between 1970 and 1990. Half of this was champagne, but British customers are notoriously quick to switch over to substitutes, e.g. *spumante, Sekt* or *cava* – whenever recession bites and/or when champagne prices 'hit the roof', as they did in 1973/74, in the early 1980s and in 1990.[198] Bubbly shipments from Australia and the USA have done well in the 1990s (see Table 4.13).

The best performers by far though, were still wines with an alcoholic strength of less than 13%. Shipments of whites did particularly well in this category, soaring more than sixfold between 1970 and 1990, from 51 to 337 million litres. They were also characterised by a rapid decline of bulk trade, from 90% to less than 50% of traded volumes during the first half of the 1970s; by 1980, their share had dipped under 40% and only amounted to 20% in 1990.[199] Bottled imports of reds and rosés increased nearly 20 times over the same 20 year period, from 7 to 138 million bottles. Reds and rosés have been gaining ground slowly but steadily since 1984, when they captured only 28.3% of the sales of still wines under 13%; their share by 1991 had increased to 32.5%.[200]

---

197 Based on C&E data.

198 Ibid.

199 Ibid.

200 *Drinks File,* 1991.

Table 4.13 British imports, 000 £ (1990)

All wines*	1988	1989	1990	1991	1992	1993	Value share, % 1991–93	Volume share, % 1991–93
France	482 444	501 036	514 468	412 411	420 573	351 054	45.8	32.9
Italy	125 600	130 961	147 927	138 072	128 590	104 149	14.4	19.9
Germany**	135 234	133 927	130 658	121 767	116 840	83 566	12.5	19.0
Spain	81 723	65 137	82 709	78 796	82 045	70 955	9.0	8.9
Australia	16 305	16 732	21 042	32 967	44 400	59 292	5.3	4.2
Portugal	43 779	34 622	38 144	34 009	33 835	30 362	3.8	2.4
USA	8 963	11 695	12 835	15 556	22 773	25 621	2.5	2.5
Bulgaria	9 929	9 067	11 701	12 532	12 583	16 983	1.6	3.2
New Zealand	2 745	2 737	4 501	5 698	9 797	10 679	1.0	0.7
S Africa	3 389	2 162	2 773	4 019	6 891	8 464	0.8	1.0
Other	21 671	25 054	26 571	28 386	30 282	29 008	3.4	5.4
World	931 781	933 129	993 330	884 212	908 609	790 133	100.0	100.0
Sparkling								
France	156 023	175 496	174 994	114 378	108 881	94 742	79.1	51.8
Italy	24 896	16 533	14 597	12 589	10 069	8 197	7.7	21.2
Spain	3 088	3 301	4 724	4 685	4 798	5 119	3.6	9.1
Australia	813	1 315	2 295	3 781	3 975	5 013	3.2	6.1
USA	502	369	388	1 416	2 653	3 032	1.8	2.0
Netherlands	1 829	766	304	300	225	2 846	0.8	1.5
Germany**	3 390	3 217	4 243	3 349	3 216	2 627	2.3	5.9
New Zealand			241	356	1 193	1 317	0.7	1.0
S Africa	98	60	99	101	163	183	0.1	0.2
Belgium	190	144	1 505	579	109	137	0.2	0.5
Other	632	952	819	622	484	1 048	0.5	0.7
World	191 460	202 151	204 208	142 156	135 766	124 261	100.0	100.0
Still								
France	322 315	322 095	336 032	295 256	308 762	253 783	41.3	33.9
Germany**	131 717	130 179	125 849	117 974	112 995	80 137	15.0	21.1
Italy	76 637	93 796	109 065	98 205	92 909	72 597	12.7	15.2
Spain	75 855	59 056	75 454	71 666	76 476	65 594	10.3	9.2
Australia	15 490	15 416	18 748	29 176	40 395	54 268	6.0	4.4
Portugal	43 700	34 550	38 118	33 982	33 753	30 291	4.7	2.7
Bulgaria	9 910	9 041	11 701	12 532	12 583	16 983	2.0	3.6
USA	8 371	11 325	12 443	13 805	16 994	15 609	2.2	2.3
New Zealand	2 745	2 737	4 259	5 342	8 604	9 362	1.1	0.7
S Africa	3 289	2 101	2 673	3 915	6 728	8 280	0.9	1.1
Hungary	1 295	1 768	2 857	3 484	4 934	5 758	0.7	1.0
Chile	950	2 387	2 443	4 144	5 617	5 731	0.7	0.8
Macedonia						2 090	0.1	0.3
Cyprus	2 876	2 115	1 945	2 175	2 053	1 569	0.3	0.5
Romania			715	1 171	1 264	1 488	0.2	0.4
Netherlands	2 818	2 938	2 290	3 292	3 268	1 319	0.4	0.8
Switzerland	534	1 090	1 026		1 177	1 004	0.1	0.1
Argentina		1 059				815	0.0	0.0
Greece	777	837	761	806	958	678	0.1	0.1
Other	9 775	9 774	11 411	11 274	9 312	3 863	1.2	1.7
World	709 053	702 265	757 789	708 199	738 782	631 217	100.0	100.0

* Including musts and vermouths   ** 1988–1990: FRG only   *Source: United Nations*

Back in 1970, Britain used to drink almost as much fortified wine (alcohol in excess of 13%) than other wines – 49 versus 51 million litres respectively. Shipments of fortified wines first increased to around 80 million litres in the late 1970s, then lost considerable ground over the 1980s, down to a mere 34 million litres in 1990 (29% down on 1970). Imports are increasingly done in bottles here as well: the share of bulk dropped from 99% in 1970 to 40% in 1990.[201]

The growing enthusiasm of the British people for wine was tempered twice by economic recession, following the oil crises of 1973 and 1979. It was much aided by decreasing real prices however, at import as well as retail levels (see Fig. 4.29). The fall in value of imports over the early 1990s was due to tumbling CIF prices. The UK joined the EU (along with Ireland and Denmark) after wine had become a freely tradeable good, as with all other agricultural commodities. This meant that UK tariffs on wine had to be scrapped on shipments from France, Germany and Italy, whilst the EU's protective trade regime – the so-called 'Common Customs Tariff' – would be adopted with respect to third countries, e.g. Australia and South Africa lost their preferential treatment at that time.[202] Wine from Greece, who joined the EU in 1981, and later from Portugal and Spain who both became members in 1986, would also be awarded EU preference. Additional reductions in wine prices occurred as the combined result of the UK's attempt at taming rising alcohol consumption by reducing duty rates on wine in relation to those for spirits and for beer, *and* EU fiscal harmonisation calling on the three new beer-producing members to stop discriminating against wine. Finally, the emergence of supermarkets as the most crucial retailing channel for wine, partly triggered by a rise in entertainment activities in people's homes and a corresponding drop in frequentation of pubs and clubs, resulted in intensified competition amongst distributors and the restructuring of many specialist shops. This helped to pass price reductions on to customers. (Even pubs started to serve hot meals in their effort to attract their deserting clientele back to the premises, thereby providing wine with a rare opportunity to make inroads in this traditionally male and beer-dominated environment.) The competitiveness of East European and New World producers has also ensured that British customers would be provided with the best value for money possible, all along the price points scale and in spite of EU preference.

201 Based on C&E data.

202 GATT, 1966.

4.29 British imports (112.1) (source: United Nations).

Trade policy

EU preference is mostly felt at the bulk end of the market. There, up until 1995, non-EU shipments faced not just tariffs but also a steep minimum price, calculated on the basis of the EU guide price for ordinary wine shipped in bulk. The best way to deal with this was to import bottled wine, albeit cheap ones, for the added value is such that the resulting CIF price was almost guaranteed to pass the hurdle. The protective trade regime of the EU has merely accelerated the shift to bottled imports. It urged retailers to buy the wines directly in the supplying country (still using a UK-based agent, as is standard business practice in Britain) and helped them meet customers' needs by the same token, who are increasingly asking for the wine to be bottled in the country of export, if not in the region of production itself, as an additional guarantee of authenticity of the wines they purchase.

The changes in trade policy imposed by joining the EU modified the set of suppliers to the British market, as bulk trade remained important in the 1970s. The biggest loser was undoubtedly Spain, which, in addition to being left out of the EU, was confronted with a declining market in fortified wines (sherries), little progress in the quality of its other offerings and lack of consistency in its pricing

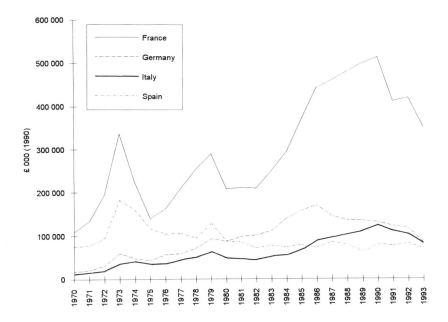

4.30 British imports from main suppliers (CIF, 112.12) (source: United Nations).

policy. Spain lost substantially in market share, from 37% in volume in 1970 (29% in value) to 25% (18%) in 1980 and 8% (8%) in 1990, see Fig. 4.30. Portugal was faced with a similar, though not as drastic a cut in market share, from 7% in volume (8% in value) in 1970, to 4% (6%) in 1980, and 2% (4%) in 1990, see Fig. 4.31. Australia used to be a minor but traditional supplier to the UK (1% in 1970), but lost its preferential trading status upon UK accession to the EU, at a time when its wine sector was on its knees, undergoing a profound transformation anyway. The comeback of the late 1980s featured a much rejuvenated industry, producing highest quality wine on most efficient terms, and eager to export. Australia broke through on its own merits and notched up a 2% market share in 1990. Other suppliers, mainly Bulgaria and Hungary, also lost in market share, from 19% of volume (9% of value) in 1970 to 6–7% (4%) in 1980 and 1990.

The greatest beneficiary of the reshuffle of the suppliers to the UK was France, which managed to increase its share from 26% in volume (42% in value) in 1970 to 38% (53%) in 1990, followed by West Germany, which boosted its slice of the growing British cake from 5% in volume (7% in value) to 22% (14%) over the same period. Italy's market share soared from 4% in volume (5% in value) in 1970 to 18% (14%) in 1990.

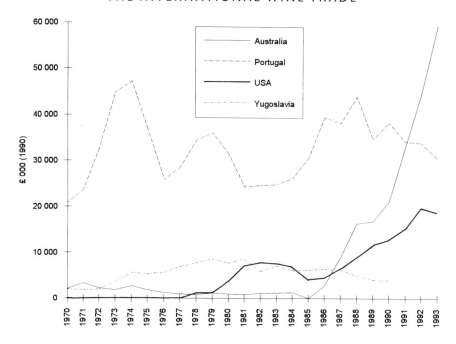

4.31 British imports from selected suppliers and challengers (CIF, 112.12) (source: United Nations).

Market and import trends

It should be noted that until the mid-1970s, the pound remained weak against the currencies of its major wine suppliers except Italy. The subsequent strengthening of the British currency (except against the Deutschmark) helped compress wine prices until the mid-1980s, when the pound came under strong pressure again.

France has benefited most from the development of the UK wine market over the 1970s and 1980s. The bubbles boom translated into soaring champagne sales until recently, and its exports of appellation and ordinary wines have progressed more or less steadily, and usually ahead of the rest of the British market. The current signs of maturation mean increasing demand for reds, not so much at the top end which is dominated by Bordeaux's classics (shipments date back to the sixteenth century when the town was in British hands) than in the middle price range where little known appellations have to deliver a fierce battle against Spanish and Chilean reds as well as against cheap varietals from Eastern Europe. Some French wines have seen their fortunes decline recently, as British buyers began to resist price hikes in some categories, in a similar situation to that of the mid-1970s.

Quality wines amounted to just over half (56%) of French shipments to the UK in terms of volume in 1990, but provided more than 83.4% of the receipts, and conversely for exports of ordinary wines, which made up 44% of the French volume sent to the UK but only contributed to 16.6% in terms of revenue. Somewhat characteristically, bulk shipments amount to less than 10% of quality wines and to a third of ordinary wines. Bordeaux outsold Burgundies and Beaujolais combined by two to one. These were followed by Muscadet and Alsatian whites. Of the ordinary wines, nearly 70% were *vins de table* (mostly whites); red and white *vins de pays* (costing 15% more on average) did equally well, reaping together the remaining 30% of the market.[203] All categories were heading down in 1990 – France actually performed worse than average in that year – except for Alsatian whites, rosés from Provence and *vins de pays*, Beaujolais, Burgundies and Muscadet were all sharply down, after prices were pushed up 'to levels which consumers could neither understand nor tolerate'.[204] UK (and other) consumers have little understanding for large price rises, and tend to feel like they are being cheated.

German exports took off in the late 1970s, during the 'white wine boom'. Its sweet white wines did particularly well with women and the exponential shape taken by its shipments to the UK were only cut by the diethylene glycol affair in 1985. German exporters reacted to the decline in sales by slashing prices in 1987, in spite of the rising Deutschmark. The move was widely perceived as a marketing error though: volumes kept steady until 1990, but at the cost of a fast deteriorating image; values plunged accordingly. German success had been achieved by focusing on a few selected white wines: 50% are Liebfraumilch, the rest Moselle and Hock; and by using essentially one designation of quality, i.e. that prevailing at EU level (quality wines called QbA in Germany).[205] The British public felt comfortable with the simplicity of German denominations and responded accordingly: of all wine types Liebfraumilch scored the highest sales in UK off-licences in 1991/92 with a market share of 16%, just ahead of Italian Lambrusco with 11.5%. French *vin de table* was next with 6.7%, followed by *vin de pays* with 6.5% and, again, German Hock with 4.3%.[206] In spite of all the recent difficulties, Germany remains the

203 Calculations based on French export data. Source: French *douanes*, as in CFCE (1992, UK, pp 25–8).

204 CFCE, 1990, p 109.

205 Ibid, p 37.

206 December 1991–January 1992, ranked by volume. Source: market research statistics in NTC's *Drink Pocket Book*, 1993, p 90.

UK's second largest supplier – and the UK Germany's major export market.

Italy's exports to the British market grew slowly but steadily until 1991. Overall sales progressed seemingly unabated by the methanol scandal, but *spumante* (originating mostly from Piemonte, where the affair took place) has been losing ground steadily since then, much to the benefit of Spanish and Australian exporters of sparkling wine, nearly all *cava* in the case of Spain. Italian wines are generally considered to be good value for money, although their image is considered fairly neutral. CIF prices fell almost uninterrupted until the mid-1980s and remain relatively low on average. Chianti, Soave and Lambrusco have all achieved recognition on the UK market. Italy is tantalisingly close to taking Germany's second place in terms of value.

Spain lost on nearly all accounts in spite of some great technical achievements – Riojas have become serious competitors to French red AOCs. Spain's problems were exacerbated by bad image – 'the least expensive and drinkable wines around'[207] – reinforced by a lack of a pricing policy which only added to consumer confusion about the quality of Spanish wines. Pricing and a serious image problem were also at the root of the downfall of the heavily concentrated sherry sector, i.e. Harvey of Bristol, Croft and Gonzales Byass with estimated brand shares of 31, 21 and 12% respectively in terms of volume in 1991.[208] An ageing image caused sherries to lose considerable ground in the 1980s. Beginning in 1987, Spain stepped up its efforts to shrug off the mediocre image of its wines by spending heavily on generic advertising. This and the roaring publicity surrounding a chain of international events in the fields of culture, commerce and sports organised in Spain recently, such as the Barcelona Olympics, contributed to a turnaround in Spanish exports to the UK in the early 1990s. Spain firmly intends to remain a major supplier to the British market, as the UK is the top destination for its wines in value (second in volume to Germany).

More intense competition is imminent, however. The combined presence of all other exporters to the British market is anything but marginal, being nearly as big as either the German or Italian presence in terms of volume.

Portugal stands apart, because of the relative steadiness of its exports in terms of volume and their relatively high average price. This is due to the high proportion of ports and Madeiras (57% in

207 CFCE, 1990, p 37.

208 Sherry survey by Harvey, in *Drinks File*, 1991.

volume and 77% in value in 1989) as well as their ability to defy gravity in an otherwise dwindling market, where sherry has suffered so badly. The rise in value of shipments was due in part to the rise of the escudo against the pound. The Portuguese currency losing 75% of its value between the mid-1970s and mid-1980s may well have played a hand in maintaining sales on average. The UK is a critical market for Portugal, being its third most valuable market for port (after France and Belgium-Luxembourg), second for Madeira (after France) and third again for its remaining wines (after Angola and the US).[209]

The success of Yugoslavian wines was undoubtedly due to price. Shipments increased steadily in volume until the late 1980s when they started to tumble. The fall in UK sales coincides with cutbacks in domestic production, weakening demand both at home and on the export markets in general.

Eastern European countries – Hungry, Romania, Bulgaria plus Cyprus – have been another casualty of EU preference. Cypriot exports rose from 18.5 to 30 million litres between 1970 and 1974, only to slide back steadily, year after year to a bare 4 million litres in 1989. Cyprus' place has been largely taken by East European wines. Hungary's strong focus on promotion led to some success in the late 1980s – shipments rose from 1.6 to 4.4 million litres between 1988 and 1990 alone – whilst Romania would still need to upgrade its wine industry if it is to claim similar results in the future.[210] Bulgaria's cheap varietal wines, particularly reds, have turned the country into one of the fastest growing exporters to the UK: shipments more than doubled between 1987 and 1990, from 9 to some 20 million litres.

Chile scored similar successes, albeit on a much smaller scale, with some outstanding and reasonably priced red varietals. Like South Africa, Chile will soon benefit from increasingly good quality and, more importantly, from its recent implementation of democratic principles.

Californian wines did well in the early 1980s but lost ground a few years later when prices rose, chiefly as the result of the pound coming under pressure against the dollar; but British buyers resumed their purchases of US wines when prices fell back again in 1990. California is poised to build on this success, admittedly with heavy promotional efforts: Gallo is the biggest advertiser in the UK market, with expenditure of nearly £3 million in 1990 and £2.6 million in 1991, well ahead of the sums spent promoting Asti Spumante (£1.5

209 Source: ICEP, IVV Lisbon, in *Marketing Jahrbuch Wein 1991/92*, p 171–2.

210 *MIVS*, July/August 1991, p 10; *Drinks File*, 1991.

million in 1990 and £1.4 million in 1991) and Piat d'Or (£2.2 million and £1.3 million).[211]

Australia turned out to be the real success story in the British market. It used to ship some 4–6 million litres to Britain back in the 1960s but saw exports dwindle to a mere 10th in the second half of the 1970s, and remain there for a decade, leaving New Zealand, Canada, Japan, the US and Sweden to become Australia's biggest export markets for years. Australia started its forceful comeback in 1985 and, within five years, the UK was back as the country's principal destination, with 12.5 million litres in the 1990/91 fiscal year, and 14 million in 1991/92.[212] Virtually gone are Australian fortified wines; exports now consist largely of still table wines, both whites and reds, as well as some sparkling nectars.

Import and distribution channels

The 'off-licence' sector retailed an estimated 70% of the wines sold in Britain in 1990. The licensed (Horeca) trade catered for the remaining 30% (Table 4.14). Hotels, restaurants and clubs accounted for an estimated half of the sales in the 'off' sector, pubs for a third (these are still largely controlled by UK brewers and the Mergers and Monopolies Commission requested that they divest heavily). Clubs and wine bars, largely responsible for the wine fad in the 1980s, make up the rest.

Much of the buoyancy of the wine market was spurred by the 'off' trade however, and in particular the food supermarkets. All of the largest food retailers – Tesco, Asda, Sainsbury and Argyll (who own Safeway and Presto) – have wine departments. Some are extremely (and justly) proud of them: Marks and Spencer, Safeway and Sainsbury sell most of their wines under their own or an exclusive label and have a longstanding, trusting clientele. An estimated 35% of supermarkets' turnover on wine was done under their own labels in 1990.[213] All major supermarkets have their own wine staff which carry out the selection of all the wines marketed in the UK. They may still use the services of an agent as is business practice in Britain, but some will go as far as inspecting the wineries abroad before signing any contract (usually 'ex-cellar', or FOB winery, in the producer's own currency).

---

211 Source: Register-MEAL Ltd, in NTC's *Drink Pocket Book*, 1993, p 109.

212 Source: AWBC, in Winemaker's Federation of Australia Inc's annual statistical reports.

213 CFCE (1990, UK, p 68).

Table 4.14 The distribution of wine in the UK

		Estimated market share 1990, by volume (%)
Off-licence trade		70
Grocers		
Multiples and Co-ops	30	
Independents	5	
Specialists		
Multiples	18	
Independents	13	
Mail order clubs	1	
Other (including cash & carries)	3	
On-licence trade		30
Hotels, restaurants and clubs	15	
Pubs	10	
Wine bars	5	

Source: Food and Wine from France, in CFCE (1990, p.64)

Most will determine the design and wording of their own corporate labels.

Independent specialist wine and liquor shops are often regional and many of them have had to join efforts in order to survive in the face of concentration. With the exception of Oddbins, controlled by Seagram, all of the major chainstores are in the hands of brewers: Victoria Wines belongs to Allied Lyons, Augustus Barnet to Bass and Thresher to Whitbread, who also acquired Peter Dominic and Bottoms Up from IDV.

Nearly all trade with the Continent is done by road. Overseas wines are also mainly shipped in bottles, in containers, and the larger volumes are sent directly to the retailer. Some exporters have set up bonded duty free warehouses, which allow them to deliver within 10 days, or even ship further to the rest of the EU.

The recent disposal of Grant of St James, the most prominent importer of bulk, followed a shift in priorities for Allied Lyons, from wholesale to retail sale[214] (it was acquired by Matthew Clark, a wines and mineral water company who had taken control of a leading drinks wholesaler, Freetraders, a few months earlier). It is also a sign of the diminishing importance of bulk trade between the UK and the rest of the world. Bulk imports have been wines 'ready for bottling'; all

214 According to Hiram Walker's director (*MIVS*, November and October 1993 issues); *The Financial Times*, June 9, 1993.

winemaking, assembling and blending operations are traditionally carried out in the producing country as importers do not want this responsibility. This is unlike coolers which are mixed in the UK, like many other 'tropical' cocktails.[215] Imports of light wines (of less than 5.5% alcohol) remain marginal by all accounts. Italians dominate in this sector with their Lambrusco 'light'.[216]

Denmark

Basically the same environment as that of Germany prevails in Denmark in as far as individual alcohol consumption is concerned. Since the Danish population has remained virtually unchanged over the 1970s and 1980s at just over 5 million inhabitants (an increase of 4% between 1970 and 1990), per capita and total consumption figures go hand in hand. Denmark ranked 10th worldwide in 1990, but most of it is beer (4th after Germany and Czechoslovakia, with 12.6 litres) and a comparatively low consumption of spirits (30th with 1.3 lpa). Total alcohol consumption was fairly stable over the 1980s, with beer increasing slowly then remaining stagnant since the mid-1980s, spirits declining since their mid-1970s peak, and rising demand for wine. In Denmark there was a transfer of consumption from high proof to lower alcoholic drinks like everywhere else in Western Europe.[217]

Wine demand has risen 6–7 times between 1960 and 1991, from 3.33 to 22 litres per head. The rise has been supported by falling CIF prices (in real terms) on average, due to the firming of the krone against the currencies of all its suppliers except Germany, and to the fact that Danish importers persist in dealing with large quantities of bulk – 53.7% of all still wine shipments in 1990.[218] Dutch importers and customers are known for seeking relatively cheap wines on the international market, wine imports may have proved nearly recession-proof in terms of volume, but not in value, see Fig. 4.32.[219]

The market is somewhat mature, sitting between the Netherlands and Belgium: reds dominated in the early 1990s, with a 58.5% market

215 *The Financial Times.*

216 CFCE (1990, UK, p 46).

217 Source: *World Drink Trends.*

218 *MIVS,* July/August 1992, p 49.

219 *MIVS,* October 1990, p 41; July/August 1991, p 12; June 1992, p 3.

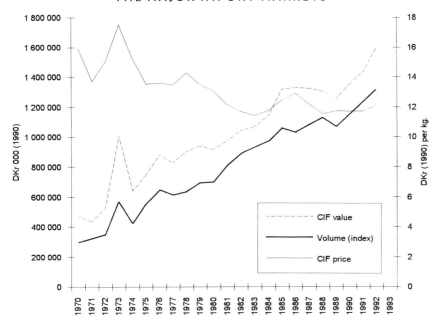

4.32 Danish imports (112.1) (source: United Nations).

share while whites made 38.4% and rosés 3.1%.[220] Interestingly, young Danes prefer whites however. As anywhere else in Western Europe, the biggest changes have come from the rapid progression of supermarkets in the retailing of wines, with price and taste the most critical factors. Country of origin and brand name seem to play more of a secondary role, except when wine is bought for a special occasion.[221] Sparkling wines only account for roughly 1% of consumption in terms of volume and less than 4% in value. Sparkling Lambrusco is doing well because of its moderate price.[222]

Market and import trends

France stormed the Danish market after it gained EU membership in 1973, and took the lion's share as they did in the Netherlands. Its

220 CFCE, undated. Market shares for 1990: reds 57.7%, whites 39.3% and rosés 3%, (*MIVS*, April 1992, p 8).

221 CFCE (1992, Denmark, p 56).

222 July/August 1991, p 50.

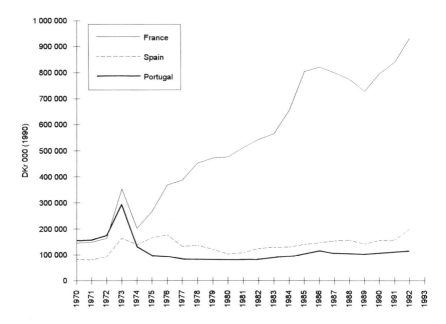

4.33 Danish imports from main suppliers (CIF, 112.12) (source: United Nations).

market share was running at 63% in volume and 62% in value in 1990, see Table 4.15 and Fig. 4.33. French wines clearly dominate at the top end of the market, but their strong presence in the middle and lower segments could come under threat however.

Spain and Portugal took a beating when Denmark joined the EU: their market share dropped significantly in terms of volume, from 20% and 53% respectively, in 1970, to 10% and 7% in 1990. The Iberian countries' situation improved again when they became EU members. Spanish wines, particularly Riojas, are highly considered by the Danes, in contrast to their poor image in the UK.

Italian wines made little progress in Denmark except in the wake of EU membership in the early 1980s. They suffered after the methanol scandal but recovered in the late 1980s, following the general upgrading of Italian exports, see Fig. 4.34.

German wines gained quickly in popularity in the mid-1970s but grew only slowly later in the decade; the price drop of 1983 stimulated growth again. The diethylene gylcol affair ruined most of these efforts and although volumes kept steady, values plunged throughout the 1980s. The 1990s appear to signal a turnaround though, as the profile of German wine has been raised again and sales have picked up.

Table 4.15 Danish imports, 000 DKr (1990)

All wines*	1988	1989	1990	1991	1992	Value share, % 1991–92	Volume share % 1991–92
France	779 710	733 739	802 588	846 882	939 638	59.0	57.6
Spain	157 269	141 649	155 195	157 309	199 133	11.8	10.2
Italy	106 476	121 153	130 226	132 163	134 751	8.8	9.2
Portugal	104 278	102 533	107 000	110 989	117 420	7.5	6.1
Germany**	94 885	70 731	70 397	77 158	84 897	5.4	7.4
Chile	4 172	12 926	17 784	24 117	28 189	1.7	2.3
USA	15 531	18 253	15 966	23 787	28 062	1.7	2.3
S Africa					15 227	0.5	0.5
Greece	6 732	9 430	13 273	13 592	12 234	0.9	0.9
Yugoslavia					6 524	0.2	0.2
Other	46 709	43 033	40 048	47 561	28 952	2.5	3.3
World	1 315 761	1 253 447	1 352 477	1 433 558	1 595 027	100.0	100.0
Sparkling							
France	39 717	40 947	44 996	35 215	38 718	64.0	31.3
Spain	4 584	9 303	9 391	8 929	15 661	21.3	31.3
Germany**	4 685	3 316	2 514	2 494	4 311	5.9	14.1
Italy	2 090	1 065	2 003	4 446	2 699	6.2	17.8
Portugal	333	398	203	480	248	0.6	1.0
Romania	80	60	31	75	156	0.2	0.5
USA	94	75	37	87	87	0.2	0.1
Belgium	152	195	6	50	46	0.1	0.2
S Africa					29	0.0	0.1
Chile	51				17	0.0	0.0
Other	311	390	333	648	1 179	1.6	3.5
World	52 095	55 749	59 514	52 424	63 151	100.0	100.0
Still							
France	733 970	686 970	750 678	803 792	894 002	60.7	60.4
Spain	152 382	132 339	145 804	148 381	183 449	11.9	10.4
Portugal	103 945	102 135	106 797	110 509	117 172	8.1	6.5
Germany**	90 091	67 250	67 673	74 440	80 066	5.5	7.6
Italy	59 000	76 200	86 825	83 231	76 668	5.7	5.1
Chile	4 121	12 926	17 784	24 117	28 172	1.9	2.5
USA	15 437	18 178	15 929	23 699	27 975	1.8	2.4
S Africa					15 198	0.5	0.5
Greece	6 732	9 430	13 249	13 405	12 216	0.9	0.9
Yugoslavia					6 524	0.2	0.2
Australia	18 192	13 481	10 014	14 353	6 357	0.7	1.0
Bulgaria	3 630	1 673	2 077	8 274	5 611	0.5	0.7
Argentina	3 348	6 362	6 667	5 842	4 242	0.4	0.7
Romania	636	968	1 214	1 496	1 780	0.1	0.1
Hungary	2 661	600	1 276	1 490	1 514	0.1	0.2
Belgium	991	615	906	929	1 450	0.1	0.1
Cyprus	730	1 350	1 066	954	861	0.1	0.1
New Zealand					728	0.0	0.0
UK					555	0.0	0.0
Other	14 931	12 926	13 045	12 595	3 762	0.6	0.6
World	1 210 796	1 143 405	1 241 003	1 327 507	1 468 303	100.0	100.0

* Including musts and vermouths   ** 1988–1990: FRG only   *Source: United Nations*

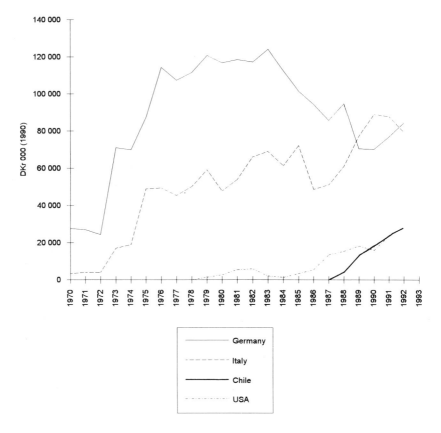

4.34 Danish imports from selected suppliers and challengers (CIF, 112.12) (source: United Nations)

Denmark now offers a new potential outlet for dry, high quality whites.[223]

Much of the threat in the lower and middle segments comes from New World wines, which have not just become cheaper but also better. Also noteworthy is the presence of Argentinian wines along with those from Chile, Australia and the US though Argentine wines suffered a setback in 1991 and 1992.

Trade policy

EU membership had significant effects, not least of which was the abolition of the state monopoly on the manufacturing and import of spirits. Wine trade used to be subject to quantitative restrictions, i.e.

223 According to the Danish wine and spirits association, in *MIVS*, June 1992, p 4.

import quotas, negotiated on a bilateral basis with supplying countries. They were also subject to apparently the heftiest import duties in Western Europe, amounting to some 76% of the CIF price in the mid-1960s.[224] Portugal and Spain could win back some lost market share, albeit much reduced and long overdue.

Import and distribution channels

Denmark is still very much a closed market.[225] Few international wine operators have managed to penetrate it so far, and this is not for lack of trying (IDV and Seagram, both of which deal mainly with spirits, are the exceptions). The wine importing and retailing activities remaining largely in the hands of Dutch firms however did not make this sector immune from strong competitive pressures, resulting in both concentration and shortening of the marketing channels, as in the rest of Western Europe.

As elsewhere in Northern Europe, the major thrust came from the increasing involvement of supermarkets in the distribution of wine – each major chain has its own wine importing firm, e.g. Dansk Supermarket Vin and Svenborg Vinkompagni, while other, smaller retailers have responded by centralising their purchases and setting up their own importing firms. Specialist shop chains each have their own importer as well, e.g. Skjolb-Burne and United Wine Import. These moves have brought about considerable changes in the import and distribution network, notably concentration and shortening of the channels as mentioned above.[226]

Many a traditional importer managed to survive by specialising on certain wines and/or concentrating on a specific type of clientele, e.g. the catering sector. Also noteworthy is the participation, in the import and distribution of wines, by brewers, e.g. Carlsberg/Tuborg who control Vingaarden, or spirits producers, e.g. Erik Andersen who set up Ankervin.[227] Unlike in the spirits business, where brands and exclusive import and distribution contracts are paramount, this practice is far less widespread, perhaps because of the importance

---

224 The combined effect of import *and* domestic duties was 230%, GATT, 1966, pp 14, 33.

225 *MIVS*, July/August 1991, p 12.

226 CFCE (1992, Denmark, p 65–8).

227 Ibid.

of bulk imports and the fact that large quantities of (especially ordinary) wine are marketed under the importer's own label.[228]

Contracts are usually made 'ex-winery' in the producer's own currency, and Danish importers prefer to make transport arrangements themselves.[229]

A surtax was introduced on bottles in an attempt to encourage their reutilisation, but this has not become universal practice yet. It has however prompted some exporters to ship reusable bottles.[230] Excise duties amounting to over 70%[231] of the CIF price of an ordinary wine produced in the EU were reduced in July 1991, in anticipation of the EU's 1992 single market. This spurred demand for wine, which was showing some signs of fatigue in that year but surged in the second half of 1991.[232] A significant part of the imported volumes – perhaps as much as a quarter – are 're-exported' to the flourishing duty-free sector (cruise ships in particular).[233]

Excise duties on wine brought DKr 1.448 billion (US$72.4 billion) in 1990.[234] This type of tax varies considerably from one country to the next and remains, with VAT, the principal barrier to growth in EU internal wine trade. The EU had set enormous hopes on resolving its wine production surplus with the 1973 enlargement of the Community, to include its three 'northern' neighbours: the UK, Ireland and Denmark. (Ireland, with its 3.5 million people preferring to stick to their beer, only imported 14.1 million litres in 1990 for a CIF value of I£28.7 million (US$47.4 million) in 1990, mostly from France.)[235] In the early 1980s, these countries were still charging excise duties which were four to nine times those imposed by Belgium and the Netherlands – those of the six founding members charging most in this respect.[236]

228 Ibid, p 66.

229 Ibid, p 68.

230 *MIVS*, October 1993, p 21.

231 Based on CFCE calculations.

232 *MIVS*, various.

233 *MIVS*, July/August 1991, p 50.

234 Against 1.982 for spirits (*MIVS*, July/August 1991, p 50).

235 Source: Irish customs/CFCE.

236 Based on calculations made by the *Corriere Vinicolo*, in Niderbacher, 1983, p 57.

Rest of Scandinavia

Subsequent enlargements of the EU (Greece in 1981, Spain and Portugal in 1986) brought in net wine exporters exclusively: in 1990, Greece imported wine representing 7% and 20% of its exports in terms of volume and value respectively.[237] The ratios stood at 13% and 3% for Portugal, 2% and 5% for Spain. The pressure upon the 'northern three' to lower their duty rates grew accordingly, but the results have not been spectacular, so great has been the reluctance of governments to relinquish such a rich and easily justifiable source of revenue, tapped with the help of 'sin taxes'.

The most recent expansion of the EU will result in similar pressures being exerted on Sweden and Finland to reduce their excise duties. Together with Norway, these countries are all heavyweights in the area of alcohol taxation, with correspondingly huge duty free markets, such as cruise liners.[238] Also, should the case of the Danish monopoly on spirits constitute any precedent, then two of the three Scandinavian state monopolies for the production, import, export and distribution of alcoholic drinks are bound to be dismantled eventually. These bodies were created in the early 1920s in Sweden and Norway and early 1930s in Finland, out of the need to curtail alcohol consumption. Sweden's Vin & Sprit, Norway's Vinmonoplet and Finland's Alko were all restructured in the mid-1980s, with retailing being divorced from import and production.

Scandinavian governments are ready for a partial liberalisation of their monopolies. They have accepted that the import side of their business will be opened up to foreign competition, but are likely to dig their heels in concerning the retailing activity of their monopolies, arguing that upholding restrictions of this type is wholly justifiable in terms of their national health care programmes and of their sovereignty. They believe that countries should be left free to pursue the health and social policies of their choice as long as they do not discriminate against products originating from other member countries.

On 21 October 1991 they signed the Treaty setting up the European Economic Area encompassing the EU and EFTA, with the exclusion of Switzerland. The EEA's dispositions on competition required members to implement free trade amongst each other by

---

237 1989–91 average, except for Portugal (1990 only), based on FAO data.

238 The Scandinavian duty free market is the largest in the world for alcoholic drinks – in excess of 10% of worldwide sales. (CFCE study on Scandinavian countries – distribution and imports).

1994. EEA legislation is very similar to, yet not as compelling as that of the EU since many sensitive areas, such as agriculture, were left out of the agreement. The prevailing view is that the EEA Treaty allows for retailing monopolies to subsist on health policy grounds, provided these are genuine aims and there is no blatant attempt at discrimination against suppliers. All three monopolies have thus already invited all potential exports to join their product list for market testing and for eventual referencing. A rolling programme picks up new products and drops the worst performers from shop shelves each year.

The withdrawal of an application for EU membership after holding a referendum as was the case with Norway, means that the dispositions of the EEA Treaty would simply continue to apply. The view of the viability of state retailing monopolies has yet to be tried in court, for what happens on the wine side may well depend on attacks launched from the spirits side: all three Nordic countries are traditional producers and exporters of white spirits, e.g. vodka and aquavit. The stakes are high. Alcohol giants and their lobbies are thus determined not to watch the game from the sideline. Take Scotch whisky for instance: one of Britain's top export items can count on Whitehall's trade diplomacy and aggressive lobbying by Guinness who controls nearly half of its production since it took over United Distillers in 1986. The Scotch Whisky Association made no secret that, EU or not, it would use all legal means at its disposal to break Sweden's resolve to maintain a retailing monopoly.[239] Sweden is the largest of the three Scandinavian markets by far, and also the most advanced regarding the dismantling of its state monopoly.

Sweden

Sweden's monopolies did succeed in reducing spirits consumption and shifting customers over to beer and wine: spirits demand per head fell from a peak of just over 3 lpa in the mid-1970s to 1.7 lpa in 1990, beer consumption oscillated between 45 and 60 litres over the same period whilst wine enjoyed steady growth. Wine sales basically doubled between 1970 and 1990, from 6.4 to 12.3 litres, having already increased by some 78% in the 1960s.[240]

---

239 This section was based on *MIVS*, July/August 1991, November 1991, January 1992, July/August 1992, January 1993, November 1993; *International Drinks Bulletin*, April 1993.

240 Source: *World Drink Trends.*

The growth in wine consumption slowed down in the reces-sionary 1990s (real GDP fell for three years in a row) but was spurred again by the reform of the excise system in July 1992, from *ad valorem* to 'per degree' taxation, at a time when alcohol consumption was reduced further. The reform also featured a deep (−36%) cut in the duties applied to wines with an alcoholic strength of less than 10%. Australian, New Zealand, German and Portuguese producers benefited most from this provision, much to the dismay of the French who keep losing ground.[241]

Market and import trends

Imports grew in line with the government policy of encouraging drinkers to shift from spirits to wine and bear little marks of economic recession in 1977–78 and 1981–82. The reason lies partly in the buying skills of the state monopoly – the Swedish market brings com-paratively low returns because it is mainly bulk – and partly in the relative firmness of the Swedish krona against its main suppliers' currencies except the French franc and, as usual, the German currency.

French wines gained most ground during the 1970s as CIF prices came down; growth slowed down as prices stabilised, and volumes tumbled in the second half of the 1980s when prices rose again, see Fig. 4.35. Vin & Sprit just started to shop elsewhere, particularly in Italy and Spain (see Fig. 4.36, 4.37 and Table 4.16). Spain, France and Portugal have all seen their market share decline substantially between 1970 and 1990 as more competitive wines were put on offer from around the world.

Germany saw orders for its wine increase when prices fell in the mid-1970s and again in the mid-1980s, in spite of the general firming of the Deutchsmark. A gloomy picture emerges for Greece and Algeria, whose wines lost in appeal and vanished from the scene in the 1980s. Yugoslav wines performed relatively well at the cheap end of the market in the late 1980s.

The clear winners in recent years were the New World wines. The price of Californian exports fell below German levels in 1987 and stayed there for some years. The Australians are the most competitive, providing outstanding quality at reasonable price; their market share soared in the second half of the 1980s as a result, from nil to over 10% of the Swedish market. And conversely for Sweden who became Australia's second largest market after the UK, swallowing a quarter of

---

241 *MIVS*, March 1993, p 11.

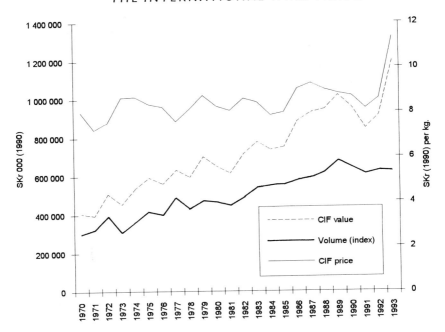

4.35 Swedish imports (112.1) (source: United Nations).

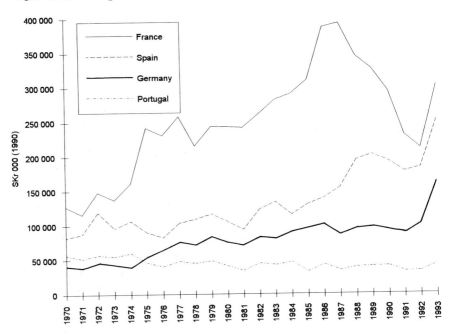

4.36 Swedish imports from main suppliers (CIF, 112.12) (source: United Nations).

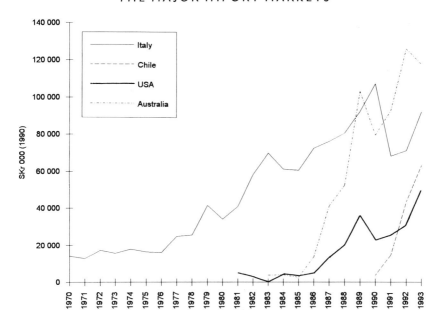

4.37 Swedish imports from selected suppliers and challengers (CIF, 112.12) (source: United Nations).

its exports in volume.[242] New World wines became fashionable amongst Swedish wine drinkers just when French products started to look overpriced (price is a dominant factor in individual purchase decisions)[243] and their image was starting to deteriorate. 1991's most sold wine brand was Chilean (Santa Emiliana); it was followed by two French (La Garonne and CTX Languedoc) and an Australian wine Lindemann's Shiraz).[244] Whether this is a move from a fad to a permanent preference for New World wines depends on the extent of the transformation of Swedish import and distribution channels. A straight application of the current EU's import regime to Sweden would soon cripple bulk imports from outside the Union, which would bump against the wall erected by EU preference (as it now stands). Only a swing of Swedish imports from bulk to bottled trade, e.g. following the entry of supermarkets and an aggressive policy on their part, would prevent the door slamming on non-EU suppliers – Australia and the US in the main. Then again, EU producers would be

242 Source: AWBC.

243 *MIVS*, March 1993, p 11.

244 Source: *Impact.*

Table 4.16 Swedish imports, 000 SKr (1990)

All wines*	1988	1989	1990	1991	1992	1993	Value share, % 1991–93	Volume share, % 1991–93
France	350 397	331 048	296 031	233 143	214 411	305 789	25.5	19.0
Spain	194 590	202 002	192 128	177 180	182 835	252 036	20.7	21.4
Germany**	95 001	97 210	92 086	87 271	100 885	162 961	11.9	10.2
Italy	117 916	133 296	140 250	102 215	102 070	125 492	11.2	9.9
Australia	52 307	102 777	79 198	92 449	125 575	117 279	11.3	14.0
Chile			3 703	14 801	43 417	63 257	4.1	4.5
USA	20 240	36 214	22 961	25 809	31 409	50 228	3.6	5.5
Portugal	38 452	39 026	39 776	31 733	32 262	42 726	3.6	2.4
Bulgaria	24 424	23 806	21 944	21 282	18 851	19 949	2.0	3.6
New Zealand			11 415	6 128	5 772	12 080	0.8	0.9
Other	55 090	55 400	54 143	54 240	53 989	44 849	5.2	8.5
World	948 417	1 020 781	953 635	846 250	911 476	1 196 647	100.0	100.0
Sparkling								
France	64 020	54 325	52 221	40 693	45 715	71 365	48.5	27.6
Spain	42 766	38 863	30 567	28 757	25 143	29 282	25.6	36.6
Italy	8 973	8 927	10 357	9 904	11 607	19 570	12.6	14.9
Germany**	13 100	11 540	9 262	8 905	9 667	11 572	9.3	12.8
Australia		1 004		1 932	5 205	3 641	3.3	7.0
USA	50	740		33	68	716	0.3	0.4
Israel	259	185	112	171	140	135	0.1	0.2
New Zealand						110	0.0	0.1
Chile								
Portugal	762	64			26		0.0	0.1
Other	467	327	154	574	182	104	0.3	0.3
World	130 398	115 976	102 673	90 969	97 754	136 494	100.0	100.0
Still								
France	280 208	271 355	240 776	189 403	165 570	230 508	23.3	19.0
Spain	151 723	162 933	161 371	148 185	157 671	222 632	21.0	21.3
Germany**	81 721	85 449	82 747	78 322	91 186	151 340	12.7	10.4
Australia	52 307	101 773	79 198	90 517	120 370	113 638	12.9	14.7
Italy	71 282	83 008	96 534	58 177	59 402	72 350	7.5	7.6
Chile			3 703	14 801	43 417	63 257	4.8	4.8
USA	20 125	35 353	22 837	25 583	31 155	49 470	4.2	5.9
Portugal	37 676	38 962	39 776	31 694	32 221	42 665	4.2	2.6
Bulgaria	24 424	23 806	21 944	21 282	18 851	19 949	2.4	3.9
New Zealand			11 415	6 128	5 772	11 970	0.9	0.9
Hungary	10 167	11 640	12 983	13 730	13 848	11 749	1.6	2.2
Argentina	2 143	3 282	3 596	5 968	9 345	8 959	1.0	1.2
Greece	4 997	2 456	2 070	3 213	5 907	5 746	0.6	0.6
Austria	7 104	5 731	6 571	5 013	4 119	3 702	0.5	0.8
Romania	8 549	8 856	5 181	4 279	4 197	3 066	0.5	1.1
Cyprus	6 227	5 097	3 779	4 085	3 786	2 472	0.4	1.1
Slovenia						1 842	0.1	0.1
Denmark	1 754	1 274			1 092	1 193	0.1	0.0
Israel	1 733	2 371	2 088	1 745	1 347	887	0.2	0.2
Other	11 432	14 103	17 182	14 702	9 168	4 204	1.1	1.6
World	773 571	857 449	813 752	716 824	778 423	1 021 600	100.0	100.0

* Including musts and vermouths   ** 1988–1990: FRG only   *Source: United Nations*

only too happy to take the shelf space left vacant by New World producers.

Import and distribution channels

Systembolaget is Sweden's retail monopoly. It operates under the umbrella of the Ministry of Health. Its principal client, apart from the catering sector, is Vin & Sprit, the 'other monopoly' taking care of the production, import, export and wholesale of all alcoholic drinks except low strength beer.

Vin & Sprit is likely to remain a major player in the wine and spirit trade for some time: it owns Absolut, a vodka brand distributed worldwide and, as the world's largest single wine buyer on the world market, it has acquired substantial skills in importing, bottling and shipping wines around the country. Restructured in 1987, it went through another extensive reorganisation in 1993, designed to sharpen its competitive edge against potential entrants. It imports most of the wines in bulk (over 70% in the late 1980s),[245] for bottling and marketing under its own brands. It also imports brands for which it acts as an exclusive agent in Sweden. Not only have production and marketing become separate functions within Vin & Sprit, but the firm also set up an affiliate, Provinum Distribution, dealing with most of the logistics involving the import, storage and shipment of wines passed on to other agents.

To the 700 wines they offered in the past, Vin & Sprit and Systembolaget added a few hundred new ones in 1994. Allowing the concentrated Swedish food sector to retail wines could actually reduce, if only temporarily, the choice of wines offered to Swedish customers; ICA, DAGAB and KF have allegedly used their dominant position to impose high margins on the food products they retail.[246] Canadian state monopolies' arguments run along similar lines. But a massive entry of supermarkets would definitely spur trade over the longer term, by placing wines amongst daily food items. This would also boost the share of bottled shipments since supermarkets are likely to cut short traditional channels and attempt to import directly from producers, as in the case of the UK.

245 Caire, 1989.

246 This section was based on *MIVS*, January 1992, pp 34–6, July/August 1992, pp. 6–7, November 1993, pp 8–9.

Outlook

The liberalisation of the Swedish market, especially the reduction in excise duties under the pressure of its EU partners, is bound to bring new life to this price sensitive market. Growth is likely to be even more spectacular in Norway and Finland though, where consumption lies at only a quarter to a third of the Swedish level and far greater yearly average rates of growth have been seen over the second half of the 1980s: 5.3% for Norway, 7.9% for Finland against 1.4% for Sweden.[247]

Austria, like Sweden and Finland, is a fresh member of the Union. Wine consumption is firmly centred around indigenous white wines and remains predominantly occasional. Demand is fairly stable at just over 260 million litres: consumption receded from 1984–86 (much of the drop came on the heels of the 1985 diethylene glycol affair) but sprang back to its previous level by 1990. Austria is momentarily awash with its own wines (80% whites) and uprooting subsidies are being handed out in order to bring supply back in line with demand. Only a fraction (2%) of production is exported – some 6.3 million litres in 1990 – mostly to Germany (65%) and Sweden (15%).[248] Imports are mostly reds originating from Italy, Hungary and France. EU membership is expected to increase the share of imported wines fourfold, from a current 7% to an estimated 30%.[249] Imports are subject to a yearly global quota of 18 million litres.[250] Austria's import regime is akin to that of neighbouring Switzerland who, in spite of its small size, remains a major player on the international wine scene.

Switzerland

Tiny Switzerland is considered a restricted but 'high value' market outlet by most exporters. It has remained attractive over the past 40 years largely because of the high disposable income of the 7 million residents, nearly a fifth of whom are foreign citizens. The predominance of German, French and Italian cultures is reflected in regional consumption patterns for alcoholic drinks: Swiss-Germans, who make

247 Ibid, June 1993, p 32.

248 Source: OSTZ, in *MIVS*, March 1992, pp 42–6.

249 According to the Austrian wine producer's association (*Journée Vinicole*, 19–20, July 1994).

250 *MIVS*, June 1993, p 11.

up the majority of the population, are keener on beer than are their *romand* and *ticinese* counterparts for instance, who drink comparatively more wine. Individual demand for wine embarked on a gentle recessionary path only recently, but looks set to follow a negative trend for some time. Overall alcohol consumption has shown clear signs of saturation since the early 1980s, as in most other Western markets.

The beer sector was first to dip into recession. Beginning in the early 1970s, consumption per capita fell by over 10% in just a few years, but then stabilised at round 70 litres.[251] The contraction of the beer market benefited those for spirits and wines where individual demand continued to grow until the early 1980s. Per capita consumption of spirits slipped by almost 20% over the following decade though, whilst that of wine managed to sustain itself at the relatively high level of 47–48 litres for more than ten years. It now stands at around 44 litres, making the Swiss the 6th heaviest wine drinkers in the world – a record for a country importing nearly two-thirds of its needs (181 million litres for SFr745 million/US$507 million in 1990).

Vineyards have dotted the Swiss landscape since Roman times. Most of their development occurred during the eighteenth/nineteenth centuries, but economic liberalism and sprawling European rail networks soon exposed local production to French surpluses. After losing well over half its vineyard acreage and over 40% of its output between 1900 and 1933, the government opted for a severe curb in imports and their subordination to the marketing of indigenous wines[252] – mostly whites.[253] These temporary measures were sanctioned by voters after the Second World War,[254] as part of an

---

251 Source: WDT.

252 Principles of *prise en charge*, whereby whenever production surpluses arose, importers were compelled to take up some of the surpluses and help market them.

253 Almost exclusively from the Chasselas grape yielding extreme variations in yields from one year to the next, but also some excellent dry whites on the shores of Lake Geneva and on steep flanks in the upper Rhône Valley (variations in yields caused just about every other region in the world to abandon the cultivation of this grape – most Alsatian production, for instance came from it.

254 The 1947 amendment to the Swiss Constitution, giving intervention powers to the Federal Government, and the 1951 review of the Federal Law on Agriculture. These provided the legal basis for the 1953 Federal Council's Decree on Viticulture and the Marketing of Domestic Products (*Statut du Vin*) and the 1958 Federal Assembly's Decree on Temporary Measures in Favour of Viticulture (limited to 10 years but renewable by Parliament).

agricultural policy aimed at self-sufficiency and a strong rural population, for self-defence purposes essentially.

Imports of wine doubled between 1950 and 1990, from 88 to 176 million litres. And so did production under the protective umbrella of Switzerland's agricultural policy, from 71 to 145 million litres. Acreage rose by a mere 14% to reach the present 14 000 ha, but yields jumped by over 80%.[255] Domestic reds benefited most from the rise in demand, doubling their share of domestic output from 20% to 40% over that period.

Trade policy

Sparkling wines and wines imported for industrial use – whether reds or whites – are not affected by any particular restrictions except tariffs. The import of still whites other than specialities is subject to a basic interdiction. Switzerland purchased them on the international market on a few occasions, purely for market stabilisation purposes.[256] Specialities are regulated by import quotas allowing for access to about 10% of the market. The opening of the market for white wines is due to begin in July 1995, in accordance with the terms laid down by GATT's 1994 Final Act: import quotas will be transformed into tariff quotas bearing present tariffs as preferential rates.[257] Additional imports will face full tariff rates, in most cases, reflecting the difference between domestic producer prices and CIF import prices during the agreed period of their calculation.[258]

Retailers have exerted relentless pressures in seeking to ease the import of still reds since the mid-1970s. They called for larger import quotas and more flexible, less secretive rules for allocating them amongst individual importers (there are presently over 500 importers of wine and the competitiveness of this sector has fallen under the scrutiny of the Swiss Cartel Commission more than once since 1970).[259] Retailers attempted to bypass restrictions on bulk by importing reds in bottles and later challenged the constitutionality of the measures limiting such trade (tariff quotas were introduced for bottled reds in the mid-1970s), but to little avail. In 1989 however,

255 Calculations based on three-year averages.

256 In 1957/58, 1973/74, 1980/81 and 1981/1982, essentially.

257 So as to ensure undiminished market access (so-called 'current access condition').

258 1986–88 are the base years for the so-called 'tariffication' process.

259 Commission Suisse des Cartels (1970, 1973, 1984).

they launched a successful referendum which brought about an early tariffication of red wines, along the lines set by GATT's draft agreement. The staged liberalisation put an end to national import quotas (stemming from bilateral agreements – multilateral treaties had eschewed the contentious issue on agricultural trade thus far) and replaced them with a single tariff quota of 162 million litres for bulk and bottled imports of red wines, irrespective of their origin. The last leg of the tariffication process took effect in 1994. The new regime is bound to have only a limited impact on the quantities of imported red wines: bulk import quotas have been slack for several years as deep, strong reds were increasingly replaced with lighter, fruitier wines, particularly rosés. As in the US, sales of imported wines tumbled after their progression came to a grinding halt in the early 1980s.

Market and import trends

The 1970s revealed by far the highest rates of increase in overall wine consumption, with 3.1% per year. They were bordered by two decades of sustained growth (1.8% and 1.7% per year for the 1960s and 1980s respectively), but the pace slowed down considerably during the 1980s, to 0.4%. The deceleration of the 1980s was due to falling demand for foreign reds and to reduced growth in the sales of whites. The decline of imported reds was triggered by a contraction in the number of foreign workers in the mid-1970s,[260] on the heels of the first oil crisis, and was compounded by the desire to drink 'less but better' on the part of many consumers – a move which benefited domestic reds and which has kept growing to date[261] (see Fig. 4.38). There was also a shift from reds to whites (see Fig. 4.39) and an explosion in sales of rosés which are widely (but wrongly) perceived as being lower strength[262] and bear the additional convenience of suiting an entire meal.[263]

Imports were subject to bilateral national quotas, and varied little over time in terms of volume, see Fig. 4.40. Between 1970 and 1990, the major changes consisted of an increase in France's share (from 22% to 33%) at the expense of Spain (from 30% to 21%) whose cheap

260 Mostly active in the highly seasonal and recession-prone hotel and construction sectors.

261 The generally more expensive domestic wines enjoy a better image.

262 Mentioning the alcohol content on the label is not compulsory.

263 Thus avoiding the need to serve a white wine with an *entrée* and a red wine with the main course, usually meat.

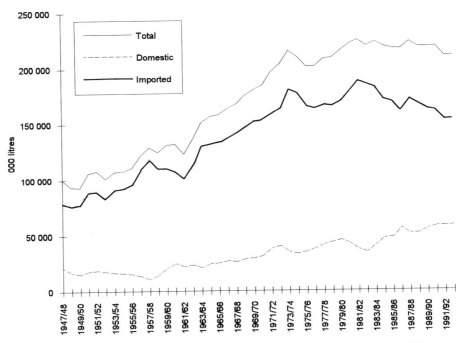

4.38 Swiss consumption, production and imports of reds (source: Office Fédéral de l'Agriculture).

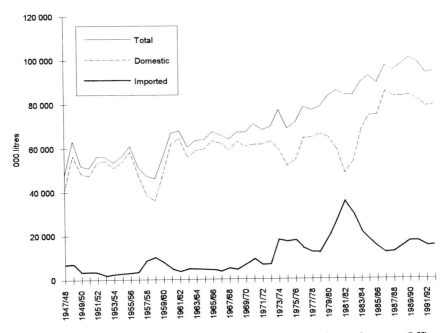

4.39 Swiss consumption, production and imports of whites (source: Office Fédéral de l'Agriculture).

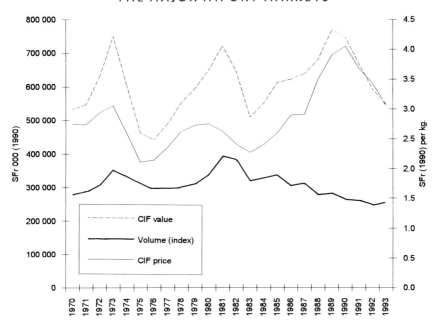

4.40 Swiss imports (112.1) (Source: United Nations).

reds had increasingly fallen out of favour.[264] The share of the third major player, Italy, remained basically unchanged at around 26–27%, see Fig. 4.41. The remaining imports came from Portugal, Algeria, Yugoslavia and a handful of other countries, see Fig. 4.42.

France enjoys the lion's share in terms of value: 65% in 1990,[265] see Table 4.17. Italy, whose wines enjoy a solid reputation as 'good value for money', came a distant second with 18%, followed by Spain with 9%. The majority of French wines are AOCs, as Swiss customers have a penchant for well known generics, especially Côtes du Rhône and Beaujolais (Switzerland is the largest export market for both), followed by Bordeaux and Burgundies.[266] The entrenched tastes of consumers also mean that generally high priced New World varietals have made little progress to date.

The sparkling segment benefited from a near doubling of sales between the mid-1980s and the early 1990s. *Sekt* is performing relatively well at the cheaper end, given the stark competition offered by (mainly Asti) *spumante* and *cava*. These sparkling wines are only

264 For still wines (112.12). Source: United Nations.

265 For still wines (112.12) Source: United Nations.

266 CFCE (1993, Switzerland, pp 57, 69).

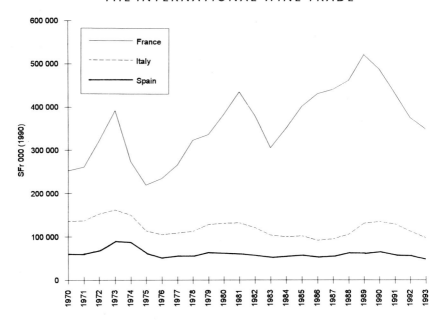

4.41 Swiss imports from main suppliers (CIF, 112.12) (source: United Nations).

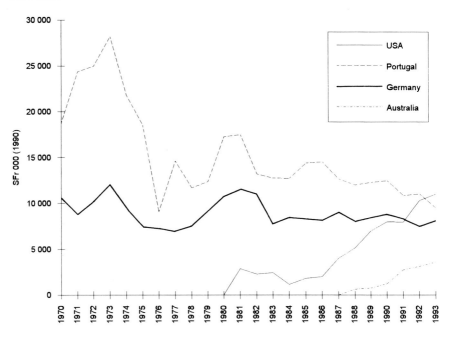

4.42 Swiss imports from selected suppliers and challengers (CIF, 112.12) (source: United Nations)

Table 4.17 Swiss imports, 000 SFr (1990)

All wines*	1988	1989	1990	1991	1992	1993	Value share, % 1991–93	Volume share, % 1991–93
France	459 949	519 261	485 623	430 019	373 565	347 471	63.9	34.1
Italy	105 880	131 533	135 221	130 068	112 736	97 948	18.9	27.3
Spain	62 853	61 907	65 954	57 862	56 825	48 892	9.1	23.9
USA	5 138	6 995	7 991	7 947	10 291	10 994	1.6	0.8
Portugal	12 005	12 268	12 434	10 850	11 023	9 500	1.7	4.3
Germany**	8 066	8 624	9 563	8 906	7 701	8 606	1.4	1.0
Australia	636	750	1 227	2 763	3 130	3 609	0.5	0.3
S Africa	1 462	1 656	1 696	2 451	2 447	2 523	0.4	0.6
Cyprus	1 681	4 011	5 852	4 128	2 873	1 805	0.5	3.2
Austria	1 759	1 750	1 745	1 576	1 460	1 487	0.3	0.2
Other	19 172	19 560	18 222	11 052	10 133	9 653	1.7	4.3
World	678 601	768 315	745 528	667 621	592 185	542 488	100.0	100.0
Sparkling								
France	142 373	168 548	156 768	135 136	116 223	118 184	87.3	64.4
Spain	5 944	5 385	7 522	7 050	7 211	7 917	5.2	16.7
Germany**	5 480	6 042	6 167	5 204	5 168	5 230	3.7	9.4
Italy	1 792	2 279	2 748	3 021	2 470	2 546	1.9	5.6
Austria	766	474	316	394	393	426	0.3	0.5
USA	146	190	208	239	106	174	0.1	0.2
S Africa	114	203	193	275	222	162	0.2	0.4
Slovenia					94	160	0.1	0.1
Australia	51	83	157	127	135	127	0.1	0.3
Portugal	54	167	153	159	361	113	0.1	0.2
Other	2 369	1 741	2 511	1 830	1 439	929	1.0	2.0
World	159 089	185 111	176 741	153 437	133 822	135 967	100.0	100.0
Still								
France	317 390	350 506	328 473	294 446	257 226	229 031	56.9	32.8
Italy	103 179	127 912	131 150	125 455	109 283	94 742	24.0	28.0
Spain	56 142	55 634	57 731	49 986	48 899	40 358	10.2	24.3
USA	4 992	6 790	7 771	7 708	10 173	10 821	2.1	0.8
Portugal	11 927	12 099	12 282	10 664	10 651	9 369	2.2	4.6
Australia	585	667	1 070	2 636	2 995	3 482	0.7	0.4
Germany**	2 555	2 403	2 635	3 126	2 353	2 878	0.6	0.6
S Africa	1 347	1 453	1 503	2 175	2 226	2 361	0.5	0.6
Cyprus	1 679	4 011	5 850	4 128	2 873	1 805	0.6	3.4
Hungary	1 907	2 036	1 698	1 575	1 185	1 194	0.3	0.8
Croatia						1 079	0.1	0.5
Austria	993	1 276	1 429	1 182	985	1 052	0.2	0.2
UK	1 989	590	1 958	1 598	1 184	1 007	0.3	0.0
Chile	384	210	958	548	939	950	0.2	0.2
Greece	871	2 532	1 156	682	769	889	0.2	0.4
Argentina	704	1 489	1 332	1 082	1 420	689	0.2	0.8
Morocco					369	402	0.1	0.2
Bulgaria	745	600	430	178		366	0.0	0.1
Slovenia					404	301	0.1	0.1
Other	10 199	10 356	8 164	3 546	2 322	1 654	0.5	1.3
World	517 588	580 563	565 592	510 715	456 254	404 429	100.0	100.0

* Including musts and vermouths   ** 1988–1990: FRG only   *Source: United Nations*

regarded as substitutes to 'the real thing', i.e. champagne, which continues to dominate this corner of the market.

Import and distribution channels

Horeca is a sizeable channel, thought excessive pricing has led to a gradual erosion of its market share which is now put at under 30%.[267] Mövenpick, the integrated restaurant chain, has successfully diversified into direct mailing, as have many wineries marketing domestic or imported crus.

More than a fifth of retail sales are made on the producers' doorsteps, especially in the French and Italian-speaking parts of the country. The business ethic of the largest food retailer, Migros, has resulted in a blunt refusal to market alcoholic drinks and tobacco thus far. This leaves Coop (the largest traditional distributor of wines) and Denner (a most aggressive discounter) as the two main players in the area, with 27% and 18% shares of retail sales respectively.[268] Usego comes a distant third with 7%, followed by smaller cash and carries, many of which supply the Horeca sector.

Restrictions on import and traditional allocation rules helped to reinforce the position of long established wine importers as long as these applied (Schenk, Coop – which has its own wineries – Egli, Scherer & Buehler and Bataillard are the largest importers). The picture could change as the result of easing licensing laws and the slackness in red wine import quotas (all imports of reds are done at preferential rates). Regarding white wines, tariffication and the gradual opening of the market will also mean that retailers will find it increasingly easy to bypass the wine trade in the coming years.

Perspectives

Owing to easier market access, imported wines get a fair chance to fight the downward trend in demand. The shift from reds to whites should continue in line with the gradual opening of the hitherto closed white wine market under GATT's tariffication process. The disappearance of national quotas means that Switzerland has broken free from traditional ties with suppliers and can now look beyond the EU for the best deals available around the globe.

267 CFCE (1993, Switzerland, p 62).

268 That is discounting Horeca sales. Source: Institut für Marktanalysen AG, Hergiswil (IHA).

The natural trend towards greater concentration in the import sector may be contained by the eagerness of domestic producers to diversify in the marketing of foreign wines, along their own product lines, in an attempt to meet the challenge posed by increased competition from abroad. Bulk shipments represented 17% of still wine imports during the 1993/94 marketing year;[269] they should continue to play a significant role for some time still, as they did in Denmark and Germany for instance, considering the know-how accumulated by domestic wineries in bottling and packaging imported wines over the years and consumer confidence in their skills and integrity as witnessed by their readiness to pay more for wine bottled in the region of production is still low compared with that in other Western countries, except for high priced crus.

Middle East and Africa

The Middle East

It is both surprising and sad to see that the virtual birth place of the wine trade did not manage more than 0.2–0.3% of world wine trade in the 1970s and 1980s. Trade did grow over the second half of the 1970s and the early 1980s, from roughly 2 to nearly 6 million litres by the time it peaked, in 1982 (see Fig. 4.43), but contracted steadily afterwards. By 1990 sales were less than 3 million litres for US$8.6 million (including Israel) – barely 50% more than Iceland's performance that year and a tenth of Austria's imports. The region is troubled by conflict and ensuing economic difficulties. Foreigners have left by the thousand, who constituted the primary customer base for wine importers throughout this century. The Middle East is now also largely under Islamic rule.

The United Arab Emirates, former British protectorates, formed in 1972 following Britain's withdrawal from the Gulf, imported 1 million litres for US$3 million in 1990, down from a peak in 1985 of 1.7 million litres. The UAE have been a major player in this area since it started reporting statistics in 1976; their purchases increased steadily, but after their peak in 1985 have receded towards the 1 million litres level. Bahrain imported up to 1 million litres in the second half of the

---

269 Source: *Office Fédéral de l'Agriculture.*

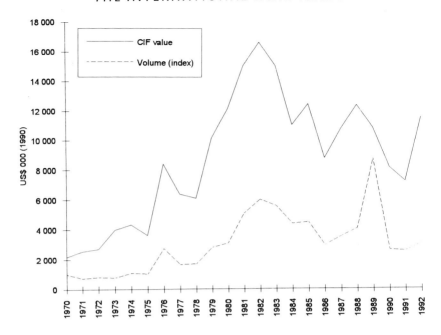

4.43 Middle East imports (CIF, 112.1) (source: United Nations).

1980s; it too has reduced its imports in the early 1990s, which now fluctuate at around 500 000 litres, for US$2–3 million. Despite this recent decline in orders, two states now virtually carry what is left of the imports to the region.

Lebanon, importing 250 000 litres for US$620 000 in 1990, is a relatively small producer and importer, compared with 1981 and 1982, when it imported over a million litres.

Syria is a small importer by any standards, with 44 000 litres for US$119 000; but did manage to cause a noticeable blip however, in 1989, by importing 6.2 million litres and pushing up the statistics for the whole region by the same token.

Iran and Iraq (220 000 litres for US$600 000 in 1990) are also small importers, despite Iraq's increase in orders in the early 1980s. Sadly, both countries have been devastated by years of war.

Israel, importing 270 000 litres for US$551 000 in 1990, also pushed imports briefly above the 1 million mark in 1982 and 1983.

Africa

Like the Middle East, Africa is also on a downward trend reflecting the decline of wine production in the once colonised north of the continent (see Fig. 4.44). Morocco, Algeria and Tunisia have only

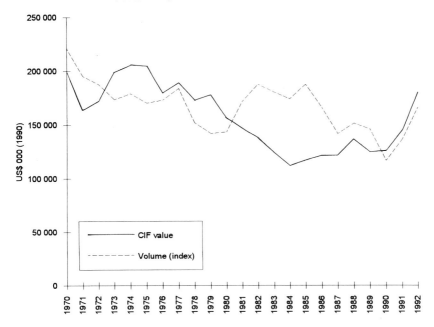

4.44 African imports (CIF, 112.1) (source: United Nations).

partially managed to divert the surpluses caused by EU preference, even though they do have limited access to the EU through the Lomé convention. In 1965, as in preceding years, French-speaking African countries constituted the main export outlet outside Europe and were worth approximately 100 million litres, against the 1 billion or so delivered to France at that time.[270] The opposite tip of the continent falls under a similar influence, that of the Republic of South Africa.

African wine imports are earmarked with past and present colonial ties – mainly with France and Portugal – and there are very few perspectives for growth on this continent. Admittedly, many countries have other priorities for trade, and wine is heavily taxed on the whole. In 1990, the African continent imported 117 million litres for US$126 million, i.e. less than Denmark and indeed any of the 12 countries analysed thus far.

Angolan imports top the league with some 30 million litres in 1990, but the vast majority came from Portugal. The Ivory Coast, Reunion (a French colony) and Gabon each imported more than 10 million litres that year. Most other African states traded significantly less than 5 million litres a year. Table 4.18 breaks down African wine imports from 1967–1991.

270 GATT, 1966, pp 7–9, 18.

Table 4.18 African imports

								tons
Volume	1967	1970	1975	1980	1985	1990	1991	1992
Angola	15 506	73 180	20 000	10 000	27 000	30 000	37 000	60 000
Cameroon	15 506	16 140	12 100	17 945	21 686	4 040	2 131	6 400
Gabon	11 337	10 500	7 000	14 750	20 000	10 723	9 000	8 500
Ivory Coast	28 270	23 601	48 825	51 000	65 467	19 000	22 500	18 300
Reunion	3 003	2 977	11 085	10 670	11 177	11 301	9 601	11 953
Senegal	6 661	4 846	5 600	6 652	4 749	9 702	7 500	8 200
Others	172 956	89 639	67 593	32 339	37 324	31 069	44 093	53 774
Total	253 239	220 883	170 203	143 356	187 403	115 835	131 825	167 127

								000 US$ (1990)
Value	1967	1970	1975	1980	1985	1990	1991	1992
Angola	67 486	68 294	19 419	15 064	27 929	36 000	46 373	70 309
Cameroon	9 011	9 516	9 467	13 193	11 004	5 871	2 129	5 867
Gabon	6 714	5 788	5 340	16 659	9 714	5 145	6 235	5 867
Ivory Coast	15 952	16 465	33 238	25 371	15 779	7 800	9 017	6 798
Reunion	2 504	2 988	13 569	14 241	9 085	18 699	14 410	19 498
Senegal	3 838	2 399	4 126	5 712	1 375	4 789	4 317	5 029
Others	98 800	94 077	119 544	66 278	42 279	50 684	63 702	69 651
Total	204 306	199 526	204 703	156 516	117 165	128 988	146 181	183 019

Source: United Nations

Latin America

The slow but steady increase in volumes of wine imported by Latin American countries over the past two decades was interrupted by two bouts of intense activity around 1980 and 1990. Shipments grew from 40 million litres in 1970 to around 60 million by the end of the decade and then suddenly jumped by over 50% into the 90–100 million range for a period of three years (see Fig. 4.45). Mainly responsible for this surge in activity was a usually import-shy Argentina who had to resort to buying nearly 20 million litres of (Italian) wines on the world market in 1979 to make up for a sizeable deficit in production at a time when consumption was at its peak (2.3 billion litres in 1977). Argentina fell back to 7 million litres in 1980 and to 5 million the following year before sinking to insignificant levels again in 1982. Mexico also contributed to the surge in Latin American imports at the end of the 1970s: figures soared from 2.6 million litres in 1978 to 11

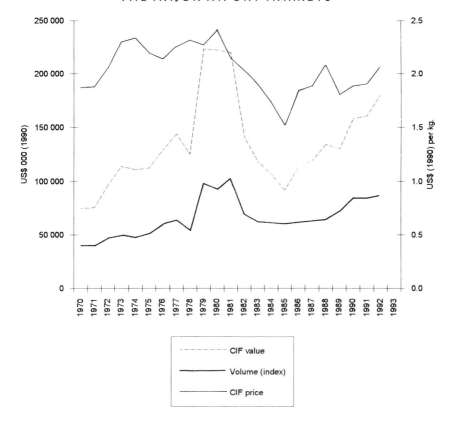

4.45 Latin American imports (CIF, 112.1) (source: United Nations).

million in 1979, to 12 million the following year and to 24 million in 1981, but then collapsed to just a few thousand litres for several years. Mexican imports broke through the 1 million litre mark in 1986 again and continued to expand rapidly afterwards, to over 3 million litres in 1987, 6 million in 1988, 13 million in 1989 and 20 million in 1990. The 27 million imported in 1991 turned Mexico into Latin America's largest importer, well ahead of Brazil with 22 million litres in 1990 and 9.5 million in 1991. Mexico is also Latin America's fourth largest producer after Argentina, Chile and Brazil, with around 200 million litres in 1990; it is a minor exporter with less than 1 million litres in 1990 and a major importer of US wines, overtaking Sweden for third place in 1991, after Japan and the UK with nearly 7 million litres. The major reason given for the surge in Mexican imports is the opening of the economy over the second half of the 1980s and, now, its full membership in NAFTA.

227

Brazil is the third largest producer in the region. Imports have followed the general Latin American trend, rising slowly during the 1970s and accelerating at the end of the decade, easing significantly over the early 1980s and expanding anew around 1990. Venezuela's imports doubled between 1970 and 1977, from 9 to over 18 million litres, then ebbed for several years, falling as low as 10 million, only to surge again towards the end of the 1970s, to 21 million in 1980. They stabilised for several years but then dropped sharply in 1985 and continued to fall, dipping even below the 7 million mark in 1989. The 7 million litres imported in 1990 were worth nearly US$12 million; Venezuela increased its orders in the following year.

The remaining other countries importing more than 5 million litres in 1990 were two overseas administrative departments of France, Martinique and Guadelope, situated in the Caribbean region. Guadeloupe increased imports steadily, from 8 to 12 million litres between the early and mid-1970s. The 11–12 million litres mark worked as a plateau until 1990, when it started to recede somewhat. Martinique's orders have kept at a flat 6 million litres throughout the past twenty years.

Medium-sized importers (2–5 million litres) include Paraguay, Colombia, French Guiana (another French overseas territory north of Brazil), Cuba and the Bahamas.

Paraguay's imports increased sevenfold between 1970 and 1980 to 2.2 million litres; this rose to 2.7 million in 1981 and 3.5 million in 1982, then fell to 1.5 million in 1983 and 1 million the following year. They broke again through the 3 million barrier in 1985 and continued their progression unabated, to reach 4.6 million in 1990 and 8 million in 1991. Colombia progressed steadily from 1970 (1 million litres) to 1982 (over 3 million) but receded towards the 2 million level for the rest of the decade. Only recently have imports increased again, to 2.6 million litres in 1991. French Guiana's imports increased from 1.6 million litres to well over 2 million in the late 1970s, then levelled off. They receded towards the 2 million level in 1991.

Cuba's orders rose steadily through most of the 1970s (3 million litres in 1977 and 1978), eased towards the 2 million mark for several years and climbed back to 3 million in the early 1980s. They fluctuated around that level for a decade and seemed to have gone higher, to an estimated 4 million litres in the early 1990s. Except for occasional burst of activity – in 1976 (2.9 million litres), 1981 and 1990 (3 million), imports by the Bahamas have kept relatively stable within a 1–2 million litre fluctuation band.

The development of the Latin American wine trade occurred at two very different speeds: while imported volumes more than doubled between 1970 and 1990, exports increased more than twelve-fold. A reverse picture emerges for the late 1980s when one turns to the value of trade expressed in US$. After years of surpluses, following the decline in consumption of the 1980s, Latin American exporters have become very competitive exporters.

Oceania

The 27.7 million litres imported in 1990 for just over US$90 million by Oceania were essentially down to Australia (10.7 million litres for US$43.3 million), New Zealand (8.1 million for US$29.2 million) and two overseas French territories, New Caledonia (3.5 million for US$7.7 million) and French Polynesia (4.1 million for US$6.4 million). Fiji and Papua New Guinea, the next largest importers, were only contributing marginally to the doubling of imports to the region between 1970 and 1990, trading a bare tenth of what the French dependencies did in 1990 (see Fig. 4.46).

French Polynesian imports have remained basically stable since 1970, fluctuating within a 4–4.6 million litre band most of the time,

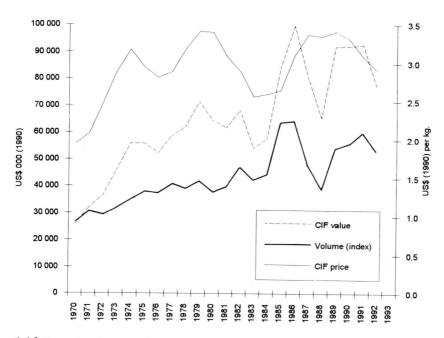

4.46 Oceanian imports (CIF, 112.1) (source: United Nations).

this tending to ease slightly in the 1990s. Much the same applies for New Caledonia, except the wider band of 3–5 million litres, which seems now to have settled round 4 million in the 1990s. French preference is fully operational there.

The growth in wine trade came from New Zealand and Australia. New Zealand's imports soared in the first half of the 1970s, from 1.6 million litres in 1970 to 2.7 million in 1974, then eased considerably until the early 1980s (2.3 million in 1981), peaking briefly at 3.9 million in 1985 only to recede again towards the 2 million mark. New Zealand imports then surged at the turn of the 1990s: 7 million in 1989; 8 million in 1990; 11 million in 1991, overtaking Australia that particular year, from which it imported the majority of its wines (zero tariffs prevail between both countries, reduced tariffs exist for developing countries such as those of South America and Eastern Europe) but even full tariffs are not particularly high – 22% of CIF in 1991, and are due to be decreased to half that level by 1996.[271]

Australian imports had grown fairly steadily and much in line with those of the region, from just below 2 million in 1970 to four times that level by the end of the 1970s, then on at a much slower pace until the mid-1980s. In 1985 and 1986, the level of imports was 19 million, double that of 1984. Orders have since settled at around 10 million a year. For the first half of the 1970s and again in the 1980s. Australia enjoyed a relatively balanced trade in wine, at least in volume. Equilibrium was breached in the late 1970s as exports plunged and imports continued to rise; it was then again disrupted by a surge in imports in 1985–86 and by soaring exports henceforth. Australia has lenient tariff rates (10–15% of CIF value); its major suppliers are Italy (nearly half of still wines), France (particularly strong with champagnes), Portugal and Germany. Total domestic demand has either fallen or stagnated since 1988 though (the buck in trend occurred two years earlier in terms of individual consumption). Continuing tax hikes are a longstanding, contentious issue between wine producers and the federal government. The 55% increase in the sales tax decreed in the middle of 1993 has cast a serious shadow on hopes for a resumption of growth on the domestic market. It is expected to hurt smaller exporters too, who may not be able to absorb the effect of the new tax.[272] Wine consumption appears to be inelastic in the short run, but becomes elastic with respect to price and income over the long

---

271 CFCE (1992, New Zealand, p 11).

272 *Drinks File*, September 3 1993.

run, at −1.3 and 2.8 respectively.[273] The future of Australian wine imports depends on the evolution of wine consumption and on that of the Australian currency. Both have performed relatively poorly in the early 1990s. But a weak exchange rate is a boon to exporters. As in many other temperate zones of the Southern hemisphere, the most ebullient sector of the wine trade is on the export side. The next chapter pans back, heading North-East; it gives a series of selected exporters' profiles on a journey back to the Old Continent.

273 Tsolakis et al, 1983.

5

Exporters' profiles

The New World

Australia

E xports from Australia have embarked on an exponential path, increasing tenfold in little more than a decade, from 7.5 million litres in the 1980/81 fiscal year to 78 million in 1990/91, and over 100 million two years later.[1] Shipments remained under the 10 million mark for the first half of the 1980s but rocketed thereafter as Australia started to feel the pinch from receding wine sales in its own backyard and began to tackle overseas markets seriously, see Fig. 5.1. Wine consumption receded between 1988 and 1991 but levelled afterwards, due to dipping sales in ordinary wines (packaged in popular bag-in-boxes, called 'casks'), which only modest growth in the demand for higher quality wines was unable to offset (individual demand actually fell from 21.6 litres in 1985/86 to 17.6 in 1990/91 and rebounded to 18.6 the following market year; it is expected to climb back to 25 by 2010).[2]

New Zealand, Japan, Canada and the UK were already supplied by Australia, if only moderately, in the mid-1980s. Shipments to these markets took off in the late 1980s (Japan, the largest with 2.7 million litres in 1990/91, was the only disappointing result: exports crossed

---

1 Source: Winemakers' Federation of Australia, (in Inglis 1993) and Australian Wine Export Council (in *Drinks File*, 3 Sept 1993).

2 Inglis, 1993, pp 6, 12–14.

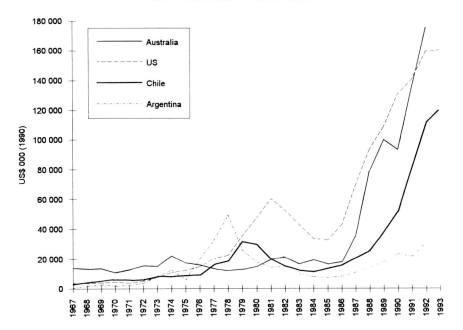

5.1 Main challengers' exports (FOB, 112.1) (source: United Nations).

the 3 million mark in 1987/88, peaked at 3.5 million the following year but have receded since then, and now reach a mere 2.3 million litres[3]). Australians managed a formidable push in the US, increasing tenfold between 1984 and 1992, a period which witnessed a 57% reduction in overseas orders by the Americans, mainly at the expense of West Europeans.[4] Sweden's imports performed even better, jumping to some 10 million litres by the late 1980s, to become Australia's largest market in volume at that time (these were large bulk shipments to Vin & Sprit, the Swedish monopoly, who increased its orders to 15 million litres but cut them again recently). The real star of the 1990s was the UK however, where sales seemed to have halted their progression just short of 10 million litres in the late 1980s, but suddenly tripled in three years, to over 30 million in 1992/93.[5] Great Britain's lead over the US, Sweden, New Zealand and Canada has widened dramatically recently (Fig. 5.2). Nearly half the shipments are directed to the British market and Australia's dependence on these five destinations is in excess of 80% (Table 5.1). Less than 40% of Australian exports are now

3 Financial years ending June. Source: Australian Wine and Brandy Corporation.

4 Inglis, 1993, p. 13.

5 Source: Winemakers' Federation of Australia (WFA), in Inglis, 1993.

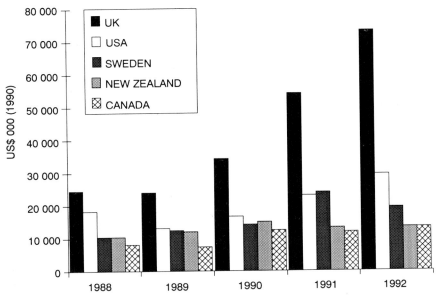

5.2 Australia's main export markets (FOB, 112.1) (source: United Nations).

done in bulk.[6] The UK, US, Sweden, Canada and Germany were acknowledged targets for the marketing efforts dispensed by the dynamic Australian Wine Export Council.[7]

Australia is a medium-cost producer of varietal wines of the highest quality, thanks to constant innovation in vineyards and wineries alike. Storage of premium grape juice without additives in order to allow all year round winemaking, and yeast and bacterial strain selection and propagation allowing full control over fermentation are just two examples of Australian innovations. Australia lacks the glamour of appellations, which they feel they are not yet ready to introduce, but their quality varietals (Chardonnay, Semillon, Cabernet Sauvignon, Shiraz and Pinot Noir) have spearheaded their thrust abroad, one of the rare segments still growing in the US but where competition is growing tougher by the day.[8] A generally weak Australian dollar allowed them to stress the 'good value for money' dimension of their wines whilst quality was monitored at the wineries'

6 Inglis, 1993, p 7.

7 Croser, 1992.

8 Croser, 1992; Inglis, 1993, pp 7–8, 17; Jackson-Grose, 1989.

Table 5.1 Australian wine exports, '000 US$ (1990)

All wines	1988	1989	1990	1991	1992	Value share, % 1991–92	Volume share, % 1991–92
United Kingdom	24 403	23 564	33 790	53 942	73 327	38.3	35.6
USA	18 398	13 032	16 268	22 714	29 391	15.7	11.9
Sweden	10 348	12 278	13 964	23 801	18 774	12.8	16.1
New Zealand	10 325	11 395	14 802	12 855	12 971	7.8	9.7
Canada	7 847	6 918	12 072	11 363	12 713	7.2	7.4
Japan	7 201	6 932	6 049	5 951	5 325	3.4	3.4
Ireland		577	2 039	2 797	4 279	2.1	1.9
Hong Kong	1 478	1 310	1 671	1 867	2 072	1.2	0.9
Singapore	792	937	988	1 681	1 964	1.1	0.9
Finland	803	438	491	1 767	1 905	1.1	1.7
Other	14 899	10 113	12 727	14 449	16 382	9.3	10.6
World	96 495	87 494	114 861	153 186	179 103	100.0	100.0
Sparkling							
United Kingdom	1 149	1 868	3 446	5 826	6 702	54.0	50.2
New Zealand	2 443	2 745	2 332	1 839	1 924	16.2	17.9
Sweden		129	21	359	925	5.5	8.5
Hong Kong	228	242	294	374	553	4.0	4.0
Japan	152	234	205	461	540	4.3	5.4
USA	807	364	384	425	377	3.5	2.6
Canada	67	50	117	123	282	1.7	2.1
Fiji	161	161	109	102	169	1.2	1.0
Singapore	73	136	131	165	141	1.3	1.2
Papua New Guinea	255	211	176	170	129	1.3	1.0
Other	603	464	744	782	840	7.0	6.0
World	5 939	6 602	7 959	10 625	12 581	100.0	100.0
Still							
United Kingdom	23 254	21 693	30 338	47 859	66 564	37.1	34.5
USA	17 591	12 669	15 884	22 274	29 014	16.6	12.6
Sweden	10 348	12 149	13 943	23 443	17 849	13.4	16.7
Canada	7 779	6 848	11 955	11 240	12 431	7.7	7.8
New Zealand	7 865	8 548	12 443	10 993	10 969	7.1	9.1
Japan	7 049	6 698	5 778	5 361	4 775	3.3	3.2
Ireland		577	2 039	2 797	4 217	2.3	2.0
Finland	803	438	491	1 767	1 905	1.2	1.8
Singapore	719	788	848	1 498	1 762	1.1	0.9
Netherlands	2 189	774	1 020	1 544	1 700	1.1	1.3
Switzerland			680	1 587	1 637	1.0	0.7
Denmark	3 309	1 731	1 338	1 678	1 534	1.0	1.4
Hong Kong	1 251	1 068	1 368	1 478	1 514	1.0	0.6
Norway	714	375	1 032	1 443	1 477	0.9	1.2
Germany**		793	1 052	1 117	1 112	0.7	0.7
France	614				852	0.3	0.6
Papua New Guinea	1 344	1 310	1 078	706	778	0.5	0.4
Fiji	905	637	761	745	693	0.5	0.5
Indonesia	338	395	617	595	663	0.4	0.6
Other	4 319	3 040	3 996	3 836	4 761	2.8	3.5
World	90 391	80 529	106 661	141 960	166 208	100.0	100.0

* Including musts and vermouths   ** 1988–1990: FRG only   *Source: United Nations*

235

gates by self-regulatory processes, in accordance with the industry's 'PIQE' motto, standing for Purity, Integrity, Quality and Economy.[9]

The key issue however, is that of maintaining market presence should New World wines drop out of fashion, by developing a durable image for Australian wines. US fashions are ephemeral, British consumers are noted for seeking advantageous prices and over-exposure to Swedish and Canadian monopolies can be a risky affair. In New Zealand and Sweden, Australia's share of the domestic market verges on 15%.[10] Reliance on North American markets has already diminished considerably, but that on the UK – where over 70% of Australian wines are positioned in the 'less than £3' segment – has now reached dangerous dimensions. Australia's reliance on a small number of markets situated in other trade blocs (the EU and NAFTA) casts some doubt on the feasibility of the export targets set for the years 1997 and 2000: a$750 million and 1 billion respectively, corresponding to a tripling and quadrupling of the a$260 million figure achieved in 1992 – in nominal terms.[11] These were considered realistic goals by the domestic wine industry, and growers have drawn their plans in accordance with them: a 30% increase in the supply of grapes is thus projected for the 1995/96 marketing year, over 1991/92 (premium grapes are planned to rise by 43%, non-premium and multipurpose grapes by 13%).[12]

For in spite of all its natural advantages and technological skills, Australia could easily find itself priced out of one or several key markets, either as the result of a temporary strengthening of its currency (or weakening of its partners'), or following a rise in grape prices with some varieties already in short supply.[13] What could also rock the prospects for increased exports and domestic supply, is the rise of other challengers, notably Argentina, Chile and South Africa. To them, a return to democracy signalled a resumption of listings in most Western supermarkets and specialist shops. The opening up of South American economies in particular has brought with it a string of foreign investments, adding technical innovation to their best

9 For example the Label Integrity Program, the Compliance Monitoring Program and the Residue Survey Program (Croser, 1992).

10 Inglis, 1993, p 8.

11 All in current Australian dollars (quoted at 1.34 against the US dollar in August 1994). Sources: *The Financial Times*; the AWBC and the Winemakers' Federation of Australia (news release of 30 Sept 1992).

12 Australian Bureau of Agriculture and Resource Economics, 1993, p 30.

13 Jackson-Grose, 1989.

advantage so far – generous natural conditions and one of the cheapest labour markets in the West.

Restructuring industry and associations also brought new life to the Australian wine market. The decade leading to 1992 saw a 25% reduction in the number of grape growers, a more than doubling of that of wineries and the fusion of three major producers' associations into the single Winemaker's Federation of Australia. The most salient aspect of the structural changes which went hand in hand with the success scored at home and abroad, is the forceful concentration of wine sales in the hands of a few firms following a spate of mergers and takeovers, and the successful flotation of previously restructured wineries. The four largest entities command an estimated 85% of Australian wine production (see Table 5.2).

Penfolds acquired Lindemans in 1990 from the US conglomerate Philip Morris and fell prey to South Australian Brewing the same year, who already controlled at least one important producer, Seppelt, and a co-operative winery. Two other major co-operatives, Berri Estates and Renmano, merged in the late 1980s, only to join strengths a few years later with family-owned Thomas Hardy; the combined business launched a successful public flotation of their stocks in 1991. Innovative Orlando, who tested pressure-controlled fermentation back in 1953, went through a management buy-out and came later under the control of France's Pernod-Ricard in 1989. Mildara Wines and Wolf Blass merged into Mildara-Blass in the summer of 1991.

Table 5.2 Australia's main wine producers

Company	Major brands	Market share %	Turnover in 1991/1992, million A$
The Penfolds Wine Group	Penfolds, Seppelts, Lindemans, Wynns	30	*320*
The BRL Hardy Wine Company	Hardys, Stanley Leasingham, Houghtons Berri Estates, Renmano	22	191
Orlando Wyndham Group	Orlando, Wyndham Estate	21	190
Mildara Blass	Mildara, Wolf Blass, Krondorf	12	*107*
S Smith & Son Pty Ltd/Yalumba	Yalumba, Hill Smith Estates	4	*33*
McWilliams Wines	McWilliams, Hanwood, Mount Pleasant	4	*33*
Brown Brothers	Brown Brothers, All Saints	3	*29*
Medium and small winemakers	Some 540 wineries	4	na

Estimates in italics
Source: *Neue Zürcher Zeitung (based on data by the Winemakers' Federation of Australia and their own investigations)*

Australia readily accepts the need for structural adjustments and firms are constantly on the lookout for synergies.

Chile and Argentina

The major consumer centres of Santiago and Buenos Aires are both fairly distant from the producing regions, leading to a concentration of domestic trade in bottling plants situated in their vicinity. Chile's acute economic crisis of the early 1980s led to a reduction in the number of vineyards and to the concentration of the winemaking activity into a few powerful hands. In the wine sector, as in all other areas of economic activity, only exceptionally strong firms had survived (acreage and yields had fallen dramatically as the result of the reduction in domestic demand for ordinary wine and many producers of such wines had been driven out of business).[14] The crisis of the wine sector survived the country's economic crisis by a few more years. Only in 1987 did a much leaner Chilean wine industry begin to see a reversal of fortune. The progressive opening of Chile to foreign capital also brought in a few investors from Spain, France and California who injected both cash and know-how in a much impoverished sector; the strains of the wine crisis of over 16 years ago are still felt today. Exports are left to a handful of wineries based around Santiago. Concha y Toro and Santa Rita are price makers on the domestic market and the situation on the US import market reflects to some extent that prevailing on the Chilean wine export scene as a whole: both best selling Chilean brands are produced by Concha y Toro's (one, Walnut Crest, was crafted specifically for the US market by its importer Banfi Vintner who had masterminded Reunite's success in the late 1970s). Together they commanded a 33% share of Chilean wine imported by the US in 1991. Adding shipments by another two large wineries, Santa Rita and Santa Carolina, brings their combined share to two-thirds in that year.[15] Another significant player is San Pedro, who used to rank a distant second exporter behind

---

14 Chile's liberalisation process had been initiated in 1974 by the so-called 'Chicago boys', soon after the bloody coup which managed to topple Allende's democratic government and substitute a most repressive system for it. The first leg of the economic reform (1974–1981) was flawed however; it led to a revaluation of the Chilean currency and ended up with a severe crisis. Only during the second leg of the liberalisation process did Chile actually manage to boost its exports. See Krieger (1993, p. 127) and United Nations Conference on Trade and Development (1992) for more details on political and economic reforms.

15 A similar situation prevailed in 1990 too (*Market Watch, May 1992, p 77*).

Concha y Toro back in 1988, with less than half its export sales but with Santa Rita hard on its heels[16] – a battle of saints!

Like Australia, Chile's fortunes were made in the second half of the 1980s, as Chile managed to offer extremely stable and low prices, all quoted directly in US$ (see Fig. 5.1). Bulk markets are losing considerably to bottled trade which, in 1992, represented just under 80% of all shipments.[17] Chile lost its German and Swiss markets in the early 1970s. Shipments to Japan are still on the increase but have lost in importance by comparison to North America where Chile is currently focusing its energies. These now take up 40% of its exports (Table 5.3 and Fig. 5.3). And the Chilean government is openly seeking membership of NAFTA (the country belongs neither to Mercosur nor to the Andean Group – South America's two main trading blocs[18]). In Western Europe, the UK, Sweden, Norway and Denmark are all new

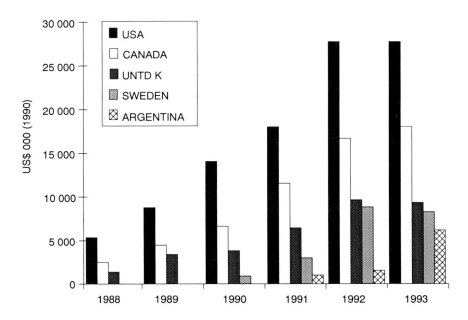

5.3 Chile's main export markets (FOB, 112.1) (source: United Nations).

16 In 1988, Concha y Toro, San Pedro and Santa Rita boasted turnovers of US$6, 2.6 and 2.15 million respectively (*MIVS*, July 1989, p 7)

17 Associacion de Exportadores y Embotelladores de Vino.

18 In April 1994, Mercosur included Brazil, Paraguay, Uruguay and Argentina; whilst the Andean Group was bringing together Venezuela, Colombia, Ecuador, Peru and Bolivia (*The Financial Times*, April 11, 1994).

Table 5.3 Chilean wine exports, 000 US$ (1990)

All wines*	1988	1989	1990	1991	1992	1993	Value share, % 1991–93	Volume share, % 1991–93
USA	5 277	8 952	14 244	18 140	28 030	27 994	23.7	24.7
Canada	2 538	4 545	6 832	11 837	17 012	18 310	15.1	15.3
United Kingdom	1 402	3 459	3 943	6 638	9 864	9 601	8.4	6.7
Sweden			995	3 170	8 925	8 484	6.6	5.8
Argentina			4	1 147	1 983	6 400	3.1	4.7
Ecuador	893	1 149	1 085	2 002	2 410	6 122	3.4	4.2
Venezuela	1 530	1 764	2 647	5 452	5 651	5 175	5.2	5.0
Norway				2 408	4 134	4 104	3.4	3.1
Colombia	2 531	2 452	2 222	2 219	3 325	4 080	3.1	2.7
Paraguay	2 204	1 783	2 536	4 450	4 368	3 282	3.9	5.0
Other	9 105	13 488	17 103	23 464	25 391	26 846	24.2	22.9
World	25 480	37 592	51 611	80 926	111 094	120 396	100.0	100.0

Sparkling

Venezuela			199	739	949	884	28.6	27.9
Argentina			4	299	508	817	18.0	18.2
Peru			158	393	228	378	11.1	10.8
Bolivia			225	276	289	375	10.4	8.3
Colombia			71	52	115	214	4.2	4.2
USA			109	375	185	186	8.3	10.5
Paraguay			42	124	74	150	3.9	4.5
Canada			45	55	156	139	3.9	4.5
Ecuador			51	124	65	39	2.5	3.2
Netherlands			21	11	6	22	0.4	0.3
Other			172	221	203	354	8.6	7.7
World			1 097	2 668	2 779	3 558	100.0	100.0

Still

USA			14 133	17 756	27 845	27 807	24.2	25.1
Canada			6 783	11 742	16 840	18 171	15.4	15.5
United Kingdom			3 939	6 638	9 864	9 601	8.6	6.9
Sweden			995	3 170	8 925	8 484	6.8	5.9
Ecuador			1 034	1 876	2 345	6 083	3.4	4.3
Argentina				848	1 471	5 583	2.6	4.3
Venezuela			2 448	4 714	4 702	4 291	4.5	4.4
Norway				2 408	4 134	4 104	3.5	3.2
Colombia			2 151	2 167	3 211	3 865	3.0	2.6
Denmark			2 312	2 997	3 932	3 169	3.3	3.4
Paraguay			2 494	4 324	4 293	3 131	3.9	5.0
Netherlands			740	1 412	2 814	2 629	2.3	1.7
Brazil			2 757	1 233	1 229	2 608	1.7	1.7
Peru			1 660	4 654	2 745	2 446	3.2	3.8
Germany				1 222	1 859	1 741	1.6	1.1
Ireland				636	1 027	1 457	1.0	0.7
Japan			1 969	2 223	1 613	1 354	1.7	2.4
Finland			690	1 492	997	1 208	1.2	1.0
Bolivia			624	698		1 032	0.6	0.5
Other			5 752	5 955	8 420	8 013	7.4	6.4
World			50 481	78 164	108 266	116 776	100.0	100.0

* Including musts and vermouths   *Source: United Nations*

outlets which have sprung up in the late 1980s. These markets, plus Benelux, accounted for about 25% of Chile's exports in volume and value in 1990 and 1991. The rest is mainly exported to other Latin American markets. The restructured Chile is, like Australia, bracing itself for major increases in grape and wine production. Some analysts forecast a trebling of the 75 million litres or so reached in 1992 by the end of the decade. This would result in a serious increase in Chile's exposure to foreign markets, which already stands at 50% of wine production (in excess of 150 million litres in that year).[19] But Chile has little to lose: none of the other commodities on which its economy is based spells a brighter future than wine. Chile may also succeed in trading its reputation as a producer of excellent but relatively cheap varietals (mainly Cabernet Sauvignon and Sauvignon Blanc) for that of an exporter of highly competitive premium wines. The sharp price increase of 1992 may just be a strategic step in that direction: this only managed to slow down the progression of sales in terms of volume, whilst values continued to soar. Chile also plans unhindered investments and trade with its giant neighbour – Argentina.

Argentina's economic difficulties only aggravated a wine industry suffering from lack of investment in the 1970s and 1980s. Argentina was faced with the same problem of tumbling demand for ordinary wines and surplus production which plagued all other major producing nations: output grew until the mid-1970s and stabilised until the late 1980s whilst demand per capita fell rapidly during the 1980s: from 71 litres in 1983 it dipped to just under 50 litres in 1992.[20] Like the EU, Argentina was attempting to support wine prices and even its set of elaborate market intervention measures (ranging from production quotas to sales interdictions via compulsory bottling in the region of production) was powerless at halting the crisis, not least because of the overlapping of provincial and national measures and lack of clear delimitation of the powers of the numerous bodies involved in regulating the Argentine wine industry.[21] The Giol winery had been acquired by the Provincial Government of Mendoza in the mid-1950s with a view to intervening in the market (Mendoza's share of national production is about two-thirds). It processed well over 300 million tons of grapes by the late 1980s (representing 10% of Argentina's production) and had a storage capacity of 280 million litres, which was often used for price support but resulted in massive

19 Hernandez, 1993.

20 IRREAL, Fundacion Mediterranea, Mendoza.

21 Juri, 1992.

stockpiling, as is usually the case with such measures.[22] Giol was also involved in exporting wine. Its restructuring in 1988 and privatisation the following year were a prelude to reforming a deeply bankrupt policy. A full deregulation of the wine market was to follow, as only oenological measures would remain in force (these are part of food and health regulations aiming at consumer protection). A national decree deregulated nearly all sectors of the economy in November 1991 and the peso was pegged later on to the US dollar, on a one-to-one parity. The result is a wholly free wine economy, mirroring that of Chile on the other side of the Andes. Argentinian exports, which used to be taxed on their way out of the country, are now set to emulate their neighbour's success. Although some time behind, it will probably happen on a much grander scale, for Argentina is one of the world's major producers – the fourth largest after Italy, France, Spain and about equal with the US; Chile produces less than a fifth of Argentina's output.

Argentina's exports experienced a short blip between 1975 and 1978, mainly as the result of production surpluses, much depressed domestic prices and massive buying by Russia which took an average 38% of its exports in volume over those years. Argentina lost nearly all its export markets during the highly inflationary years of 1979 and 1980 when prices rose massively and the peso was revalued. The doldrums lasted until the mid-1980s. Soon after the Falklands/Malvinas clash with Britain (the UK has never been a serious buyer of Argentinian wines), rock bottom prices prompted Japan, its primary client at that time, with an export share of about a third in terms of volume and a large buyer of musts, Canada, the US plus a handful of EU states to resume their purchases. Dollar prices were not nearly as stable as those for Chilean wines over the late 1980s, but remained quite attractive. In dire contrast to the situation prevailing in Chile, over two-thirds of Argentine exports are done in bulk.[23] Japanese orders have displayed little growth since 1988, but those of the US have increased steadily (Fig. 5.4). The US and Canada have also become keen buyers of concentrated musts of late and prompted export figures to grow from 1 to 5 million litres in just half a decade.[24] The most recent bout of activity in the wine sector was provided by

---

22 See Juri and Mercau (1990) for more details on Giol and the market situation in the late 1980s.

23 Calculated on the basis of still and sparkling wine shipments realised in 1991, which appeared to be a typical year (source: Instituto Nacional de Vitivinicultura).

24 1989–91 versus 1985–86 (source: Instituto Nacional de Vitivinicultura).

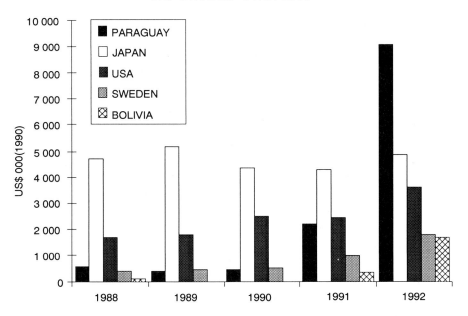

5.4 Argentina's main export markets (FOB, 112.1) (source: United Nations).

two Mercosur members though, as exports to Paraguay and Uruguay rocketed in the early 1990s. Half the shipments went to Paraguay, Japan and the US in those years (see Table 5.4).

The United States

As with anything else in the US, wine exports are fairly recent history. Californian wines only gained attention in the late 1970s, after snatching first place from the best French crus, both for whites and reds, in an international contest organised by Steven Spurrier in Paris. But the real impetus came from the production surpluses of the early 1980s, which forced Californians to fight off imported wines and to turn to a few, well targeted foreign markets. Lower prices caused a first surge in US exports, but these were mostly excess bulk wines diverted on to the Canadian market and volumes retreated to more realistic levels a few years later. The real export boom took place in the second half of the decade when Canada, Japan, the UK and several other Western European states (particularly Sweden, Switzerland, Belgium and Denmark) started to raise their orders.

Canada, the UK and Japan are the US's largest customers: together they take up nearly two-thirds of its exports (Table 5.5). The Japanese market started to lose some of its fizz in 1991 though, and figures

Table 5.4 Argentinian wine exports, 000 US$ (1990)

All wines*	1988	1989	1990	1991	1992	Value share, % 1991–92	Volume share, % 1991–92
Paraguay	524	349	390	2 211	9 070	21.3	24.4
Japan	4 669	5 152	4 326	4 302	4 889	17.4	19.8
USA	1 650	1 755	2 458	2 435	3 573	11.4	6.9
Sweden	351	423	451	951	1 797	5.2	4.6
Bolivia	81			318	1 674	3.8	4.5
Netherlands	155	378	980	1 384	1 501	5.5	4.1
Uruguay	270	221	280	836	1 158	3.8	3.3
Germany**				576	1 076	3.1	2.0
Canada	704	1 205	1 820	1 062	999	3.9	5.0
Venezuela	563	619	718	618	874	2.8	1.4
Other	5 229	7 947	11 647	6 933	4 632	21.9	24.0
World	14 195	18 048	23 070	21 627	31 244	100.0	100.0
Sparkling							
Venezuela				317	637	43.2	60.0
Uruguay				164	144	14.0	9.7
Paraguay				54	93	6.7	5.2
Peru				19	36	2.5	1.3
USA				15	35	2.3	1.4
Chile				51	34	3.9	2.7
Brazil				30	15	2.0	1.6
Bolivia				16	12	1.3	0.6
Spain					5	0.2	0.6
Japan				47	2	2.2	1.9
Other				270	209	21.7	15.0
World				982	1 223	100.0	100.0
Still							
Paraguay				2 117	8 815	22.9	25.8
Japan				1 979	4 840	14.3	17.0
USA				2 329	3 411	12.0	6.9
Sweden				937	1 797	5.7	4.9
Bolivia				300	1 632	4.1	4.8
Netherlands				1 384	1 501	6.1	4.4
Germany**				576	1 076	3.5	2.1
Uruguay				660	1 012	3.5	3.4
Canada				1 003	971	4.1	5.1
Brazil				970	508	3.1	1.5
Spain					479	1.0	0.3
France				292	441	1.5	1.9
Denmark				788	358	2.4	2.4
United Kingdom				772	350	2.4	1.7
Chile					305	0.6	0.7
Venezuela				301	237	1.1	0.5
Peru				240	219	1.0	0.7
Norway				403	215	1.3	1.7
Finland				453	208	1.4	1.2
Other				2 634	1 174	8.0	13.0
World				18 139	29 548	100.0	100.0

* Including musts and vermouths ** 1988–1990: FRG only *Source: United Nations*

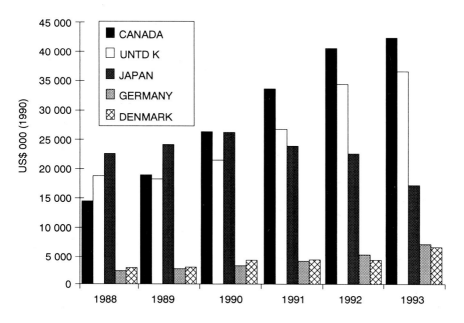

5.5 Main US export markets (FOB, 112.1) (source: United Nations).

dipped further as economic recession reduced consumer spending on wine; Japan was thus clearly outpaced by the other two, even in the sparkling segment where it once enjoyed undisputed leadership (Fig. 5.5). Other nations' shares and rates of increase are strikingly more modest, with perhaps the exception of Holland which more than doubled its orders between 1990 and 1991.

About 30% of exports of still wines (of less than 15% alcohol) are done in bulk, but their contribution to earnings was reduced significantly at the turn of the decade as their price tumbled in real terms whilst those for bottled shipments managed to keep their level more or less unchanged (Fig. 5.6). Canada is the largest purchaser of bulk wines (over 60% in 1992), followed by Japan (16%). The UK comes a distant third with a share of only 3.5%. Belgium, France and Switzerland follow suit, as traditional importers of bulk, but bottled shipments are still preferred in those countries too, at a rate of 3 to 1 (Fig. 5.7). NAFTA member Mexico orders as much bulk as bottled wines. The UK outranks Canada on the bottle front. Japan and other, mainly Northern European countries, are the next largest customers; their shares range from 10% in the case of Japan to 3% in that of Belgium. Orders by EU members have increased steadily.

Table 5.5 United States' wine exports, 000 US$ (1990)

All wines*	1988	1989	1990	1991	1992	1993	Value share, % 1991–93	Volume share, % 1991–93
Canada	14 449	18 824	26 034	33 619	40 480	42 205	26.2	27.5
United Kingdom	18 830	18 255	21 476	26 643	34 402	36 335	21.9	19.6
Japan	22 626	24 018	26 115	23 718	22 318	16 933	14.2	13.9
Germany**	2 193	2 381	2 926	3 527	5 382	6 446	3.5	3.9
Denmark	2 677	2 491	3 905	3 865	4 499	5 883	3.2	4.4
Netherlands	653	1 593	1 795	4 720	4 199	4 789	3.1	2.2
Switzerland	3 002	2 905	4 235	4 010	4 037	3 891	2.7	2.7
Belgium	2 684	2 536	3 761	3 306	4 168	3 832	2.5	2.3
Oth. Asian economies	1 138	1 278	1 892	1 505	2 199	3 434	1.6	2.0
France	1 718	2 170	3 711	3 349	3 075	2 347	2.0	2.0
Other	18 036	22 075	24 580	26 264	29 953	29 336	19.2	19.7
World	88 006	98 525	120 430	134 525	154 712	155 431	100.0	100.0
Sparkling								
United Kingdom		164	271	1 814	3 127	4 098	21.7	23.9
Canada		2 248	1 577	1 821	2 432	2 339	15.8	11.5
Japan		4 516	4 697	2 826	5 920	1 674	25.0	30.8
France		413	184	177	921	524	3.9	5.4
Belgium		215	155	393	372	408	2.8	2.4
Neth. Antilles		356	246	405	419	324	2.8	1.6
Oth. Asian economies		159	415	118	423	308	2.0	1.5
Netherlands			136	104		287	0.9	1.1
Mexico		77	87	125	114	260	1.2	1.4
Hong Kong		152		163	179	186	1.3	1.3
Other		2 832	2 069	2 923	4 090	2 390	22.6	19.0
World		11 133	9 837	10 868	17 996	12 799	100.0	100.0
Still								
Canada		16 465	24 457	31 798	38 048	39 866	28.0	31.2
United Kingdom		17 892	21 121	24 614	31 270	32 222	22.5	20.3
Japan		18 910	20 736	15 484	15 870	14 796	12.6	10.8
Germany**		2 284	2 926	3 527	5 208	6 431	3.9	4.5
Denmark		2 388	3 798	3 616	4 478	5 883	3.6	5.2
Netherlands		1 593	1 532	4 410	4 199	4 478	3.3	2.4
Switzerland		2 895	4 108	3 889	4 037	3 891	3.0	3.1
Belgium		2 321	3 571	2 913	3 786	3 367	2.6	2.4
Hong Kong		1 726	1 437	1 319	1 666	2 007	1.3	1.2
Oth. Asian economies		1 061	1 477	1 340	1 743	1 883	1.3	1.3
Mexico		1 400	1 802	1 251	2 507	1 862	1.4	1.9
France		1 515	3 521	3 169	1 979	1 791	1.8	1.5
Ireland					728	1 769	0.6	0.7
Sweden		3 453	5 096	3 914	3 753	1 581	2.4	2.6
Bermuda		871	917	842	1 201	1 477	0.9	0.8
Bahamas		885	908	998	1 059	1 414	0.9	1.0
Finland		409		976	832	1 129	0.8	0.8
Neth. Antilles		1 186	1 157	946	1 349	988	0.8	0.8
Singapore		443	718	697	1 045	982	0.7	0.6
Other		7 894	8 868	10 223	8 780	11 348	7.7	6.7
World		85 592	108 150	118 927	133 538	139 164	100.0	100.0

* Including musts and vermouths   ** 1988–1990: FRG only   *Source: United Nations*

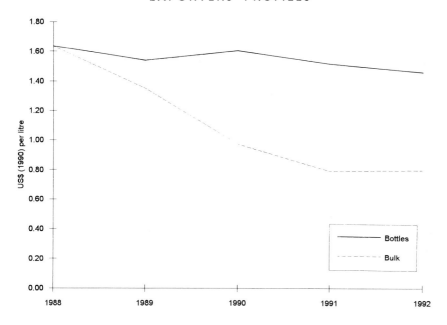

5.6 US FOB prices for still wine (<15%) (source: Bureau of the Census).

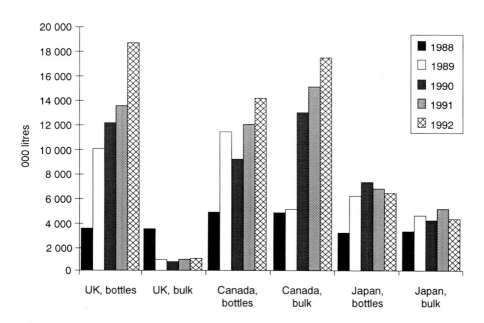

5.7 US bulk and bottled shipments to selected markets (still wine <15%) (source: Bureau of the Census).

247

US exporters are Californian producers in most cases. Export outlets have continued to gain in importance since the peak in US wine consumption in the early 1980s and now account for 7% of production in the 'Golden State'.[25] Its northern neighbour, Canada, has shown some signs of fatigue recently: the real value of orders increased only slightly in real terms in 1993 and receded by over 8% in volume over the preceding year. South of its border, Mexico is not expected to become a sizeable market for years, in spite of joining NAFTA recently. The acquisition of Heublein and its large wine interests by Grand Metropolitan/IDV in the late 1980s and the efforts deployed by California's Wine Institute in Britain (recall that in 1991, Californians spent nearly a million pounds on generic advertising alone[26]) certainly helped its rise to prominence, but for how long? Californian wines have ceased to be a 'fad' and now must sell on the basis of their intrinsic value.[27] This also applies to continental Europe where Belgium, Holland and Germany are thought to yield the best potential for immediate growth.[28] All these markets are situated within the dominion of EU producers. Thus no wonder that Californians are turning west – that is to Asia – for long term growth; the Pacific Rim is expected to become a keen buyer of US wine as soon as proper infrastructures are set in place.[29] This is already taking place in Japan where US wines are increasingly channelled to consumers via supermarkets – and the US is best placed for pushing its brands on them.

The Old Continent

France

France is the world's second largest exporter in volume, after Italy, but by far the first in value. In 1990, some 1.25 billion litres were shipped

---

25 According to the head of export program set up by California's Wine Institute (*Wines & Vines*, May 1994).

26 Which was more than any other nation (NTC, 1992).

27 *Wines & Vines* (May 1994).

28 Ibid.

29 Ibid.

worldwide, for US$4.28 billion. Exports have regressed slightly in the following years, both in volume and real value (see Fig. 5.8). France lost valuable market shares in North America since 1985 but gained ground in Asia, especially in Japan. The core of France's business is realised in Western Europe however, and particularly the EU which accounts for over 70% of sales.[30] Just over half of French exports go to Germany, Britain and Belgium alone; their contribution to earnings is slightly lower as the cheapest wines tend to be shipped to those destinations as well as to Holland, Denmark and Canada; Sweden is another major buyer of bulk (see Table 5.6 and Fig. 5.9). The highest average export prices are billed to US, Japanese and Swiss customers, but price increases led to a contraction of sales in terms of volume in the 1990s. Even in the UK the price of some wines has gone beyond psychological barriers – the severe recession of champagne sales in the early 1990s was caused by hefty price increases. Shipments to Italy consist almost exclusively of champagne and the clientele has reacted swiftly to price increases there too: imports were cut by a third in 1993 and fell below Swiss levels that year. The loss of bulk business (with Germany) to Italy and, more recently, to Spain, was offset in part by the success of her *vins de pays* (upper quality

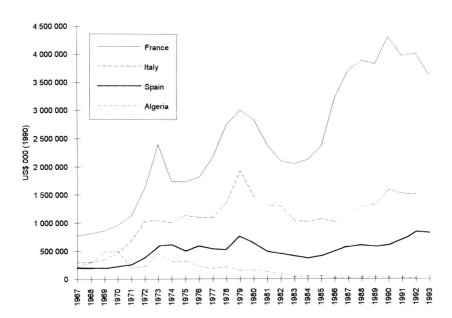

5.8 Leading exporters (FOB, 112.1) (source: United Nations).

30 1989–90 average. Source: CFCE and French customs.

Table 5.6 French wine exports, 000 US$ (1990)

All wines*	1988	1989	1990	1991	1992	1993	Value share, % 1991–93	Volume share, % 1991–93
Germany**	665 956	611 459	717 911	715 899	700 569	654 447	18.0	23.9
UK	790 525	763 625	880 635	728 212	741 205	637 985	18.3	20.3
USA	523 865	498 588	460 011	436 365	497 648	474 252	12.2	6.2
Belgium	411 767	389 806	469 030	464 100	487 768	400 290	11.8	11.3
Switzerland	321 492	320 040	353 707	308 201	274 035	257 254	7.3	4.6
Netherlands	233 387	224 739	257 078	264 408	270 780	249 312	6.8	9.6
Denmark	122 060	110 828	135 604	136 871	156 371	133 737	3.7	5.7
Canada	139 089	171 297	163 203	148 415	130 104	128 513	3.5	4.7
Japan	119 720	170 197	206 464	151 440	129 935	121 024	3.5	2.1
Italy	137 696	145 598	184 351	184 876	153 765	99 690	3.8	2.1
Other	406 703	400 750	453 098	414 015	429 541	423 458	11.0	9.4
World	3 872 258	3 806 926	4 281 092	3 952 802	3 971 721	3 579 961	100.0	100.0

Sparkling

	1988	1989	1990	1991	1992	1993	Value share, % 1991–93	Volume share, % 1991–93
Germany**	182 090	172 748	226 090	226 647	214 160	213 921	19.0	30.4
USA	215 038	197 892	182 745	169 504	159 265	183 809	14.9	8.0
UK	252 494	264 254	297 693	199 521	187 966	171 268	16.2	17.1
Switzerland	104 044	108 029	120 957	98 667	84 541	91 153	8.0	5.7
Italy	122 536	124 775	156 870	159 490	134 872	90 587	11.2	6.2
Belgium	78 002	78 499	98 895	89 660	89 361	89 718	7.8	8.8
Netherlands	26 571	27 557	27 466	28 453	23 665	25 136	2.2	2.4
Japan	16 171	23 676	31 635	21 118	16 217	18 885	1.6	1.5
Guadeloupe	13 834	11 678	16 438	13 904	14 266	16 267	1.3	2.4
Canada	16 799	22 166	17 299	14 349	12 530	12 702	1.1	1.0
Other	172 859	170 824	196 578	188 322	198 905	190 392	16.7	16.4
World	1 200 437	1 202 098	1 372 666	1 209 636	1 135 747	1 103 837	100.0	100.0

Still

	1988	1989	1990	1991	1992	1993	Value share, % 1991–93	Volume share, % 1991–93
UK	531 991	493 153	577 045	524 394	548 240	463 705	19.3	20.8
Germany	480 293	432 991	490 571	488 574	483 094	434 896	17.7	23.4
Belgium	324 359	305 950	364 514	369 466	393 431	305 319	13.4	11.6
USA	305 695	298 126	273 936	264 305	335 841	288 337	11.2	6.0
Netherlands	206 226	196 513	228 150	233 876	243 473	219 536	8.8	10.3
Switzerland	217 154	211 521	232 160	208 729	189 060	165 612	7.1	4.6
Denmark	111 325	100 050	123 185	126 436	145 755	124 737	5.0	6.3
Canada	117 603	144 524	142 214	130 306	114 374	112 772	4.5	5.0
Japan	102 556	144 767	172 143	128 868	113 075	100 987	4.3	2.1
Sweden	40 985	37 830	36 539	30 872	33 058	30 206	1.2	1.6
Ireland	18 902	19 640	24 594	23 849	22 155	24 618	0.9	0.8
Hong Kong	9 782	9 262	11 739	8 988	10 856	12 472	0.4	0.2
Norway	18 117	11 235	14 336	12 361	12 576	11 622	0.5	0.6
Guadeloupe	9 622	9 165	11 392	9 609	9 757	11 134	0.4	0.5
Austria	8 458	7 830	9 593	8 433	8 289	8 676	0.3	0.2
Italy	14 082	18 237	25 199	24 356	17 852	8 238	0.6	1.7
Reunion	7 428	7 316	7 949	8 163	9 664	8 084	0.3	0.6
Singapore	5 670		8 054	7 385	8 020	8 063	0.3	0.1
Finland	12 078	13 230	15 341	15 740	9 387	7 531	0.4	0.4
Other	90 036	104 521	100 669	84 823	93 028	93 671	3.4	3.1
World	2 632 364	2 565 863	2 869 323	2 709 503	2 800 986	2 440 218	100.0	100.0

* Including musts and vermouths ** 1988–1990: FRG only   *Source: United Nations*

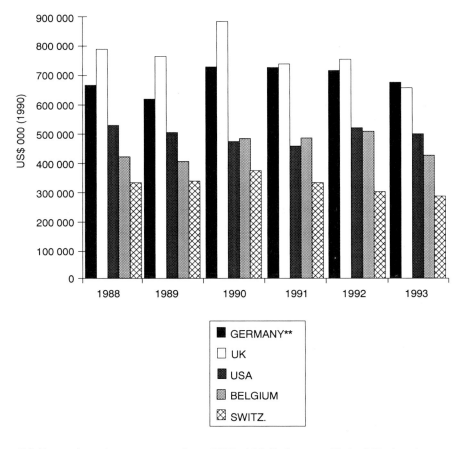

5.9 France's main export markets (FOB, 112.1) (source: United Nations).

ordinary wines which cannot be blended with products from other members states).

Appellation wines are France's trump card; their steady progression and the insistence, by the French, on shipping AOCs almost exclusively in bottles, has added value to exports and allowed France to compensate for falling volumes and keep values more or less steady. Wines from Bordeaux have been excellent performers ever since the British decided to ship some to their drinking élite back home. They are probably the best example of a cleverly crafted image and astute marketing: a strict hierarchy of a relatively small number of out-standing and (too) much talked about crus has been maintained since 1855. All crus taken together, including second-rate *crus bourgeois*, make up a tiny minority – perhaps as little as 5% – of the 450 million litres of AOC wines produced by Bordeaux each year; their image is used to push the rest to a largely undiscerning clientele. Some 37% are exported, and a quarter of them reach North American shores.[31] Bordeaux exports have trebled since 1970 and 80% is done in bottles.[32]

Four out of the ten largest French exporters are based in Bordeaux: Grand Terroirs Associés, Barton & Guestier, Groupe Taillan and Société des Vins de France, see Table 5.7. Many of the most prestigious and largest Bordeaux négociants have since come under their control or under that of financial and foreign entities: Barton & Guestier was the first to fall in overseas hands, those of Seagram, in 1955; CVBG (Consortium Vinicole de Bordeaux et de Gironde) is owned by the Dutch drinks manufacturer Bols; Cordier became owner of the Compagnie Financière de Suez in 1984 (who also runs the Compagnie des Salins du Midi), and Calvet was bought by Allied Lyons in 1982; Louis Eschenauer went to John Holt of Liverpool in 1959 but eventually returned to a group of private investors in 1990 after brief ownership by Brent Walker; de Luze also went to a British (paper) group first and is now in the hands of the Cognac firm Rémy Martin.[33] Foreign companies are also present in Champagne: Seagram, and Allied Lyons in a joint venture with Marne & Champagne; Seagram and Marne & Champagne are second only to Moet-Hennessy who has a cross-shareholder agreement with Guinness.

Native Bordeaux firms can also excel in the acquisitor's role. Castel (founded in 1949) went on a buying spree in the late 1980s, buying up a chain of specialist shops in France (Nicolas) and a Dutch

Table 5.7 France's ten largest exporters, 1991 sales (million Francs*)

	Export	Total
Grand Terroirs Associés	385.0	700.0
Grands Chais de France	360.4	424.0
Barton & Guestier	324.0	360.0
Les Vignerons du Val d'Orbieu	300.0	1 200.0
Georges Duboeuf	297.9	470.1
Groupe Taillan	264.5	955.0
IDV France	246.9	277.4
Société des Vins de France	233.2	530.0
Les Chais Beaucairois	232.0	751.0
Rémy Pannier	223.3	489.7

* 1 US$ = 5.3 FFr

Source: *Revue Vinicole Internationale*

31 *Neue Zürcher Zeitung* (1 December 1992).

32 Fouguet, 1989.

33 Bichsel, 1991 and Peppercorn, 1992.

distributor (LFE) in 1988, in the run up to the EU's single market. Its greatest coup however was the acquisition of Société des Vins de France (SVF) in a friendly takeover from Pernod-Ricard in 1992. The deal turned Castel – who already owned over 700 hectares of vineyard in Bordeaux and a Californian winery – into the second largest wine group in the world, just behind Gallo.[34] The purchase of SVF gave Castel a range of successful brands, such as La Villageoise and Vieux Papes (best performing French ordinary wine brands, domestically and worldwide, ahead of Castel's own brand, Castelvins[35]) and Classiques (France's fifth most successful AOC brand) and a much sought after critical mass for supporting them domestically and internationally. This also prompted a need for further concentration in the ordinary wine segment, such as a recent joint-venture between two giants of the French *Midi* – Val d'Orbieu and Salins du Midi.[36] Pernod-Ricard retreated in its core business of spirits and in the upper quality segments just as Seagram did in the US in the late 1980s; Pernod kept Orlando – acquired in 1989 – and Wyndham for whom it had launched a successful takeover bid nine months earlier. In 1992, Pernod took a 50% stake in one of Argentina's oldest and main producers of fine wines – Arnold Etchard.

Perspectives for French varietal wines are improving in line with the gradual reconversion of the Midi's vineyards to better varieties, particularly Cabernet Sauvignon and Merlot. By selling on that basis rather than adopting the traditional generics approach (e.g. Bordeaux, Burgundy, Côtes du Rhône), the French wine trade is attempting to upgrade the bland image of its ordinary wines (*vins de table* and *vins de Pays*) both in the eyes of domestic and international customers, and to exploit the potential tapped so successfully by the New World wines.

Italy

Italian exports fluctuated between 200 and 300 million litres in the 1960s. Shipments soared to over 1 billion litres in the first two years of

---

34 Estimated wine sales are 450 and 490 million litres respectively. Castel had a total turnover of about FFr 10 billion (US$ 1.7 billion) in 1993, which was roughly split as follows: 46% in wine, 15% in mineral waters (Castel bought most of the brands Nestlé had to dispose of when it took over Perrier), 35% in beer (with large interests in Africa and Vietnam) and other activities – according to Piere Castel, in an interview with *Impact* (January 1, 1994).

35 *Revue Vinicole Internationale* (December 1991, special supplement).

the formal establishment of free trade in wine in the EU in January 1970. Most of it went to France in replacement of Algerian wines. Exports rose further in the late 1970s, when home consumption started to tumble, and reached 2 billion litres in 1982, their all-time peak. The contraction of the US market – Italy's largest customer taking just under 30% of exports in value at that time – together with the international repercussions of the methanol scandal nearly halved exports in just four years. Figures picked up again towards the end of the 1980s as recollections of it faded, to total 1.4 billion litres in 1990, for US$1.6 billion, but eased off slightly thereafter.

Compared with that of France, Italy's overall strategy is based on even great reliance on a few, well targeted markets: Germany, the US, the UK and France together account for 82% of exports in terms of volume and 76% in value (Table 5.8 and Fig. 5.10). The German market is the prime outlet for Italian wines with a share of about a third in volume and value. Reunification added about 100 million litres to German orders which broke through the 400 million mark in 1990.[37] France was outranked as Italy's main export market in terms of volume that year, as shipments plunged from 540 to 380 million litres between 1989 and 1990.[38] These are almost exclusively cheap blending wines and shipments to France have decreased steadily over time, first as the result of trade disruptions in 1974 and 1980, and then simply because the market for the resulting blended wines of relatively high strength simply disappeared. What was lost to the French was thus gained in Germany, and mostly at the expense of French exporters. Similarly for bottled trade: the contraction of the US market in the first half of the 1980s led to a concentration of sales efforts on the British market. Their respective shares were 9% and 11% in volume for 17% and 14% in terms of value (see Table 5.8). Switzerland is only a secondary but stable customer, the fifth largest in value with 6%, and 4% of exported volumes, though orders have decreased recently, through lack of demand. The Netherlands, Finland, Ireland and Japan have increased their purchases of Italian wines during the late 1980s and early 1990s whilst Romania appears to have made huge purchases of cheap bulk in 1992. Despite these successes, overall exports have again embarked on a downward trend in the 1990s, losing over 15% on their 1989 peak. Their ability to keep and even raise the value of their shipments over that period is due to a

36 Journée Vinicole (May 28, 1994).

37 ISTAT.

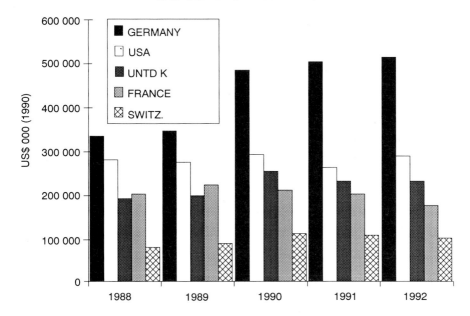

5.10 Italy's main export markets (FOB, 112.1) (source: United Nations).

rising share of bottled trade and to a repositioning of their wines in higher quality segments.

Well over half of Italian exports were shipped in bulk in the late 1980s, but only contributed to a fourth of earnings. Exporters have been moving slowly from bulk to bottled trade over the years. They also put greater emphasis on appellation wines; these amounted to just under 30% of the volumes shipped in 1991 for instance, but accounted for over half of exports earnings that year.[39] Some countries, like Holland, are now supplied predominantly with wines bottled in the region of production. The dramatic fall in export volumes which had taken place in the 1980s would have had a far more serious impact on earnings had this repositioning not occurred. Italy's strategic – if only gradual – shift away from ordinary wine appears to be slowly paying off: DOC white wines have turned out to be its best weapon in the attempt to fend off the drive of Spanish competitors in German territory for instance. White wines are also the main instrument of Italy's progress in Japan where they have displaced the US into fourth place. Their innovations in the production of low-alcohol wines have earned them a share of nearly 90% in that particular segment of the British market in 1991.[40]

38 ISTAT.

39 ISTAT.

Table 5.8 Italian wine exports, 000 US$ (1990)

All wines*	1988	1989	1990	1991	1992	Value share, % 1991–92	Volume share, % 1991–92
Germany**	332 433	337 928	478 738	494 831	502 873	33.1	34.5
USA	277 788	266 782	282 452	248 284	275 142	17.4	8.9
United Kingdom	184 628	186 651	237 101	215 885	212 591	14.2	11.0
France	194 475	212 286	198 694	186 644	158 554	11.5	27.8
Switzerland	69 966	78 141	96 350	90 493	79 066	5.6	3.7
Canada	34 995	40 133	40 200	43 760	37 414	2.7	1.6
Belgium	31 686	31 140	36 522	36 427	35 544	2.4	2.2
Austria	22 756	25 271	30 149	31 471	28 260	2.0	1.3
Netherlands	19 595	21 928	25 121	27 404	27 160	1.8	1.4
Japan	7 915	10 487	16 706	19 713	17 329	1.2	0.4
Other	83 380	112 357	119 902	115 169	126 177	8.0	7.3
World	1 259 615	1 323 105	1 561 935	1 510 079	1 500 109	100.0	100.0
Sparkling							
Germany**	68 898	49 767	67 596	81 798	101 188	46.7	50.4
USA	68 868	65 594	60 757	49 770	49 444	25.3	19.7
United Kingdom	23 473	20 358	22 761	20 036	15 629	9.1	10.4
France	3 887	2 872	3 087	5 159	4 139	2.4	3.0
Switzerland	1 113	1 329	1 634	1 974	1 672	0.9	0.7
Canada	2 684	3 221	3 254	2 611	2 206	1.2	1.3
Belgium	1 008	1 003	1 418	1 113	1 332	0.6	0.5
Austria	285		437	571	477	0.3	0.2
Netherlands	886	613	826	1 381	1 184	0.7	0.4
Japan	1 010	1 589	2 665	2 595	2 250	1.2	0.7
Other	8 630	12 945	17 139	19 203	26 187	11.6	12.7
World	180 741	159 292	181 574	181 210	205 707	100.0	100.0
Still							
Germany**	251 745	274 419	388 763	390 405	379 623	32.8	34.8
USA	191 596	186 730	205 582	184 759	212 235	16.9	8.2
United Kingdom	130 363	137 953	180 216	158 349	154 295	13.3	8.9
France	181 197	186 899	178 009	170 839	145 413	13.5	31.4
Switzerland	68 028	75 876	93 571	87 262	76 525	7.0	4.3
Canada	26 899	31 639	31 866	35 523	31 207	2.8	1.5
Belgium	23 799	23 339	27 845	28 380	27 722	2.4	2.0
Austria	21 106	23 798	28 272	29 541	26 053	2.4	1.4
Netherlands	16 621	19 233	22 654	23 886	23 096	2.0	1.4
Japan	5 507	7 871	12 878	15 703	14 004	1.3	0.3
Denmark	8 514	10 670	13 381	12 595	11 300	1.0	0.6
Sweden	10 597	11 604	13 417	9 789	11 017	0.9	0.7
Free zones	4 739	6 488	5 593	7 406	5 273	0.5	1.2
Australia	4 935	5 948	6 837	6 472	5 200	0.5	0.3
Finland	1 624	2 096	3 293	3 874	4 154	0.3	0.3
Ireland	2 267	2 374	3 511	3 487	3 569	0.3	0.2
Nigeria					3 077	0.1	0.1
Romania				1 372	3 027	0.2	1.3
Norway	1 357		1 475	1 917	1 580	0.1	0.1
Other	14 307	28 535	19 544	20 193	20 845	1.7	1.1
World	965 200	1 035 475	1 236 707	1 191 751	1 159 215	100.0	100.0

* Including musts and vermouths   ** 1988–1990: FRG only   *Source: United Nations*

The most active exporters, Riunite and the Gruppo Italiano Vini (GIV), are both in the hands of the giant Lega delle Cooperative. Riunite was best known at the beginning of the 1980s as the company sold nearly 100 million litres of sparkling Lambrusco to the US. Credit for their success rests solely with their New York importer, Villa Banfi, who 'designed' the wine for the needs of US consumers at that time with such remarkable clarity of vision. The Lambrusco phenomenon is largely over, sales having crashed during the 1980s, but they have picked up again recently. Villa Banfi invested their profits in Tuscan vineyards at Montecalcino and hope to repeat their success with Brunello, a hitherto little known grape variety (but so was Lambrusco, which was only commercialised as a white wine and enjoyed a rather low profile in its 'native' North of Italy). A similar approach lies behind Banfi's highly successful marketing of a Chilean Chardonnay under the *Valnut Crest* brand: having noted the reluctance of US consumers to accept South American wines, they launched it with a name and label which were highly reminiscent of Californian varietals with which the wine was intended to compete.[41] The Gruppo Italiano Vini (GIV) is another major player on the North American scene as well as in Germany, its main market. GIV is the uncontested leader of the quality segment, ahead of Chianti Ruffino, Cavit and Bolla. Based in the Veronese region, GIV boasted a turnover of 126 billion lira (US$105 million) in 1990, a 3% share of domestic production and a 10% stake in Italian exports. In 1993, GIV bought a majority stake in Wildman, a US importer, from the hands of Allied Lyons. Many medium-sized wineries became involved with imports in the late 1970s and early 1980s, yet all too often in an episodic way. Several exporters refocused their activity on to the domestic market in the late 1980s in the face of the difficulties met on the US and French markets. Most exports of vermouth and Asti *spumante* are concentrated in the hands of just two firms, Martini & Rossi and Cinzano which is now fully controlled by IDV. Large co-operative wineries based in the south of the country and in Sicily are usually responsible for the biggest consignments of bulk to Germany and France, as well as for most production surpluses. The Instituto per il Commercio Estero (ICE) backs Italian exporters with prospecting and large promotional campaigns on strategic markets. The major strength of Italian exporters lies in their development of strong brands along with appellations; their greatest weakness resides in the poor image of Italian wines and in the string of scandals which stained the 1980s.[42]

40 ISMEA.

41 Market Watch (May 1992).

Recent export successes achieved with sparkling wines can do little to alleviate the painful downsizing of the Italian wine industry. Exports have stalled in the 1990s and sales tumbled on the domestic market: wine consumption has shrivelled by more than a third and shed well over 2 billion litres since the early 1970s;[43] the rate of decline has slowed but the trend remains negative. The expansion of the Italian production sector during the 1970s – growth continued unabated until the end of the decade – was nearly wholly based on French and US demand for their wines. Substantial setbacks in both countries in the 1980s compelled most Italian exporters to concentrate their efforts on stopping the haemorrhage at home or to turn their attention to the German and British markets. But even there their ordinary wines come under intense competition from inexpensive New World varietals and cheaper generics from Spain who has to wrestle with identical, if only less pronounced trends on its domestic market.

Spain

Spain's exports grew steadily in the post-war period, reaching 100 million litres in the early 1950s, 200 million in the mid-1960s, 300 million in 1970 and double that amount again in the mid-1970s. They kept fluctuating within a 4–600 million litre band, with a slight downward trend, until Spain became a fully fledged Member of the EU, in January 1993 (although Spain had acceded in 1986, its wine 'exports' to other Member States had been subjected to annual quotas during a long transition period). Exports increased sharply in 1991 and 1992 as restrictions were progressively lifted in anticipation of the establishment of the EU's single market; they broke through the 1 billion litres ceiling the following year.

Recent shipments included massive consignments of bulk to France for the first time in two decades. It was not just in France that Spain was successful at shaking Italy's dominance of the EU market for blending wines. The generally lower prices commanded by Spanish ordinary wines have also made them increasingly attractive to German producers who purchased them for blending with their own still wines as well as base wines for the production of *Sekt*. Even Russians could be enticed into ordering over 70 million litres in 1993 – still likely with the help of generous EU export subsidies (it is hard to imagine how Spain could have displaced Russia's traditional Eastern

42 *MIVS* (March 1994).

European suppliers without them[44]). Although some have disputed Spain's ability to challenge its neighbour at the high end of the wine business in any significant way,[45] the French consider Spanish producers – particularly those based in La Rioja – as a potential threat to their appellation wines.

Spain's wine exports broke down as follows in 1992: a good third of the volumes shipped were ordinary wines, another third were appellation wines and the rest was split between higher strength wines, sparkling wines and musts.[46] Three-quarters of the shipments of still wines were exported in bulk that year.[47] To become an international supplier of cheap bulk was not exactly the objective sought by Spain, but such are the subtleties of the EU's common wine policy (the Mancha region near Madrid is awash with surplus wines and even generous uprooting premiums seem powerless at reducing Spain's production potential[48]). Confronted with the mediocre image of their wines, some producers undertook a strategic turn in 1985 and began to ship higher value products. A rising proportion of appellation wines were bottled in the region of production; La Rioja went as far as making this practice compulsory. A Belgian importer and the EU Court of Justice took another view (it was a clear breach of the EU provision on free trade), but La Rioja's *Consejo Regulador* responded by making all its producers, including the largest two (AGE Bodegas Unidas and Frederico Paternina), abstain from selling bulk: of the 31 million litres exported in 1992, 97% were bottled shipments.[49]

The change of tack was mostly felt by the US which had become the prime destination for Spain's most valuable still wines (Americans command a 4.5% share in value with only 1.1% in terms of volume – see Table 5.9) and their orders decreased accordingly. The US is also a major outlet for sparkling wines, essentially *cava*, even though volumes have regressed considerably over the 1990s, in line with the general contraction of the American sparkling segment; Germany

---

43 Domestic consumption stood at 3.5 billion litres in 1992.

44 In an expression of their concern about recent GATT arrangements, Spanish wine professionals warned that a phasing out of export subsidies would seriously undermine the competitiveness of their bulk exports to markets situated outside the EU (*MIVS*, March 1994).

45 Peris and Taylor (1993).

46 *MIVS* (March 1994).

47 Ibid.

48 Ibid. Spahni (1988) warned that Spain would soon come to help drain EU finances if no one had the courage to put an end to price support distillation programmes.

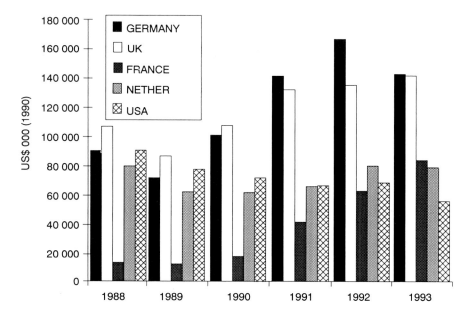

5.11 Spain's main export markets (FOB, 112.1) (source: United Nations).

is about to take the lead in terms of value in this sector too. The Dutch have remained reliable clients since around 1970 and stand close behind France in the overall ranking for 1993 even though they ordered nearly five times less in terms of volume that year. The UK has steadily increased its purchases of still wines since 1989, in both volume and value (see Fig. 5.11); Britain is also a non-negligible outlet for sparkling wines. Overtaken by the Russian Federation in 1993; although they ranked third and fourth, Britain and Russia stood well behind the US and Germany who are coming close to dominating Spain's export scene. Despite this and in sharp contrast to Italy, Spain has maintained a diverse palette of clients, none of which commands a strategic share of exports.

Only accredited *criadores exportadores* can ship to foreign markets. These are large industrial vinifiers and negociants who are traditionally based in the sherry-brandy sectors and in the blending (*assemblage*) of wines for export, all fairly concentrated sectors of activity. Much of the sherry business is in the hands of just three firms: Osborne, Domecq (now fully controlled by Allied Lyons) plus Gondalez Byass. That of *cava* is the near exclusivity of Codorniu and Freixenet. The steady contraction of the bulk business led traditional, large exporters of bulk, e.g. Vinival (controlled by Bodegas y Bebidas), Vicente Gandia and Schenk, to increase their bottled shipments and

Table 5.9 Spanish wine exports, 000 US$ (1990)

All wines*	1988	1989	1990	1991	1992	1993	Value share, % 1991–93	Volume share, % 1991–93
Germany**	90143	71890	101158	143008	170046	146969	19.5	24.0
UK	106706	87007	109989	135410	138641	146259	17.8	8.4
France	11293	11982	18060	42577	67236	87832	8.4	21.3
Netherlands	79714	62272	63373	67388	82522	82436	9.8	5.7
USA	89707	78143	72811	67872	71275	59482	8.4	2.4
Sweden	25597	25659	28457	30382	37812	43191	4.7	2.9
Russian Federation					2485	37213	1.7	3.3
Denmark	24633	20166	25627	25861	31667	34536	3.9	2.0
Switzerland	39980	37425	41608	38754	37190	32471	4.6	5.3
Belgium	20659	14813	17452	21013	19982	19856	2.6	1.8
Other	112625	164750	134912	125178	179429	136375	18.7	23.0
World	601057	574106	613447	697443	838284	826620	100.0	100.0

Sparkling

	1988	1989	1990	1991	1992	1993	Value share, % 1991–93	Volume share, % 1991–93
USA	49661	42965	40118	37901	35927	31589	26.1	27.8
Germany**	14758	15584	22556	23044	29930	27771	20.0	25.8
Russian Federation					2485	10116	3.1	3.5
UK	5125	4672	7611	7540	7377	8668	5.8	7.1
Switzerland	3710	3068	5073	4725	5311	5990	4.0	4.4
Sweden	6116	4401	5234	4227	5170	4059	3.3	4.7
Canada	4603	6280	5011	4374	3750	3528	2.9	3.9
Japan	2188	2495	2790	2788	4111	3168	2.5	2.7
Netherlands	1089	1594	2354	2634	2623	2421	1.9	2.1
Norway	1348	1232	1499	1728	2197	2176	1.5	2.1
Other	12237	13938	17743	18681	77164	20229	28.8	15.8
World	100836	96229	109989	107644	176046	119716	100.0	100.0

Still

	1988	1989	1990	1991	1992	1993	Value share, % 1991–93	Volume share, % 1991–93
UK	97550	78707	98795	124075	129914	137048	20.9	8.7
Germany**	70508	52275	68441	107595	124617	110324	18.3	21.8
Netherlands	78500	60506	60879	64605	79735	79782	12.0	6.2
France	9600	9684	13984	37774	59886	79032	9.5	22.3
Sweden	19417	21258	23223	26154	32642	39132	5.2	3.1
Denmark	23657	18853	23412	24407	29181	32413	4.6	2.1
Russian Federation						26719	1.4	3.5
Switzerland	35765	32781	36045	33503	31406	26083	4.9	5.7
USA	36186	31950	29725	27144	31395	25221	4.5	1.1
Belgium	17440	13331	15671	19128	17869	17775	2.9	1.9
Portugal		56938	8486			12095	0.6	1.7
Canada	8280	7875	7146	6543	7541	6278	1.1	0.8
Mexico	5729	5162	4598	5570	8777	6053	1.1	0.2
Ireland	6426	4281	5454	5549	6722	5982	1.0	0.3
Norway	5556	4171	4946	4721	5710	5214	0.8	0.5
Not specified		2888	3718			5106	0.3	0.6
Andorra	4493	4419	5244	5072	4592	4079	0.7	0.6
Côte d'Ivoire	4003	3398		3588	3087	4069	0.6	2.5
Japan	4569	6519	6541	5127	5859	3692	0.8	0.3
Other	48302	42454	59583	58407	49269	53866	8.7	16.3
World	475981	457450	475891	558963	628203	679963	100.0	100.0

* Including musts and vermouths   ** 1988–1990: FRG only   *Source: United Nations*

even to acquire appellation vineyards. Others, like Augusto Egli or the co-operative Cristo de la Vega have specialised in exporting *mistelles*, fizzy musts whose fermentation has been prevented by the addition of alcohol – the drink has a strength usually in excess of 10%. Rioja is Spain's equivalent to Bordeaux, yet few firms have really specialised in the export of fine wines so far; Fausto Martinez is a well known exception.

Most of these firms have long expanded internationally: Freixenet has a production unit in California, as does Torres who also invested in Chile. Bodegas y Bebidas set up a new company in Latvia in association with two local wineries recently, and Codorniu opened an affiliate in Russia in 1993. The British background of many sherry producers had helped them trade with the UK at an early stage. The three largest British traders of wine and spirits today (Guinness with a market capitalisation of 10.6 billion pounds in 1992, Grand Metropolitan with 8.1 billion pounds and Allied Lyons with 5.3 billion pounds[50]) have all reached worldwide proportions but their origins are deep-rooted in beer manufacturing:[51] Allied Breweries was the result of a 1961 merger between three regional English brewers which brought J Lyons in 1978 and the spirits division of the Canadian Hiram-Walker in 1986;[52] the Grand Metropolitan hotels group acquired the leading English brewer Watney Mann in 1972 and, with it, International Distillers and Vintners (IDV).[53] Their diversification into the wine sector was only a natural move out of their embattled domestic markets for spirits and beer. There were also considerable synergies to achieve at the distribution level, especially with tied pubs and specialist shops. Their expansion outside British borders led them to countries belonging to the 'Anglo-Saxon' model first, with a similar consumption trend towards more wine (and less spirits or beer) and synergies to be realised at the supplying and distribution stages. As they grew bigger and more dependent on the value of their publicly quoted shares (market capitalisation), they started to lay more and more emphasis on owning a portfolio of strong, internationally recognised brands which they would produce and push to consumers through their distribution network spanning the globe. A web of joint ventures and acquisitions during the deregulation of financial markets

49 *MIVS* (July–August 1993).

50 17.5 billion US$, 13.4 billion US$ and 8.8 billion US$ respectively (*The Financial Times*, 1993, p.35, 40).

51 Guinness' origins date back to 1759.

52 It is selling its tea and food activities and renaming itself Allied-Domecq.

in the 1980s allowed them to keep as much control as possible over the distribution of their brands and, thereby, on retail prices and margins. Greater control in terms of brand price policy led to more coherent marketing and greater possibilities for global advertising (e.g. spreading a similar image across countries in as far as this is possible). Brands also appeared in some balance sheets as intangible assets: Guinness and Grand Metropolitan put their brand valuation at 2.5 and 1.4 billion pounds respectively, which some accountants considered a most risky practice.[54] Many are inclined to share this view since 'Marlboro Friday'.[55]

Unlike sparkling wines, sherries, ports and vermouths, still wines do not lend themselves easily to global branding. Paul Masson, Piat d'Or, Mateus, Riunite, La Villageoise are amongst the few exceptions which are distributed worldwide and are still capable of commanding enough consumer franchise to bring substantial benefits to their owners (e.g. the possibility to rejuvenate the brand, as was the case with Paul Masson Light in the UK) or could allow for global advertising. International wine and spirits traders have systematically pruned their portfolio of brands and shed the weaker ones with the result that table wines have rarely stayed for long at the core of their business e.g. the recent disposal, by IDV, of its US ordinary wine brand Almaden; they almost invariably came back to large operators in the ordinary wine segment. Of the global traders, Seagram is probably the most patient as it least suffers under the need to produce 'quick results' to its annual meeting of shareholders (a large portion of the shares still rests with the Bronfman family). Accounting considerations linked with the issue of brand valuation may become more prominent as firms 'go public' in an increasing fashion in their hunt for fresh capital. The search for synergies at distribution level remains the logic behind most acquisitions in any event.

A nice portfolio of wines does help push brandies and other spirits in the Horeca sector for instance, which is of considerable importance in the embryonic markets of Asia. Closer to Europe, brands allowed German exporters to penetrate brand-hungry America with relative ease in the 1970s, and they remain the most valuable instrument at the disposal of *Sekt* producers and spirits traders now

53 Green, 1990.

54 Smith, 1992, Chapter 11.

55 Philip Morris, the tobacco *cum* food conglomerate, had to cut the price of its premium cigarette brand by about 20% on 2 April 1993, in response to losing market share to cheaply priced cigarettes (*The Financial Times,* 23 July 1993; *The Economist,* December 4, 1993).

moving into Eastern Europe. Brands also helped Portugal export its rosés and ports – with a little help from global traders.

Portugal

Portugal also had to wait for EU accession, in 1986, to buck the downward trend of foreign shipments (see Fig. 5.12). Holland, Denmark, Germany and Italy have remained secondary but fairly stable markets since 1970. Britain has remained an important outlet for Portuguese wines since the 1703 Methuen Treaty freed trade between the two countries, but shipments have fluctuated much in volume and value over the past two decades. Belgian orders rose substantially in the wake of Portugal's accession to the EU and are now closing in on the British. But overall, Portugal's export figures bear the

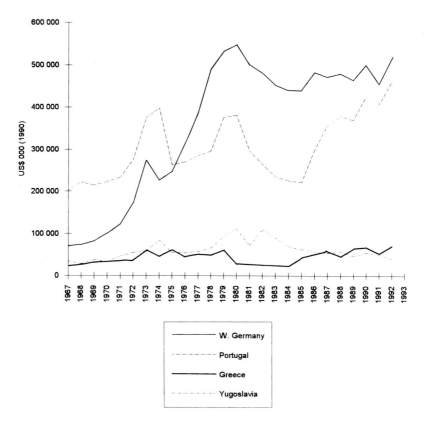

5.12 'Middle field' exporters (FOB, 112.1) (source: United Nations).

Table 5.10 Portuguese wine exports, 000 US$ (1990)

All wines*	1988	1989	1990	1991	1992	Value share, % 1991–92	Volume share, % 1991–92
France	103716	100156	109560	103741	123569	25.8	22.8
United Kingdom	65294	47005	58262	52507	57728	12.5	7.2
Belgium	53253	43743	57299	51727	56054	12.2	7.6
Angola	8978	20598	23409	25746	50720	8.7	18.6
Netherlands	23385	22350	27614	32189	35346	7.7	4.7
Germany**	24710	20658	26278	25212	25283	5.7	5.1
Italy	19719	19833	19104	21748	24738	5.3	6.0
USA	28216	24030	19990	18509	18773	4.2	3.4
Denmark	14383	13418	16148	15666	18699	3.9	3.6
Spain	5898	6135	7390	6716	8702	1.7	4.4
Other	48219	53927	55058	54241	54406	12.3	16.6
World	395771	371853	420112	408003	474021	100.0	100.0

* Including musts and vermouths
** 1988–1990: FRG only
Source: United Nations

imprint of the evolution of two critical markets, those of the US and France, who took a decisively different turn over the years. Shipments to the US increased sharply until the mid-1970s, when Portugal's military dictatorship was toppled, and then plunged into near oblivion. The French took exactly the opposite course: orders soared upon instigation of democracy in 1976 and then gradually increased until the 1990s. France is the largest importer of ports, and together with Belgium and the UK took up half of Portuguese exports in value in the early 1990s (just under 40% in volume, see Table 5.10). Another important outlet is Angola – a former Portuguese colony which still commands a share of over 18% in volume, but less than half that figure in terms of value.

Portugal's largest exporter is Sogrape, known for its Mateus brand; rosés make up 90% of its production and the firm exports an alleged third of the bottles exported by the country.[56] Fonseca, set up as a joint venture with IDV, ranks second with Lancers. Both brands deal essentially with rosés. Vinho Verde, with its 8% strength, is the lightest of all traditional wines and is exported mostly on that basis. The market structure of ports stems from the eighteenth century; the 30000 growers of the Douro Valley, represented by the Casa do Douro, are pitted against an association of about twenty port shippers on the other, dominated by the 'big three' (Allied Lyons, IDV and Seagram).

56 *Vinum* (May 1993) and *MIVS* (March 1993).

Germany

The 1980s brought an abrupt end to German ambitions in North America, but the addition of the five new *Länder* provides it with an excellent platform from which to penetrate the former Eastern bloc. German exports grew nearly tenfold in volume between 1970 and 1984, their all-time high. They peaked four years earlier in terms of value though, after their expansion in the US had ground to a halt. Exporters had responded to the degradation of their position on the US market with swift and deep price cuts worldwide, which managed to boost exported volumes for a few more years. British and Dutch orders soared. The UK market had followed the US lead with a short time lag and overtook it as soon as US orders started to weaken, and it took the diethylene-glycol affair of 1985 to wrench them into a more stable course (whilst precipitating their decline on the other side of the Atlantic). Britain has remained Germany's main export market ever since and now commands a market share of roughly 50% (see Table 5.11). Japanese orders doubled in volume between the mid and late 1980s and later stabilised at their current level; they are Germany's second outlet in value but come only fourth in terms of volume, behind Holland and a shrivelled US market.

Most Liebfraumilch[57] stems from Rheinessen and Rheinpfalz

Table 5.11 German wine exports, 000 US$ (1990)

All wines*	1988	1989	1990	1991	1992	Value share, % 1991–92	Volume share, % 1991–92
United Kingdom	219 615	206 496	230 954	205 050	228 768	44.6	52.9
Japan	37 325	41 005	51 208	37 652	45 306	8.5	4.6
Netherlands	39 493	38 047	39 293	41 653	43 617	8.8	9.4
USA	58 517	49 941	46 552	32 464	41 629	7.6	5.1
Sweden	14 247	14 137	14 109	17 139	26 114	4.4	3.8
Denmark	18 465	13 364	15 709	14 646	16 873	3.2	4.0
Canada	22 666	22 153	21 180	19 434	20 146	4.1	2.8
Belgium	9 712	10 038	11 510	14 168	13 537	2.8	3.0
Norway	8 844	7 609	8 386	8 547	8 601	1.8	1.9
Finland	2 660	3 100	5 539	8 138	8 274	1.7	2.0
Other	43 972	55 167	56 297	56 226	64 879	12.4	10.4
World	475 518	461 056	500 737	455 118	517 743	100.0	100.0

* Including musts and vermouths
** 1988–1990: FRG only
Source: United Nations

57 This type of wine can be produced from any combination of grape variety sanctioned for the production of appellation wines, provided the final blend contains at least 70% of Riesling, Silvaner, Müller-Thurgau or Kerner (Jamieson, 1991, p 67).

today, and is produced by large co-operative wineries and Sichel who owns the Blue Nun brand. The major German operators deal mostly with spirits and sparkling wines (Racke is perhaps the main exception, with its well-known Ameslfelder and Viola brands). Henkell & Söhnlein, for instance, has become a dominant figure on the wine scene since these two leading producers of *Sekt* merged in 1986; they also acquired a majority stake in Hungarovin in 1992, the largest producer in the country.

The former Yugoslavia

Exports by the former Yugoslavia increased until the early 1980s but regressed just as steadily afterwards, mainly because of tumbling orders by the former Eastern bloc (COMECON[58]) with which it enjoyed special status but failed to be a proper member. Yugoslavia became increasingly dependent on the West German market whose orders increased steadily during the 1970s and 1980s. It accounted for 40% of shipments in volume and contributed 45% to total earnings in 1989–1990.[59] The second largest outlet for Yugoslav wines was the UK, which took up 13% of exports in volume and 10% in value, though they had become less popular since the mid-1980s. The US with its 4% share in volume (6% in value) and Japan with its 3% (both in volume and value) were only minor outlets. For the rest, Yugoslavia used to rely heavily on its Eastern European partners. The former GDR, for instance, used to take up a quarter of Yugoslavia's exports at the time of the fall of the Berlin wall and Poland was another large customer.[60] Between 1986 and 1992, the former Yugoslavia exported 18% of production on average.

Individual wine consumption has been receding since its peak at 8.8 litres in the mid-1970s; it stood at a mere 6.6 in the early 1990s.[61] Production followed suit in the 1980s, at a slower pace, whilst exports were increased all along, until the mid-1980s. Most of the output is concentrated in Slovenia, which produces the best white wines, and

---

58 Also called CMEA (Council for Mutual Economic Assistance) see Chapter 6.

59 Average value; 1990 is the last year for which export data are available (source: United Nations).

60 FAO, 1992, p 16.

61 WDT.

yields are low by international standards.[62] The vast majority of Yugoslav exports occur in bulk, for bottling in the region of production is usually more expensive than in the importing country. Only the best wines – originating mostly from Slovenia – are estate bottled. Serbia is the largest producer of ordinary wines, mostly whites, but can hardly get access to foreign markets since the assault on Bosnia-Herzegovina in 1992 estranged the country from the international community. The combination of a contraction of domestic demand and shrivelled export markets – following the disintegration of Comecon in 1990 and economic sanctions imposed by some Western countries since 1992 – have raised the prospect of surpluses in war-torn Yugoslavia for the 1990s.

Greece

Greek exports fell significantly in volume in the early 1970s, in the wake of the setting up of a common market in wine within the EU. Belgium was Greece's principal client by far, but orders collapsed within a decade and Germany was left as the only significant buyer by 1980. French and Italian orders rose substantially in the mid-1980s, following Greek accession to the EU, though Italian orders have fluctuated considerably ever since. Germany remained Greece's best client, followed by France and Italy; Greece's reliance on these three markets has reached alarming proportions: their 1991–92 average share exceeded 80% in volume and 70% in value (see Table 5.12). Altogether, the EU absorbed 87% of Greek exports in 1992. The wines shipped to Germany were bottled consignments in most cases, but the vast majority of French and Italian purchases were cheap bulk for blending. Foreign shipments represented 15% of the decreasing quantities of wines supplied by Greece in the early 1990s (output has been falling since 1973). Production consists mostly of white wines, and only 8% of the wines supplied have a right to an appellation.[63] Here as well as in the rest of the EU, the sector of ordinary wines is going through an acute crisis.

62 27 hl/ha (FAO, 1992, p 16).

63 *MIVS* (January 1991).

Table 5.12 Greek wine exports, 000 US$ (1990)

All wines*	1988	1989	1990	1991	1992	Value share, % 1991–92	Volume share, % 1991–92
Germany**	14 943	17 579	26 383	26 070	33 549	48.0	42.8
France	5 374	9 209	16 000	8 220	14 478	18.3	21.8
Italy	748	12 951	6 561	3 168	4 724	6.3	15.8
USA	2 140	2 322	2 942	2 524	4 242	5.4	2.9
Belgium	1 558	2 755	2 092	2 316	3 457	4.6	3.8
Canada	1 503	2 505	2 431	1 904	2 192	3.3	2.3
Netherlands	828	803	1 375	1 376	1 691	2.5	1.6
United Kingdom	758	969	1 023	1 055	1 403	2.0	1.3
Not specified	694	871	885	948	1 043	1.6	0.8
Austria	562	612	743	603	995	1.3	1.0
Other	4 076	13 656	6 837	3 394	4 957	6.7	5.9
World	33 183	64 232	67 272	51 578	72 731	100.0	100.0

* Including musts and vermouths
** 1988–1990: FRG only
Source: United Nations

Other exporters

Cyprus

Cyprus exports concentrate on a few markets. Like Greece, the island is heavily dependent on Germany which takes nearly half of them in value (two-thirds in volume). Britain, Cyprus's colonial master until 1960, follows suit with over a quarter of its shipments in value and 10% in volume. Swiss orders rose in the late 1980s but decreased again thereafter; they consisted of industrial wines in most cases, and accounted for 11% of Cypriot exports in value and 15% in volume. Sweden is the next largest destination with just over 3% in value and volume; no other country commands a share in excess of 2%. Cyprus is working hard at renewing its vineyards with 'classic' varieties such as Chardonnay, Riesling, Cabernet Sauvignon and Cabernet Franc, and the wine laws are getting ever more 'Euro-compatible'.[64] Three-quarters of the island's production are concentrated in the hands of just four wineries.

64 *MIVS* (April 1994).

North and South Africa

The demise of exports and production of North African countries – Tunisia, Morocco and especially Algeria – coincided with the retreat of colonies and, later, the advance of Islamic fundamentalism. The gradual loss of foreign and domestic outlets, together with the inability of their wine industries to switch over to bottled trade, severely cut down shipments originating from North Africa. Algerian exports, for instance, collapsed in the early 1980s as can be seen in Fig. 5.8. The 26 million litres shipped in 1990, for US$24 million, represented little more than Austrian exports at around that time. Algeria's principal customer remains France, but trade between the two is only a fraction of what it used to be. In 1992 for instance, France imported 3 million litres from its former colony, 95% less than in 1970. France ceased to be a significant trading partner for Tunisia in 1989, which is left with Germany as its main buyer with six to seven million litres on average each year. The area of the Tunisian vineyard devoted to the production of wine has contracted by half since 1980 – it is now barely bigger than that of Switzerland – and production has shifted to growing table grapes.

In dire contrast to the situation in the North, the African Continent witnesses a boom in shipments from its southern tip. South Africa is a much larger producer though (ranking eighth behind Germany) and has benefited from the lifting of economic sanctions since the abolition of apartheid. Exports more than doubled between 1991 and 1992. The UK and Germany (neither of whom had imposed an embargo on South African wines) remain the country's largest client. Britain had imported an average US$5 million worth of wines between 1988 and 1991; orders leapt to US$12 million (roughly 7 million litres) in 1992.[65] Germany came a distant second with only half the British figures that year. Holland, Denmark, the US, Switzerland and Belgium followed suit, with orders ranging between three and one million dollars.[66] South Africa had long concentrated on bulk shipments, but bottled exports are expected to increase rapidly. The giant Kooperative Wijnbouwers Vereniging (KWV) is the main exporter. The quasi-monopolistic structure of the wine industry which has prevailed thus far is loosening up as the country unfolds to the world.

---

65 CIF; dollar figures are expressed in real (1990) terms as usual. Source: United Nations.

66 Idem.

China

Radical changes are affecting all strands of life in the states belonging to the former Soviet Bloc, now all undergoing a painful transition to free market economies, and cracks start to appear in China's wall.

Communist China and affiliated states in the South-East peninsula trade lightly in wine. As in Africa, these are poorly developed countries with more important trade priorities than boosting wine imports, which is generally considered to be a luxury item. China has an enormous potential for growing and making wine of its own and is currently developing it, sometimes with the help of foreign investors (e.g. recent joint ventures by Pernod-Ricard and Rémy-Cointreau).

The present economic and political outlook for China is such that its 'free enterprise zones' which are getting in ever closer contact with the West are quite likely to begin to import wine, yet still essentially for festive purposes. Hong Kong works as a hinge to the Chinese market for at least two reasons. Firstly, the profusion of unofficial channels between the British colony and the Southern provinces is a powerful incentive for avoiding administrative delays and hefty taxes.[67] Secondly, Hong Kong acts as a 'window to the West' for most Chinese and is used accordingly by Western manufacturers eager to display their products to a huge potential market of 1.2 billion customers. Mainstream China looks set to drink Chinese wine for some time still.[68]

All remaining states of interest to the wine trade, which used to have centrally planned economies, are located in Central and Eastern Europe.

---

67 *MIVS* (May 1994). Hong Kong also re-exports significant volumes of spirits and wines to Japan in order to supply the so-called 'parallel' import channels.

68 Wine ('Ju') is a term covering all alcoholic drinks, including spirits, and distilleries are particularly inefficient. Grape wine production is only marginal and thought to amount to little more than a few hundred thousand litres.

6

Formerly planned economies

Poland, the former Czechoslovakia, Hungary, Romania, Bulgaria, the German Democratic Republic and the former USSR made up what was known as the Soviet bloc from 1945 until 1989, when revolutions swept through Central and Eastern Europe, severing the ties between the satellite states and their political master. The USSR lost a number of its republics in the process but managed to consolidate what was left into the CIS two years later. The Soviet bloc was an economic as well as a political and military entity. COMECON[1] ensured the integration of all its members' centrally planned economies; it was essentially autarkic and reinforced the control of the USSR over them. COMECON members shunned GATT (even though some of them were founding members) and their currencies were non-convertible. COMECON was officially dissolved in 1990, but Soviet interest and co-operation amongst members had already fallen significantly on the heels of the USSR's own domestic reforms initiated in the mid-to-late 1980s. The 1980s meant stagnation for most Soviet bloc members, and the 1989 revolutions brought about recession. Heavy indebtness (accumulated largely in the 1970s and 1980s and forcing some members, such as Hungary, to export to the West in an attempt to service their debts),[2] lack of competitiveness

---

1 The Council for Mutual Economic Assistance (CMEA) was founded in 1949 and it included Mongolia, Cuba and Vietnam, but neither Albania or the former Yugoslavia ever became full members.

2 Kadar, 1992, p 348.

and, in many cases, unwillingness on the part of the former *nomenclatura* to give up its privileges, have crippled the former members' ability to sustain the prolonged pain of economic transition to Western style market economies.[3]

The disintegration of COMECON, the severe recession affecting all of its former members soon after they shrugged off Soviet domination and, ultimately, the collapse of the Soviet market which stood at its core, meant that COMECON's traditional wine suppliers were suddenly faced with the grim reality of structural production surpluses. Forty years of COMECON membership have left Hungary, Bulgaria and Romania with outdated technologies, a drive for quantity at the expense of quality,[4] a severe shortage of marketing skills and the daunting task of putting their production potential back into private hands – some 852 billion litres in all.[5] They turned briskly to Western markets in an attempt to save their wine industries from total collapse, searching for both investors and customers. A concomitant effort to restructure production has been slowly put into gear, partly financed by Western institutions such as the EBRD, the EU's PHARE program and the US's VOCA.[6] The planned revival of Eastern Europe's winegrowing and winemaking should bring with it not only better access to Western outlets, but also a rejuvenation of their own, stale wine markets while Russia composes itself before resuming imports eventually.

The quality of bottled exports by former COMECON members confines their immediate ambitions to a shrivelled Eastern European market and to the cheap end of Western markets however, while their own domestic markets remain of little interest to Western exporters of quality wines for some time yet (unlike those for spirits). This and the dire financial need in which most Eastern European producers find themselves force them to market the majority of their output in bulk, and set them on a collision course with EU producers (some of them have already re-routed part of their surpluses to Russia). Rough estimates for Eastern Europe's surplus put it at around 350 million litres for 1992, while EU figures suggest something in excess of 2

---

3 This section was partly based on *The Oxford companion to politics of the world* 1993, pp 119–20, 202–3, 861–7.

4 A variant of *déresponsabilisation* which ruined the EU wine market.

5 Average production for Hungary, Bulgaria and Romania over the 1986–90 period. Source: OIV.

6 European Bank for Reconstruction and Development; Volunteers for Overseas Cooperative Assistance (a Washington-based, private non-profit organisation).

billion litres in the same year. The intense competition raging at the commodity end of the international wine market will not wither away easily. The collapse of demand for wine in former Soviet bloc countries and the dissolution of COMECON, its swift replacement with preferential trade agreements with the EU by a few Central European states and/or resumption of GATT membership, have triggered a turbulent rearranging of trade flows across Europe, which is bound to send more than just ripples across the international wine market.

Major importers

East Germany

Individual alcohol consumption nearly trebled in the former East Germany between 1960 and 1990; wine revealed the strongest growth, increasing from just over 3 to more than 12 litres per head over that period, but still well below West German levels.[7] Wine imports doubled in volume between 1970 and 1989, progressing steadily from 104 to 210 million litres, but then fell abruptly in 1990 when Germany was reunited. Their progression was almost equally impressive in real value terms, from 143 to 238 billion over the same period (see Fig. 6.1). The transfer of the five *Länder* to the West and to the EU camp amounted to the loss of one of the most precious outlets for COMECON exporters and a boon to West German producers and importers, as well as to other EU members who could bank on EU preference for pricing their Eastern competitors out of the German market.

Poland

Poland (with a population of 38.4 million in 1990) is well ahead of the others in reforming its economy and could become a valuable market in the long term. Serious discrepancies between wine consumption

---

7 Official statistics revealed a most arguable jump from 12 to 20 litres between 1989 and 1990. Data for 1991 onward are included in those for unified Germany. Declining West German wine consumption stood at around 70 litres per head in 1990. Source: *World Drink Trends.*

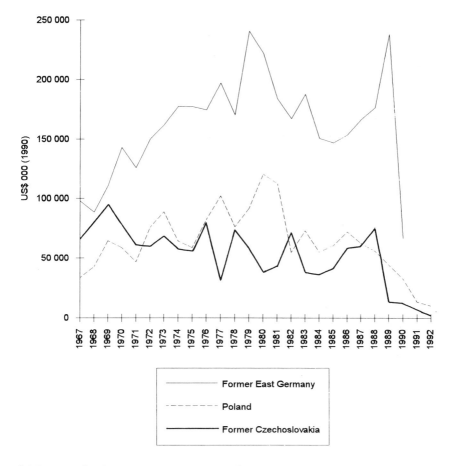

6.1 Imports by former East Germany, Poland and former Czechoslovakia (CIF, 112.1) (source: United Nations).

and trade figures prevent the identification of precise patterns prior to 1988,[8] though demand appears to have risen throughout the 1960s and 1970s and receded thereafter to an estimated 100 million litres in the years leading to 1990.[9] Imports grew correspondingly from under 50 million litres in 1979 to double that amount ten years later (see Fig. 6.1).[10]

8 Either because official consumption figures were inflated (presumably in order to curb the consumption of alcoholic drinks) or because huge quantities were smuggled into the country, or both.

9 Representing a mere 2 litres per head, according to OIV; Poland's Central Statistical Office (Glowny Urzad Statystyczny) in Warsaw puts the figure at 7.4 (in *World Drink Trends*).

10 97.4 and 114.8 million litres for US$56 billion and $44 billion in 1988 and 1989 respectively. Source: FAO.

The buck in trend came in 1990 as the result of tariff and steep tax increases which were intended to reduce consumption and imports of wine as well as spirits – the demand for beer and non-alcoholic drinks soared – and wine import figures dipped to 70 million litres in 1990 (for US$32.6 million). Trade and fiscal measures together with the mounting difficulties met by the country in the early stages of economic transition suppressed wine demand and imports even further in the following years, to just below the 40 million mark in 1991 (for US$14 million and to 30 million litres (for US$11m).[11]

In 1990, about a third of Polish imports stemmed from the EU in terms of value: France led the pack with a 30% share of EU exports to Poland, closely followed by Spain and Italy (with a quarter each) plus Germany (with just under 20%). Italian and German sparkling wines accounted for more than three-quarters of EU shipments in that category. Spain shipped the most still wines, half of them in bulk, just ahead of France. French exports consisted of bottled wines almost exclusively. The poor economic indicators at present would hint at a continuing trend for bulk shipments (only a minority of Poles can afford higher quality wines).[12]

The Czech and Slovak Republics

The Czech and Slovak Republics (with a combined population of 15.7 million people in 1990) are small wine producers of similar size to Switzerland, producing 120 million litres from 1986–90 on average, and 134 million in 1992).[13] Production increased in the 1970s but fell away during the following decade. Plans are now being made for a renewed increase in acreage and output with the aim of satisfying domestic needs; a mere 2% is exported.[14] Most of the production is white (87%)[15] and situated in Slovakia, which became a new exporter after the dissolution of its political union with the Czech Republic in January 1993.[16] The major problem for Czech and Slovakian producers is somewhat typical of all post-Communist regimes, that

11 Source: FAO.

12 *Journée Vinicole*, April 1992, pp 6–7.

13 Source: OIV.

14 FAO, 1992, pp 6–8.

15 Ibid, p 7.

16 Jennings & Wood, 1993, p 28.

of operating the smoothest transition possible from producing large quantities with little concern for quality, to adopting the quality standards expected in the West. This is not just a matter of wineries switching over to new technologies (particularly regarding filtration and bottling equipment) but of adopting a policy of producing and controlling quality so as to prevent yearly variations which Western consumers are increasingly reluctant to accept.[17]

Czechoslovakia was a typical beer consuming country. Wine consumption increased until the mid-1970s and has been receding ever since; demand climbed as high as 17.2 litres per head in 1977, but declined gently but continuously in subsequent years.[18] Total wine consumption fell further from 182 million litres in 1990 to 172 million in 1991 and 139 million in 1992. The Slovaks have a tendency to drink more wine and slightly less beer than the Czechs.[19]

Imports stood at around 30 million litres for most of the 1980s and over 80% stemmed from the former USSR and Hungary.[20] Figures contracted to some 19 million litres in 1990 (for US$12.5 million) and to 18 million litres in 1991 (for US$7 million), then virtually collapsed in 1992, for similar reasons to those at work in Poland.[21]

The former USSR

The biggest shock wave is likely to come from the former USSR which was one of the largest wine producers, consumers and importers in the world; in 1990, the USSR held a sixth of the earth's land surface and a population approaching 290 million. The authorities tried to curb alcohol consumption from the mid-1980s, cutting individual demand by over two-thirds in barely six years and wine consumption by nearly half, to an estimated seven litres per head in 1990. This is about the level at which it stood in the mid-1960s (demand soared in the late 1960s and peaked at over 16 litres before stabilising during the 1970s).[22]

---

17 Ibid, p 34.

18 Source: *World Drink Trends.*

19 Jennings & Wood, 1993, p 26–7.

20 FAO, 1992, p 7.

21 Source: OIV (recent figures from OIV and FAO are identical for basically all former planned economies).

22 Source: *World Drink Trends.*

The reduction in demand was basically achieved by cutting output: Gorbachev's uprooting programme reduced Soviet vineyards by 22%, from 1.3 million hectares in 1986 to 1 million in 1990. Acreage is spread over the republics of Moldova (200 000 ha), Azerbaijan (180 000 ha), Ukraine (170 000 ha), Russia (150 000 ha), Uzbekistan (130 000 ha), Georgia (120 000 ha), Armenia and Tadjikistan. Total production averaged 1.8 billion litres in 1991 and 1992. A return to mid-1980s levels is planned for the year 2000, to around 3.4 billion litres.[23] The former Soviet Union exported a mere 1% of its production. Moldova and Georgia were the most active on foreign markets, followed by Russia and Ukraine with their sparkling wines. The USSR's outlets were the former East Germany and Hungary.[24] Russian exports fluctuated in a 10–20 million litre band from 1970 until 1985 and then increased significantly over the second half of the 1980s, venturing into the 60–90 million litres territory, only to fall back to previous levels: 26 million litres were brought out of the country in 1990 for nearly US$80 million and 20 million the following year, for a mere US$54 million.[25]

Imports stood at above 700 million litres for most of the time in the period between 1970 and 1985 but plunged into a lower band (100–200 million) soon after, and they now fluctuate erratically within this range. About 140 million litres were imported in 1990 for a value of US$285 million.[26] Barring the occasionally large imports of bulk designed to compensate for poor harvests at home, e.g. from Argentina in the late 1970s and later from Spain and Algeria, shipments consisted mainly of fine wines which were almost exclusively from Hungary and Bulgaria.

Within the Soviet Union, Russia used to import vast quantities of wine in bulk and musts which were used for blending with its domestic production. Georgia and Moldova were two major suppliers and their relationship with Russia was largely based on barter trade. The intangible nature of barter trade, the dismantling of former distribution channels and the proliferation of new, 'parallel' ones, together with the acute instability of both the Russian system and that of the whole Commonwealth of Independent States, make it difficult for anyone to guess the nature and size of future trade flows between the former Soviet republics and the rest of the world. The Moldovan

23 FAO, 1992, p 11.

24 Ibid, p 14.

25 Ibid.

26 Ibid.

case helps illustrate this point, showing how difficult it is for former Soviet states to sever the ties woven by their former Russian masters.

Moldova is a landlocked state situated to the east of Romania and to the sough-east of Ukraine, of a similar size to Belgium but with a population of only 4.4 million people. The official wine promotion agency had the exclusive right to dispose of wine production until 1991, and Moldova enjoyed a cosy relationship with its sole client, the Russian central purchasing authority. Only in 1992 were Moldovan producers given the opportunity to sell a third of their production to other outlets, including export markets. This 'window of opportunity' was shut the following year however, when it became clear that Moldova would need to trade all available wine for the raw materials desperately needed from Russia.[27]

The Russian Federation is known for having revised its import taxes on numerous occasions. In February 1993, tariffs on still wines were set at 10, 20 and 40% of their CIF value, depending on whether the exporter was a developing nation, a country enjoying 'most favoured nation' (MFN) status with the Russian Federation (as do the EU and the US for instance) or some other relationship.[28] The web of bilateral treaties amongst CIS members could cause a far-reaching reshuffling of Russia's traditional supply lines for wine since, for instance, Georgia and Moldova now appear to be subject to the import tax whereas Azerbaijan and Ukraine are exempt from it. This has led some exporters to establish distribution joint ventures on Russian soil, with a clear view to displacing Georgia and Moldova as traditional suppliers.[29] And if one needed any proof of it, EU exports to the former Soviet Union sprung from less than half a million litres in 1989 to nearly 2 million in 1990 and 5 million in 1991 (for a value of 4.3 million ECUs), albeit with the help of export subsidies.[30] These were mainly surplus table wines from Spain.

Romania, Hungary and Bulgaria

Romania bought small amounts of foreign bulk from Spain, Italy and Argentina, for blending with domestic production essentially, as did

---

27 See Lamont, 1993, for more details.

28 *Horticultural Products Review*, May 1993, p 29.

29 Ibid.

30 Source: Eurostat, in *Horticultural Products Review*, May 1993, p 30–1.

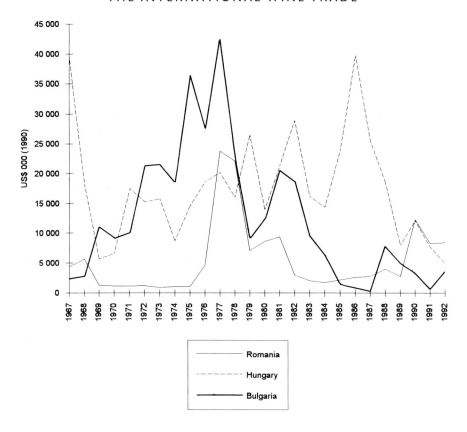

6.2 Imports by former Romania, Hungary and Bulgaria (CIF, 112.1) (source: United Nations).

Hungary who tapped the southern European and Algerian markets. Hungary imported 47 million litres in the first half of the 1980s on average, but this dropped to some 23 million litres in 1990, for an estimated value of US$12 million.[31] Bulgaria imports little wine; 2.5% of production, compared to Hungary's 10% in the 1980s,[32] see Fig. 6.2.

31 FAO and the Hungarian Winetraders' Association, *The Hungarian Economy,* June 1993.

32 1981–90 average (OIV).

Leading exporters

Hungary

In its transition to a market economy, Hungary (with a population of 10.6 million) steered clear of shock therapy from the outset. It is seeking the active co-operation of foreign companies in the form of joint ventures and aims at freeing up trade gradually; relationships with former COMECON members are handled with in the framework of bilateral agreements, and broader association agreements have been signed with EFTA and the EU. Both types of agreement are based on the principle of 'asymmetrical free trade', whereby Hungarian (as well as Bulgarian and Romanian) exporters are granted easier terms for access to West European markets than are EU or EFTA exporters in those three countries.[33] The sensitive issue on wine trade was dealt with in a separate agreement with the EU.

Hungarians have a long tradition in producing and exporting wine. The country also stands at the forefront of innovation in Eastern Europe. It used to export over 300 million litres in the mid-1980s and as much as 200 million litres until 1989, but shipments dropped sharply in 1990, to 160 million litres (exports then subsided to 90 million and 110 million litres in 1991 and 1992 respectively). Some 83 million litres went to the former USSR in 1990, and its successor republics remain Hungary's principal client in spite of the dramatic cut in their consumption.[34] The defection of Hungary's second largest customer to the West – the Eastern German *Länder* – resulted in the loss of valuable sales: the combined imports of West and East Germany for instance fell from 77.1 million litres in 1988 to 32.2 million in 1990. The Czech and Slovak Republics imported a further 16.4 million litres from Hungary. They were followed by the UK, the US and Canada, all minor customers with purchases ranging between 200 000 and 400 000 litres.[35] Less than a quarter of shipments were done in bulk in 1989 and 1990, but in 1992, its exports were roughly split between bottles and bulk.[36]

---

33 Kadar, 1992, pp 350, 358.

34 Source: FAO.

35 441 000, 220 000 and 200 000 litres respectively. Source: Hungarian Winetraders' Association (in *Marketing Jahrbuch Wein 1991/2*).

36 Based on data reported in OIV, *The Hungarian Economy*, June 1993.

Hungary exported half its production in the second part of the 1980s.[37] The collapse of the COMECON markets left its producers with years' worth of stocks and calling for further cuts in output (production had already been reduced from 500 to 400 million litres between the first and second half of the 1980s; 70% of the acreage is planted with white varieties and 30% with red).[38] Hungary alone held an estimated 350 million litres of unsold wine in stock in 1992, representing more than an entire harvest. Some 200 million litres a year were predicted to find no purchasers and the crisis was deemed so acute that the government decided to send some 30 million litres of surplus wines to the distilleries, on the 'EU model'.[39] The wine legislation currently in preparation is intended to be 'Euro-compatible'.

These difficulties only added to the strains caused by falling domestic demand, which had been receding since the early 1970s and averaged 236 million litres in 1986-90,[40] whilst beer enjoyed a continuously rising popularity, as indeed did spirits until recently. The collapse of wine consumption in 1989 brought the Hungarian government to raise taxes on beer and spirits and to reduce that on wine, and demand swung back to levels it enjoyed in the early 1980s (per capita consumption stood at 30 litres per head in 1991 and 1992).[41] The upturn in consumption may be due to the success of the 'new style' varietals. These wines are produced in ever greater amounts by Hungarian wineries and are making serious advances on Western markets, particularly in the US and in the UK.

'New style' wines are based on a few classic varieties (Chardonnay and Sauvignon Blanc for the whites; Cabernet Sauvignon, Cabernet Franc and Merlot for the reds) and the wines are made on the Australian and American model (foreign winemakers have been hired in many cases). This is in stark contrast to the varietals produced before the 1990s by the large state-owned *kombinat* wineries such as Egervin, Hungarovin, Pannonvin and Balaton Boglar.[42] The successful wines are made and marketed by joint ventures in most cases, e.g. with British capital in the case of Gyöngyös in the Eger region and Balaton Boglar in South Balaton. Foreign capital is also flowing in Tokaj which

---

37 1986–90 average.

38 OIV, *The Hungarian Economy*, June 1993.

39 CFCE, *Marketing Jahrbuch Wein 1992/93*, p 143.

40 Source: OIV.

41 Source: OIV and *World Drink Trends*.

42 Williams, 1993.

produces Hungary's best-known traditional sweet wines. Most ventures concentrate on the production side, though some of the investors are global drinks manufacturers seeking to establish a major presence in the country and, undoubtedly, access for other products they manufacture, whether spirits or non-alcoholic drinks.[43] AOC legislation is being drawn up on the European model whilst EU and US co-operation programmes assist Hungary in its attempt to approach Western markets in a much more aggressive way, by raising the image of its wines with the help of generic advertising amongst other things.[44] 'Excellent value for money' is what Hungarians are aiming for; if successful, the strategy would result in positioning their products above Bulgarian varietals and dangerously close to Australian wines.

Bulgaria

Bulgaria (with a population of 9 million) has been faced with a slow decline in individual demand for wine since the early 1970s, from 26–27 litres per head to 20–23 in the early 1990s. Spirits consumption rose until the mid-1980s and beer sales soared until 1989 (rising more than fourfold between 1960 and 1990 and falling abruptly in 1991).[45] Domestic demand accounted for a mere 40% of the 380 million litres of wines produced in the 1980s and the main destination was the USSR. Many of its wines were shipped to Western markets as well, particularly Germany and the UK, where they scored a string of successes in the lowest price points – the 'cheap varietals' segment (Bulgaria has long regarded wine production as a means of generating hard currencies). Other export outlets include the Scandinavian countries plus Denmark, Switzerland, Japan and the USA.[46] Bottled shipments first reached US consumers in 1979 through PepsiCo's international wine and spirits division, Monsieur Henri Wines, while Pepsi concentrate was imported by Bulgaria's state monopoly as part of the agreement.[47]

---

43 For example, Seagram acquired Hungarovin recently.

44 Williams, 1993.

45 Source: *World Drink Trends.*

46 FAO, 1992, p 4.

47 Philpott, 1989, p 190.

Bulgaria remained COMECON's largest exporter until Hungary caught up with it in the early 1980s, but the average value of its wines was generally lower than those of its competitor (see Fig. 6.3). Bulgarian exports rose from 200 million litres in the early 1970s to well over 300 million in barely 12 years. They fell to 200 million following the collapse of the Soviet market in 1986 and dipped again dramatically at the turn of the decade, plunging to 127 million litres in 1990 (for US$213 million FOB) and to half that amount a year later.[48] Unlike Hungary, Bulgaria has not granted any export subsidies since privatisation of its agricultural sector.

Production is heavily mechanised. It rose until the early 1980s, stopping short of 500 million litres and declined steadily afterwards; figures dipped below the 300 million mark in 1989 and totalled only

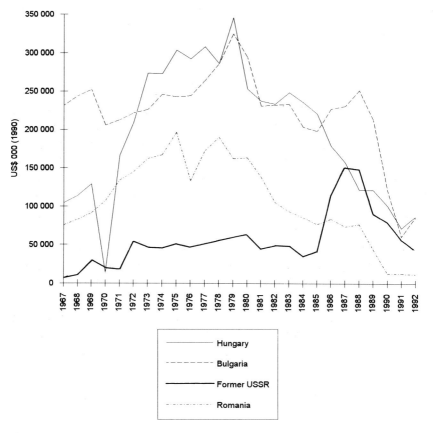

6.3 Exports by Hungary, Bulgaria, the former USSR and Romania (FOB, 112.1) (source: United Nations).

48 Source: FAO.

200 million in 1992.[49] An AOC legislation was first introduced in 1978 and reinforced in 1985.[50] State co-operatives have been broken up by liquidation committees and land restituted in accordance with the 1991 land law, but with little tangible success so far, since this has brought the farming sector back to subsistence level, particularly in terms of the technology employed. Large collective farms' machinery is often proving too large for working individual plots of land and much of it stands idle. The allocation of land is proving difficult in a country whose orthodox communist regime destroyed all records related to private property and whose economy was the most closely linked with that of the former Soviet Union. The GNP was halved after the breakup of COMECON, which used to take up 80% of exports, and the former *nomenclatura* is still proving the biggest hurdle in privatising the rest of the economy (Bulgaria is considered the laggard of all former Soviet satellites in this respect).[51]

Romania

Romania (with 23 million inhabitants) is faced with roughly similar conditions to those in Bulgaria in terms of domestic demand for alcohol, with the exception of spirits consumption, which has remained stable since the early 1970s. Individual demand for wine fell from about 30 litres in the 1970s to 20 litres in the early 1990s.[52] The domestic market remains the largest of the former Soviet satellite countries, even though it shrunk from 650–700 million litres in the 1980s to a mere 450 million in 1991 and 1992.[53]

Romania built a favourable reputation and scored early successes in the West in the 1970s for the outstanding wines it used to market at that time. Exports stood at around 70 million litres in the early 1970s, broke briefly through the 100 million mark on three occasions (in 1975, 1980 and 1981), but receded steadily in the 1980s. Exports had lost 30% of their volume by 1989 and collapsed to the 10–15 million litres range in the early 1990s.[54] An estimated 16 million litres were

49 Source: OIV.

50 Philpott, 1989, p 51.

51 *The Financial Times*, 5 May 1993.

52 Source: *World Drink Trends* and OIV.

53 Source: OIV.

54 Source: UN, OIV.

exported in 1990, for an FOB value of US$13 million.[55] Its major Western markets were Germany, the US and the UK.[56] Romania is far less dependent on exports than are either Hungary or Bulgaria: foreign demand accounted for 5–7% of domestic output prior to the export crash and it only imported 1% of its domestic needs.

Bulk imports originate mainly from Spain, followed by Argentina and Italy.[57] They soared to over 20 million litres in 1991 and 1992 and shifted Romania into the net importers' camp, if only temporarily.[58] Its wine industry has deteriorated markedly over the past 15 years and only huge investments would seem to be able to bring it back up to winemaking standards prevailing in other export countries. Production has decreased from the 800 million litre level prevailing before the 1989 revolution to a current 500 million litres, while the country is facing economic and social disintegration by and large. An estimated 20% has fallen out of production thus far whilst some vineyards are undergoing restructuring. Like all other former COMECON producers, Romania intends to restore past production levels.[59] An uphill struggle lies ahead of it.

Trade between the EU and former COMECON members

The EU is Eastern Europe's closest trading partner. The two blocs managed to develop a few trade links before the dissolution of COMECON, in spite of their autarkic/protectionist tendencies.

There was a near balance in wine trade between the EU and former COMECON members in volume terms in the early 1990s, with the flow in either direction standing at around 70 million litres. Not including the former Yugoslavia which never was a full member, COMECON's exports to the EU amounted to 63 and 73 million litres in 1990 and 1991 respectively and were mainly attributable to Bulgaria, Hungary and Romania. Imports from the EU totalled 64 and 75 million litres in those same two years and went principally in the direction of

55 Source: FAO.

56 FAO, 1992, p 10.

57 Ibid.

58 1986–90 averages (OIV).

59 FAO, 1992, p 9.

Table 6.1 EU external trade: imports and exports (000 litres)

Imports	1987	1988	1989	1990	1991
Former Yugoslavia	57 079	58 101	46 560	62 584	66 521
Bulgaria	15 638	21 498	22 866	35 090	40 660
Hungary	18 022	17 406	15 428	14 745	19 717
Romania	8 787	9 772	9 580	10 335	10 181
Former USSR	2 898	2 755	3 407	3 211	2 710
Former Comecon	45 345	51 431	51 281	63 380	73 267
Former Comecon's share	28%	31%	34%	32%	32%
Total	159 462	165 253	152 503	198 696	231 404

Exports	1987	1988	1989	1990	1991
Former Yugoslavia	148	167	356	1 510	17 463
Bulgaria	29	80	47	4 790	7 631
Hungary	20 982	15 265	50 769	20 992	4 961
Romania	56	39	27	17 755	16 846
Former USSR	159	169	348	1 940	4 798
Poland	1 203	7 856	20 612	12 251	36 055
Czechoslovakia	4 043	305	787	6 592	5 164
Former Comecon	26 471	23 715	72 589	64 322	75 454
Former Comecon's share	2%	2%	7%	6%	8%
Total	1 069 375	1 048 377	1 068 807	1 015 725	958 288

Source: Eurostat (in Cahier de conjoncture, no. 3, March 1994, pp 120–1).

Poland and Romania. Wine trade between the two former trading blocs has gone through significant changes over the past 20 years.

The EU's exports to the former COMECON started from the relatively modest base of 22 million litres in the first half of the 1970s on average. They soared in the late 1970s following huge orders from the former USSR and even passed the 150 million mark in the early 1980s. EU export figures fell within a 40–60 million litre fluctuation band following the collapse of the Russian market. East Germany (30–40 million litres) and Hungary (5–20 million litres) became the major outlets for EU wines in the mid-1980s. With Hungarian exports having regressed considerably in the meantime, the market is currently driven by Romania (17 million litres in 1991) and Poland (36 million), see Table 6.1.

COMECON's exports to the EU rose from an average 27 million litres in the first half of the 1970s to over 70 million in the early 1980s. Figures had contracted somewhat to 40 million by the mid-1980s but recovered steadily afterwards, reaching some 73 million in 1991. Hungarian exports to the EU totalled 20 million litres in that year, half the volume exported by its closest rival, Bulgaria. Bulgarian shipments rose sharply in the second half of the 1980s, due in great part to the enormous success of its varietals on the British market; its second largest EU client was West Germany. Romanian exports to the EU declined gently throughout the first half of the 1980s but rose again later, returning to the 10 million litre level they used to enjoy in the late 1970s. Shipments by the former USSR totalled as much as 4–5 million litres in the late 1970s but now average 3 million; they are almost exclusively marketed in what was West Germany.

Although balanced, trade between the EU and COMECON did not have the same importance to the European Union: whereas EU shipments represented only 8% of its worldwide exports in the early 1990s (1 billion litres), wines originating from COMECON accounted for nearly a third (32%) of its imports at that time (200–230 million litres).[60] The difficulties of the former Soviet bloc (economic recession and dipping demand for wine) made COMECON switch from a net *importing* capacity of nearly 70 million litres in the first half of the 1980s, to a net *exporting* potential of 350 million in the second half.

The CIS experienced a contraction of demand in the late 1980s, which was far greater than the reduction in production, causing a swing from being a net importer of over 150 million litres during the first half of the 1980s to a net exporter of some 140 million litres in the second half. CIS demand sprang back in the course of the 1990s though, turning it into a net importer again, of around 100 million litres. This is significantly less than the 200 and 500 million litres of net imports realised during the 1970s however, as shown in Fig. 6.4.

Exports by non-CIS members doubled to over 200 million litres between the first and second half of the 1980s, and increased further to 280 million and 430 million in 1991 and 1992 respectively. The curtailing of COMECON's production potential outside the CIS[61] had fallen short of the reduction in demand here as well, by over 100 million litres. The defection of the GDR to the EU – worth an estimated 140 million litres – and the collapse of the Polish market (from over 300 million litres to under 200 million between the first and second half of the 1980s) were particularly severe. Demand regressed by some 20 million litres in Czechoslovakia and the traditional markets of Hungary, Bulgaria and Romania decreased by a combined 150 million litres over the same period. Conditions deteriorated further almost everywhere in the course of the early

---

60 This section rests on EU data issued by the Commission of the EU and Eurostat, who publish wine trade data in volume only.

61 350 million litres.

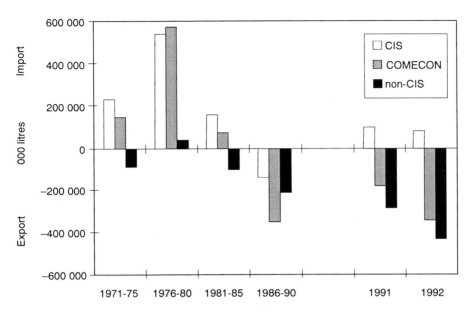

6.4 Notional imports by former COMECON (source: OIV).

1990s, except in Hungary, where domestic demand bounced back to an estimated 310 million litres in 1992.

The former COMECON members drank 2.92 billion litres in 1992 but produced over 3.27 billion, meaning it would need to export 350 million litres outside its trading area to keep its production capacity intact. The transfer of the East German *Länder* to the West and the temporary shrivelling of traditional COMECON markets have stripped Hungarian, Bulgarian and Romanian exporters of a significant part of their clientele and generated momentary surpluses which are unmarketable in the West, much like EU 'distillation wines'. The quality of bottled exports to former COMECON members being low by Western standards, the current tendency is for Eastern European producers to dispose of their wines most cheaply and in bulk when dealing with Western buyers, so dire is their need for hard currencies. Bottled trade is thus likely to see its share rise over the longer term whilst conditions on the new style varietals segment is bound to stiffen considerably in the international market now led by American and Australian producers. Former COMECON producers will be forced to sell bulk for as long as they have not restructured production to a higher quality level *and* until they have established a durable presence in Western markets with either cheap, heavily branded generics or new style varietals. Bulk trade is thus heading for collision between EU and the former Eastern Europe surpluses in a depressed European market. Russia will use the contest to its own advantage, being eager to import the cheapest bulk on offer in order to keep its 'wine factories' running (just like Japan) while waiting for demand to spring back to life. The best way to avoid a damaging price war is to resize production while spurring consumption by lowering prices and widening consumer choice. Both objectives can be met within the framework of GATT/WTO.

Stemming a likely overspill of Eastern European wines, waiting to be diverted to West European destinations in the aftermath of the collapse of COMECON's main consumer markets, became a priority for the EU. Five-year agreements were passed in November 1993 regulating the use of wine designations and limiting wine flows between the EU and the three most successful exporters on its eastern flank, i.e. Hungary, Bulgaria and Romania. The wine accords were negotiated separately from all other sectors of economic activity including agriculture. They offered them tariff quotas worth a combined 65 million litres for 1993, just short of the 71 million the EU imported in 1991 (see Table 6.1). Hungary, Bulgaria and Romania were awarded 18.7 million, 33.3 million and 11 million litres respectively while each conceded tariff quotas to EU exporters worth 9 million, 4.3 million and 6 million litres. The quotas are scheduled to increase by about 10% each year. The EU's preferential rate is set at 80% of the basic import duty, to be lowered to 40% at the end of the five-year period. The EU's partners put it at 90% (due to a decrease to 70–75% over the same five years).[62] Wine trade with Poland and the Czech and Slovak Republics is governed by bilateral association agreements signed earlier, in December 1991, as well as by subsequent interim arrangements.

The association agreements are often viewed as a means of keeping the EU's new partners at arm's length, in spite of the general commitment to open up markets to Eastern European goods, since the EU happens to erect the highest barriers in exactly those areas where its trading partners are proving most competitive.[63] The same could be said of the wine agreements: keeping Eastern European wine exports under check was more crucial to the EU over the short and medium term, than attempting to carve new markets in the East,

---

62 *Official Journal of the European Community*, No 1, 337.

63 Particularly in agriculture. See *The Financial Times*, 11 May 1992, 8 March 1994, and *The Economist*, 13 March 1993, for more details. The same can be said of the EU commitment at the 1992 Edinburgh summit to let Central Europeans join; Hungary and Poland formally applied in 1994 but are unlikely to join in the immediate future.

where unsubsidised exports would prove uncompetitive anyway.[64] Besides, the EU was negotiating its latest enlargement at that time, thereby hoping to secure privileged access to a fresh set of relatively rich consumer markets by simple application of 'community preference' – a further blow to those Eastern European exporters who had concluded with EFTA members general association agreements of the same vein as those negotiated with the EU.

The series of bilateral association agreements passed between Western and Eastern European states aim at establishing asymmetrical trade flows between developed market economies on the one hand and formerly planned economies – now in transition – on the other. Their prime objective is to prevent imports by Eastern Europe from rising faster than their exports to the Western European states, as was the case with 'agrifood' trade between 1988 and 1990.[65] Are these bilateral agreements mere preambles to EU membership and would it not be better, over the longer term, for Eastern European wine economies to focus on the opportunities offered by a worldwide multilateral trade agreement? This option burst into the open in April 1994, in Marrakesh, with the signing of GATT's Uruguay Round's Final Act, which will bring about sweeping changes in world trade.

Most Central and East European states are contracting parties at GATT: Poland, the Czech and Slovak Republics plus Hungary are founding members; Romania is a contracting party enjoying 'developing nation' status. Bulgaria and Slovenia are about to become full members of GATT's successor, the World Trade Organisation (WTO). Less advanced negotiations are also under way for the admission of Croatia and Albania. Most of the CIS states have observer status, signifying their intention to join.

---

64 Not least because Central European currencies are momentarily undervalued in terms of international purchasing power parity. Central Europe is deemed to become one of the fastest growing economic regions of the world (*The Economist,* 13 March 1993).

65 Poignant, 1992, p 29.

CHAPTER

7

After Marrakesh

In April 1994, representatives of the 111 countries which have become contracting parties to GATT since its founding in 1947, signed the Final Act of the eight year old Uruguay Round of negotiations. For agriculture, it entails binding commitments in the areas of market access, export competition and domestic support over a period of six years, beginning in January 1995 (ten years for developing countries). The Final Act also offers better protection of wine designations and trademarks. GATT's existing but separate agreement on technical barriers, its *Standards Code*, was revised and made applicable to all the Final Act's signatories, who also agreed on a set of rules and disciplines in the areas of sanitary and phytosanitary measures. Much stricter provisions will govern the use (and abuse) of technical measures as a result. By clearing a series of major obstacles, Marrakesh brings a sluggish international wine trade to the threshold of a renewed phase of competition and growth, which could match that of the 1970s.

Technical standards, sanitary and phytosanitary measures

GATT's agreement on technical barriers to trade – hitherto applicable only to certain countries – was extended to all members of the WTO. With regards to wine, and with the exception of packaging and labelling requirements, the discipline introduced by the adoption of the principles enshrined in the *Standards Code* should prove more important than the actual provisions themselves, for it is sanitary and phytosanitary measures which have the greatest potential to restrict international wine exchanges. They are handled separately from WTO provisions on standards and include processing and production methods (new technological applications); certification, testing and inspection procedures; methods for evaluating the potential adverse effect on health arising from the presence of additives, pesticide residues and contaminants. Taken together, sanitary and phytosanitary measures constitute a true minefield to any wine producer venturing out of his home country. The broad definitions, basic rights and obligations of WTO members, as well as the terms for ensuring transparency of the measures, have been clearly spelled out in the Final Act, and the 125 signatories have agreed to abide by them.

The aim of the agreement on sanitary and phytosanitary measures is to minimise their negative effects on trade, not just by ensuring their transparency and their non-discriminatory character (an important topic since wines are essentially differentiated on the basis of their origin), but also their justifiability on the basis of scientific evidence. Rules for notification of the planned introduction of new measures and procedures for appeal against them are already in place. A committee on sanitary and phytosanitary measures is established, which should put erstwhile negotiations on harmonising existing measures on new tracks. It will be able to bank on previous efforts provided to that end, particularly in the framework of the FAO's *Codex Alimentarius* and that of recent bilateral wine agreements, in much the same way as GATT did for intellectual property issues: here, it was able to draw on past work carried out mainly by the Office International de la Vigne et du Vin and the World Intellectual Property Organisation.

Geographical indications and appellations of origin

The Final Act's chapter on intellectual property rights secures virtually worldwide protection when geographical indications identify that a wine has a particular quality, reputation or other characteristic because it originates from a specific geographical area. Such indications must not be used on other wines. However, WTO member countries in which a particular indication has already become a generic name are not required to provide this protection for the wine in question. A similar exception applies to pre-existing trademarks. A third exception relates to semi-generic terms, e.g. Californian Chablis and Australian Lambrusco, in countries where they have been in use for more than ten years – and have thus become traditional household names – but their use must not increase in scale or nature. These exceptions will be subject to further negotiations between the countries concerned, with the aim of phasing them out. Future disagreements between member countries about the compatibility of national laws with their obligation to provide these rights against the use or misuse of denominations, designations, appellations and other wine epithets (in all languages) will be subject to WTO's dispute settlement procedure.[1]

Market access

The Final Act requires, for each category of wine import or 'tariff line', the translation of all non-tariff measures which applied from 1986–88 into a single tariff (customs duty) equivalent. This process is called 'tariffication'. Border measures include quantitative import restrictions (import quotas), minimum import prices, variable import levies, discretionary import licensing, restrictions maintained through state trading and voluntary export restraints. Tariffication takes place with quite a detailed level of description of the goods (usually at the 8-digit level of the Harmonised System code; tariff equivalents are basically calculated as the difference between domestic and CIF prices for each type of good. The resulting initial tariffs – whether specific, *ad valorem* or mixed – must become effective in the course of 1995 and reduced by 36% on average over a period of six years. The 36% rate of reduction must be met by the agricultural sector as a whole and a minimum rate of 15% applies to each tariff line.

Access opportunities prevailing in 1986–88 (usually offered in the form of bilateral arrangements providing for country-specific import quotas or tariff quotas) must be maintained. Whether these were fully used at that time is irrelevant. Any expansion of tariff quotas must take place on an MFN basis, which effectively rules out the conclusion of new preferential agreements amongst WTO members.[2]

---

1 Take the recent agreements between the EU and Hungary, Bulgaria and Romania for instance, which devoted a hundred pages each to listing protected EU wine denominations alone.

Existing ones will erode over time as preferential and full tariff rates are reduced simultaneously.

Minimum access of 3% of the market must be provided for under any circumstances, at the beginning of the 6-year period, in terms of a tariff quota bearing low or minimal tariff rates; it must be expanded to reach 5% by the end of the implementation period. This provision is aimed at the most protected markets; its objective is to ensure that trade takes place in spite of potentially prohibitive initial tariff rates, i.e. where the difference between domestic and import prices is so high as to deny imported goods any significant share of the domestic market.

Schedules comprising the initial tariff equivalents (including tariff quotas) and the proposed reductions were submitted by each contracting party and accepted before Marrakesh. They become binding commitments upon ratification of WTO by each member state. Figures 7.1 to 7.3 show the initial and bound tariffs applying to a litre of still wine in bulk (worth US$1.5 CIF), of still wine in bottles (US$4.5 CIF) and of sparkling wine in bottles (US$4.5 CIF) shipped by Australia to the US, the EU and Japan. The full schedule is reproduced in Tables 7.1–7.3.

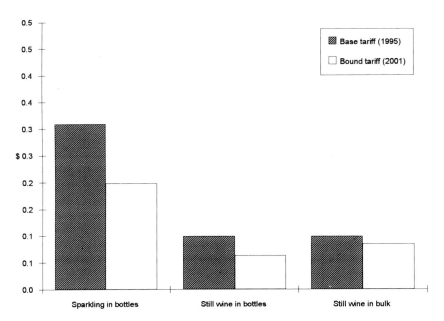

7.1 Base and bound tariffs for the US (source: GATT/WTO).

2 Except in cases aiming at the establishment of a customs union.

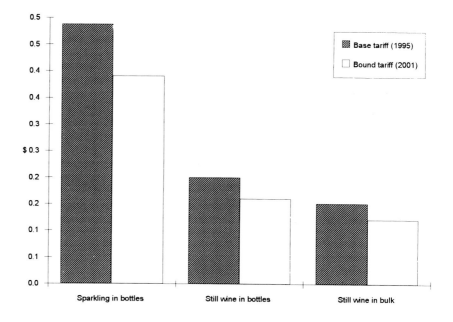

7.2 Base and bound tariffs for the EU (source: GATT/WTO).

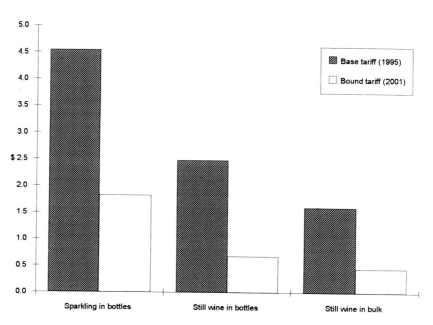

7.3 Base and bound tariffs for Japan (source: GATT/WTO).

Table 7.1 Base and bound tariffs for the United States of America

Tariff item number	Description of products	Base rate of duty (U- Not bound)	Bound rate of duty	Implemen-tation period from/to	Special safeguard	Initial negotiating right	Other duties and charges
1	2	3	4	5	6	7	8
2204	Wine of fresh grapes, including fortified wines; grape must other than that of heading 2009:						
2204.10.00	Sparkling wine	30.9¢/litre	19.8¢/litre				
2204.21	Other wine: grape must with fermentation prevented or arrested by the addition of alcohol: In containers holding 2 litres or less:						
2204.21.20	Effervescent wine	30.9¢/litre	19.8¢/litre				
	Other: Of an alcoholic strength by volume not over 14% vol.:						
2204.21.30	If entitled under regulations of the United States Internal Revenue Service to a type designation which includes the name 'Tokay' and if so designated on the approved label	9.9¢/litre	6.3¢/litre				
2204.21.50	Other	9.9¢/litre	6.3¢/litre				
	Of an alcoholic strength by volume over 14% vol.:						
2204.21.60	If entitled under regulations of the United States Internal Revenue Service to a type designation which includes the name 'Marsala' and if so designated on the approved label	8.3¢/litre	5.3¢/litre				
2204.21.80	Other	26.4¢/litre	16.9¢/litre				

297

Code	Description		
2204 (con.)	Wine of fresh grapes, including fortified wines; grape must other than that of heading 2009 (con.): Other wine: grape must with fermentation prevented or arrested by the addition of alcohol (con.):		
2204.29	Other: In containers holding over 2 litres but not over 4 litres:		
2204.29.20	Of an alcoholic strength by volume not over 14% vol	9.9¢/litre	8.4¢/litre
2204.29.40	Of an alcoholic strength by volume over 14% vol	26.4¢/litre	22.4¢/litre
	In containers holding over 4 litres:		
2204.29.60	Of an alcoholic strength by volume not over 14% vol	16.5¢/litre	14¢/litre
2204.29.80	Of an alcoholic strength by volume over 14% vol	26.4¢/litre	22.4¢/litre
2204.30.00	Other grape must	6.9¢/litre + 49¢/pf. litre	4.4¢/litre + 31.4¢/pf. litre
2205	Vermouth and other wine of fresh grapes flavoured with plants or aromatic substances:		
2205.10	In containers holding 2 litres or less:		
2205.10.30	Vermouth	5.5¢/litre	3.5¢/litre
2205.10.60	Other	6.¢/litre	4.¢/litre
2205.90	Other: Vermouth:		
2205.90.20	In containers each holding over 2 litres but not over 4 litres	5.¢/litre	3.¢/litre
2205.90.40	In containers each holding over 4 litres	8.¢/litre	3.¢/litre
2205.90.60	Other	6.¢/litre	4.¢/litre

Source: GATT

Table 7.2 Base and bound tariffs for the European Union

Tariff item number	Description of products	Base rate of duty	Bound rate of duty	Implemen- tation period from/to	Special safeguard	Initial negotiating right	Other duties and charges
1	2	3	4	5	6	7	8
2204	Wine of fresh grapes, including fortified wines: grape must other than that of heading No 2009:						
22041049	Sparkling wine	40.0 ECU/hl	32.0 ECU/hl				
	Other wine: grape must with fermentation prevented or arrested by the addition of alcohol:						
220421	In containers holding 2 l or less:						
22042110	Wine other than that referred to in subheading 2204 10 in bottles with 'mushroom' stoppers held in place by ties or fastenings: wine otherwise put up with an excess pressure due to carbon dioxide in solution of not less than 1 bar but less than 3 bar, measured at a temperature of 20°C	40.0 ECU/hl	32.0 ECU/hl				
	Other:						
22042124	Of an actual alcoholic strength by volume not exceeding 13% vol	16.4 ECU/hl	13.1 ECU/hl				
22042134	Of an actual alcoholic strength by volume exceeding 13% vol but not exceeding 15% vol	19.2 ECU/hl	15.4 ECU/hl				
	Of an actual strength by volume exceeding 15% vol but not exceeding 18% vol:						
22042141	Port, Madeira, sherry, Tokay. (Aszu and Szamorodni) and Setubal muscatel	18.5 ECU/hl	14.8 ECU/hl				
22042149	Other	23.3 ECU/hl	18.6 ECU/hl				
	Of an actual alcoholic strength by volume exceeding 18% vol but not exceeding 22% vol:						

Tariff item number	Description of products	Base rate of duty	Bound rate of duty	Implementation period from/to	Special safeguard	Initial negotiating right	Other duties and charges
1	2	3	4	5	6	7	8
22042151	Port, Madeira, sherry, Tokay (Aszu and Szamorodni) and Setubal muscatel	19.8 ECU/hl	15.8 ECU/hl				
22042159	Other	26.1 ECU/hl	20.9 ECU/hl				
22042190	Of an actual alcoholic strength by volume exceeding 22% vol	2.19 ECU/%vol/hl	1.75 ECU/%vol/hl				
220429	Other:						
22042910	Wine other than that referred to in subheading 2204 10 in bottles with 'mushroom' stoppers held in place by ties or fastenings: wine otherwise put up with an excess pressure due to carbon dioxide in solution of not less than 1 bar but less than 3 bar, measured at a temperature of 20°C	40.0 ECU/hl	32.0 ECU/hl				
	Other:						
22042924	Of an actual strength by volume not exceeding 13% vol	12.4 ECU/hl	9.9 ECU/hl				
22042934	Of an actual alcoholic strength by volume exceeding 13% vol but not exceeding 15% vol	15.1 ECU/hl	12.1 ECU/hl				
	Of an actual alcoholic strength by volume exceeding 15% vol but not exceeding 18% vol:						
22042941	Port, Madeira, sherry and Setubal muscatel	15.1 ECU/hl	12.1 ECU/hl				
22042945	Tokay (Aszu and Szamorodni)	16.4 ECU/hl	13.1 ECU/hl				
22042949	Other	19.2 ECU/hl	15.4 ECU/hl				
	Of an actual alcoholic strength by volume exceeding 18% vol but not exceeding 22% vol:						
22042951	Port, Madeira, sherry and Setubal muscatel	16.4 ECU/hl	13.1 ECU/hl				
22042955	Tokay (Aszu and Szamorodni)	17.8 ECU/hl	14.2 ECU/hl				

Code	Description			
22042959	Other			
22042990	Of an actual alcoholic strength by volume exceeding 22% vol	26.1 ECU/hl	20.9 ECU/hl	
220430	Other grape must:			
22043010	In fermentation or with fermentation arrested otherwise than by the addition of alcohol	2.19 ECU/%vol/hl	1.75 ECU/%vol/hl	
	Other:			
22043091	Of a density of 1.33 g/cm3 or less at 20°C and of an actual alcoholic strength by volume not exceeding 1% vol	40.0%	32.0%	
	Concentrated	28.0% + 164 ECU/hl + 257 ECU/T	22.4% + 131 ECU/hl + 206 ECU/T	SSG
	Other	28.0% + 34 ECU/hl + 257 ECU/T	22.4% + 27 ECU/hl + 206 ECU/T	SSG
22043099	Other			
	Concentrated	50.0% + 151 ECU/hl + 257 ECU/T	40.0% + 121 ECU/hl + 206 ECU/T	SSG
	Other	50.0% + 34 ECU/hl + 257 ECU/T	40.0% = 27 ECU/hl + 206 ECU/T	SSG
2205	Vermouth and other wine of fresh grapes flavoured with plants or aromatic substances:			
	In containers holding 2 l or less:			
22051010	Of an actual alcoholic strength by volume of 18% or less	17.0 ECU/hl	10.9 ECU/hl	
22051090	Of an actual alcoholic strength by volume exceeding 18% vol	1.4 ECU/%vol/hl + 10.0 ECU/hl	0.9 ECU/%vol/hl + 6.4 ECU/hl	
220590	Other:			
22059010	Of an actual alcoholic strength by volume of 18% vol or less	14.0 ECU/hl	9.0 ECU/hl	
22059090	Of an actual alcoholic strength by volume exceeding 18% vol	1.4 ECU/%vol/hl	0.9 ECU/%vol/hl	

Source: GATT

301

Table 7.3 Base and bound tariffs for Japan

Tariff item number	Description of products	Base rate of duty	Bound rate of duty	Implemen- tation period from/to	Special safeguard	Initial negotiating right	Other duties and charges
1	2	3	4	5	6	7	8
2204	Wine of fresh grapes, including fortified wines; grape must other than that of heading 2009.						
2204.10	Sparkling wine	455yen/l	182yen/l				
2204.21	Other wine: grape must with fermentation prevented or arrested by the addition of alcohol: In containers holding 2 l or less:						
	Sherry, port and other fortified wines	280yen/l	112yen/l				
	Other	55% or 280 yen/l, whichever is the less, subject to a minimum customs duty of 150yen/l	15% or 125 yen/l, whichever is the less, subject to a minimum customs duty of 67yen/l				
	–						
2204.21 (continued) 2204.29	Other: In containers holding 150 l or less	55% or 280 yen/l, whichever is the less, subject to a minimum customs duty of 150yen/l	15% or 125 yen/l, whichever is the less, subject to a minimum customs duty of 67 yen/l				

Code	Description		
2204.30	Other	160yen/l	45yen/l
	Other grape must: Of an alcoholic strength by volume of less than 1% vol: Containing added sugar:		
	Not more than 10% by weight of sucrose, naturally and artificially contained +7	35.9%	23%
	Other + 1 l	46.5% or 35.9 yen/kg, whichever is the greater	29.8% or 23 yen/kg, whichever is the greater
	Other:		
	Not more than 10% by weight of sucrose +5	29.9%	19.1%
	Other + 9	39.8%	25.5%
	Other	256yen/l	45yen/l
2205	Vermouth and other wine of fresh grapes flavoured with plants or aromatic substances.		
2205.10	In containers holding 2 l or less	126yen/l	69.3yen/l
2205.90	Other:		
	Of an alcoholic strength by volume of less than 1% vol + 5	29.9%	19.1%
	Other	126yen/l	69.3yen/l

Source: GATT

303

Unlike any other nation, the EU was able to renounce tariffication for fear of having to meet minimum access requirements. It raised existing tariffs slightly in order to include the countervailing charge imposed on exports shipped to the EU below its minimum import price.[3]

Export subsidies

Export subsidies will be reduced by 21% and 36% over the same six years, from their 1986–88 level, in terms of quantities eligible for aid and expenditure respectively. All publicly funded measures aimed at reducing the cost of shipping and marketing wines overseas will thus be dismantled gradually, with the exception of advisory services on marketing and promotion. The commitment by the contracting parties not to apply measures aimed at circumventing those abolished should result in stopping the current practice of handing out cash to the importer-distributor for unspecified promotional purposes, which almost invariably end up as price discounts and have a similar effect to export subsidies.

The tacit agreement amongst wine producing countries, not to use export subsidies against each other, has largely prevented exporters from engaging in damaging outbidding races. The EU, for instance, does not grant export refunds to any American country (except Venezuela), South Africa, Algeria, Australia, Austria, Cyprus, Israel, Morocco, Switzerland, Tunisia, Turkey and the former Yugoslavia.[4] Export refunds could result in pretty awkward situations nonetheless, as was demonstrated recently.[5] Taking the fairly common case of a shipment of red wine in bulk, of 12% strength, it turned out that the minimum CIF price at which a wine could enter the EU, in 1990/91, without facing any countervailing duty was 42 ECU/hl.[6] An export refund of 20 ECU/hl was available for a similar wine produced in the EU (for which the 'guide price' was 39 ECU/hl) but destined for

3 In 1990/1, for instance, the so-called 'reference price' (inclusive of tariff) was some 36% over the 'guide price', itself close to the market price for bulk (cf below).

4 OJL202 of 31/7/1990.

5 Swinbank and Ritson (1992, p 29).

6 Equal to the difference between the 'reference price' of 52.44 and the then applicable import duty of 10.9 ECU/hl.

export; its export price was thus 19 ECU/hl, some 55% below the minimum CIF price prevailing on the import side.[7,8] Most African, Asian and East European destinations (Russia, Bulgaria, Hungary and the Czech and Slovak republics) benefited from such refunds.

By bringing in discipline in this area, GATT has removed the spectre of damaging price wars. EU export refunds will be reduced from the yearly 64.5 million ECUs awarded for 308 million litres in 1986-88 on average, to less than 31.3 million ECUs and 243 million litres by the year 2000,[9] (see Table 7.4). US export assistance programmes face a similar fate and 'promotional dollars' expenses will need to be severely cut if not scrapped altogether in the light of the commitment not to introduce or re-introduce subsidies which were not provided for in 1986-88. GATT's contracting parties have also pledged to adopt enforceable international rules on the provision of export credits, credit guarantees and insurance programmes.

Domestic support

The undertaking by GATT parties to reduce the level of domestic support programmes which do not fall in the 'green box' of permitted income support measures by 20% is the most critical commitment after market access. It helps resolve the issue on export subsidies indirectly, by reducing the gap between domestic and international prices, which export refunds are usually designed to compensate for.

'Green box' measures must be transparent, which effectively rules out transfers from consumers to producers. They must also not distort trade in any significant way. This can only be achieved by decoupling producers' subsidies from the type and volume of output as well as from prices. Permitted 'green box' measures include advisory and research services as well as direct payments granted to producers, within the framework of decoupled income support programmes, income insurance, relief from natural disasters, producer or resource

---

7 1.65 ECU/% vol.

8 Presuming this wine would have found a buyer for the EU guide price of 38.52 prevailing in that year. Most wines did not: French and Italian red wines (R1, 12%) sold at 37.7 and 37.5 ECU/hl respectively (based on the recorded average prices of 3.145 and 3.128 ECU/% in France and Italy respectively (Source: Commission).

9 GATT (EC schedule LXXX, Part IV, Sect 3).

Table 7.4 Export subsidies: budgetary outlay and quantity reduction commitments

Description of products and tariff item numbers at HS six digit level	Base outlay level (million ECU)	Base Calendar/other year applied	Annual and final outlay commitment levels 1995–2000 (million ECU)						Base quantity (000 t)	Base Calendar/other year applied	Annual and final quantity commitment levels 1995–2000 (000 t)						Relevant supporting tables and document reference
	2	3	1995	1996	1997	1998	1999	2000	5	6	1995	1996	1997	1998	1999	2000	
1								4								7	8
Wheat and wheat flour	1 783.0		2 069.4	1 883.7	1 696.1	1 512.4	1 326.8	1 141.1	17 008.1		19 118.6	17 982.1	16 845.7	15 709.3	14 572.8	13 436.4	
Coarse grains	1 379.5		1 296.7	1 214.0	1 131.2	1 048.4	965.6	882.9	12 624.5		12 182.6	11 740.8	11 296.9	10 857.1	10 415.2	9 973.4	
Rice	61.8		58.1	54.4	50.7	47.0	43.3	39.6	183.7		177.3	170.8	164.4	158.0	151.6	145.1	
Rapeseed	32.2		30.3	28.3	26.4	24.5	22.5	20.6	100.4		96.9	93.4	89.9	86.3	82.8	79.3	
Olive oil	85.9		80.7	75.6	70.4	65.3	60.1	55.0	148.0		142.8	137.6	132.5	127.3	122.1	116.9	
Sugar (1)	776.5		730.0	683.3	636.7	590.1	543.6	497.0	1 617.0		1 560.4	1 503.8	1 447.2	1 390.6	1 334.0	1 277.4	
Butter and butteroil	1 325.4		1 245.9	1 166.3	1 086.8	1 007.3	927.8	848.2	463.4		447.2	431.0	414.7	396.5	382.3	366.1	
Skim milk powder	370.1		347.9	325.7	303.5	281.3	259.1	236.9	308.0		297.2	286.4	275.7	264.9	254.1	243.3	
Cheese	439.2		505.2	460.4	415.6	370.7	325.9	281.1	386.2		406.7	386.4	366.1	345.7	325.4	305.1	
Other milk products	1 008.1		947.6	887.1	826.7	766.2	705.7	645.2	1 187.9		1 161.4	1 116.8	1 072.2	1 027.6	983.0	938.4	AG ST/EEC
Beef meat	1 967.8		1 900.6	1 772.3	1 644.1	1 515.9	1 387.6	1 259.4	1 034.3		1 118.7	1 058.4	996.1	937.7	877.4	817.1	
Pigmeat	183.4		172.4	161.4	150.4	139.4	128.4	117.4	508.6		490.8	473.0	455.2	437.4	419.6	401.8	
Poultry meat	143.2		137.8	128.5	119.3	110.1	100.8	91.6	367.8		440.1	410.2	380.3	350.4	320.5	290.6	
Eggs	39.8		37.4	35.0	32.7	30.3	27.9	25.5	105.4		107.2	102.4	97.7	92.9	88.1	83.3	
Wine	64.5		60.6	56.8	52.9	49.0	45.2	31.3	3 080.4 (2)		2 972.6	2 864.8	2 757.0	2 649.2	2 541.4	2 433.5	
Fruit and vegetables, fresh	102.9		96.7	90.5	84.4	78.2	72.0	65.9	1 148.0		1 107.8	1 067.6	1 027.5	967.3	947.1	906.9	
Fruit and vegetables, processed	15.4		14.5	13.6	12.6	11.7	10.8	9.9	200.8		193.8	186.7	179.7	172.7	165.7	158.6	
Raw tobacco	62.9		95.0	84.1	73.1	62.1	51.2	40.2	142.5		190.4	174.9	159.3	143.7	128.2	112.6	
Alcohol	150.2		141.2	132.2	123.2	114.2	105.1	96.1	1 452.4 (2)		1 401.6	1 350.7	1 299.9	1 249.1	1 196.2	1 147.4	
Incorporated products	572.5		646.1	590.1	534.2	478.3	422.3	366.4	–		–	–	–	–	–	–	

(1) Does not include exports of sugar of ACP and Indian origin on which the Union is not making any reduction commitments. The average export in the period 1986 to 1990 amounted to 1.6 million t.
(2) 000 hl
Source: GATT

retirement programmes, investment aids, environmental and regional assistance programmes.

Implementation and monitoring of the reduction of the level of domestic support requires the calculation of an 'aggregate measurement of support', defined as the gap prevailing between international (CIF import) prices and domestically administered prices, multiplied by the quantity eligible for support during the base period. Failing to do so, an equivalent measure must be used, such as budgetary outlays used to support domestic producer prices during 1986–88.

A glance at the world's largest wine producing nations in the Table in the Introduction reveals that the EU, which actively supports wine prices, will again be most affected. The EU accounts for over 60% of the world's wine production but is responsible for nearly all the world's surplus.[10] Few if any of the remaining major producers – Argentina, the former USSR, the USA, South Africa, and Romania – have recourse to direct price support measures, and no other nation contributes to more than 2% of world wine output.

The challenge was to police an increasingly marketing-driven industry (this requires much room for innovation) with agriculture-oriented policies seeking fair revenues to producers and sustainable, traditional production practices, without derailing into generating surpluses. And WTO will eventually succeed where the EU has failed for nearly two decades – in changing the ruinous course of a policy deeply rooted in 1930s French-style interventionism. The structural surplus of the EU is so massive and so persistent (pledges to eradicate them date back to 1978) that it deserves close attention.[11]

The present imbalance grew out of the basic unwillingness to let free trade be established and production relocated within the EU – as was requested in the Treaty of Rome, and the common market regime introduced for wine and other agricultural products in 1970 – and from pressures to use distillation in order to balance national markets

10 1986–90 average (OIV); *Bulletin Européen de Conjoncture Viti-vinicole*, Nov 1992, p 75.

11 Measures aiming at removing what was then identified as a clear structural surplus were first implemented in 1979 (Commission, 1978) and later renewed in a series of dull programmes whilst price support measures were reinforced simultaneously (including the introduction of a minimum price in 1982), resulting in the EC9's surplus growing from an estimated 600–1000m in the late 1970s to about 3bn litres just before the Iberian enlargement (Greece, Portugal and Spain were responsible for an additional 1.5bn at that time). Surplus estimates are based on the Commission's own views at the time, expressed in its revamped '1980–86 action programme for a progressive establishment of balance on the market in wine' and in its proposal on stabilisers (Commission, 1988). See Spahni (1988, 1990) for a thorough discussion on this and on the shortcomings of the EU's common wine policy.

instead. The Community's vineyards started to shrink in 1977. Production continued to rise for a few more years, however, in spite of a general decline in demand, because price support measures were strengthened radically in 1976. These measures consisted of storage aid and distillation for the most part. Distillation of excess wines was meant to be carried out on a strictly occasional basis initially (with a view to removing isolated surpluses stemming from, say, a succession of unusually large harvests) but was used to remove chronic surpluses from then on.[12] Price support arrangements were reinforced again in 1982: a minimum price equal to 82% of the guide target price was introduced and distillation of part of the production surplus began to be carried out on a compulsory basis.[13] Although price support measures were restricted to ordinary wines, they helped maintain the prices of higher quality wines too, albeit indirectly, since many appellation wines produced in excess of permitted maximum yields per hectare are merely downgraded (*déclassés*).[14]

EU guide prices are set for ordinary wine in basically the same manner as for the other agricultural commodities subject to a common market organisation, at the yearly meeting of EU agricultural ministers. Heads of state agreed in Dublin, in December 1984, to freeze guide prices until market balance was restored; this was also a precondition to enlarging the EU to include Portugal and Spain. A new 5-year structural programme was decreed for the years 1985/86 – 1989/90, which was just as ineffective as its predecessors. The policy of pursuing guide prices was abandoned altogether in the late 1980s because of their lack of realism (save for a few brief spells, table wine prices had been stagnating well below target levels since 1980). Guide prices were kept as a reference for setting up minimum import prices and the Commission of the EU concentrated on quantitative market management thereafter. It aimed at a swift removal of excess production on a mainly compulsory basis, immediately after harvest, to avoid depressing prices. The Commission also attempted to limit production by introducing a heavy penalty for higher yields.

The capping of expenses caused by distillation only occurred

---

12 The measure was appropriately called 'exceptional distillation' then and was rechristened 'support distillation' later (EC Reg 816/70, art 7). The 1976 review introduced 'preventive distillation' which was systematically used to remove surpluses soon after harvest (EC Reg 1160/76, art 6b).

13 Provisions for a minimum price and compulsory distillation of surpluses were introduced in a second review of the wine regime, by art 3a and 41 of EC Reg 2144/82, whilst preventive distillation was reinforced.

14 Others are sent to distillation (e.g. in Bordeaux).

when the EU faced the grim but real prospect of insolvency. 'Budget stabilisers' were introduced for wine and other surplus agricultural products in 1988.[15] The financial responsibility of individual producing members was also increased in an attempt to bridle the cost of distilling surpluses, then running to the tune of 634 million ECUs a year (1986–88 average).[16] Much more attractive abandonment premiums (exceeding land prices in some instances) were offered in an attempt to bring some 700 000 ha out of production and balance the market by January 1996.

The failure of stabilisers to drain the estimated 4.5 billion litre wine lake on schedule was quite predictable then, for the EU kept allocating the vast majority of the money available to distilling surpluses rather than to programmes aiming at uprooting vines:[17] less than half the planned amount were taken out of production by mid-1993, and one would probably have to wait for another seven years to meet the target.[18] Even so, the Commission reckoned in its 1993 proposal for reforming the wine regime, that the EU would still be left with a surplus of 3.9 billion litres by the year 2000.[19]

The proposed reformed wine regime is scheduled to take effect with the 1995/96 marketing year.[20] The revamped policy works on the basis of some 15.4 billion litres deemed marketable without the help of subsidies and a production surplus of 3.6 billion litres. Its key elements are the introduction of national quotas and the financial correspondency for member states;[21] the extension of distillation measures to all wines (restricted to ordinary wines hitherto); the

15 Wine stabilisers were the last package to emerge because of a serious rift between agricultural ministers, over the proposed use of compulsory distillation, together with uprooting premiums, in order to reduce output. The structural programme made no assumptions as to the future development of demand and yields, which had been falling and rising respectively, over the 1980s, at a yearly rate of about 2%.

16 Including 250m in alcohol stocks depreciation (FEOGA, in Club de Bruxelles, 1992, p 1.24). Other domestic support measures include private storage aid and rehousing aids for wine stocks. Individual states have sometimes topped EU measures with national measures as well. The EU schedule at GATT was not readily available at the time of writing.

17 Spahni (1990).

18 Institut Européen de Conjoncture Viti-vinicole, *Cahier de conjoncture*, Mars 1994.

19 The surplus was put at 3.7bn litres in 1992/93 (Commission, 1993).

20 It has yet to be accepted undiluted by the EU Council of Ministers (the EU's executive body so to speak).

21 Southern Italy, Castilla la Mancha and Central Portugal have been identified as regions primary responsible for 'producing for distillation' (so to speak).

drawing of regional structural plans for eliminating excess production and for bringing the winegrowing activity back up on to the hillsides where it was meant to be kept originally. Finally, the long-awaited shift of emphasis will occur, from financing inadequate distillation measures to spending more heavily on uprooting and other structural programmes.[22] The aim is to bring distillation back to its original function, i.e. an occasional means of removing accidental production surpluses. Distillation would be used sparingly, for a maximum of 600 million litres per year, beginning in 1997/98.[23]

Marrakesh was timely. It will ensure that wine trade develops not just within economic blocs but in all possible directions. It is good news not just for EU taxpayers but also for unassisted wine exporters who are likely to benefit from more sustained international prices by the year 2000 as the world surplus is increasingly brought under control and trade embarks on a renewed growth cycle.

Bulgaria and South Africa have a high and rising rate of self-sufficiency (now in excess of 140%) comparable with that of France, Italy, Spain and Portugal. Bulgaria is determined to fully exploit the commercial potential of its attractively priced varietals, as is South Africa, whose rejection of apartheid has helped win the hearts and wallets of American and European consumers. Austria, the former Yugoslavia, the former USSR and Chile are also becoming increasingly dependent on export markets but still retain modest degrees of self-sufficiency. Romania, Argentina (a sleeping giant), Brazil and Australia all have medium but stable self-sufficiency levels. Germany and the USA – two large importers – have carved themselves profitable shares in selected import markets.

The USA, Australia, New Zealand, Chile, Argentina, Hungary and Bulgaria are all liberal or newly liberalised markets and most eager to take up the challenge sealed in Marrakesh. They will pose the greatest threat to EU exporters. Competition is thus likely to continue to intensify on the international market, but on much fairer terms. The winners will be those who open up their gates to trade and let their consumers benefit from a wider choice of wines. Some nations have managed to develop and keep a significant domestic wine industry and yet have relatively large imports: the USA, Germany and Switzerland are good examples. Two of them have succeeded in securing significant export markets as well, giving proof that the international

22 For 1993, though, the FEOGA estimated expenditure on distillation (900 million ECUs) is still twice the amount spent on uprooting premiums (450 million ECUs) in *Cahier de conjoncture*, Mars 1994.

23 *La journée vinicole*, 21 May 1994.

wine trade is indeed 'two-way' and that there is nothing to fear from it. There *is* scope for yet more trade particularly since the curtain fell on GATT's successful Final Act. So cheers to the spirit of Marrakesh; may it enliven a few more rounds!

References

Atkinson A B, Gomulka J and Stern N H (1990) 'Spending on alcohol: evidence from the Family Expenditure Survey 1970–1983, *The Economic Journal*, vol 100, pp 808–27.

Australian Bureau of Agricultural and Resource Economics (1993) *Wine grapes – projections of wine grape production and winery intake to 1995–96*, ABARE, Canberra.

Baker P and McKay S (1990) *The structure of alcohol taxes: a hangover from the past?*, The Institute for Fiscal Studies, London.

Barrett J T (1992) 'Straight from the heart – *60 Minutes* broadcast boosts red wine sales, *Market Watch*, November 1992, pp 32–9.

Berman T (1993) 'Présentation de l'audit stratégique de la filière vinicole française réalisé la demande de l'ONIVINS' [Strategic audit of French wine market structure] in *Quelles stratégies d'entreprises pour maintenir notre leadership mondial?* [Which strategies in order to maintain our leadership in the world? – Conference Proceedings]. Paris: Fédération Nationale des Syndicats Régionaux du Négoce Eleveur des Vins de France.

Bichsel R (1991) 'Bordeaux' Handel im Wandel' [Bordeaux' trade in transformation], in *Vinum* 91(11), 20–57.

Bock K-H (1977) *Weinabsatz im Gastgewerbe in der Bundesrepublik Deutschland – Untersuchungen zur Preisgestaltung und Verkaufspolitik* [The distribution of wine in the West German Horeca sector – Analysis of price determination and sales policy] (Dissertation), Justus-Leibig Universität, Giessen.

Boulet D, Montaigne E and Gaufres M (1990) *Crise viticole et innovation* [Wine crisis and innovation], INRA, Montpellier.

Bousigon J C (1979) *Les montants compensatoires monétaires et le marché du vin – l'exemple français (thèse).* Université de Toulouse, Toulouse.

Caire D (1989) *Stratégies à l'exportation des principaux pays européens* *producteurs de vins tranquilles <15°: le cas de la France, l'Italie, l'Espagne et l'Allemagne* [Export strategies of the main producers of still wines: the case of France, Italy, Spain and West Germany] (diplôme), ENSAM, Montpellier.

Centre Français du Commerce Extérieur (1990) *Circuits d'importation et de distribution des vins et spiritueux au Royaume-Uni* [UK import and distribution channels for wine and spirits], CFCE, Paris.

Centre Français du Commerce Extérieur (1992) *Guide de l'exportateur de vins et spiritueux* [The wine and spirits exporters' guide], CFCE, Paris.

Centre Français du Commerce Extérieur (1993) *Circuits d'importation et de distribution des vins et spiriteux en Suisse* [Swiss import and distribution channels for wine and spirits], CFCE, Paris.

Clawson J B (1993) 'Non-tariff obstacles to trade, discriminatory trade practices, and GATT', *How to facilitate trade in products of the vine* (proceedings of the OIV's 73rd general assembly in San Francisco), Office International de la Vigne et du Vin, Paris.

Commission of the European Communities (1978) 'Progressive establishment of balance on the market in wine – action programme 1979–85 and report from the Commission', *Bulletin of the European Community*, supplement 7/78.

Commission of the European Communities, (1988) *Propositions de règlements du Conseil modifiant l'organisation commune du marché viti-vinicole (suites du Conseil Européen de Bruxelles)* [Proposed Council regulations modifying the common organisation of the wine market], Commission discussion paper COM(88) 125 (final), Brussels.

Commission of the European Communities (1993) *Development and future of wine sector policy*, Commission discussion paper COM(93) 380 (final), Brussels.

Commission Suisses des Cartels (1970, 1973) 'Importations de vins' [Wine imports], *Veröffentlichungen der Schweizerischen Kartellcommission*, no 2 and no 4, Bern.

Commission Suisses des Cartels (1984) 'Les conditions de concurrence sur le marché romand des vins' [Competition on the Swiss-French wine market], *Veröffentlichungen der Schweizerischen Kartellcommission*, no 4, Bern.

Cooke G M, Reed A D and Keith R L (1977) *Sample costs for construction of table wine wineries in California*, University of California, Berkeley.

Cour de Justice des Communautés Européenne (1983) *Arrêt de la Cour du 22 Mars 1983 dans l'affaire 42/82 (libre circulation des marchandises – importations de vin italien en France)*, [Ruling of 22 March 1983 on case 42182 (free circulation of goods – French import of Italian wines)], Luxembourg.

Crooks E (1989) *Alcohol consumption and taxation*, The Institute for Fiscal Studies, London.

Croser B (1992) 'The Australian wine industry: taking a leadership role', *Wine Industry Journal*.

Davidson D (1992) *A guide to growing winegrapes in Australia*, Dianne Davidson Consulting Services, Adelaide.

DiNardo J and Lemieux T (1992) *Alcohol, marijuana, and American youth: the unintended effects of governmental regulation*, working paper no 4212, National Bureau of Economic Research, Cambridge, Massachusetts.

Drinks File (various issues).

The Economist (various issues).

The Economist, (1992) *Guide to economic indicators: making sense of economics*, Century Business, London.

Escudier J-L (1993) 'Les nouveaux produits de la vigne: intérêt et perspectives', *Bulletin de l'OIV*, vol 66, 747-8.

The Financial Times (various issues).

The Financial Times (1993) *FT 500 – a guide to the top European companies*, The Financial Times, London.

Fisher J (1992) 'The international market place for wine: United States perspective', *International wine markets: business opportunities and legal challenges* 1992 Napa Valley Conference, International Wine Law Association, Brussels.

Fitch P G (1993) 'Non-tariff obstacles to trade; discriminatory trade practices; GATT – an Australian perspective' (paper presented at the OIV's 73rd general assembly in San Francisco), DPIE Wine and Brandy Section, Canberra.

Folwell R J and Baritelle J L (1978) 'The US wine market', *Agricultural Economic Report*, no 417, US Department of Agriculture, Washington DC.

Foulonneau (1991) *Guide pratique de la vinification* [a guide for winemaking practice], Armand Colin, Paris.

Fouquet F (1989) 'La commercialisation des vins de Bordeaux' [The marketing of wines from Bordeaux] in *Comptes rendus de l'Académie d'Agriculture de France*, 75(7), 37-40.

GATT (1966) *World trade prospects for ordinary wine*, Trade Intelligence Paper No 8, *GATT*, Geneva.

Gille P (1992) *Le rôle de la grande distribution dans la filière vinicole française – essai d'analyse* [supermarkets and wine market structure], INRA, Montpellier.

Green R (1990) *La stratégie des multinationales de boissons face aux changements de l'économie* [The strategy of drinks multinationals faced with changes in their economic environment], INRA, Ivry.

Hallgarten F (1986) *Wine scandal*, Sphere Books, London.

Harding R J (1991) 'Alcohol consumption in the United Kingdom', *Bulletin de l'OIV*, vol 64, 725-6.

Harpers (various issues).

Heien D (1993) 'Higher excise taxes: revenue source or social experiment?' *How to facilitate international trade in products of the vine*, (proceedings of the OIV's 73rd general assembly in San Francisco), Office International de la Vigne et du Vin, Paris.

Henderson B D (1984) *The logic of business strategy*, Ballinger, Cambridge, Massachusetts.

Hernandez A (1993) *Estimacion de las nuevas plantaciones de vid y cantidades probables de vinos 'calidad exportacion' para el quinqenio 1993-1998* [Estimation of new plantings and likely production of wine of 'export quality' for the years 1993-1998], Pontifica Universidad Catolica de Chile, Santiago de Chile.

Hooley G J and Saunders J (1993) *Competitive positioning: the key to market success*, Prentice Hall, Hemel Hempstead.

Impact (1982) *American wine market review and forecast*, Shanken

Communications, New York.

Inglis T (1993) *The Australian Wine Industry* (conference paper), Winemakers' Federation of Australia, Adelaide.

International Wine Law Association (1992) *International wine markets: business opportunities and legal challenges*, 1992 Napa Valley Conference, Brussels.

INRA-ENSA-Montpellier (1987) *L'économie viticole française* [The French wine economy], INRA, Paris.

INRA-ONIVINS (1991) *La consommation du vin en France en 1990 – évolution 1980–90 & projections 1995–2000* [Wine consumption in France in 1990 – trends and projections], INRA, Montpellier.

Instituto Nacional de Vitivinicultura (1991) *Especificaciones analiticas para exportar vinos – segun pais de destino* [Analytical specifications for wine exports – arranged by country of destination], INV, Mendoza, Argentina.

Jackson-Grose D (1989) 'Australian exports: hit or myth?', *Wine Industry Journal*, February 1989.

Jamieson I (1991) *German wines*, Faber and Faber, London.

Japan Tariff Association (1992) *Customs Tariff Schedules of Japan – 1992*, JTA, Tokyo.

Jarrige F (1987) *Les exportations françaises de vins et spiritueux aux Etats-Unis* [French wine and spirits exports to the US](mémoire DEA), Université des sciences économiques, Dijon.

Jennings D and Wood C (1993) 'Czechoslovakian wine: strategic development for UK export', *International Journal of Wine Marketing*, vol 5, no 2, pp 26–38.

Johnson H (1989) *The story of wine*, Mitchell Beazley, London.

Juri M (1992) 'El proceso de desregulacion vitivinicola y sus efectos' [The deregulation process and its effects on the wine and grape industries] in *Noveades Economicas*, February 1993, 28–30.

Juri M and Mercau R (1990) 'Privatizacion en la Argentina: el caso de Bodegas y vinedos Giol' [Privatisation in Argentina: the case of the winery Giol] in *Estudios*, January–March 1990, 3–19.

Kadar B (1992) 'Hungary', *The European Community after 1992 – perspectives from the outside*, Border S and Grubel H (eds), MacMillan, London.

Kasimatis A N, Bearden B E and Bowers K (1979) *Wine grape varieties in the North coast countries of California*, University of California, Berkeley.

Kierzkowski H (1985) 'Models of international trade in differentiated goods', *Current issues in international trade: theory and policy* (Greenway D ed), pp 7–24, MacMillan, London.

MacKinnon L and Larue B (1990) *The demand for wine in Ontario* (working paper WP90/21), University of Guelph, Guelph.

Kotler P (1988) *Marketing management: analysis, planning, implementation and control* (6th ed), Prentice Hall, Englewood Cliffs.

Kotler P and Armstrong G (1991) *Principles of marketing* (5th ed), Prentice Hall, Englewood Cliffs.

Krieger J (ed) (1993) *The Oxford companion to politics of the world*, Oxford University Press, Oxford.

Krugman P and Obstfeld M (1991) *International economics: theory and policy* Harper Collins, New York.

Lamont J (1993) 'Perestroika, monopoly, monopsony and the marketing of

Moldovan wine', *International Journal of Wine Marketing*, vol 5, no 2, pp 48–59.

Lancaster K (1979) *Variety, equity and efficiency*, Blackwell, Oxford.

Léglise M (1976) *Une initiation à la dégustation des grands vins*, Divo, Lausanne.

Lindsey P (1987) *An analysis of the effects of exchange rates and trade barriers on the United States wine trade* (Ph.D. thesis), University of California, Davis.

Marché International des Vins et Spiritueux (MIVS) (various issues).

Michaud M G (1991) *Supermarket sales of Texas wines: a profile* (AUIV paper), AUIV-OIV, Paris.

Mitchell V W and Greatorex M (1989) 'Risk reducing strategies used in the purchase of wine in the UK' in *International Journal of Wine Marketing*, 1(2) 31–46.

Moulton K (1991) *Situation and outlook for wine in the United States – 1991*, University of California, Berkeley.

Moulton K and Zepponi G (1988) 'Economics of the wine industry in the United States', *Economics of food processing in the United States* (ed.), Academic Press.

Niderbacher A (1983) *Wine in the European Community*, European Documentation, Office for Official Publications of the European Communities, Luxembourg.

Nishiura K C (1993) 'Technical barriers to wine trade and the General Agreement on Tariffs and Trade: current disciplines and Uruguay Round implications' (paper presented at the OIV's 73rd general assembly in San Francisco), USDA, Washington.

NTC (1992) *The drink pocket book 1993*, NTC, Henley-on-Thames.

OCED (1990) *Les systèmes de financement des crédits a l'exportation dans les pays membres de'l OCDE* [Export credit financing systems in OECD member countries], (4th ed), OECD, Paris.

OIV (1993) *How to facilitate international trade in products of the vine* (proceedings of the OIV's 73rd general assembly in San Francisco), Office International de la Vigne et du Vin, Paris.

Ough C S (1992) *Winemaking Basics*, Food Products Press (Haworth Press), Binghampton.

Peppercorn D (1992) *Guide to the wines of Bordeaux*, Mitchell Beazley, London.

Peris S M and Taylor J W (1993) 'The coming crisis in the Spanish wine industry', *The International Journal of Wine Marketing* 5(1), 5–22.

Peron A and Camous P (1989) *Canaux de distribution et consomations en Europe* [Distribution channels and consumption in Europe], Economica, Paris.

Peynaud E (1987) *The taste of wine: the art and science of wine appreciation*, Macdonald, London.

Philpott D (1989) *Wine and food of Bulgaria*, Mitchell Beazley, London.

Poignant A (1992) 'Les échanges de produits agro-alimentaires entre la CEE et les pays de l'Europe centrale et orientale: analyse géographique et sectorielle des exportations communautaries' [Trade in agro-food products between the EC and Central Eastern European countries: geographical and sectional analysis of the Community's exports], *Europe* *de l'Est: la grande mutation (transition et perspectives)*, Romillat, Paris.

Pompelli G K (1987) *Consumer demand for wine by households in the United States* (Ph.D. dissertation), University of California, Davis.

Pompelli G K and Heien D (1991) 'Discrete/continuous consumer demand choices: an application to the US domestic and imported white wine markets', *European Review of Agricultural Economics*, vol 18, pp 117-30.

Rankine B (1989) *Making good wine: a manual of winemaking practice for Australia and New Zealand*, Sun, Australia.

Ribéreau-Gayon J et al (1975) *Traité d'oenologie – sciences et techniques du vin*, Dunod, Paris.

Ribéreau-Gayon P (1991) *Le Vin*, Que Sais-Je? (Presses Universitaires de France), Paris.

Ritson C and Tangermann S (1979) 'The economics and politics of monetary compensatory amounts', in *European Review of Agricultural Economics*, no 6, pp 119-64.

Robinson J (1986) *Vines, grapes and wines: the wine drinker's guide to grape varieties*, Mitchell Beazley, London.

Sichel P (1989) 'The ingredients for a succesful international wine industry', *Wine 2000* (16–18 August conference proceedings), the Australian Wine and Brandy Corporation, Adelaide.

Singleton V L (1992) 'Wine and enology: status and outlook, *American Journal of Viticulture*, vol 43, no 4.

Smith T (1992) Accounting for growth – stripping the camouflage from company accounts, Century Business (Random House), London.

Spahni P (1988) *The common wine policy and price stabilization*, Avebury, Aldershot.

Spahni P (1990) 'Wine budget stabilizers – a question of true balance', *Food Policy*, vol 15, no 2, pp 167-72.

Spawton A L (1991) 'Grapes and wine seminar – prospering in the 1990s: changing our view of the consumer', *International Journal of Wine Marketing*, 3(2) 32-42.

Stuller J and Martin G (1989) *Through the grapevine*, Wynwood Press, New York.

Sudraud P (1992) 'Le défi de la qualité', *Revue des Oenologues*, no 65.

Swinbank A and Ritson C (1992) *A guide to EEC wine policy*, Horton, Bradford.

Tarditi S (1978) 'Currency interference in common agricultural policy: monetary compensatory amounts', *Economic Notes*, vol 7, no 1, pp 65-100.

Tarrou D (1976) 'L'organisation monétaire de la Communauté Economique Européenne et la concurrence entre la France et l'Italie sur le marché du vin' [European exchange mechanisms and competition between France and Italy on the wine market], *Economie Mériodionale*, no 94.

Tsolakis D, Riethmuller P and Watts G (1983) 'The demand for wine and beer', *Review of Marketing and Agricultural Economics*, vol 51, no 2.

United Nations Conference on Trade and Development (1992) *Trade liberalization in Chile: experiences and prospects*, United Nations, New York.

Unwin T (1991) *Wine and the vine: an historical geography of viticulture and the wine trade*, Routledge, London.

Vigiaré A (1987) 'Rôle et évolution des transports internationaux' [Function and evolution of international transport] *Cahiers français: le commerce international*, no 229, January 1987, supplement.

Vivuen, 1993, (1).

Watson A (1990) *Finance of international trade* (4th ed), The Chartered Institute of Bankers, London.

White D and Blandford G B (1988) *The competitive position of the United States grape and wine industry*, Cornell University, Ithaca.

Williams J L (1993) 'New initiatives in the Hungarian wine industry: foreign innovation and investment', *International Journal of Wine Marketing*, vol 5, no 2, pp 39–47.

Wine Institute (1987) *Wine in the United States – 1934 to 1937*, San Francisco.

Wine Institute (various issues) *Wine industry statistical report*, San Francisco.

Wine Institute (various issues) *Internal grape and wine statistics*, San Francisco.

Wines and Vines (various issues).

Wines and Vines (1993) *Buyer's guide*, The Hiaring Company, San Rafael.

Wohlgenant M K (1985) *An econometric model of the US wine industry* (paper no B-1507), Texas A&M University, College Station.

World Drink Trends (various issues).

Index

Abbreviations used:

Measures:
cl (centilitre = 0.1 litre)
ha (hectare = 10 000 square metres = 2.47 acres)
hl (hectolitre = 100 litres)
l (litre = 0.22 UK gallons = 0.2642 US gallons)
lpa (litres of pure alcohol)

Names:
AIDV (Association Internationale des Juristes pour le Droit de la Vigne et du Vin/International Wine Law Association)
AOC (Apellation d'Origine Contrôlée)
AWBC (Australian Wine and Brandy Corporation)
AWEC (Australian Wine Export Council)

BLEU (Belgium–Luxembourg Economic Union)

C&E (Customs and Excise)
CCT (Common Customs Tariff)

CFCE (Centre Français du Commerce Extérieur)
CIF (Cost, Insurance and Freight)
CIS (Commonwealth of Independent States)
CO_2 (carbon dioxide)
COFACE (Compagnie Française d'Assurance pour le Commerce Extérieur)
CPI (Consumer Price Index)
CSO (Central Statistical Office)

EEA (European Economic Area)
EFTA (European Free Trade Agreement)
ENSA (Ecole Nationale Supérieure Agronomique)
EU (European Union)

FAO (Food and Agriculture Organisation of the United Nations)
FAS (Free alongside ship)
FEOGA (Fonds Européen d'Orientation et de Garantie Agricoles [European Agricultural Guidance and Guarantee Fund/EAGGF])

FOB (Free on board)
FRG (former Federal Republic of Germany)

GATT (General Agreement on Tariffs and Trade)
GDP (Gross Domestic Product)
GIV (Gruppo Italiano Vini)

Horeca (hotels–restaurants–cafés)
HS (GATT/WTO's Harmonised System)

ICE (Instituto Nazionale per il Commercio Estero)
IDV (International Distillers and Vinters)
INAO (Institut National des Appellations d'Origine)
INRA (Institut National de la Recherche Agronomique)
INV (Instituto Nacional de Vitivinicultura)
IRREAL (Instituto de Studios Economicos sobre la Realidad Argentina y Lationoamericana)
ISTAT (Instituto Centrale di Statistica)
LVMH (Louis Vuitton – Moët Hennessy)

MCA (Monetary Compensatory Amounts)
MITC (Methylisothyocyanate)

MIVS (Marché International des Vins et Spiritueux)

NAFTA (North Amercian Free Trade Agreement)
NFO (National Family Opinion)
NPD (National Panel Data)

OECD (Organisation for Economic Cooperation and Development)
OIV (Office International de la Vigne et du Vin)
ONIVINS (Office National Interprofessionel des Vins)
OSN (Other Special Natural wines)

R&D (Research and development)
Reg (Regulation)

SITC (United Nations' Standard International Trade Classification)
SO$_2$ (sulphur dioxide)
SVF (Société des Vins de France)

UN (United Nations)

VAT (Value added tax)
VDQS (Vins Délimités de Qualité Supérieure)
VQPRD (Vins de Qualité Produits dans des Régions Déterminées)

WDT (World Drink Trends)
WTO (World Trade Organisation)

abstinence 52, 183
abuse 1, 60
accompanying document 100
acidity 18-19, 21, 26, 98, 99
acquisitions (see also concentration and restructuring) 53, 248, 262-263
additives 29-30, 98
advertising (law on) 50-51, 70-71
Africa 224-226
  exports 270
  imports 225-226
  production 224-225
ageing 27
agents (see brokers)
agricultural policy viii, 1, 90
Albania 291
Albert Heijn 6, 159-60
alcohol (consumption) 44; (defined) 5
alcoholic strength (see strength)
Aldi 160, 171
Algeria
  consumption viii
  exports ix, 10-11, 90, 145, 152, 175-177, 209, 219, 223, 254, 270, 278, 280
Allied Lyons/Allied Domecq 143, 199, 252, 257, 260, 262, 265
Almaden 82, 263
analytical checks 22, 30
Andean Group 239
Angola (imports) 265
AOC 25, 31, 251, 253
appeal against new measures 293
appellation wine (defined) 31
appellations (see also AOC) 3, 6, 17, 30-33, 95, 184, 195, 234, 251, 255, 257, 258, 268, 282, 285,
arbitrage/urs 89
arbitration (see trade disputes)
Argentina 238, 253, 310
  consumption viii, 241
  exports 108, 115, 142, 158, 202, 236, 241-243, 278, 279, 286
  imports 226
  market intervention 90, 241-242
  production 17, 227
  trade policy 242
Armenia 5, 278

aroma (see flavour)
Asia 46, 50, 105, 119-120, 263; (imports) 248, 249
association agreements (between the EU and Central European states) 281, 290-291
asymmetrical free trade 281, 291
auctions 89
Australia 3, 93, 310
  consumption 230-231, 232
  exports 65, 108, 119, 121, 122, 135, 181, 191, 192, 196, 198, 202, 209-211, 230, 232-238, 289
  imports 229-231
  production 17, 20, 25, 31-32
  trade policy 4, 10, 100, 101-102, 230
Australian Wine Export Council (AWEC) 101
Austria 4, 310
  consumption viii
  exports 170-171, 172, 214
  imports 214
  production 17, 214
  trade policy 214
Azerbaijan 278, 279

Bahrain 223-224
base wine (defined) 167
Beaujolais 25, 133, 149, 195, 219
Beaujolais Nouveau 23, 27, 46, 83, 184
Belgium-Luxembourg Economic Union (BLEU) 146-153
  consumption 147-148
  import and distribution channels 152-153
  imports 148-152, 239, 243, 245, 248, 249, 264, 265, 268, 270
  production 146
bilateral agreements 4, 10, 94, 98, 99, 100, 174-175, 207, 279, 290-291
bill of lading 100
blending ix, 2, 4, 8, 10, 26-27, 111, 126, 164, 175-176, 179, 184, 258, 260, 279-280
Blue Nunn 267
Bodegas y Bebidas 260, 262
Bordeaux 11, 25, 27, 65-66, 92, 102, 133, 149, 151, 156, 194, 195, 219, 251-253

bottling in the region of production
(illegality of compulsory
measures) 259
brands 1, 6, 53, 55, 66-67, 72, 82, 83,
84, 113-114, 116, 135-137, 144,
183, 205-206, 211, 253, 257,
267; (international/global
brands) 262-264; (brand
rejuvenation) 263; brand
portofolio (262-263)
brandy 41, 260, 263
Brazil 85, 135, 227-8, 310
British wine (defined) 56
brokers 8, 88, 93, 114, 136, 153, 164
Bulgaria 272, 291, 310
consumption 283, 288
exports 65, 90, 115, 158, 170, 174,
192, 197, 278, 283-284, 286,
287-288, 289, 290
imports 280
production 17, 273, 283-285
Bureau of Alcohol, Tobacco and
Firearms (BATF) 70, 72
Burgundy 253

California 6, 36, 67-69, 72, 92, 108,
114, 123, 139, 143, 197, 209, 238,
243, 248, 253, 262
California Commission 84
Canada 120-128
consumption 121-122
import and distribution channels
125-128
imports 122-125, 232-234, 236,
242, 243, 245, 248, 249, 281
production 122
trade policy 98, 125-128
Canada-US Free Trade Agreement 123
Canadaigua 82
Canadian wine 122, 128
carbon dioxide 22, 26, 28
carbonated wine 26, 41
Caribbeans 228
cartels (see monopolies)
Castel 53, 55, 252-253
catering (see Horeca)
cava (defined) 260
centralised purchasing 144
certificate of chemical analysis 87
certificate of origin 98-100

certification 98, 99-100, 293
champagne 249, 252
chaptalisation (see sugaring)
character and style (see also style) 21,
26-28, 87; (UK) 66-67; (US) 80
chemical agents 10
chianti 17, 32-33, 45
Chile 93, 242, 262, 310
exports 65, 84, 85, 90, 108, 122,
123, 135, 142, 194, 197, 202, 211,
236, 238-239
market intervention 90
production 227, 238
China 107-108, 271
CIF 10, 88
Cinzano 167, 257
CIS/Russia 70, 262, 272, 273, 291, 310
consumption 277-278, 288
exports 167, 278, 288, 290
import and distribution channels
278
imports 242, 258, 260, 278, 281,
283, 287
production 278
trade policy 279
classic varieties 17
clonal selection 16
Cobden's Treaty 56
Codex Alimentarius 98, 293
Codorniu 260, 262
cold ducks 72
Colombia 228
colour 2, 21, 23, 45, 65-66, 80, 87
COMECON 12, 65, 161, 267, 268, 272,
273, 281, 284, 285, 286, 288, 289,
290
Common Customs Tariff (CCT) 144-
145, 191
common wine policy (see EU wine
policy)
Commonwealth of Independent
States (see CIS)
communication 79
community preference 140
Compagnie Française d'Assurance
pour le Commerce Extérieur
(COFACE) 101
comparative advantage viii
competitive positioning 3
composition of trade ix

concentration 36-37, 54-55, 103, 114, 144-5, 167, 196, 237, 238, 260, 269, 270
Concha y Toro 238
Conseil Interprofessionnel des Vins de Bordeaux (CIVB) 102
consumer attitudes (see consumer preferences)
consumer awareness 117
consumer benefits/welfare 2-3
consumer expenditure 57-58
consumer loyalty 130
consumer preferences 1, 2, 3, 5, 46, 72-3, 80, 99, 144, 223
consumer protection (see health)
consumer resistance 28, 84, 257
consumer tastes (see consumer preferences)
consumer tax (see taxation)
consumption (3 basic models) 47-50; (traditional market) 50-55; (new markets) 55-86
container (shipping) 28, 92-93
container 2, 21, 28-29, 54, 99, 206
contaminants 29-30, 33, 293
contract price (see price)
Convergent Mix of Alcoholic Beverages 47
coolers (see wine coolers)
cost advantage 19
cost cutting 4
costs 234
  intermediaries 88
  law of ever-diminishing costs 91
  marketing (aid for) 101-2
  production: (fixed) 36-37; (operating) 37
  transport and insurance 88, 91-93
countervailing charge/duty 145, 304
credit insurance (see export credit insurance)
criadores exportadores 260
critical mass (see economies of scale)
Cuba 228
Cyprus
  exports 145, 170, 197, 269
  production 269
Czechoslovakia (Czech and Slovak Republics) 272, 291
  consumption 277, 288

imports 175, 277, 281, 290
production 276-277

dealcoholised wine (defined) 41
decoupling 305
Delhaize Le Lion 152
Denmark 200-206
  consumption 200-201
  import and distribution channels 205-206
  imports 201-204, 239, 243, 249, 270, 283
  trade policy 204-205
deregulation 7, 238, 242, 262-263
designations 292, 293-294
dessert wine defined 32, 41
diethylene glycol 4, 29, 65, 72, 108, 133, 161, 170, 195, 202, 214, 266
direct sourcing ix, 6, 159
discrimination 3, 9, 60, 88, 94, 110, 120, 126, 128, 138, 144-145, 208
dispute settlement 294
distillation (see market intervention)
distribution (in general) 3, 7, 102-103, 262-263
documentary credit 100
domestic subsidies (see market intervention)
Douro 30, 265
duties (see Taxation)

Eastern Europe
  exports 110, 115, 194, 197, 230, 258-259
  imports 264, 266, 267
Egypt 5
European Union 9-10, 90, 207-208, 310
  exports 84, 279
  import and distribution channels 144-5
  imports 245, 248
  market intervention 9-10, 12, 54, 169, 174, 178-179, 307-310
  production 25, 31
  taxation 60-61, 143-145
  trade policy 4, 11, 98, 100, 102, 144-146, 191, 174-175, 290-291, 295, 296, 297-299, 304, 305
  wine policy 176-179, 307-310

economic rents 90
economies of scale 2, 36–37, 38, 253
Eger 282
Egervin, 282
elasticity of demand 37, 46, 53, 58–
    59, 73, 129–130, 185–186, 201,
    230–231
enoteca 186
environment 4, 33–34, 98, 99, 206
ethyl alcohol, 30, 41
EU association agreements (see
    association agreements)
EU-Canadian Agreement 126
EU-US wine accords 140
European Bank for Reconstruction
    and Development (EBRD) 273
European Economic Area (EEA) 207–
    208
European Free Trade Agreement
    (EFTA) 207, 291
Evian agreements 11, 176
ex-winery price 88
exchange rates (see also monetary
    compensatory amounts) 3, 47,
    88–91
excise duties (see taxation)
export credit insurance 101–102,
    305
export promotion 100–101, 139, 145,
    257
export subsidies 9, 87, 95, 102, 258,
    279, 284, 304–305
exports (exposure to) 90, 236, 239,
    254, 260, 267, 268, 286

Faber 167
fads/fashions 44, 63, 72, 83, 132, 211,
    236, 248
FAS 88
fermentation 22–23
fighting varietals 74, 135
finance (in production) 34–38;
    (profitability of US wineries) 69–
    70; (instability of US corporate
    finance) 70
financial deregulation (see
    deregulation)
financial instruments (see also risk)
    91
financing 7, 37–38, 262–263

Finland 214
    import and distribution channels
        207
    imports 254
flavour 19, 21–22, 24, 26, 29
flavoured wine (defined) 40
FOB 10, 88
Food and Agriculture Organisation of
    the United Nations (FAO) 293
food retailers (see supermarkets)
foreign investment 238, 239, 262–
    263, 271
fortified wine (defined) 23–24, 41
France 9, 10, 12, 70, 107, 175–182,
    238, 242, 310
    consumption viii, 47, 50–55, 175–
        176
    exports ix, 3, 26, 64, 65, 83, 85, 117,
        121, 128, 132–133, 135, 148–
        151, 156, 168–169, 174, 184,
        192, 194, 195, 201–202, 206,
        209, 211, 214, 217–219, 225,
        230, 254, 276
    imports ix, 3, 90, 175–182, 245,
        248–253, 254, 257, 258, 260,
        264, 268, 270
    production 17, 20, 31
    trade policy 10–11, 101, 175–179,
        182
fraudulent wines 4, 29–30, 67, 98,
    125, 164, 171
Freixenet 260, 262
French overseas departments 228, 229
French Paradox 72

Gabon 225
Gallo 40, 74, 82, 85, 135, 140, 197,
    253
General Agreement on Tariffs and
    Trade (GATT) 10, 41,120, 138,
    140-2, 273, 290, 310; (HS code)
    41–43; (panel rulings) 110, 126,
    128; (Final Act) 292; (Standard
    Code) 292; (Uruguay Round) 95,
    145, 216, 222, 291, 292–307,
    310–311
generic names 293–294
generic promotion 101–102, 248
generic wines 10, 69, 81, 82, 253,
    258, 289–290

genetic engineering 16
geographical designations (see appellations)
Georgia 278–279
Germany 3, 4, 9, 13, 160–175, 310
    consumption 161–163
    exports 64, 65, 72, 83, 85, 90, 108, 117, 121, 122, 125, 133, 151, 156–158, 181, 185, 192, 195–196, 202, 209, 230, 266–267, 276,
    import and distribution channels 171–173
    imports ix, 12, 26, 90, 163–171, 214, 234, 239, 248, 249, 254, 255, 257, 258, 259–260, 264, 267, 268, 269, 270, 274, 281, 283, 286, 287, 288
    production 17, 20, 31, 161
German reunification 160–1, 173–175, 254
Giol 241–242
global advertising 263
global operators/players (see international drinks companies)
Grand Metropolitan (see International Distillers and Vintners)
grape varieties 2, 16–17, 69
Greece 5
    exports 151, 158, 170, 179, 185, 191, 207, 209, 268
    production 31, 268
green box measures 305
Gruppo Italiano Vini (GIV) 172, 257
Guinness 116, 208, 252, 262, 263
Günther Reh 167

hardy 237
harmonisation (of EU duty and consumer tax rates) 94; (of technical standards) 98; 144
Harmonised System (HS) Code 41–43
health 1, 4, 54, 56, 60, 64, 67, 71, 72, 84, 98, 110, 207–208, 213, 242
heavy drinking 58, 79
hedging (see risk)
Henkell 167, 267
Heublein (see also IDV) 82, 135, 140, 248
higher quality wine (defined) 31

Hiram-Walker 136, 262
Hong-Kong 107, 120, 271
Horeca 7, 55, 78, 103, 107, 116, 152–3, 171, 222, 263
Hungarovin, 282–283
Hungary 3, 272, 291, 310
    consumption 283, 288–289
    exports 90, 142, 161, 170, 174, 192, 197, 214, 278, 282–283, 284, 286, 287, 289, 290
    imports 280, 287
    production 17, 273, 281, 283–284

import quotas (see quantitative trade restrictions)
imports (exposure to) 90
INAO 33, 52
indication of origin (see appellations)
Indonesia 108, 120
innovation 6, 20, 30, 234, 237
Institut National des Appellations d'Origine (INAO) 52
Instituto Nazionale per il Commercio Estero (ICE) 257
intellectual property rights 95, 141, 293–294,
International Distillers and Vintners (IDV) 82, 135, 143, 199, 205, 248, 257, 262, 263, 265
international drinks companies 6, 7, 12, 40, 89, 262–263
international prices (see price transmissions)
international standards (harmonisation of) 95
International Trade Commission (ITC) 139
ion exchange process, 98, 141
Iran 224
Iraq 224
Ireland 60, 206; (imports) 254
Israel 224
Italy 4, 12, 70, 90, 107, 182–188, 242, 310
    consumption viii, 182–184
    exports ix, 26, 64, 65, 72, 83, 85, 108, 110, 117, 121, 122, 125, 132, 135, 151, 158, 164, 168, 174, 178, 179, 192, 196, 214, 219, 226, 248, 249, 253–258, 258, 276, 279, 286

import and distribution channels 186-187
imports 184-188, 264, 268
production 17, 31-3, 258
Ivory Coast 225

Japan 10, 13, 105-120
consumption 106-108, 113-114
exports 290
import and distribution channels 114-117
imports ix, 12, 105-106, 108-109, 117-120, 232, 239, 242-243, 245, 248, 249, 254, 255, 266, 283
production 111-113
trade policy 110-111, 296, 302-303
Japanese wine 111-113
jug generics 73, 82, 83
jug wine 32, 69, 73, 77
justifiability of measures 293

Kendall-Jackson 6
Korea 107-108, 120
Koshu 113

La Villageoise 263
labelling 4, 292; (requirements) 98-100
Lambrusco ix, 83, 85, 132, 195, 200, 201, 257
Latvia 262
Lebanon 224
lead 98
legislation 4
Liebfraumilch 133, 158, 195, 266-267
light wine 63, 200
Lindemans 237
liqueur wine (defined) 41
litigation (see trade disputes)
Loi Evin 50-51
Lomé convention 225
London gin epidemic 60
Louis Vuitton Moët Hennessy (see Moët Hennessy)
low alcohol drinks 110
low alcohol wine 24, 40, 41
low strength wines 44, 255

made wine (defined) 56
Malaysia 108, 120
marc 34
market access 95, 216, 294-304
market capitalisation 262-263
market intervention 9-10, 12, 54, 90, 95, 102, 145, 282, 305-310
Marrakesh 95
Martini & Rossi 257
Mateus 263, 265
maturity ix, 13, 50, 67
mechanisation 19-20, 35, 37, 111, 284
Mendoza 241
Mercian 111-114
Mercosur 95, 239, 243
mergers and acquisitions 137, 262, (see also acquisitions)
methanol 29-30, 72, 98, 132, 161, 254
méthode champenoise 24
Methuen Treaty viii, 264
methylisothyocyanate (MITC) 98, 110, 119, 141
Mexico 226-227; (exports) 142, 245, 248
Middle East 223-224
minimum access 295
Mistelles (defined) 41, 262
moderation 10, 44, 70, 72, 217
Moët Hennessy 116, 136, 143, 159, 167, 252
Moldova 278-279
Monetary Compensatory Amounts (MCA) 177-178, 185
monopolies/monopsonies 4, 77-78, 103, 120, 125-128, 135, 198, 204, 207-208, 209, 213
monopolisitic competition ,
Morocco (exports) 223, 270
multilateral agreements 94-95, 100
must 23, 41-43, 242

Napa 6, 18, 45, 116
National Family Opinion (NFO) 73
neo-prohibitionism 70-71, 129
Netherlands 154-160
consumption 155
import and distribution channels 159-160

imports 156-159, 245, 248, 254, 255, 259, 264, 266, 270
New Guinea 226
new markets (see consumption)
new style varietals 282, 289
New Zealand 310
    exports 65, 198, 209
    imports 229-230, 232-3, 236, 249
    production 25
    trade policy 230
non-discriminatory character of measures 293
North American Free Trade Agreement (NAFTA) 95, 126, 142, 227, 236, 239, 245, 248
Norway 214
    import and distribution channels 207
    imports 239
North Africa (exports) 110
notification of new measures 293
novello 184

oenological practices 4; (recognition of) 29, 98-99, 140
Oetker 167
off-licence sector 64, 66, 78
Office International de la Vigne et du Vin (OIV) 293
ordinary wine (defined) 31-32
organic wine (defined) 33
origin of product 3, 21, 44, 45, 65, 83-84, 87
Orlando 237, 253

packaging 4, 46, 84; (requirements) 292
Paraguay 228; (imports) 243
pallets 92
Paul Masson 82, 263
payback period 18, 35, 37
Penfolds 237
Pernod Ricard 136, 159, 181, 237, 253, 271
phylloxera 4, 17-18
Piat d'Or 263
Poland 291
    consumption 274-276, 288
    imports 175, 267, 276, 287, 288, 290
pop wine (defined) 40, 81

port (defined) 24, 265
Portugal 308, 310
    exports 65, 83, 85, 119, 135, 152, 170, 181, 185, 191, 192, 196-197, 202, 207, 209, 219, 225, 230, 264-265
    production 17, 31
    trade policy viii
positioning (see product positioning)
premium generics 83
premium varietals 73
premium wine (defined) 32, 73, 77
price 21, (collective bargaining) 37, 90; (UK retail prices) 64; (US retail prices) 73-74; (contract price) 88-89; (price makers) 238
price consciousness (see also elasticity of demand) 154, 155
price support (see market intervention)
price transmissions viii, 47, 88-91
price versus quality 3, 47, 65, 66, 191, 219, 234, 248, 283
pricing 7, 115
primeur wine 23
privatisation 242
procymidone 98, 141
product attributes/characteristics 2, 3, 20-21
product differentiation vii, 2, 3, 5, 47, 53, 143
product mix 2, 3, 21
product positioning vii, 20-21, 236, 239, 259
production hazards 17-18
production quotas 309
production subsidies (see market intervention)
production surplus (see surplus)
prohibition 67, 77
promotion 6, 7, 87, 101-102, 114
promotional cash/discount 102, 304
protection/ism viii, 4, 46, 47, 84, 129, 138, 143, 175, 215-216

quality 2, 15, 21; (perceived) 20
quality control 4, 30-33, 234-236, 277
quality wine produced in a specific region (PSR) (defined) 31

reference price 145
repeal 67, 77
research and development 17, 38-39
residues 193
restaurants (see Horeca)
restrictive legislation 6, 8, 33, 38, 40,
    183-184
restructuring 237, 242, 257, 286, 289,
retailing channels (in general) 103
reunification (see German
    reunification)
Reunite 257, 263
Rioja 17, 196, 202, 259, 262
risk 6, 11, 17, 18, 35, 37; (consumer
    risk) 66-67; (exchange rate risk)
    91, 101, 115; (risk of insolvency)
    100; (buyer/credit risk) 101,
    136-137; (country risk) 101;
    (speculation) 108
Romania 3, 272, 291, 310
    consumption 285, 288
    exports 65, 115, 174, 197, 286, 288,
    289, 290
    imports 254, 279-280, 286, 287
    production 17, 273
rootstock 17- 18
Russia (see CIS)

sales tax (see taxation)
sanitary and phytosanitary measures
    10, 95, 292-293
Santa Rita 238
Scandinavia 207-208
    exports 285-286
    imports 283
    production 286
Seagram 40, 82, 85, 112, 116, 136,
    140, 143, 159, 167, 265, 199, 205,
    252, 263, 283
seasonality of sales 66, 76, 167
segment 47, (US) 73-74, 77
segmentation 2, 3
Sekt 26, 165-166, 267
self-sufficiency (rate of) 310
semi-generic names 294
semi-generic wines 10, 32, 82, 99,
    140-141
sensory evaluation 22, 30
Share of Intake Panel (SIP) 73
sherry (defined) 24, 196, 260

Singapore 108, 120
SITC code (defined) 41-3
sochu 106, 110
social acceptance viii, 5
Société des Vins de France (SVF) 53,
    55, 252-253
Söhnlein 167
Sonoma 6, 18
sorbic acid (see SO2)
South Africa 45, 65, 310; (exports)
    115, 191, 225, 236, 270
South America (exports) 110, 230
Soviet bloc ix, x, 12, 271, 272, 273,
    288
Spain 90, 107, 238, 242, 308, 310
    consumption viii
    exports 26, 64, 65, 83, 85, 108, 115,
    119, 121, 122, 133-135, 152,
    156, 168, 169-170, 174, 179,
    181, 184, 185, 191, 192-3, 196,
    194, 202, 207, 209, 217, 219, 249,
    255, 258-262, 276, 278, 279, 286
    production 17, 31
sparkling wine (defined) 24, 41
specialist shops 103
speculation (see risk)
spumante 26
stabilisation 216
Standards Code 95
still wine (defined) 41
strategic groups of exporters
    (defined) x
strength 2, 21, 23-24, 39, 55, 64, 80,
    87, 265
style 2, 21-22, 26-28, 46
sugar 18-19, 21, 24-25
sugaring 25
sulphur dioxide (SO2) 33, 98
Suntory 111-112, 114, 115, 143
supermarkets ix, 6, 53, 54-55, 66, 78,
    103, 144-145, 148, 152-153,
    159-60, 164, 171, 172, 181, 201,
    205
surplus 7, 9, 25, 54, 72, 91, 102, 123,
    129, 137-8, 146, 176, 215, 223,
    241, 243, 257, 258, 272-273,
    279, 282, 307
sustainable viticulture 33
Sweden 208-214
    consumption 208-209

import and distribution channels 213

imports 209-213, 214, 233-234, 236, 239, 243, 249, 269

trade policy 211

sweet wine (defined) 23, 24-25

Switzerland 214-223, 310

consumption 215

import and distribution channels 222

imports 90, 217-222, 239, 243, 245, 249, 254, 269, 270, 283

production 25, 215-216

trade policy 216-217

table wine (defined) US 31; EU 32

Tadjikistan 278

Taiwan 120

tariff equivalents 294-295

tariff quota 145, 294-295

tariff rates (base/initial) 295; (bound) 295

tariff schedules 295-303

tariffication 95, 216-7, 294, 304

tariffs (see also trade policy, for the major importing countries) 8, 47, 88, 93-97, 294-295

taxation viii, 4-5, 8-9, 60-61, 70-71, 77-78, 88, 89, 90, 93-97, 110, 126, 139, 142, 143-144, 147, 191, 206, 207-208, 209, 230, 276,

technical barriers 10, 292

technical specifications 87, 98-100

technological change ix, 6

temperance 56, 64

testing and inspection 293

Thailand 108, 120

Tokaj/Tokay 17, 283

trade agreements 8, 10

trade barriers 8-10

trade blocs 8-9, 94-95

trade disputes 10, 82, 294

trade disruptions 141-142, 254

trade diversion 161

trade missions 100-101

trade restrictions (quantitative) 90, 94-95, 204-205, 216-217, 258, 294; (non-quantitative) 95, 293, 294

trade statistics/data used (defined) x

trademarks 95, 292

traditional markets (see consumption)

traditional producing regions 8

transparency of measures 293, 305

transportation costs 8

Treaty of Rome 11, 146, 307

Tunisia 90; (exports) 145, 164, 170, 223, 270

two way trade 2-3, 47, 90, 187, 310

UCCOAR 53, 55

Uzbekistan 278

Ukraine 278, 279

United Arab Emirates (UAE) 223

United Kingdom 91, 121, 189-200, 262

consumption 50, 55-67, 191

import and distribution channels 198-200

imports ix, 12, 189, 194-198, 168, 232-324, 236, 239, 242, 243, 245, 248, 249, 254, 255, 258, 260, 264, 266, 267, 269, 270, 281, 283, 286

production 55

trade policy viii, 56, 191-193, 208

United States 9, 10, 91, 121, 129-143, 310

consumption 50, 67-86, 129

exports 3, 243-248, 117, 119, 121, 122, 123, 125, 128, 181, 197, 209, 211, 227, 289,

import and distribution channels 135-138

imports ix, 3, 12, 85-86, 90, 129-135, 233-234, 236, 242, 254, 254, 257, 259, 260, 263, 264, 266, 267, 270, 281, 283, 286

production 20, 31-32, 67-70

trade policy 4, 84, 98, 102, 138-142, 295, 300-301

Uruguay (imports) 243

Val d'Orbieu 53, 55, 172, 253

value added tax (VAT) (see taxation)

value for money (see price versus quality)

varietal wines 17, 81, 82-83, 234, 239, 253, 258, 269, 282, 283, 289

varieties (see grape varieties)
VDQS (defined) 31
Venezuela 228
vermouth (defined) 41
Villa Banfi 257
Vinho Verde (defined) 265
vins de pays (defined) 249–251, 253
vitis vinifera 15, 16, 17
voluntary self-restraint 110
VQPRD (defined) 31

wine and democracy 45
wine and tourism 45
wine coolers (defined) 41, 69
Wine Equity Act 139
Wine Institute of California 102, 248
wine stabilisers 309
wine wars 178
wine-based drink 38–41, 44, 81–82
Winemakers' Federation of Australia 237

winemaking 4, 15, 20–33; (standards) 98–99; (all year round) 234
World Intellectual Property Organisation (WIPO) 293
world price trends 91
world wine consumption 12–13, 44, (main features and trends) 45–50
world wine trade (trends) 10–13, 104–105
wrap-around cases 92

Yamanashi 45, 113
yields 16, 18, 25, 308
yields versus quality 18
x-Yugoslavia 286, 291, 310
consumption 267
exports 45, 65, 108, 135, 164, 170, 197, 209, 219, 267–268
production 17, 267–268
x-USSR (see CIS)